The Gardener's Reading Guide

Copyright © 1993 Text by Jan Dean; Foreword by Allen Lacy

Facts On File, Inc.
460 Park Avenue South
New York NY 10016

Library of Congress Cataloging-in-Publication Data
Dean, Jan. 1939-
The gardener's reading guide / Jan Dean.
p. cm.
Includes bibliographical references and index.
ISBN 0-8160-2754-4 (hc) (alk. paper)
ISBN 0-8160-3012-X (pb)
1. Gardening—Bibliography. I. Title.
Z5996.A1D43 1993
[SB450.97]
016.635—dc20 92-24321

A British CIP catalogue record for this book is available from the British Library.

Facts On File books are available at special discounts when purchased in bulk quantities for businesses, associations, institutions or sales promotions. Please contact our Special Sales Department in New York at 212/683-2244 (dial 800/322-8755 except in NY).

Jacket design by Donna Sinisgalli
Composition by Facts On File, Inc./Grace M. Ferrara
Manufactured by R. R. Donnelley & Sons
Printed in the United States of America

10 9 8 7 6 5 4 3 2 1

This book is printed on acid-free paper.

THE

GARDENER'S

READING

GUIDE

JAN DEAN

FOREWORD BY ALLEN LACY

Facts On File

For

Rick

and

Mimi

If thou of fortune be bereft

And in thy store there be but left

Two loaves, sell one and with the dole

Buy hyacinths to feed thy soul.

———————————

JAMES TERRY WHITE

CONTENTS

PART III: SPECIFIC GARDENING METHODS

PART IV: SPECIAL TYPES OF GARDENS

PART V: REGIONAL GARDENING

PART VI: MISCELLANEOUS GARDENING TOPICS

FOREWORD

For Americans in whom the passions for gardening and for reading about gardening coincide, one of the unfortunate facts of our national life is that the best books on the topic can be elusive. Few libraries except those that are part of such institutions as botanical gardens and horticultural associations have in their holdings more than a handful of titles that cover gardening, and those that they do have are apt to be strictly practical guides instructing us how and when to do what in our home plots. The discount bookstore chains that dominate the marketplace today have at best a scrappy assortment of gardening books, and the ones they do offer are increasingly likely to be British imports that are long on toothsome photography and short on pleasurable and highly readable text. A tiny number of bookstores in America—I can think of just five from one coast to the other—specialize in horticultural books, and there are a couple of mail-order firms that do likewise, but there must be many readers who are unaware of the existence of these resources. Furthermore, even these companies necessarily do not stock books that have gone out of print. Used-book dealers can be helpful in locating such titles, but on a very haphazard basis.

Meanwhile, there are surely people who would delight in some particular gardening book, but who haven't yet learned of its existence.

My own gardening library has been built up over many years through constant games of hide-and-seek in junk stores and at garage sales—and by browsing through the catalogs of antiquarian book dealers specializing in horticulture, such as Booknoll Farm in Hopewell, New Jersey. Along the way, there has been many a discovery of wonderful writers I had previously missed. The roster of their names includes Neltje Blanchan, David Fairchild, Charles Dudley Warner, Celia Thaxter and many others. Hide-and-seek has been pleasant, but it is a slow and highly inefficient affair.

Now there comes Jan Dean's *The Gardener's Reading Guide*, which is all that its title promises. With pleasant and brief but chatty commentary, Jan Dean offers an informed and intelligent survey of the world of books on gardening. Her own book opens doorways for those of us who are passionate both about gardening and about the printed word.

Allen Lacy

PREFACE

The Gardener's Reading Guide is for those who enjoy gardening with their hands, but get better results gardening in their heads. I am one of those people.

Having grown up in New Orleans, and then lived for 15 years on the Mississippi Gulf Coast, I was accustomed to an evergreen world and prolific plants. Thanks to the climate, this abundance was achieved with little effort on my part.

In 1979, I moved to Fort Worth, Texas, bought a house, and planted a bed of azaleas which did not survive the rigorous winter. Following a few more years of large and small gardening failures, I finally realized that some of my favorite plants would only grow in this climate if I was willing to pamper them outrageously. I wasn't.

Compromise was the answer. I planted attractive, minimal care plants, and with the extra time I had, I indulged my love of "how I did it" gardening books. With these books, I not only had the pleasure of vicariously creating a garden, but I also had glimpses into the gardener's everyday life.

As I browsed the bookstore and library shelves and rummaged through used-book stores, I searched for these books. If I could unearth enough of them, I would be able to endure the terrible heat of a north

Texas summer when I yearned to read about a cool New England garden.

Two summers ago, the search for these books became my daytime occupation, while reading the sought after books was my evening diversion. By the time summer was over, I had compiled quite a list of personal narrative gardening books and mysteries involving gardening.

When Facts On File expressed an interest in publishing an annotated bibliography of gardening books, I had the added pleasure and challenge of seeking out more books. But because there are so many wonderful ones, it was difficult deciding what to include and what to omit. If I had included every one I wanted, this book would be unmanageable in size.

I hope you find many books here that you weren't aware of, and that they bring you great pleasure. I've tried to include a thoughtful representation in each category, but if I haven't included a book (or other resource) that you feel is appropriate, please write to me at 3454 Guadalupe Road, Ft. Worth, TX 76116, and tell me about your favorites. I'd love to hear from you.

—*Jan Dean*
Fort Worth, TX

ACKNOWLEDGMENTS

My special thanks to the Fort Worth Central, Ridglea and Southwest Regional public libraries. I spent months there researching and asking questions, and they were always helpful and encouraging.

To Paula Sanders, reference librarian at Texas Wesleyan University, thanks for finding the publication dates I was missing.

To the Fort Worth Botanic Garden for use of their lovely little library. I spent many happy hours dipping into their shelves of old gardening books, and then settling by the window overlooking the fountain and fragrance garden.

To the Dallas Downtown Public Library and the Southern Methodist University library, my thanks.

There were so many individuals who helped, but my special thanks to Dr. Michael T. Stieber and Ian Mac-Phail at the Morton Arboretum, Virginia Henrichs, Head Librarian at the Chicago Botanic Garden library, Jane Gates at the National Agricultural Library, Kathi Keville at the American Herb Association, Victoria Robb Creech at the American Orchid Society, Walter and Gloria Oakes of the International Lilac Society, Jeane Stayer at The American Iris Society, Betty Hotchkiss at the American Camellia Society, Jeri Grantham at the American Hibiscus Society, Barbara Hall at the American Rhododendron Society, Barbara Pryor at the New England Wildflower Society, Dr. Robert Gilman at the North American Lily Society, Betty Tufenkian at the International Geranium Society, Mary Lou Gripshover at the American Daffodil Society, and Jacques Mommens at the American Rock Garden Society.

The booklists of the Massachusetts Horticultural Society and the American Horticultural Society were a great help in getting me started. Joe Keyser, Director of Programs at AHS and overseer of their book program, even offered to look over the manuscript if I needed him.

To Joy McCann, author of the *Gardener's Index*, and Paula Oliver at Northwind Farms, thank you for responding to my requests so promptly.

The Garden Club of America, the American Bonsai Society, Bonsai Clubs International, The Herb Society of America, the Hydroponic Society of America, the Bromeliad Society, The American Fuchsia Society and the American Rose Society were all helpful.

To Barbara Barton, because whenever I thought I was going to drown in a sea of Rolodex cards, I glanced at her book, *Gardening by Mail*, and was inspired by the fantastic job she did.

To Babs Winter for her continued interest in the project, and for sending me Samuel Johnson's quote, "A man will turn over half a library to make one book." It sits by my computer.

To Elaine Ridings for sharing many beautiful English gardens and for waiting patiently in an inordinate number of English bookshops while I scanned the shelves and forgot the time.

To Allen Lacy, whose essay, "Old Gardening Books" in *Farther Afield*, started me on this journey, and to my editor, Kathy Ishizuka, for making it a fun trip.

CRITERIA FOR INCLUSION

1. The books selected were ones that would be of interest to the average gardener. If you are looking for titles of a highly specialized nature, contact the appropriate plant society for information or a list of recommended technical books.

   For addresses of plant societies not given here, check *North American Horticulture: A Reference Guide*, edited by Barbara Ellis and the staff of the American Horticulture Society. Also, look under "Gardening" in the keyword index of the *Encyclopedia of Associations* at your library. You will find numerous gardening associations listed. Turn to the page number given for in-depth information about the society.

2. Because of the enormous number of gardening books, I tried to limit the books to those published within the last 15 years. Exceptions were made in the case of classics, and, I must admit, for some of my personal favorites. This is not only an annotated bibliography, it is also an opinionated one.

3. Nursery catalogues and newsletters are not included in this bibliography. Even though these are excellent reading material, they are adequately covered in *The Gardener's Book of Sources* by William Logan.

4. The category to which a book belongs was not always clear-cut. When a book could fit into more than one category, I placed it in the most obvious (to me) section, and cross-referenced it to the other section or sections. Here are some examples:

   a. *Herbs and Flowers of the Cottage Garden* by Jennifer Wilkinson was put in the "Cottage Gardens" section and cross-referenced in the "Herbs" section.

   b. *Behind Those Garden Walls in Historic Savannah* by L. F. Wood was put in the "U.S. & Canadian Gardens" section and cross-referenced twice, once to "Plans" because it contains so many garden plans, and once to "Small and City Gardens" because the book's suggestions are appropriate for small gardens. (There were not many double cross-references needed, thank heavens.)

   c. The above mention of "Plans" reminds me that every book containing garden plans is not cross-referenced to "Garden Plans," only those books that contain a significant number of plans.

   d. And finally, I did not cross-reference everything that I could have. If I had, the "related books" section at the end of the chapter would have, at times, been longer than the chapter. I tried to place myself in your shoes and figure out how to make the book the most usable and enjoyable without making it cumbersome. My aim was to provide you with suggestions for related reading, not overwhelm you.

5. Not all the entries have a description. Either the title was self-explanatory, or the book was recommended by a knowledgeable gardener, and I didn't have the opportunity to examine it. I've tried to keep these "no description" books to a minimum, and debated whether to remove them entirely, but decided a recommended title without a description was better than no title at all.

WHERE TO FIND THE BOOKS

The hardest part of compiling a bibliography is discovering new books at the last minute and not being able to include them, but in order to meet a publishing deadline, a cut-off point is necessary. Personally, I'm still collecting titles and searching library and bookstore shelves and book catalogues. Here are some of my favorite places for finding gardening books:

1. **Public libraries** If your library doesn't have a book you want, ask if they can obtain it through Interlibrary Loan from another library which owns the book. There is generally no charge for this service.

2. **Special horticultural libraries** These are scattered around the United States and have wonderful collections of old gardening books. Since their specialty is horticulture, they have a bigger selection than the public libraries. Also, many of the larger horticultural libraries are affiliated with Interlibrary Loan. For a comprehensive listing of these libraries, check Barbara Barton's *Gardening by Mail*.

3. **Mail order (new books)** If you haven't discovered Capability's Books, put down this book, call 800-247-8154, and get on their mailing list. Their yearly 80-page catalog (with updates several times a year) is the ultimate for a garden book lover.

    Another mail order source that handles gardening books, but not exclusively, is Edward R. Hamilton, Falls Village, CT 06031-5000. They specialize in remainders so the books are generally older titles, but very good buys.

    Both the American Horticultural Society (P.O. Box 0105, Mount Vernon, VA 22121, 800-777-7931) and the Massachusetts Horticultural Society (300 Massachusetts Avenue, Boston, MA 02115) offer extensive catalogs of gardening books.

    Timber Press (9999 S.W. Wilshire, Suite 124, Portland, Or 97225, 800-327-5680) specializes in books for gardeners, horticulturists and botanists.

    Sterling Publishing (387 Park Avenue South, New York, NY 10016, 800-367-9692) offers a gardening book catalogue.

4. **Book clubs** There are two gardening book clubs. When you join, you receive periodical bulletins about the latest gardening books they offer by mail. Their addresses are:

    The Garden Book Club, 3000 Cindel Dr., Delran, NJ 08075, 800-257-8345

    The Organic Gardening Book Club, P.O. Box 4514, Des Moines, IA 50336, 800-678-5661

5. **Mail order (used books)** An excellent source for out-of-print books are the many used book dealers who specialize in gardening and horticultural books. The names and addresses of many of these can be found in *Buy Books Where - Sell Books Where: A Directory of Out-of Print Booksellers & Their Author-Subject Specialties* compiled by Ruth Robinson. The 1992 to 1993 (8th) edition lists 24

booksellers under "Gardens & Gardening." Also, many of the used book dealers advertise in the gardening magazines.

6. Don't forget the bookstores, both new and used, in your area. They all have some gardening books, and the bigger ones generally have a large gardening section.

7. Finally, be on the lookout at garage and estate sales, thrift shops (especially the Salvation Army and Goodwill), and annual public library sales. All of these are wonderful sources of gardening books.

LOCATION KEY TO
BOOK PUBLISHERS

Note: Some of these publishers, especially of the older titles, are no longer in business. For the publishers still in existence, their complete addresses can be found in one or more of the following reference books at your library:

Books in Print, Volume 8: Publishers (R.R. Bowker)
Literary Market Place lists U.S. and Canadian publishers and *International Literary Market Place* lists publishers in all other countries (R.R. Bowker).
Publishers Directory (Gale Research)

   Also, if you want to contact the publisher, many of them have 800 numbers for ordering purposes. These 800 numbers can be found in the above directories.

Abbeville Press, New York, NY
Abrams, New York, NY
Acres USA, Kansas City, MO
Acropolis, Reston, VA
Addison-Wesley, Redding, MA
AGPS (Australian Government Publishing Service), New York, NY
Alaska Northwest, Bothell, WA
Algonquin Books, Chapel Hill, NC
Allison & Busby, New York, NY
Alpine Garden Society, Woking, Surrey, England
American Association of Botanical Gardens and Arboreta, Wayne, PA
American Book Co., New York, NY
American Botanist, Chillicothe, IL
American Philosophical Society, Philadelphia, PA

Amphoto (Watson-Guptill imprint), New York, NY
Anaya Publishers, London, England
Andmar Press, Mills, WY
Angus & Robertson (HarperCollins imprint), New York, NY
Antelope Island Press, Berkeley, CA
Antique Collector's Club, Wappingers Falls, NY
Arch Cape Press (Outlet Book Co. imprint), New York, NY
Architectural Book Publishing, Stamford, CT
Archon Books (Shoe String Press imprint), Hamden, CT
Arco Publishing, New York, NY
Arnold, London, England
Arrowood Press, New York, NY
Associated University Presses, Cranbury, NJ
Atheneum (Macmillan imprint), New York, NY
Atlantic Monthly Press, New York, NY
Avery Publishing Group, Garden City Park, NY
Avon Books, New York, NY
Ayer Co., Salem, NH
G. J. Ball Publishing, Geneva, IL
Ballantine, New York, NY
Bantam, New York, NY
Barnegat, Barnegat Light, NJ
A.S. Barnes (Oak Tree Publications imprint), Stamford, CT
Barron, Hauppauge, NY
Barrows, New York, NY
Batsford (Trafalgar Square imprint), North Pomfret, VT

Beacon Hill Garden Club, Boston, MA

Beautiful America Publishing, Wilsonville, OR

Beekman Publishing, Woodstock, NY

Binfords & Mort, Portland, OR

Black Cat Press, Menlo Park, CA

Blandford Press (Sterling Publishing imprint),
   New York, NY

Geoffrey Bles, London, England

Bobbs-Merrill, New York, NY

Books Nippan, Carson, CA

Bookworm Publishing, Russelville, AR

Botany Books, Bremerton, WA

Bramhall House (Outlet Book Co. imprint),
   New York, NY

Brevard Rare Fruit Council, Melbourne, FL

Brick House Publishing, New Boston, NH

Brooklyn Botanic Garden, Brooklyn, NY

R. L. Bryan Co., Columbia, SC

Buccaneer Books, Cutchogue, NY

Bullbrier Press, Ithaca, NY

California Action Network, Davis, CA

Cambridge University Press, New York, NY

Camden House, Charlotte, VT

Capability's, Deer Park, WI

Caprilands Herb Farm, Coventry, CT

Carroll & Graf, New York, NY

Cassell (Sterling Publishing imprint), New York, NY

Caxton Printers, Caldwell, ID

Celestial Publishing, New Orleans, LA

Century (Trafalgar Square imprint), North Pomfret, VT

Chartwell Books, Secaucus, NJ

Chatto & Windus (Trafalgar Square imprint), North
   Pomfret, VT

Chelsea Green Publishing, Post Mills, VT

Chicago Review Press, Chicago, IL

Chicot Press, Atlanta, GA

Chilton, Radnor, CA

Chronicle Books, San Francisco, CA

Claitor's Publishing, Baton Rouge, LA

Earl M. Coleman Enterprises, Crugers, NY

Collier Books (Macmillan imprint), New York, NY

Collingridge Books (Octopus Publishing Group imprint),
   London, England

Collins (HarperCollins imprint), New York, NY and
   London, England

Columbia University Press, New York, NY

Columbus Books, London, England

CompuDex Press, Kansas City, MO

Congdon & Weed, Chicago, IL

Connecticut College Arboretum, New London, CT

Contemporary Books, Chicago, IL

Continuum, New York, NY

Coons, Brownsville, TX

Cornell Cooperative Extension, Ithaca, NY

Cornell University Media Services, Ithaca, NY

Cornell University Press, Ithaca, NY

Cornerstone Library, New York, NY

Countryman Press, Woodstock, VT

Countryside Books, Clearwater, FL

Crescent Books, New York, NY

Croom Helm (Routledge, Chapman & Hall imprint),
   New York, NY

Crossing Press, Freedom, CA

Thomas Crowell, New York, NY

Crown Publishers, New York, NY

DaCapo Press, New York, NY

David & Charles (Sterling Publishing imprint),
   New York, NY

Delacorte Press, New York, NY

de la Mare, New York, NY

J. M. Dent, London, England

Desert Biological Publications, Dona Ana, NM

Devin-Adair, Greenwich, CT

Dial Books, New York, NY

The Dial Press (Doubleday imprint), New York, NY

Diamond Books, Berkeley, CA

Beverly Dobson, Irvington, NY

Dodd, Mead, New York, NY

Dorset Press, New York, NY

Doubleday, New York, NY

Doubleday Doran, Garden City, NY

Dover, New York, NY

Down East, Camden, ME

Dragonflyer Press, Upland, CA

Dufour, Chester Springs, PA

Duke University Press, Durham, NC

Dutchess County Conifers, LaGrangeville, NY

Dutton (NAL/Dutton imprint), New York, NY

Endangered Species Press, Tustin, CA

Evans, New York, NY

Faber & Faber, Winchester, MA

Facts On File, New York, NY

Falcon Press, Scottsdale, AZ

Farrar, New York, NY

Farrar, Straus & Giroux, New York, NY

Fawcett, New York, NY

Fawcett Columbine (Fawcett imprint), New York, NY

Feline Press, Gainesville, FL

Fiberworks Publications, Austin, TX

Firefly Books, Buffalo, NY

Fisher Books, Tucson, AZ

Floraprint USA, Chicago, IL

W and G Foyle, London, England

Fulcrum Publishing, Golden, CO

Funk and Wagnalls (HarperCollins imprint), New York, NY

Gallery Books (Smithmark imprint), New York, NY

Garden Way (Storey Publishing imprint), Pownal, VT

Garland Publishing, Hamden, CT

J. Paul Getty, Malibu, CA

Globe Pequot, Chester, CT

David Godine, Boston, MA

Golden Coast, Savannah, GA

Golden Press (Western Publishing imprint), New York, NY

Gollancz (Trafalgar Square imprint), North Pomfret, VT

Good Earth Publications, Burlington, VT

Great Basin, Reno, NV

Green Books, Bideford, Devon, England

Greenhouse Press, Clinton, NC

Greenwich Book Publishers, New York, NY

Grossett and Dunlap (Putnam Publishing Group imprint), New York, NY

Grove Weidenfeld, New York, NY

Grower Books, London, England

Gryphon Books, Brooklyn, NY

Gulf Publishing, Houston, TX

Robert Hale, London, England

Hale, Cushman & Flint, New York, NY

Hamish Hamilton (Viking Penguin imprint), New York, NY

Hamilton's Publishing, Carlsbad, CA

Hancock House, Blaine, WA

Hand-D-Cap Publishing, Phoenix, AZ

Harbor Crest, Bainbridge Island, WA

Harcourt, New York, NY

Harcourt Brace and Co., New York, NY

Harcourt Brace Jovanovich, San Diego, CA and other locations

Hardy Plant Society of Great Britain, Clevedon, Avon, England

Harmony Books (Crown Publishers imprint), New York, NY

Harper, New York, NY

HarperCollins, New York, NY

Harper International (HarperCollins imprint), New York, NY

Harper Perennial (HarperCollins imprint), New York, NY

Harper & Row, New York, NY

Hartley & Marks, Point Roberts, WA

Harvard Common Press, Boston, MA

Harvard University Press, Cambridge, MA

Hastings House, Mamaroneck, NY

Hawthorn Books, New York, NY

Hearst Books, New York, NY

Hearthside Press, New York, NY

Herb Society of America, Mentor, OH

Hippocrene Books, New York, NY

Historic Savannah, Savannah, GA

Hodder & Stoughton (Trafalgar Square imprint), North Pomfret, VT

Henry Holt, New York, NY

Holt, Rinehart & Winston, New York, NY and Ft. Worth, TX

Home Planners, Tucson, AZ

Homestead Design, Bellingham, WA

Hood, Putney, VT

Horizons West, Flagstaff, AZ

Houghton Mifflin, Boston, MA

Howell Press, Charlottesville, VA

HP Books (see Price Stern Sloan)

HSMP Press, Amherst, MA

Hurst, London, England

Interport USA, Portland, OR

Interweave Press, Loveland, CO

Ironwood Press, Tucson, AZ

ISBS (International Specialized Book Services), Portland, OR

Jack, London, England

Japan Publications USA, Briarcliff Manor, NY

Johns Hopkins, Baltimore, MD

Johnson Books, Boulder, CO

Michael Joseph (Viking Penguin imprint), New York, NY

Keats, New Canaan, CT
Klutz Press, Palo Alto, CA
Knopf, New York, NY
Kodansha, New York, NY
Land Design Publications, San Dimas, CA
Larousse, Paris, France
Lavender Hill Herb Farm, Hughes Springs, TX
Libraries Unlimited, Englewood, CO
Lippincott, Philadelphia, PA
Little, Bridge, Grand Rapids, MN
Little, Brown, Boston, MA
Liveright, New York, NY
Long, London, England
Longmans Green, London, England
Longmeadow Press, Stamford, CT
Longstreet Press, Marietta, GA
Loompanics Unlimited, Port Townsend, WA
Lyons & Burford, New York, NY
Macdonald, London, England
B. B. Mackey Books, Wayne, PA
Macmillan, New York, NY
Macmillan Child Group, New York, NY
Madison Square Press (Watson-Guptill imprint),
   New York, NY
Mad River Press, Eureka, CA
Magna Print Books (Thorndike Press imprint),
Thorndike, ME
Mallard Press, New York, NY
Maupin House, Gainesville, FL
McGraw-Hill, New York, NY
McGraw Hill Ryerson, Ontario, Canada
David McKay, New York, NY
McQuerry Orchid Books, Jacksonville, FL
The Medici Society, London, England
Melrose Garden Press, Melrose, FL
Meredith Books, Des Moines, IA
Merrimack Publ. Circle, Topsfield, MA
Metamorphic Press, Santa Rosa, CA
Methuen (Routledge, Chapman, & Hall imprint),
   New York, NY
Milldale Press, Washington, DC
Minnesota Landscape Arboretum, Chanhassen, MN
Mist'er Rain, Auburn, WA
MIT Press, Cambridge, MA
Mitsumura Suiko Shion (Books Nippan imprint),
   Carson, CA

William Morrow, New York, NY
Mother Earth News, Arden, NC
John Muir, Santa Fe, NM
Museum of New Mexico Press, Santa Fe, NM
Mutual Publishing, Honolulu, HI
The Mysterious Press, New York, NY
National Council of State Garden Clubs, St. Louis, MO
National Gardens Scheme Charitable Trust, Guildford,
   Surrey, England
National Graphics, Garden Grove, CA
National Historical Society, Harrisburg, PA
Naturegraph Publishers, Happy Camp, CA
New Amsterdam Books, New York, NY
New England Wildflower Society, Framingham, MA
New Leaf, Green Forest, AR
New York Botanical Garden, Bronx, NY
North Atlantic Books, Berkeley, CA
North Light Books, Cincinnati, OH
Northeastern University Press, Boston, MA
Northwind Farm, Shevlin, MN
Northword, Minocqua, WI
W. W. Norton, New York, NY
Oasis Maui, Kahului, HI
Octopus Books, New York, NY
Odhams, London, England
Offshoot Publications, Eugene, OR
Old Westbury Gardens, Old Westbury, NY
Oracle Books, Los Angeles, CA
Ortho Books, San Ramon, CA
Outlet Book Co., New York, NY
Overlook Press, New York, NY
Oxford Illustrated Press, Yeovil, Somerset, England
Oxford University Press, New York, NY
Oxmoor House, Birmingham, AL
Pacesetter Press, Houston, TX
PAJ Publications, New York, NY
Pantheon, New York, NY
Park Seed Co., Greenwood, SC
Parnassus Imprints, Orleans, MA
Stanley Paul (Trafalgar Square imprint),
   North Pomfret, VT
PDA Publications, New York, NY
Peachtree, Atlanta, GA
Pelham Books (Viking Penguin imprint), New York, NY
Pelican, Gretna, LA
Penguin (Viking Penguin imprint), New York, NY

Pennsylvania State University, University Park, PA
Philosophical Library, New York, NY
Pictorial Histories Publishing, Missoula, MT
Pidcock Press, Gardenville, PA
Pineapple Press, Sarasota, FL
Plume (NAL/Dutton imprint), New York, NY
Plumeria Specialties, Houston, TX
Pocket Books, New York, NY
Pomegranate Press, Studio City, CA
Portland House (Outlet Book Co. imprint),
   New York, NY
Potomac Valley Press, Washington, DC
Clarkson Potter (Crown Publishers imprint),
   New York, NY
Prentice-Hall, New York, NY
Price Stern Sloan (HP Books), Los Angeles, CA
Princeton Architectural Press, New York, NY
Princeton University Press, Princeton, NJ
Pruett Publishing, Boulder, CO
Puckerbrush Press, Orono, ME
Puffin Books, New York, NY
Purchase Publishing, Purchase, NY
G.P Putnam, New York, NY
Quadrangle Books, New York, NY
Quill (William Morrow imprint), New York, NY
Quiller, London, England
Quinlan Press, Boston, MA
Raindrip, Chatsworth, CA
Rancho Santa Ana Botanic Garden, Claremont, CA
Random House, New York, NY
RD (Reader's Digest) Association, New York, NY
Reed, Wellington, New Zealand
Regency, Evanston, IL
Reston Publishing, Reston, VA
Reynal & Co., New York, NY
Rinehart, New York, NY
Rizzoli, New York, NY
Rodale Press, Emmaus, PA
Ronald Press (John Wiley imprint), New York, NY
Jeanne Rose Herbal Publications, San Francisco, CA
Routledge Press, New York, NY
Royal Horticultural Society, London, England
Running Press, Philadelphia, PA
Rutgers University Press, New Brunswick, NJ
Sagapress, Sapaponack, NY
St. Martin's Press, New York, NY

Salem House, Topsfield, MA/Salem, NH
San Juan Naturals, Friday Harbor, WA
Santa Barbara Botanic Garden, Santa Barbara, CA
Sasquatch Books, Seattle, WA
Scarbrough House, Chelsea, MI
Scarecrow Press, Metuchen, NJ
Scribner's (Macmillan imprint), New York, NY
Sears, New York, NY
Sedgewood Press, New York, NY
Seed Savers Publications, Decorah, IA
Sentinel Books, Orlando, FL
Seven Hills Books, Cincinnati, OH
Shearer Publishing, Fredericksburg, TX
Shepherds Garden Pub., Felton, CA
Shigo & Trees Associates, Durham, NH
Sierra Club Books, San Francisco, CA
Signet (NAL/Dutton imprint), New York, NY
Silkmont-Count, New Orleans, LA
Simon & Schuster, New York, NY
W. H. Smith, New York, NY
Smithmark, New York, NY
Smithsonian Institution Press, Washington, DC
Souvenir Press, Concord, MA
Sparks Press, Raleigh, NC
Spoon River Press, Peoria, IL
Stackpole, Harrisburg, PA
Stanford University Press, Stanford, CA
Starwood Publishing, Washington, DC
Stein & Day, New York, NY
Stemmer House, Owings, Mills, MD
Sterling Publishing, New York, NY
Stewart, Tabori & Chang, New York, NY
Stipes Publishing, Champaign, IL
Stockton Press, New York, NY
Stokes, New York, NY
Storey Publishing, Pownal, VT
Stump Publishing, Ontario, CA
Summit Books, New York, NY
Sun Bulb Co., Inc., Arcadia, FL
Sunset Books, Menlo Park, CA
Surrey Books, Chicago, IL
Sweetbrier Press, Palo Alto, CA
TAB Books, Blue Ridge Summit, PA
Taplinger, New York, NY
Jeremy Tarcher, Los Angeles, CA
Taunton Press, Newtown, CT

T. M. Taylor Co., Palm Bay, FL
Taylor Publishing, Dallas, TX
Ten Speed Press, Berkeley, CA
Texas Gardener Press, Waco, TX
TFH Publications, Neptune City, NJ
Thames & Hudson, New York, NY
Theophrastus, Little Compton, RI
Thomson Publications, Fresno, CA
Tiger Books, Twickenham, Middlesex, England
Timber Press, Portland, OR
Time-Life Books, Alexandria, VA
Times Books (Random House imprint), New York, NY
Trafalgar Square, North Pomfret, VT
Treasure Press (Octopus Ill. Publishing imprint),
  London, England
C. E. Tuttle, Boston, MA
Unipub, Lanham, MD
Universe Books, New York, NY
University of Arizona Press, Tucson, AZ
University of California Press, Berkeley, CA
University of Hawaii Press, Honolulu, HI
University of Illinois Press, Champaign, IL
University of Iowa Press, Iowa City, IA
University of Maine Press,, Orono, ME
University of Massachusetts Press, Amherst, MA
University of Miami Press, Baltimore, MD
University of Minnesota Press, Minneapolis, MN
University of New Mexico Press, Albuquerque, NM
University of North Carolina Press, Chapel Hill, NC
University of Oklahoma Press Norman, OK
University of South Carolina Press, Columbia, SC
University of Texas Press, Austin, TX
University of Washington Press, Seattle, WA
University of Wisconsin Press, Madison, WI
University Press of Kansas, Lawrence, KS
University Press of New England, Hanover, NH
University Press of Virginia, Charlottesville, VA
University Presses of Florida, Gainesville, FL

Unwin, London, England
Unwin Hyman, New York, NY
Vandamere Press, Arlington, VA
Vanguard Press, New York, NY
Van Nostrand Reinhold, New York, NY
Van Patten Publishing, Portland, OR
Vendome Press, New York, NY
Viking Penguin, New York, NY
Viking Press, New York, NY
Villard Books (Random House imprint), New York, NY
Voyageur Press, Stillwater, MN
Walker & Co., New York, NY
Ward Lock (Sterling Publishing imprint), New York, NY
Frederick Warne, New York, NY
Warner Books, New York, NY
Watson-Guptill, New York, NY
Weatherhill, New York, NY
Webber Gardens, Damascus, MD
Weidenfeld & Nicolson, Littleton, CO
Wellfleet Press, Secaucus, NJ
Wessels & Bissell, London, England
Whetsone Publishing, Brattleboro, VT
Whitcoulls Publishers, Auckland, New Zealand
Wieser & Wieser, New York, NY
John Wiley, New York, NY
Williamson Publishing, Charlotte, VT
Winston, Philadelphia, PA
Woodbridge Press, Santa Barbara, CA
Wooden Angel, Franklin, WV
The Woodland Press, Moscow, ID
Woodsong Graphics, New Hope, PA
Workman, New York, NY
Worth Publishers, New York, NY
Wynwood Press, Tarrytown, NY
Wyrick & Co., Charleston, SC
Yale University Press, New Haven, CT
Yankee Books, Camden, ME

Part I:

The
Personal
Side
of
Gardening

"HOW I DID IT"

Alsop, Gulielma Fell
APRIL IN THE BRANCHES (Dutton, 1947)
She is a physician at Barnard who, with a college professor friend, buys and fixes up a cottage in Connecticut. A book in the tradition of Beverley Nichols.

Barnard, Charles
STRAWBERRY GARDEN (Winston, c1871)
The subtitle says it all: "How it was planted, What it cost, What came of it financially and sentimentally. A Very Practical Story."

Brumbach, W. C.
THE ROMANCE OF DAFFODILS (Greenwich Book Publishers, 1959) This small book (47 pages) is a charmer. In 1944, after reading "Daffodils in Old Gardens" from Elizabeth Lawrence's *A Southern Garden*, he goes to Raleigh, North Carolina, to meet her, and is so inspired he begins a lifelong hunt for daffodils for his Pennsylvania garden.

Carter, Annie Burnham
IN AN HERB GARDEN (Rutgers University Press, 1947) With the help of her Italian gardener, she creates an herb garden 35 miles from New York City. The book evokes a time that will never be again when people "motor" to visit friends.

Castle, Agnes and Egerton
OUR SENTIMENTAL GARDEN (Lippincott, 1914) A romantic account of their garden in Surrey, England.

Courtauld, George
AN AXE, A SPADE AND TEN ACRES (Farrar, Straus & Giroux, 1985) He begins with a letter to the Editor of *The Morning Post*:

"In view of the recent gloom about the falling standards of living, I suggest that there are only three necessities and three luxuries which are needed in life: the former being a spade, an axe and ten acres; the latter being an adequate supply of hot water, books and lavatory paper."

He gardens in England on the Essex/Suffolk border.

Cummins, Julia H.
MY GARDEN COMES OF AGE (Macmillan, 1927) Over a period of 21 years, she converts an old 25-acre Adirondacks farm into a year-round home.

DeNevi, Angela A.
A YEAR IN MY GARDEN (Great Basin, 1989)

Dickey, Page
DUCK HILL JOURNAL: A YEAR IN A COUN-
TRY GARDEN (Houghton Mifflin, 1991) How she
transforms, over a nine-year period, one scrubby
acre of land near New York City into a garden;
includes plans for her white garden, herb garden,
main garden, hedges, shrub roses, nasturtium border,
etc.

Donald, Henry
BUNCH OF SWEET PEAS (Trafalgar Square,
1989) What happens when a poor Scottish minister
and his bride enter a sweet pea competition.

Eddison, Sydney
A PATCHWORK GARDEN: UNEXPECTED
PLEASURES FROM A COUNTRY GARDEN
(HarperCollins, 1990) With the help of friends, she
turns eight disastrous New England acres into a garden
of perennial borders, rock gardens and more.

Ellacombe, Canon
IN A GLOUCESTERSHIRE GARDEN (Trafalgar
Square, 1987) About a 19th-century English Cotswold
garden.
IN MY VICARAGE GARDEN AND ELSE-
WHERE (Arnold, 1986)

Ellis, Lucy M.
AS ONE GARDENER TO ANOTHER (Crowell,
1937) She has three gardens—one at her home in the
city, one on the Canadian shore of Lake Erie, and one
in Connecticut at the foothills of the Berkshires.

Ely, Helena Rutherfurd
A WOMAN'S HARDY GARDEN (Macmillan, 1990,
reprint of 1903 edition) Covering one year's work in her
garden, she tells about her failures, her favorites, her
shortcuts and her ideas on garden design and preparation.
She was one of the founders of the Garden Club of
America.

Fairchild, David
THE WORLD GROWS ROUND MY DOOR
(Scribner's, 1947) Creation of his tropical home and
garden in south Florida.

Farrer, Reginald
IN A YORKSHIRE GARDEN (Theophrastus,
1973, reprint of the 1909 edition)

Fish, Margery
WE MADE A GARDEN (Faber & Faber, 1984) The
creation of her garden at East Lambrook Manor, England.

Fox, Helen Morgenthau
ADVENTURE IN MY GARDEN (Crown, 1965) A
season by season account of her Westchester, New
York garden.

Gathorne-Hardy, Robert
THREE ACRES AND A MILL (Macmillan, 1940)
He describes 12 years of gardening on a small estate
near London and the traveling he does in search of rare
plants.

Goldsmith, Margaret Olthof
FRIDAY-TO-MONDAY GARDENING (Mc-
Graw-Hill, 1937) A New York businesswoman buys
property with a quarry, brook, waterfall and a six-room
cottage in Redding, Connecticut, and transforms it on
weekends into a country retreat.

Goodman, Richard
FRENCH DIRT: THE STORY OF A GARDEN
IN THE SOUTH OF FRANCE (Algonquin, 1991)
How he took a year off from the rat race and created a
vegetable garden on a borrowed piece of 30' x 40'
French land.

Griffith, Mary Smith
GARDENING ON NOTHING A YEAR (Hale,
1937) She creates a garden in Westchester County,
New York, where only rocks once flourished.

Grissell, Eric
THYME ON MY HANDS (Timber Press, 1987) The
successes and failures of his gardening efforts near
Washington. In the Beverley Nichols tradition.

Haggard, H. Rider
A GARDENER'S YEAR (Longmans Green, 1905)
He describes his two gardens, one on the eastern shore
of Suffolk and the other at Ditchingham where he
grows, among other things, aquatic plants and special-

izes in orchids. At Ditchingham, he has three acres, two gardeners, six greenhouses and two ponds.

Hays, Helen
A LITTLE MARYLAND GARDEN (Putnam, 1909) A transplanted Californian, she establishes a Maryland garden while yearning for the "luxuriant growth of the Far West."

Hill, Anna
FORTY YEARS OF GARDENING (Stokes, 1938) She gardens in the Hudson Valley and eastern Long Island.

Hill, Susan
THE MAGIC APPLE TREE (Hamish Hamilton, 1982) A year of village life at Moon Cottage in Barley near Oxford; includes gardening, cooking, village festivals and the villagers themselves.

Hollingsworth, Buckner
GARDENING ON MAIN STREET (Rutgers University Press, 1968) In her mid-60's, she creates a 20'x30' garden in her front yard in a Vermont village. One of my personal favorites.

Jacob, Dorothy
FLOWERS IN THE GARDEN (Taplinger, 1968)(subtitled "A Personal Reminiscence of Seventy Years of Gardening") In talking about how quickly time flies while working in a garden, she says, "If you are incapable of judging the time, if possible, get someone in the house to come and give you a gentle reminder. I had an aunt, a fanatical gardener, who came in one day soaked to the skin and said indignantly, 'You *might* have told me it was raining.'" She gardens in England.

Jekyll, Gertrude
WOOD AND GARDEN and HOME AND GARDEN (Antique Collector's Club, 1984) How she created her famous house and garden at Munstead Wood.

Johnson, A.T.
GARDEN IN WALES (Longmans, 1927)

Keeble, Midge Ellis
TOTTERING IN MY GARDEN: A GARDENER'S MEMOIR WITH NOTES FOR THE NOVICE (Camden House, 1989) Covers her experiences and knowledge gained through 40 years of gardening and the creation of six memorable gardens in Canada.

Kellaway, Deborah
THE MAKING OF AN ENGLISH COUNTRY GARDEN (Random House, 1989) After buying a thatched-roof cottage in Norfolk, the Kellaways struggle to produce a garden on a difficult site.

King, Caroline
THIS WAS EVER IN MY DREAM (Caxton Printers, 1948) She attempts to make a garden out of a Pennsylvania hillside.

Kirkus, Virginia
A HOUSE FOR THE WEEK ENDS (Little, Brown, 1940) All about re-doing a Connecticut country home and garden.

Leighton, Clare
FOUR HEDGES, A GARDENER'S CHRONICLE (Macmillan, 1935) (engravings by the author) A month-by-month account of her garden in the Chiltern Hills, England, 80 miles from the sea.

Lequenne, Fernand
MY FRIEND THE GARDEN (Doubleday, 1965) (English translation of work originally published in France in 1941) Charming reflections about his garden in Rouergue.

Lisle, Clifton
GROWING YEAR (Farrar, Straus, 1954) A month-by-month account of work in his Chester Springs, Pennsylvania garden.

Longgood, William
VOICES FROM THE EARTH: A YEAR IN THE LIFE OF A GARDEN (Norton, 1991) What happens in his 60' x 90' vegetable garden on Cape Cod.

McFarland, John H.
MY GROWING GARDEN (Macmillan, 1915) How he turns "two acres of San Jose, Pennsylvania scale with a house attached" into a beautiful garden.

Meade, Julian R.
ADAM'S PROFESSION AND ITS CONQUEST BY EVE (Longmans, Green, 1936) The author, a novelist, gardens in Danville, Virginia. A delightful

book about the family garden, the family and the neighbors.

Nichols, Beverley
DOWN THE GARDEN PATH (Doubleday, 1932) (with illustrations by Rex Whistler) Beverley Nichols's first gardening book, written in his early 30s, tells how he restored the derelict garden of a thatched cottage in Glatton, Huntingdonshire County, England. Wonderful chapters on growing winter flowers and building a rock garden.
A THATCHED ROOF (Doubleday, 1933) How he turns the cottage at Glatton into a home.
A VILLAGE IN A VALLEY (Doubleday, 1934) The eccentric comings and goings of the other inhabitants of Glatton.

These books—*Down the Garden Path, A Thatched Roof* and *A Village in a Valley*—have been condensed into *The Gift of a Garden or Some Flowers Remembered*, edited by John Cross (Dodd, Mead, 1972). Even if you read the three books in their original version, you will still want to read the foreword in *The Gift of a Garden*. Written by Beverley Nichols 40 years after *Down the Garden Path*, it is a fitting closure for the creation of his first garden.

And still more Beverley Nichols—
GARDEN OPEN TODAY (Dutton, 1963) (drawings by William McLaren) Nichols invites his readers to drop by and visit the garden at Ham Common that he and his gardener, Kenneth Page, created.
GARDEN OPEN TOMORROW (Dodd, Mead, 1969) (drawings by William McLaren) Chapter 11, "The Feline Touch," will appeal to all cat lovers who believe, like Nichols, that cats and gardens belong together.
GREEN GROWS THE CITY (Harcourt, 1939) How he transforms the back garden in a London suburb.
MERRY HALL (Dutton, 1952) (drawings by William McLaren) How Nichols makes a garden, including a water garden, and furnishes a Georgian house near London where Nichols lived for 10 years. Sequels are *Laughter on the Stairs* and *Sunlight on the Lawn*. The three books are condensed in *The Gift of a Home* (Dodd, Mead, 1973).

O'Brien, Harry R.
DIARY OF A PLAIN DIRT GARDENER (Dodd, 1934)

Osler, Mirabel
A GENTLE PLEA FOR CHAOS: THE ENCHANTMENT OF GARDENING (Simon & Schuster, 1989) How she handles trees, water, walls, roses, and bulbs on 1½ acres in Shropshire, England near the Welsh border. A kindred spirit who believes that "You don't have to garden to garden; gardening in the mind is a gentle vice with an impetus of its own."

Pardee, Alice DeWolf
ANYONE CAN HAVE A GREEN THUMB (Hearthside Press, 1968) (with humorous illustrations by Nancy Pardee Swenson) Includes her 10-point program for casual gardeners and her favorite plan for a perennial bed. She gardens 30 feet from Narragansett Bay.

Parker, Jill
THE PUREST OF PLEASURES: CREATION OF A ROMANTIC GARDEN (Trafalgar Square, 1989) How she created a Cotswold garden from a run-down five-acre farm.

Pryor, William Clayton
THE LAZY GARDENER (Longmans, Green, 1947) (nicely illustrated by Jessie Robinson) He refers to his gardening in Falls Church, Virginia as "taming our small Virginia wilderness." Chapter 2, "Gardening in Bed," is fun reading.

Sarton, May
PLANT DREAMING DEEP (Norton, 1968) At 46, novelist and poet May Sarton buys her first house. How she transforms "a broken-down house, a barn, and thirty-six acres in a remote New Hampshire village" is part of the charm of this book.

Sibley, Celestine
THE SWEET APPLE GARDENING BOOK (Doubleday, 1972) (illustrations by John Kollock are delightful) A warm, loving book that will appeal to anyone who has fallen in love with a piece of land. The story about the magnolia tree she receives for Christmas is one you will long remember. She gardens in Georgia, 30 miles north of Atlanta.

Silber, Terry
A SMALL FARM IN MAINE (Houghton Mifflin, 1988) How the Silbers go from urban careers to a self-sustaining rural life and garden business.

Smith, Martha
BEDS I HAVE KNOWN: CONFESSIONS OF A PASSIONATE AMATEUR GARDENER (Macmillan, 1990) A humorous account of her gardening experiences.

Tangye, Derek
A GULL ON THE ROOF (Michael Joseph, 1961) The first book in the series tells how Derek and Jeannie Tangye (and their cat, Monty) abandoned their sophisticated London life to establish a commercial flower farm in Cornwall. Read one and you're hooked. Other books in the series are *A Cat in the Window, Escape to a Sanctuary, A Cornish Summer, Somewhere a Cat Is Waiting, Sun on the Lintel, A Cat Affair, The Winding Lane, The Ambrose Rock, Jeannie, A Drake at the Door, Lama, A Donkey in the Meadow, When the Winds Blow, The Way to Minack, Cottage on a Cliff, The Cherry Tree, The Minack Chronicles, A Quiet Year*.

Thomas, Graham Stuart
THREE GARDENS (Capability's, 1983, American edition) About his English gardens.

Thomas, Rose Fay
OUR MOUNTAIN GARDEN (Dutton, 1915) Development of her garden in the White Mountains of New Hampshire.

Twomey, Katherine
A GARDENER'S YEAR (Arco, 1973) All about her garden in Hot Springs, South Dakota.

Verey, Rosemary
A COUNTRYWOMAN'S YEAR (Little, Brown, 1991)

Von Arnim, Countess (Elizabeth Russell)
ELIZABETH AND HER GERMAN GARDEN (Buccaneer Books, 1989 reprint)

Warner, Charles Dudley
MY SUMMER IN A GARDEN (Houghton Mifflin, 1871)

Welch, Maude S.
IN A WEEK-END GARDEN (Sears, 1933) A month-by-month account of how she, working on the week-ends only, transforms a Long Island garden.

West, Elizabeth
GARDEN IN THE HILLS (Faber & Faber, 1980) How she and her husband create a water garden, a woodland, and a garden of herbs, fruit and vegetables on a Welsh moorland 1,000 feet above sea level.

Wheeler, Candace
CONTENT IN A GARDEN (Houghton Mifflin, 1901)

Whitman, Georgia Squiers
WITHIN MY GARDEN WALLS (Putnam, 1939) Her gardening activities in Westchester County, New York. Her garden plan includes a "useful spot" where she stashes a shed, compost pile and a variety of vines.

Whittle, Tyler
SOME ANCIENT GENTLEMEN (Taplinger, 1966)

Wilder, Louise Beebe
ADVENTURES IN A SUBURBAN GARDEN (Macmillan, 1931) About her perennial, rock and wild gardens 30 minutes from New York City.
MY GARDEN (Doubleday, 1916) She wrote this book to answer questions that perplexed her when she started gardening. Chapters include "In the Making," "The Day before Spring and the Next," "May in the Garden," "June Magic," "July Problems," "Autumn Beauty" and more.
WHAT HAPPENS IN MY GARDEN (Macmillan, 1991) New edition of the 1935 book covering seasonal happenings in her garden.

Wright, Mabel Osgood
THE GARDEN OF A COMMUTER'S WIFE (Macmillan, 1902) An interesting story about the creation of a garden and the people who occupy the commuter's house.

Wright, Richardson L.
TRULY RURAL (Houghton, 1922) How a young couple buys a lovely old country house and restores it and the garden.

ESSAYS

Since I never know what I'll feel like reading before turning out the light, my nightstand resembles a mini-library—a couple of mysteries, a book or two on a new interest, a few magazines and more often than not, a book of gardening essays. Here are some favorites of mine and other gardeners'.

Capek, Karel
THE GARDENER'S YEAR (University of Wisconsin Press, 1984) Originally published in 1929, this witty little book discusses the pleasures and agonies of gardening.

Colette, Sidonie-Gabrielle
FLOWERS AND FRUIT (Farrar, Straus & Giroux, 1985)

Cook, Ferris
GARDEN DREAMS (Stewart, Tabori & Chang, 1991) Vita Sackville-West, Allen Lacy, Russell Page, Henry Mitchell, Josephine Nuese, E. H. Wilson, Samuel Parsons, Marion Cran and Louise Beebe Wilder describe their idea of a perfect garden.

Cox, Jeff
THE SPIRIT OF GARDENING (Rodale Press, 1986) Essays on 51 plants in or near his Pennsylvania garden.

Cruso, Thalassa
TO EVERYTHING THERE IS A SEASON (Knopf, 1973) Short essays on each month of the gardening year in New England. Shorter versions originally appeared as columns in the Boston Sunday *Globe* and *McCall's*.

Earle, Alice Morse
OLD TIME GARDENS (Macmillan, 1901) The essays cover such topics as front dooryards, a blue flower border, a moonlight garden and gardens of the poets; includes wonderful black-and-white photos.

Finch, Robert
COMMON GROUND: A NATURALIST'S CAPE COD (Godine, 1981) Thirty-two essays, including one titled "Going to Seed."

Francis, Mark, and Hester, Randolph Jr.
THE MEANING OF GARDENS (MIT Press, 1992) Thirty essays explore gardens as an expression of faith, power, order, culture, personality and healing.

Hersey, Jean
GARDENING AND BEING (Continuum, 1982) One essay for each month of the year.

Hyams, Edward S.
OF GARDENS AND GARDENERS (A. S. Barnes, 1969) Approximately 75 short essays on a variety of plants, people and the seasons.

Lacy, Allen
FARTHER AFIELD: A GARDENER'S EXCURSIONS (Farrar, Straus & Giroux, 1986) Fifty-six essays covering his personal garden plus the gardens of others, garden reading, old gardening books and much more; includes lists of mail order nurseries, organizations and societies, and recommended reading.
THE GARDENER'S EYE AND OTHER ESSAYS (Atlantic Monthly Press, 1992) Practical advice and personal opinions reflect his knowledge and love of gardening; covers a variety of topics (from the pleasure of a reel lawn mower to animals in the attic) and plants (mountain mint, paulownia tree, caladiums, hostas, phlox and more).
HOME GROUND: A GARDENER'S MISCELLANY (Ballantine, 1985) As he says in the preface, the "book is about some of the plants I have lived with and loved (and a few that I have disliked or that did not return my affection) over a lifetime of gardening."

Lawrence, Elizabeth
GARDENING FOR LOVE: THE MARKET BULLETINS (Duke University Press, 1987) We meet the people she encountered through the small classified ads for plants and seeds found in the market bulletins. Her first subscription to the bulletins was a gift from Eudora Welty.
THROUGH THE GARDEN GATE (U. of North Carolina Press, 1990) A selection of 144 of the popular weekly articles she wrote between 1957 and 1971 for *The Charlotte Observer*.

Lloyd, Christopher
THE ADVENTUROUS GARDENER (Random House, 1983) Essays divided into four categories: "Taking Care and Making More," "Mainly Woody," "Seasons and Situations" and "People, Plans and Plants."

MacKnight, Nancy (editor)
DEAREST ANDREW (Puckerbrush, 1984) A collection of letters exchanged from 1951 to 1962 between Vita Sackville-West and Andrew Reiber.

Mitchell, Henry
THE ESSENTIAL EARTHMAN: HENRY MITCHELL ON GARDENING (Farrar, Straus & Giroux, 1983) Strong opinions, information, humor.
ONE MAN'S GARDEN (Houghton Mifflin, 1992) Covers a year in his garden.

Nichols, Beverley et al.
HOW DOES YOUR GARDEN GROW? (Doubleday, 1935) Essays on gardening given originally on the radio by Beverley Nichols, Compton Mackenzie, Marion Cran and Vita Sackville-West.

Page, Ruth
RUTH PAGE'S GARDENING JOURNAL (Houghton Mifflin, 1989) Essays combining instruction, humor and anecdotes and which were originally given as radio talks for the National Gardening Association.

Perenyi, Eleanor
GREEN THOUGHTS: A WRITER IN THE GARDEN (Random House, 1982) Seventy-two essays about the pleasures and aggravations she has found in 30 years of gardening.

Pollan, Michael
SECOND NATURE: A GARDENER'S EDUCATION (Atlantic Monthly, 1991) He covers practical gardening information (composting, planting trees, mowing, etc.) but, more important, he discusses the importance of gardening as a way to learn how to live more satisfactorily.

Rothery, Agnes
THE JOYFUL GARDENER (Dodd, Mead, 1971) Originally published in 1927, it covers all kinds of gardens: beginner's, childhood, sentimental, traveler's, clock, gardens in the air, etc.

Sackville-West, Vita
COUNTRY NOTES IN WARTIME (Doubleday Doran, 1941) A lovely little book of poignant short essays written in the first years of World War II. In one, she tells about the bags filled with soil and stacked against the walls and windows of a hospital for protection. When spring came, seeds sprouted through the "cracks of the sacking and now the whole grim barricade blows with yellow daffodils."

GARDEN BOOK (Macmillan, 1979) Selections from her various garden books and newspaper columns arranged according to season.

JOY OF GARDENING: A SELECTION FOR AMERICANS (Harper, 1958) Selections from two of her books published in England (*In Your Garden Again* and *More for Your Garden*); arranged by the seasons of the year.

Schenk, George
GARDENING WITH FRIENDS (Houghton Mifflin, 1992) What happens every four months when he moves to a different part of the world (North Vancouver, Manilla or Auckland) to visit friends and work in one of the eight gardens he has created for his mostly non-gardening friends.

Scott-James, Anne
GARDENING LETTERS TO MY DAUGHTER (St. Martin's Press, 1990) Because of advancing years, she feels she may no longer be able to garden, so she writes about her gardening experiences in a series of letters to her daughter.

Swain, Roger
EARTHLY PLEASURES: TALES FROM A BIOLOGIST'S GARDEN (Macmillan, 1982) How all aspects of life are related and still provide great diversity.

THE PRACTICAL GARDENER: A GUIDE TO BREAKING NEW GROUND (Little, Brown, 1989) Advice for the beginning gardener written during the first five years in his new house, 20 Columbus Street, the title of his monthly column in *Horticulture* magazine.

White, Katharine S.
ONWARD AND UPWARD IN THE GARDEN (Farrar, Straus & Giroux, 1979) These wonderful essays first appeared in *The New Yorker* between 1958 and 1970. In one of them, she says, "All gardeners who like to get down on their knees and grub enjoy reading

books by others who do, especially if the authors write well and are good gardeners." Exactly!

Wright, Richardson L.
ANOTHER GARDENER'S BED-BOOK: A SECOND CROP OF SHORT AND LONG PIECES FOR THOSE WHO GARDEN BY DAY AND READ BY NIGHT (Lippincott, 1933) Essays covering his hobbies, likes and dislikes, and failures and successes in his Connecticut garden. There are anecdotes, quotations, personal recollections and advice for each day of the year.

THE GARDENER'S BED-BOOK: SHORT AND LONG PIECES TO BE READ IN BED BY THOSE WHO LOVE HUSBANDRY AND THE GREEN GROWING THINGS OF EARTH (PAJ Publications, 1988, reissue of the 1929 edition with an added preface by Allen Lacy) An entry for each day consisting of one short, terse piece of horticultural advice appropriate to the season and a longer piece on a variety of topics.

THE GARDENER'S DAY BOOK (PAJ Publications, 1989, reissue of 1938 edition) Practical tips, opinions, reflections and humorous anecdotes for every day of the year.

GARDENER'S TRIBUTE (Lippincott, 1949) Chapters on various people related to gardening (gardening editors, botanists, landscapers, etc.).

GREEDY GARDENERS (Lippincott, 1955) Miscellaneous tidbits related to his garden on a Cape Cod headland and the problems and solutions for such a site.

A SMALL HOUSE AND LARGE GARDEN: BEING A JOURNAL OF THE SAME WITH NOTES (Houghton Mifflin, 1924) Essays on a variety of topics, many dealing with his Connecticut country home and garden.

WINTER DIVERSIONS OF A GARDENER (Lippincott, 1934) Five essays on such topics as flower painting, summer houses and the addiction of clerics to gardening.

ANTHOLOGIES

Best, Claire, and Boisset, Caroline (editors)
LEAVES FROM THE GARDEN: TWO CENTU-
RIES OF GARDEN WRITING (Norton, 1987) If
horticultural history is your bag, this is for you. Essays
by more than 50 British garden writers (Jekyll, Roper,
Robinson, Chatto, Sackville-West, etc.) on such topics as rock gardens, wild gardens, formal gardens, ornaments, roses, borders and more.

Betts, Edwin M. (editor)
THOMAS JEFFERSON'S GARDEN BOOK
(American Philosophical Society, 1981) Selections
from the garden books that Jefferson kept from 1766
to 1824, plus other writings of his on gardening; reprint
of the 1944 edition.

Buchan, Ursula (editor)
A BOUQUET OF GARDEN WRITING (Godine,
1987) She selects certain topics such as garden design,
herbaceous plants, bulbs, water gardens, etc., and then
lets writers such as Bowles, Farrer, Jekyll, Robinson and
Sackville-West "speak" on the subjects; includes biographies of each garden writer.

Hobhouse, Penelope
GERTRUDE JEKYLL ON GARDENING (Ran-
dom House, 1985) Selections from Jekyll's various
books.

Jekyll, Gertrude
GARDENER'S TESTAMENT (Antique
Collector's Club, 1982) Anthology of selected articles
written over a 40-year period.

Krutch, Joseph Wood (editor)
THE GARDENER'S WORLD (G. P. Putnam,
1959) There are 11 sections such as "The Pleasures of
Gardening," "Fashions in Gardens" and "Gardens
without Gardeners," and, within these sections, 128
well-known writers express their views.

Lacy, Allen (editor)
THE AMERICAN GARDENER: A SAMPLER
(Farrar, Straus & Giroux, 1988) Contains the work of
over 50 writers covering the period 1805-1987 with
mini-biographies of each contributor; sections are "To
Make a Garden (why people garden), "Color," "Fra-

grance," "Native Plants," "Naming Plants," "Pests and Poisons" and "Lawns or Enclosed Gardens?".

Marranca, Bonnie (editor)
AMERICAN GARDEN WRITING: GLEAN-INGS FROM GARDEN LIVES THEN AND NOW (Viking Penguin, 1989) A variety of writings (letters, essays, travel journals, seed catalogues, etc.) from colonial times to today; includes work of Alice Morse Earle, Katharine S. White, Eleanor Perenyi and Amos Pettingill.

Sackville-West, Vita
THE ILLUSTRATED GARDEN BOOK: A NEW ANTHOLOGY BY ROBIN LANE FOX (Macmillan, 1989) A selection of Vita Sackville-West's London *Observer* columns on such topics as thyme lawns, old roses, clematis, mixed borders, the White Garden and more; includes color photos of Sissinghurst and watercolors.

Seager, Elizabeth (compiler)
GARDENS AND GARDENERS (Oxford University Press, 1984) A small book containing bits and pieces of garden writing.

Sitwell, Edith
A BOOK OF FLOWERS (Macmillan, 1952) Pieces in praise of flowers written by gardeners, philosophers, and poets; includes herbal recipes.

Spry, Constance
A CONSTANCE SPRY ANTHOLOGY (Crowell, 1954)

Wheeler, David
BY PEN AND BY SPADE: AN ANTHOLOGY OF GARDEN WRITING FROM HORTUS (Summit Books, 1991) A selection of articles from the British gardening journal; writers include Stephen Lacey, Rosemary Verey, Penelope Hobhouse and Hazel LeRougetel.

Whiting, John R. (editor)
A TREASURY OF AMERICAN GARDENING (Doubleday, 1955) Ten articles written by a variety of garden editors and horticulturists.

BIOGRAPHIES OF FAMOUS GARDENERS

Brown, Jane
LANNING ROPER AND HIS GARDEN (Rizzoli, 1987)
VITA'S OTHER WORLD: A GARDENING BIOGRAPHY OF VITA SACKVILLE-WEST (Penguin, 1988)

Chivers, Susan, and Woloszynska, Suzanne
THE COTTAGE GARDEN: MARGERY FISH AT EAST LAMBROOK MANOR (Trafalgar Square, 1991) Covers the things that influenced her gardening and the creation of her garden; also an account of the restoration of the garden by its present owner and 59 color photos.

Eliovson, Sima
THE GARDENS OF ROBERTO BURLE MARX (Timber Press, 1991) Marx, a Brazilian landscape architect, has been called "the real creator of the modern garden"; contains 163 color photos.

Henry, Blanche
NO ORDINARY GARDENER: THOMAS KNOWLTON (1691–1764) (ISBS, 1986) Insight into the horticultural world of the 18th century.

Hinde, Thomas
CAPABILITY BROWN: THE STORY OF A MASTER GARDENER (Norton, 1987)

Hollingsworth, Buckner
HER GARDEN WAS HER DELIGHT (Macmillan, 1962) Biographies of 20 women gardeners, botanists, botanical artists, plant collectors and garden writers born between 1607 and 1863.

Karson, Robin
FLETCHER STEELE, LANDSCAPE ARCHITECT: AN ACCOUNT OF THE GARDENMAKER'S LIFE 1885–1971 (Abrams, 1989) The designer of approximately 700 gardens, Steele was a link between 19th-century formalism and modern garden design.

LeRougetel, Hazel
THE CHELSEA GARDENER: PHILIP MILLER (1691–1771) (Timber Press, 1990) The life and works of the outstanding 18th-century gardener who made the Chelsea Physic Garden the best botanic garden in Europe.

Massingham, Betty
MISS JEKYLL: PORTRAIT OF A GREAT GAR-DENER (Trafalgar Square, 1985) The story of an independent woman far ahead of her time.

Spens, Michael
GARDENS OF THE MIND (Antique Collector's Club, 1991) A biography of Sir Geoffrey Jellicoe, Britain's famous landscape architect.

Stroud, Dorothy
CAPABILITY BROWN (Faber & Faber, 1984)

Tankard, Judith B., and Van Valkenburgh, Michael
GERTRUDE JEKYLL: A VISION OF WOOD AND GARDEN (Timber Press, 1989) Covers the sources and significance of her work, plus 84 photos taken by Jekyll herself.

Wells, R. W.
PAPA FLORIBUNDA: A BIOGRAPHY OF EU-GENE S. BOERNER (Brooklyn Botanic Garden, 1989)

Zuylen, Gabrielle van
THE GARDENS OF RUSSELL PAGE (Stewart, Tabori & Chang, 1991) Descriptions and 250 color photos of his best gardens in Europe and America; includes information from his private files and unpublished writings.

PLANT HUNTERS

Dodge, Bertha
IT STARTED IN EDEN: HOW THE PLANT HUNTERS AND THE PLANTS THEY FOUND CHANGED THE COURSE OF HISTORY (McGraw-Hill, 1979) Describes the adventures and difficulties the plant hunters encountered in remote regions of the world.

Fairchild, David
THE WORLD WAS MY GARDEN: TRAVELS OF A PLANT EXPLORER (Scribner's, 1945) The famous USDA explorer tells about his explorations and meetings with famous men of his time.

Farrer, Reginald
AMONG THE HILLS (Hippocrene Books, 1986) The "hills" are the Alps, and the year is 1911.
THE DOLOMITES (Timber Press, 1987) Farrer's travels with E. A. Bowles in search of new primulas and other European alpines; reprint of 1913 book.
RAINBOW BRIDGE (Timber Press, 1987) Discovery of *Gentiana farreri* and other Chinese plants; reprint of 1921 book.

Kingdon-Ward, Frank
HIMALAYAN ENCHANTMENT: AN ANTHOLOGY (Seven Hills Books, 1991) A compilation of his writings.
MYSTERY RIVERS OF TIBET (Timber Press, 1987) Searching for new plants in Tibet; reprint of 1923 book.
PLANT HUNTER'S PARADISE (Hippocrene Books, 1986) Hunting in 1930 Burma for rare orchids and other plants.
PLANT HUNTING ON THE EDGE OF THE WORLD (Timber Press, 1985) Searches on the India-Burma border; reprint of 1930 work.

Lancaster, Roy
PLANT HUNTING IN NEPAL (Timber Press, 1981) Describes modern plant hunting in the Himalayas.
TRAVELS IN CHINA: A PLANTSMAN'S PARADISE (Antique Collector's Club, 1989) Details on a large number of Chinese plants and their use in Western gardens.

Whittle, Tyler
THE PLANT HUNTERS (PAJ Publications, 1988)
Surveys the lives of famous plant hunters and how their discoveries changed modern garden design.

Wilson, Ernest H.
A NATURALIST IN WESTERN CHINA (Timber Press, 1987) Hunting and collecting plants in Hupeh, Szechuan, and across the Chino-Tibetan border; reprint of 1921 work.
SMOKE THAT THUNDERS (Hippocrene Books, 1986) Searching for plants around Victoria Falls in Africa, and in Australia and New Zealand; reprint of 1927 work.

GARDENS IN FICTION

MYSTERIES

"Gardeners and crime writers have quite a lot in common, not least that they are both fond of a good plot"—from Avon Curry's essay, "Gardening: Thou Bleeding Piece of Earth," in *Murder Ink* by Dilys Winn (Workman Publishing, 1977).

(Note: English mysteries are sometimes published under one title in England and another in America. When there is a difference, I have given the title used by the American publisher.)

Adams, Herbert
THE CRIME IN THE DUTCH GARDEN (Lippincott, 1930) A very good period piece.

Adamson, Lydia
A CAT BY ANY OTHER NAME (Signet, 1992) Cats and gardening.

Aird, Catherine
PASSING STRANGE (Doubleday, 1981) Inspector C. D. Sloan, a rose grower, becomes involved with

murder at the Almstone Flower Show and Horticultural Fair.

Anderson, J. R. L.
DEATH IN THE GREENHOUSE (Scribner's, 1983) An amateur botanist is found dead in his greenhouse in an English village.

Babson, Marian
GUILTY PARTY (St. Martin's, 1991) An American artist rents the gardener's cottage in an English village, and then she finds the gardener's body in the bushes.

Barth, Richard
A RAGGED PLOT (The Dial Press, 1981) An American Miss Marple gets involved with a group of young gardeners on Manhattan's Upper West Side.

Black, Lionel
DEATH HAS GREEN FINGERS (Walker, 1971) Kate Theobald, journalist, and her husband, Henry, are spending the weekend in an English village with a group of rose growers when a murder occurs. Since the murdered man is trying to produce a blue rose, the book includes

quite a bit of information on breeding hybrid roses. (The first U.S. edition gave Anthony Matthews as the author.)

Block, Lawrence
THE TOPLESS TULIP CAPER (Allison & Busby, 1987)

Burns, Rex
SPEAK FOR THE DEAD (Harper & Row, 1978) A young woman's severed head is found in the Denver Botanic Gardens.

Campbell, R. T. (pseudonym of Ruthven Todd)
All of the following books published in the United Kingdom by Westhouse feature a botanist, John Stubbs, as the detective:

UNHOLY DYING (1945)
ADVENTURES WITH A GOAT (1946)
BODIES IN A BOOKSHOP (1946)
THE DEATH CAP (1946)
DEATH FOR MADAME (1946)
SWING LOW, SWEET DEATH (1946)
TAKE THEE A SHARP KNIFE (1946)
    The only one of these I've had any luck locating is _Bodies in a Bookshop_ reissued by Dover in 1984.

Cannell, Dorothy
DOWN THE GARDEN PATH: A PASTORAL MYSTERY (St. Martin's, 1985) Primrose and Hyacinth Tramwell of the Cloisters manor house in the English Cotswolds are not as they appear.

Capek, Karel
TALES FROM TWO POCKETS (Macmillan, 1943) A mystery from the well-known author of _The Gardener's Year._

Christie, Agatha
MURDER AT THE VICARAGE (Dodd, Mead, 1930) Observing what goes on in the village from her garden, Miss Marple learns all she needs to know about the crime. As she says, "Gardening is as good as a smoke screen."
NEMESIS (Dodd, Mead, 1971) Miss Marple goes on a tour of stately Homes and Gardens.

Clark, Douglas
BOUQUET GARNI (Gollancz, 1984) The Garden of Eden nursery is vandalized and two women who work there are poisoned.

Clarke, Anna
POISON PARSLEY (Magna Print Books, 1983) What happens when a widow gets mixed up with a married herbalist.

Collins, Wilkie
THE MOONSTONE (Harper, 1868) Features Sergeant Cuff whose hobby is roses.

Connington, J. J. (pseudonym for A. W. Stewart)
MURDER IN THE MAZE (Little, 1927) Twin brothers are murdered in their garden maze.

Constantine, K. C.
THE MAN WHO LIKED SLOW TOMATOES (Godine, 1982) Jimmy Romanelli, who produced ripe tomatoes much earlier in the season than is normal, goes missing.

Craig, Alisa (pseudonym for Charlotte MacLeod who, in private life, is an officer in her Canadian garden club.)
    The following books feature the Grub and Stake Gardening and Roving Club of Lobelia Falls, Ontario:
THE GRUB-AND-STAKERS MOVE A MOUN-TAIN (Doubleday, 1981)
THE GRUB-AND-STAKERS QUILT A BEE (Doubleday, 1985)
THE GRUB-AND-STAKERS PINCH A POKE (Avon, 1988)
THE GRUB-AND-STAKERS SPIN A YARN (Avon, 1990)

Craig, Philip R.
Jeff Jackson, a former Boston cop who moved to Martha's Vineyard to enjoy gardening, fishing, and cooking, gets involved in crime solving:
A BEAUTIFUL PLACE TO DIE (Scribner's, 1989)
THE WOMAN WHO WALKED INTO THE SEA (Scribner's, 1991)
THE DOUBLE-MINDED MEN (Macmillan, 1992)

Daly, Elizabeth
DEADLY NIGHTSHADE (Farrar, 1940) New York City book expert, Henry Gamadge, becomes involved with wildflower poisonings in Maine.
ANY SHAPE OR FORM (Farrar, 1945) Henry Gamadge again, and this time, it's murder in a rose garden.

Dorner, Marjorie
FREEZE FRAME (Morrow, 1990) Wisconsin college professor, Beth Conroy, on a 2½-month sabbatical in Cambridge, England, indulges her passion for visiting and photographing formal gardens.

Drummond, John Keith
Matilda Worthing and Martha Shaw, two elderly ladies living in a small, well-to-do California town, love gardening and teas, but seem to get involved in mayhem:
THY STING, OH DEATH (St. Martin's, 1985)
'TIS THE SEASON TO BE DYING (St. Martin's, 1988)

Drummond, June
FUNERAL URN (Gollancz, 1976) Margot Wooten, a botanist, discovers a gravestone in an English village and realizes from the plants on it that the dead woman was a poisoner.

Ferrars, E. X.
The following books feature Andrew Basnett, an amateur detective and retired English botanist (like Ferrars's husband).
SOMETHING WICKED (Doubleday, 1984)
THE ROOT OF ALL EVIL (Doubleday, 1984)
THE CRIME AND THE CRYSTAL (Doubleday, 1985)
THE OTHER DEVIL'S NAME (Doubleday, 1987)
A MURDER TOO MANY (Doubleday, 1988)
SMOKE WITHOUT FIRE (Doubleday, 1991)

Fitt, Mary
MIZMAZE (Michael Joseph, 1959) Murder in a garden maze at an English country house.

Ford, Leslie
MURDER WITH SOUTHERN HOSPITALITY (Scribner's, 1942) The Garden Club Pilgrimage of Natchez, Mississippi is the setting for this mystery.

Forester, C. S.
PAYMENT DEFERRED (Little, Brown, 1942) A man with money problems commits murder and buries the body in his back garden.

Forrest, Richard
These books feature Lyon and Bea Wentworth. He writes children's books and she is a Connecticut politician and gardener.
A CHILD'S GARDEN OF DEATH (Bobbs Merrill, 1975)
THE WIZARD OF DEATH (Bobbs Merrill, 1977)
DEATH UNDER THE LILACS (St. Martin's, 1985)

Fraser, Anthea
SIX PROUD WALKERS (Doubleday, 1989) The word "murder" is spelled out with red flowers in an English garden.

Fraser, James (pseudonym for Alan White)
THE EVERGREEN DEATH (Harcourt, 1969) A gardener finds the mutilated body of a teenage girl under the evergreens.
A COCK-PIT OF ROSES (Harcourt, 1970) A party at the manor house ends in death in the rose garden.

Fremlin, Celia
THE SPIDER ORCHIDS (Doubleday, 1978) Rita's husband prefers his spider orchids to Rita.

Fyfield, Frances
A QUESTION OF GUILT (Pocket Books, 1988) A garden is a refuge that leads to new friendships.

Graham, Caroline
THE KILLINGS AT BADGER'S DRIFT (Avon, 1989) After locating a coral root orchid, Emily Simpson is found dead.
MURDER AT MADINGLY GRANGE (Morrow, 1991) Laurel Hannaford would rather garden than play hostess at a murder mystery weekend at her great-aunt's English estate.

Granger, Ann
SAY IT WITH POISON (St. Martin's, 1991) Alan Markby, Chief Inspector and fervent gardener, investigates a murder done with poisonous herbs; set in the English Cotswolds.

Hadley, Joan
Featuring Theo Bloomer, a retired Connecticut florist who tends to view the world through his knowledge of flowers and botanical folklore:
NIGHT BLOOMING CEREUS (St. Martin's, 1986)
THE DEADLY ACKEE (St. Martin's, 1988)

Heyer, Georgette
DETECTION UNLIMITED (Dutton, 1969) A newcomer to a small English village is murdered at a garden party.

Hill, Reginald
DEADHEADS (Macmillan, 1984) An accountant with a passion for roses seems to be killing people who stand in his way on the corporate ladder.

Holton, Leonard
All of the following feature avid gardener Father Joseph Breeder of the Convent of Holy Innocents in east Los Angeles:
THE SAINT MAKER (Dodd, Mead, 1959)
A PACT WITH SATAN (Dodd, Mead, 1960)
SECRET OF THE DOUBTING SAINT (Dodd, Mead, 1961)
DELIVER US FROM WOLVES (Dodd, Mead, 1963)
FLOWERS BY REQUEST (Dodd, Mead, 1964)
OUT OF THE DEPTHS (Dodd, Mead, 1966)
A TOUCH OF JONAH (Dodd, Mead, 1968)
A PROBLEM IN ANGELS (Dodd, Mead, 1970)
THE MIRROR OF HELL (Dodd, Mead, 1972)
THE DEVIL TO PLAY (Dodd, Mead, 1974)
A CORNER OF PARADISE (St. Martin's, 1977)

Innes, Michael
DEATH BY WATER (Dodd, Mead, 1968) Village tale with a garden party and a body in a gazebo.
A NIGHT OF ERRORS (Dodd, Mead, 1947) Has a maze.

Jackson, Muriel Resnik
THE GARDEN CLUB (St. Martin's, 1992) Transplanted New Yorker Merrie Lee Spencer becomes involved in gardening and mysterious happenings in Davis Landing, North Carolina.

Jepson, Edgar A.
THE GARDEN AT NO. 19 (Wessels & Bissell, 1910) The occupant at #20 Walden Road wonders about the strange things going on in the garden at #19.

Johns, Veronica P.
SERVANT'S PROBLEM (Doubleday, 1958) Webster Flagg, a black ex-actor and retired butler, tries to find out what is buried in his New York City garden.

Kenney, Susan
GARDEN OF MALICE (Scribner's, 1983) Set at Montfort Abbey, a medieval English manor with beautiful gardens which are destroyed by vandals.

Lathen, Emma
GREEN GROW THE DOLLARS (Simon & Schuster, 1982) Featuring John Putnam Thatcher, a Wall Street banker, and an expert amateur gardener who is pitted against professional plant developers.

Law, Janice
INFECTED BE THE AIR (Walker, 1991) Alice Bertram, partner in an organic vegetable and herb business, tries to find out why her ex-husband was murdered.

Lemarchand, Elizabeth
SUDDENLY, WHILE GARDENING (Doubleday, 1979) Climbing roses that need to be tied result in death.
CHANGE FOR THE WORSE (Walker, 1981) Trouble at Fairlynch Manor, the beautiful house and gardens that belong to the Heritage of Britain Trust.

Marsh, Ngaio
GRAVE MISTAKE (Little, Brown, 1978) Finding a gardener in a small English village is not easy.

Marsh, Richard
THE GARDEN OF MYSTERY (Long, 1911)

Matteson, Stefanie
MURDER AT TEATIME (Diamond Books, 1991) Set on an island off the Maine coast, an herb garden and a famous botanical library are featured.

McMullen, Mary
A GRAVE WITHOUT FLOWERS (Doubleday, 1983) What can happen when you tour English gardens in June.

Melville, Jennie
MURDER IN THE GARDEN (Macmillan, 1987)
The Garden is a London enclave where three women
friends live.

Michaels, Barbara
VANISH WITH THE ROSE (Simon & Schuster,
1992) Diane Reed, posing as a landscape architect
who specializes in old roses, tries to discover what
happened to her brother.

Mitchell, Gladys
DEATH OF A DELFT BLUE (Michael Joseph,
1964) Psychologist Dame Beatrice Lestrange Bradley
becomes involved with a family of bulb growers and
diamond merchants.
DEATH CAP DANCERS (St. Martin's, 1981) Some
chapter titles are wood sage, wild thyme, maiden pink,
and acrid lobelia.

Moody, Susan
PENNY BLACK (Macmillan, 1984) Murder and a
competition between orchid growers to produce the first
black orchid.

Moyes, Patricia
MANY DEADLY RETURNS (Holt, Rinehart, 1970)
Have roses caused the death of Lady Balaclava at her
birthday party?
BLACK WIDOWER (Holt, Rinehart, 1975) Henry
and Emmy Tibbett take the Georgetown Garden
Tour and get involved in murder at Maycroft House.

Nash, Anne
SAID WITH FLOWERS (Doubleday, 1943)
CABBAGES AND CRIME (Doubleday, 1945)

Nichols, Beverley
In addition to his "how I did it" gardening books,
Beverley Nichols also wrote mysteries featuring Horatio
Green, an English detective who gardened in Surrey:
NO MAN'S STREET (Dutton, 1954)
THE MOONFLOWER MURDER (Dutton, 1955)
DEATH TO SLOW MUSIC (Dutton, 1956)
THE RICH DIE HARD (Dutton, 1958)
MURDER BY REQUEST (Dutton, 1960)

Paar, Angelica
WATCHER IN THE GARDEN (Pocket Books,
1989) White roses are a murderer's signature; set in
London and Yorkshire.

Pedneau, Dave
The following feature Whit Pynchon, the district
attorney's chief investigator, who uses his flower garden
as a means of escape from his job:
A.P.B. (Ballantine, 1987)
D.O.A. (Ballantine, 1988)
B.O.L.O. (Ballantine, 1989)
A.K.A. (Ballantine, 1990)
B. and E. (Ballantine, 1991)

Peters, Ellis
The following feature Brother Cadfael, a 12th-century
monk and herbalist who believes "when you have done
everything else, perfecting a conventional herb garden
is a fine and satisfying thing to do":
A MORBID TASTE FOR BONES (Morrow, 1978)
ONE CORPSE TOO MANY: A MEDIEVAL
   NOVEL OF SUSPENSE (Morrow, 1980)
MONK'S-HOOD: THE THIRD CHRONICLE OF
   BROTHER CADFAEL (Morrow, 1981)
SAINT PETER'S FAIR: THE FOURTH
   CHRONICLE OF BROTHER CADFAEL (Mor-
   row, 1981)
THE LEPER OF SAINT GILES: THE FIFTH
   CHRONICLE OF BROTHER CADFAEL (Mor-
   row, 1982)
THE VIRGIN IN THE ICE: THE SIXTH
   CHRONICLE OF BROTHER CADFAEL (Mor-
   row, 1983)
THE SANCTUARY SPARROW: THE SEV-
   ENTH CHRONICLE OF BROTHER
   CADFAEL (Morrow, 1983)
THE DEVIL'S NOVICE: THE EIGHTH
   CHRONICLE OF BROTHER CADFAEL
   (Morrow, 1984)
THE PILGRIM OF HATE: THE TENTH
   CHRONICLE OF BROTHER CADFAEL (Mor-
   row, 1984)
DEAD MAN'S RANSOM: THE NINTH
   CHRONICLE OF BROTHER CADFAEL
   (Morrow, 1985)

AN EXCELLENT MYSTERY: THE ELEVENTH CHRONICLE OF BROTHER CADFAEL (Morrow, 1985)

THE RAVEN IN THE FOREGATE: THE TWELFTH CHRONICLE OF BROTHER CADFAEL (Morrow, 1986)

THE ROSE RENT: THE THIRTEENTH CHRONICLE OF BROTHER CADFAEL (Morrow, 1986)

THE HERMIT OF EYTON FOREST: THE FOURTEENTH CHRONICLE OF BROTHER CADFAEL (Mysterious Press, 1988)

THE CONFESSION OF BROTHER HALUIN: THE FIFTEENTH CHRONICLE OF BROTHER CADFAEL (Mysterious Press, 1989)

THE HERETIC'S APPRENTICE: THE SIXTEENTH CHRONICLE OF BROTHER CADFAEL (Mysterious Press, 1990)

THE POTTER'S FIELD: THE SEVENTEENTH CHRONICLE OF BROTHER CADFAEL (Mysterious Press, 1990)

THE SUMMER OF THE DANES: THE EIGHTEENTH CHRONICLE OF BROTHER CADFAEL (Mysterious Press, 1991)

Pim, Sheila
COMMON OR GARDEN CRIME (Hodder and Stoughton, 1945) Murder at a flower show in an Irish village near Dublin.

Radford, Edwin I. and Mona A.
LOOK IN AT MURDER (Long, 1956) Features Inspector Manson and a flower show.

Rendell, Ruth
TALKING TO STRANGE MEN (Ballantine, 1988) The unbalanced boss at Trowbridge's Garden Center is trying to get his ex-wife back while also dealing with schoolboys pretending to be spies.

Rhode, John
THE FATAL GARDEN (Dodd, Mead, 1949) Two people are murdered in the garden of a secretive inventor.

Roosevelt, Elliot
MURDER IN THE ROSE GARDEN (St. Martin's, 1989) A Washington society matron and blackmailer is found dead in the White House rose garden.

Rothenberg, Rebecca
THE BULRUSH MURDERS: A BOTANICAL MYSTERY (Carroll and & Graf, 1991) MIT Microbiologist Claire Sharples moves to California to do agricultural research and gets involved in a murder investigation.

Rowlands, Betty
A LITTLE GENTLE SLEUTHING (Walker, 1990) While digging in a Cotswolds woods for leaf mould to put on her garden, Iris Ash discovers a body.

Sayers, Dorothy
BUSMAN'S HONEYMOON (Harcourt, 1937) Both victim and murderer have been a part of the large garden at the honeymoon cottage of Lord Peter Wimsey and Harriet Vane.

Sherwood, John
The following feature Celia Grant, landscape designer, owner of a garden center, and amateur detective. The books contain much authentic horticultural information, and are liberally footnoted so the reader can find the references that are of interest. They are wonderful!
GREEN TRIGGER FINGERS (Scribner's, 1984) Celia finds a corpse while digging in a garden.

A BOTANIST AT BAY (Scribner's, 1985) On a trip to New Zealand searching for a rare Mount Cook lily, Celia becomes involved in a murder.

THE MANTRAP GARDEN (Scribner's, 1986) Gertrude Jekyll's famous garden at Monk's Mead is the setting for murder.

FLOWERS OF EVIL (Scribner's, 1987) Murder in an English country garden that Celia has been commissioned to replant.

MENACING GROVES (Scribner's, 1988) Murder and a tour of Italian gardens.

A BOUQUET OF THORNS (Scribner's, 1989) Celia judges a village flower show and helps her assistant when he is charged with murder.

THE SUNFLOWER PLOT (Scribner's, 1990) Celia designs an Elizabethan garden and takes a loss on her alpines in an attempt to save her nursery business.

THE HANGING GARDEN (Scribner's, 1993)

Sibley, Celestine
AH, SWEET MYSTERY (HarperCollins, 1991) Kate Mulcay loves to garden and read gardening books, but she

doesn't have much time for either once she starts investigating a murder.

STRAIGHT AS AN ARROW (HarperCollins, 1992) Kate Mulcay is back, this time investigating murder on Ila Island.

Simonson, Sheila
LARKSPUR (St. Martin's, 1990) Lark Dailey, owner of the mystery bookstore, Larkspur Books, becomes involved when a poet is poisoned with larkspur.

Stout, Rex
SOME BURIED CAESAR (Farrar, 1939) On his way to an orchid show, Wolfe gets into an automobile accident.
BLACK ORCHIDS (Farrar, 1942) Wolfe's desire for a very rare black orchid involves him in some shady dealings.
(Note: Rex Stout was the brother of Ruth Stout of organic gardening fame. An interest in gardening must be genetic.)

Taylor, Edith
THE SERPENT UNDER IT (Norton, 1973) Cats and gardens are featured.

Thomson, June
DEATH CAP (Doubleday, 1977) A classic English village tale involving mushroom poisoning.

Van Deusen, Delia
THE GARDEN CLUB MURDERS (Bobbs-Merrill, 1941) Death among the hardy perennials.

Webb, Jack
The following feature Father Joseph Shanley, who cultivates roses in Los Angeles:
THE BIG SIN (Rinehart, 1952)
THE NAKED ANGEL (Rinehart, 1953)
THE DAMNED LOVELY (Rinehart, 1954)
THE BROKEN DOLL (Rinehart, 1955)
THE BAD BLONDE (Rinehart, 1956)
THE BRASS HALO (Rinehart, 1957)
THE DEADLY SEX (Rinehart, 1959)
THE DELICATE DARLING (Rinehart, 1959)
THE GILDED WITCH (Regency, 1963)

Wentworth, Patricia
THE GAZEBO (also called *The Summerhouse*) (Lippincott, 1956) Maud Silver, a retired English schoolteacher becomes a professional private detective and investigates the murder of an elderly woman in a gazebo.

Whitechurch, Victor L.
THE CRIME AT DIANA'S POOL (Unwin, 1927) Murder at a lawn party.

Wood, Sally
MURDER OF A NOVELIST (Simon & Schuster, 1942) Ann Thorne, a spinster sleuth, becomes involved in murder in a Middlebury garden.

Woods, Sara
TARRY AND BE HANGED (Holt, Rinehart, 1971) Children find a body while playing in a doctor's garden.

Wright, Willard H.
GARDEN MURDER CASE (Scribner's, 1935; Paperback library, 1963) A Philo Vance story involving a garden.

NOVELS

Arkell, Reginald
OLD HERBACEOUS (Harcourt, Brace, 1951) An old-fashioned story about an English gardener. A. J. Cronin called it "enchanting, fresh as an English spring, fragrant as sweet lavender."

Austin, Alfred
IN VERONICA'S GARDEN (Macmillan, 1902) A poet's experiences in English gardens.

Bassani, Giorgio
THE GARDEN OF THE FINZI-CONTINIS (Harcourt Brace Jovanovich, 1978) Story of a Jewish family in postwar Ferrara, Italy. There is also a movie.

Bell, Neil (pseudonym for Stephen Southwold)
PINKNEY'S GARDEN (Doubleday, 1937) Mary Pinkney struggles with her children and her market garden in an English coastal village.

Burnett, Frances Hodgson
THE SECRET GARDEN (originally published in 1911) Mary Lennox, an unhappy little girl, finds solace in a secret walled garden. (Maytham

Hall in Kent, England, the site of Burnett's "secret garden" is open to the public on a limited basis. There's an interesting article about Burnett and Maytham Hall in the April 1991 issue of *Victoria* magazine.)

Cushman, Clarissa F.
BUT FOR HER GARDEN (Little, Brown, 1935) In an attempt to escape New York City life, Judith moves to the country and makes a beautiful garden.

Dennis, Nigel
A HOUSE IN ORDER (Vanguard, 1966) A horticulturist is imprisoned in a greenhouse through the winter.

Garfield, Leon
THE PLEASURE GARDEN (Viking Press, 1976) Terror in 18th-century London's Mulberry Pleasure Garden.

Godden, Jon
IN HER GARDEN (Knopf, 1981) What happens when a 75-year-old English widow falls in love with her 30-year-old gardener.

Godden, Rumer
AN EPISODE OF SPARROWS (Puffin Books, 1989) A child creates a secret garden in a London bomb hole.

Goudge, Eileen
GARDEN OF LIES (Viking, 1989) Two girls are switched at birth. One grows up in a fashionable brownstone with a rose garden.

Hammond, Lily
IN THE GARDEN OF DELIGHT (Crowell, 1916) An invalid records the events of her life and the changing scenery of her garden.

Hauck, Louise (pseudonym for Peter Ash and Louise Landon)
GARDENIAS FOR SUE (Dodd, Mead, 1942) A wartime love story between a designer in a California aircraft factory and a girl who loves gardening.

Hillmore, Susan
THE GREENHOUSE (New Amsterdam Books, 1988)

James, Edward
THE GARDENER WHO SAW GOD (Scribner, 1937) The head gardener on an English estate has a vision on the same day he loses at a London flower show.

Kosinski, Jerzy
BEING THERE (Harcourt Brace Jovanovich, 1970) A man spends all his time tending his garden and watching TV.

Oates, Joyce Carol
A GARDEN OF EARTHLY DELIGHTS (Vanguard, 1967) Clara, migratory worker, elevates herself.

Pilcher, Rosamunde
THE SHELL SEEKERS (St. Martin's, 1988) Penelope Keeling, avid gardener, lives in a Cotswold village and reminisces about her past.

Read, Miss (pseudonym for Dora Jesse Saint)
She writes a series of charming books set in English villages. Although the books do not have gardening as a primary focus, many of the villagers are gardeners. If you are interested in sampling one of these, start with her first, *Village School* (Michael Joseph, 1955). Be warned, however, that they are addictive.

Running, Corinne
GARDEN SHOWER (Morrow, 1948) A baby shower in a garden doesn't come off as planned.

Santmeyer, Helen
HERBS AND APPLES (St. Martin's, 1987)

Sharp, Margery
FOUR GARDENS (Putnam, 1935) Caroline's four English gardens: childhood garden, war garden, formal garden, and a roof garden in her old age.

Stewart, J. I. M.
ANDREW AND TOBIAS (Norton, 1980) Andy, the gardener, turns out to be the lost brother of Toby, the adopted son of the wealthy Englishman for whom Andy works.

Sullivan, Faith
THE CAPE ANN (Crown, 1988) A young girl and her mother dream of building their own home and having a garden.

Tate, Peter
GARDENS ONE TO FIVE (Doubleday, 1971) Inhabitants of the five gardens are observed by an unseen force in this allegorical fantasy.

Trevor, William
THE SILENCE IN THE GARDEN (Viking, 1988) Something happened in the summer twilight in an Irish garden on the eve of World War I.

West, Jessamyn
FRIENDLY PERSUASION (Harcourt, Brace, 1945) Features Jess Birdwell, a Quaker nurseryman.

Wheatley, Vera
SATURDAY AT HAZELDINES (Dutton, 1936) Saturday is gardening day at the Hazeldines, an upper middle class English family.

Wilson, Angus
THE MIDDLE AGE OF MRS. ELIOT (Viking Press, 1959) Meg Eliot's brother, David, and his friend, Gordon, own a nursery and write botanical books.
HEMLOCK AND AFTER (Viking Press, 1952) Ella Sands seeks refuge from life in her gardening.

SHORT STORIES

Gottlieb, Jane (photographer)
GARDEN TALES: CLASSIC STORIES FROM FAVORITE WRITERS (Viking Studio, 1990) Five famous short stories featuring a garden—"The Garden Party" by Katherine Mansfield, "A Curtain of Green" by Eudora Welty, "The Chrysanthemums" by John Steinbeck, "Rappaccini's Daughter" by Nathaniel Hawthorne and "The Occasional Garden" by Saki.

For a comprehensive listing of short stories with a gardening theme, check the *Short Story Index* at your library. It is a multi-volume reference work and contains listings of thousands of short stories. Look under both "Gardens" and "Gardeners" in each of the volumes, and you will find the titles of many stories with a gardening focus.

Part II:

How-To
Gardening

REFERENCE

Anglade, Pierre (editor)
LAROUSSE GARDENING AND GARDENS
(Facts On File, 1990) Covers plant descriptions, gardening techniques, types of gardens, garden styles around the world and famous gardeners and designers; includes over 1,000 color photos.

Bailey, L. H.
HOW PLANTS GET THEIR NAMES (Dover, reprint of 1933 edition) Explains the reasons behind scientific nomenclature, the history of the terms, and more.
THE STANDARD CYCLOPEDIA OF HORTI-CULTURE (Macmillan, 1941, 3 volumes) Outdated, but of interest historically.

Bailey, L. H. and Ethel
HORTUS THIRD: A CONCISE DICTIONARY OF PLANTS CULTIVATED IN THE U.S. AND CANADA (Macmillan, 1976) Describes 281 families, 3,301 genera, 20,397 species, and numerous subspecies, varieties, forms and cultivars of North American plants; alphabetized by genus.

Barnett, Carol
BOTANICAL AND HORTICULTURAL BOOKS: A PRICE GUIDE (Spoon River Press, 1991) Contains 2,500 titles (alphabetized by author) published before 1976; gives publisher, date of publication, page count, book's condition and recent price in dollars and pounds; includes a list of dealers, mainly U.S. but some Canadian and British, whose specialty is older gardening books.

Barton, Barbara
GARDENING BY MAIL: A SOURCE BOOK (Houghton Mifflin, 1990) A directory of mail-order resources for gardeners in the U.S. and Canada, including seed companies, nurseries, suppliers of all garden necessaries and ornaments, horticultural and plant societies, magazines, libraries and a list of useful books on plants and gardening. Mind- boggling—you had best set the timer when you sit down with this book, otherwise hours will go by and you'll never notice.

Baumgardt, John P.
HOW TO IDENTIFY THE FLOWERING PLANT FAMILIES (Timber Press, 1982) Using the techniques he teaches, you can correctly place American flowering plants into their families.

Bernhardt, Peter
WILY VIOLETS AND UNDERGROUND ORCHIDS: REVELATIONS OF A BOTANIST (Morrow, 1989)

Brickell, Christopher (editor)
THE AMERICAN HORTICULTURAL SOCI-
ETY ENCYCLOPEDIA OF GARDEN PLANTS
(Macmillan, 1989) Describes over 8,000 plants and
includes over 4,000 color photos.

**Brookes, John; Beckett, Kenneth;
and Everett, Thomas**
THE GARDENER'S INDEX OF PLANTS AND
FLOWERS (Macmillan, 1987) Describes 4,000 species and varieties of annuals, perennials, trees, shrubs,
climbers, cacti, bulbs and water plants.

Bruce, Marlene and Hank
GARDENING TRIVIA (Quinlan Press, 1988) Find
out how much you know (or don't know) when you
take these true-false, multiple choice and matching
pairs quizzes.

Capon, Brian
BOTANY FOR GARDENERS (Timber Press,
1990) Presents information on the anatomy and functions of plants relevant to gardening.

Coombes, Allen J.
A DICTIONARY OF PLANT NAMES (Timber
Press, 1985) Common and botanical names for thousands
of plants, plus correct and preferred pronunciations.

Coughlin, Roberta
THE GARDENER'S COMPANION: A BOOK
OF LISTS AND LORE (HarperCollins, 1991) Over
350 lists covering such diverse topics as "narrow-growing
trees," "sources for raspberries," "public rose gardens of the
U.S.," etc. plus a chapter detailing which plants are
needed for special gardens (biblical, Middle Ages,
Shakespeare, witch, colonial, Victorian, wedding, fire-re-
sistant and allergy-free); interesting book to thumb
through at random.

Crockett, James Underwood
CROCKETT'S TOOL SHED (Little, Brown, 1979)
Describes specific tools and how they are used in
gardening.

Dietz, Marjorie J. (editor)
10,000 GARDEN QUESTIONS: ANSWERED BY
20 EXPERTS (HarperCollins, 1990, 4th edition) Answers to a gardener's most important questions.

Ellis, Barbara (editor)
NORTH AMERICAN HORTICULTURE: A
REFERENCE GUIDE (Macmillan, 1990, rev. ed.)
The staff of the American Horticultural Society com-
piled this list of horticultural societies and organiza-
tions, botanical gardens, periodicals, etc.

Ettlinger, Steve
THE COMPLETE ILLUSTRATED GUIDE TO
EVERYTHING SOLD IN GARDEN CENTERS
(EXCEPT THE PLANTS) (Macmillan, 1990) A gardening version of the Sears catalogue covering soil, fertilizers, plant food, pesticides, grass seed, garden tools,
personal gear and many other things; explains what to
buy and how to use it.

Evans, Mary
GARDEN BOOKS, OLD AND NEW (Gryphon
Books, 1971) Originally published by the Pennsylva-
nia Horticultural Society in 1926.

Everett, Thomas H.
THE N.Y. BOTANICAL GARDEN ILLUS-
TRATED ENCYCLOPEDIA OF HORTICUL-
TURE (Garland Publishing, 1982) Ten volumes
covering over 3,600 genera with over 10,000 photos.

Fell, Derek
THE ESSENTIAL GARDENER: THE BEST
PLANTS FOR DESIGN AND CULTIVATION
(Arch Cape Press, 1990) A complete guide to the 650
best annuals, perennials, bulbs, roses, trees, shrubs,
herbs and vegetables; 900 color photos.

Ferguson, Nicola
RIGHT PLANT, RIGHT PLACE (Summit Books,
1984) A handbook for selecting the right plant depending on the requirements of the site and the purpose of the plant; over 1,400 color photos.

Gibbons, Bob
THE SECRET LIFE OF FLOWERS: A GUIDE TO
PLANT BIOLOGY (Sterling, 1990) Discusses plant
classifications, structure, photosynthesis, reproduction
and more.

Gledhill, David
THE NAMES OF PLANTS (Cambridge University Press, 1989, 2nd edition) Covers how plants are named and the meaning of the names.

Goode, Patrick, and Lancaster, Michael (editors)
THE OXFORD COMPANION TO GARDENS (Oxford University Press, 1991) Contains 1,500 entries on a variety of topics including history, terminology, garden plans, 700 famous gardens and garden designers.

Halpin, Anne M.
THE NAMING OF FLOWERS (HarperCollins, 1990) Explains botanical names and classifications to help gardeners recognize common traits, colors and scents in plants; includes floral lore.

Hardin, James W., and Arena, Jay M.
HUMAN POISONING FROM NATIVE AND CULTIVATED PLANTS (Duke University Press, 1974) Organized by plant families, the lists of poisonous plants use the plant's common name.

Hay, Roy, and Synge, Patrick
THE COLOR DICTIONARY OF FLOWERS AND PLANTS (Crown, 1982) Descriptions and 2,048 color photos make this a very complete dictionary.

Hedrick, Ulysses P.
A HISTORY OF HORTICULTURE IN AMERICA TO 1860 (Timber Press, 1988) A reprint of the 1951 edition with the addition of Elisabeth Woodburn's addendum of horticultural books published from 1861 to 1920.

Heriteau, Jacqueline, and Cathey, H. Marc
THE NATIONAL ARBORETUM BOOK OF OUTSTANDING GARDEN PLANTS (Simon & Schuster, 1990) Descriptions and growing information for over 1,700 flowers, trees, shrubs, ground covers, vines, ornamental grasses, aquatics and herbs that the people at the National Arboretum consider the most beautiful, durable and adaptable for North American gardens; includes 450 color photos and regional advice.

Herwig, Rob
HOUSE AND GARDEN PLANTS (Crown, 1986) A photograph, description of habits and needs, and cultivation and garden use data for each of the 855 houseplants and 2,007 garden plants.

Hessayon, Dr. D. G.
THE ARMCHAIR BOOK OF THE GARDEN (Sterling, 1991) Contains gardening lore, information on great gardens in history, world-record growing feats, gardening oddities and more.

Ingwersen, Will
CLASSIC GARDEN PLANTS (Timber Press, 1980) His choices for the best garden plants.

Isaacson, Richard T.
ANDERSON HORTICULTURAL LIBRARY'S SOURCE LIST OF PLANTS AND SEEDS (Minnesota Landscape Arboretum, Box 39, Chanhassen, MN 55317, 1989) Contains sources for 400 catalogs and 40,000 plants and seeds.
GARDENING, A GUIDE TO THE LITERATURE (Garland, 1985) A bibliography of 524 gardening books categorized under the following headings: reference, landscape design, ornamental gardening plants, methods of growing and using plants, gardening practices and plant problems and miscellaneous gardening topics.

Johnson, Hugh
THE PRINCIPLES OF GARDENING: A GUIDE TO THE ART, HISTORY, SCIENCE AND PRACTICE OF GARDENING (Simon & Schuster, 1984) Numerous color photos and illustrations combined with the variety of topics make this a most interesting read.

Lancaster, Roy
GARDEN PLANTS FOR CONNOISSEURS (Timber Press, 1988) Descriptions of 100 of his favorite trees, shrubs, climbers, conifers and perennials.

Logan, William Bryant
THE GARDENER'S BOOK OF SOURCES (Penguin, 1988) Sources for nurseries, societies, periodicals and services. Fun to browse through, but I find it difficult to locate specific items.

Mabberley, D. J.
THE PLANT BOOK (Cambridge University Press, 1987) Dictionary of flowering plants using Cronquist's classification method.

Makower, Joel
THE NATURE CATALOG (Random House, 1991) A sourcebook of places, events, publications, organizations and other things that have to do with nature (e.g., bird watching, wildlife refuges, minerals, nature travel, etc.)

Martin, Laura
GARDEN FLOWER FOLKLORE (Globe Pequot, 1987) Covers history, cultivation, legend, uses and more for 100 garden flowers.

McCann, Joy
GARDENER'S INDEX FOR 1986-1990 (Compu-Dex Press, P.O. Box 27041, Kansas City, MO 64110) Indexes articles in *Flower and Garden, Fine Gardening, Horticulture, National Gardening* and *Organic Gardening*.

McMahon, Bernard
McMAHON'S AMERICAN GARDENER (Funk & Wagnalls, 1976) Reprint of 1857 edition; of historical interest as it affords a view of what gardening was like and which plants were used in the mid-19th century.

Morgan, Hal
MAIL ORDER GARDENER (Harper & Row, 1988) Over 1,500 mail order sources organized by plant types (e.g., herbs) and subjects (e.g., garden furniture).

Morrow, Baker H.
A DICTIONARY OF LANDSCAPE ARCHITECTURE (University of New Mexico Press, 1987) Covers technical terms, plus important periods and individuals in landscaping.

Neal, Bill
GARDENER'S LATIN: A LEXICON (Algonquin, 1992) Definitions of Latin terms used in describing plants; includes gardening lore and information on famous gardens and gardeners.

Ortho
PLANT SELECTOR (Ortho, 1991) Over 150 lists help in the selection of flowers, trees, shrubs, vines and ground covers for different types of gardens.

Pereire, Anita
THE PRENTICE-HALL ENCYCLOPEDIA OF GARDEN FLOWERS (Prentice-Hall, 1989) Alphabetized descriptions of over 2,000 species of flowering plants; includes over 1,000 color photos.

Perry, Frances (editor)
SIMON & SCHUSTER'S COMPLETE GUIDE TO PLANTS AND FLOWERS (Simon & Schuster, 1976) Color photos, descriptions, and growing information for hundreds of indoor and outdoor plants.

Philip, Chris
THE PLANT FINDER (Hardy Plant Society of Great Britain, 5th edition) Covers 50,000 species, cultivars and varieties of plants available from over 500 British nurseries; includes addresses, phone numbers, prices and export policy.

Preston, Deborah (editor)
HEALTHY HARVEST III: A DIRECTORY OF SUSTAINABLE AGRICULTURE AND HORTICULTURE ORGANIZATIONS 1989–1990 (Potomac Valley Press, 1989) Over 1,000 listings and descriptions of organic growers associations, organic food distributors, schools and workshops, seed exchanges, publishers, and suppliers in the U.S. and foreign countries; includes a subject and geographic index.

Raven, Peter H.; Evert, Ray; and Eichhorn, Susan
THE BIOLOGY OF PLANTS (Worth Publishers, 1986, 4th edition) An in-depth textbook.

Reader's Digest
A GARDEN FOR ALL SEASONS (RD Association, 1991) Covers over 1,000 plants arranged according to season, plus 1,200+ color photos and illustrations to make selection easy.
GUIDE TO CREATIVE GARDENING (RD Association, 1987) Describes 1,000 annuals, biennials, perennials, alpines, roses, shrubs, bulbs, climbers and plants for a water garden; includes 1,250 color photos

and drawings, plus ideas for combining the plants in 230 different ways.

Royal Horticultural Society
THE NEW ROYAL HORTICULTURAL SOCIETY DICTIONARY OF GARDENING (Stockton Press, 1991) A four-volume set covering over 55,000 plants and their cultivation requirements, plus numerous articles on practical topics and 250 biographies of people famous in the plant world.

Seymour, L. D. (editor)
THE WISE GARDEN ENCYCLOPEDIA (HarperCollins, 1990, revised edition) An A to Z guide to 5,000 indoor and outdoor plants, plus articles from 26 horticultural experts; includes 300 color photos and 600 line drawings.

Smith, Geoffrey
A PASSION FOR PLANTS (Trafalgar Square, 1990) Covers every aspect of indoor and outdoor ornamental gardening; includes information on plant hunters and explanation of Latin names.

Stearn, Dr. William T.
BOTANICAL LATIN: HISTORY, GRAMMAR, SYNTAX, TERMINOLOGY AND VOCABULARY (Trafalgar Square, 1983) A handbook of use to any serious gardener; an illustrated guide to descriptive terminology.

Swenson, Allan
YOUR BIBLICAL GARDEN: PLANTS OF THE BIBLE AND HOW TO GROW THEM (Doubleday, 1981)

Takhtajan, Armen
FLORISTIC REGIONS OF THE WORLD (University of California Press, 1986) Classifies and describes the world's floristic kingdoms, regions and provinces; includes maps.

Toogood, Alan
THE HILLIER GUIDE TO CONNOISSEURS' PLANTS (Timber Press, 1991) Describes 1,500 of the best trees, shrubs, roses, conifers, climbers, perennials, bulbs, ferns, grasses and alpines.

Tootill, Elizabeth, and Blackmore, Stephen (editors)
FACTS ON FILE DICTIONARY OF BOTANY (Facts On File, 1984) Defines over 3,000 terms used in taxonomy, anatomy, biochemistry, cell biology, plant pathology, genetics and ecology.

Wilkins, Malcolm
PLANTWATCHING (Facts On File, 1988) Describes how plants remember, tell time, form relationships and more.

Wright, Michael
THE COMPLETE HANDBOOK OF GARDEN PLANTS (Facts On File, 1984) Identification guide and descriptions of over 9,000 species of perennials, annuals, biennials, trees, shrubs and bulbs; includes over 2,500 color drawings.

Wyman, Donald
WYMAN'S GARDENING ENCYCLOPEDIA (Macmillan, 1987, updated 2nd edition) Composed of nearly 10,000 articles, there is advice on all gardening issues for amateurs and experts.

MANUALS

Abraham, George and Katy
THE GREEN THUMB GARDEN HANDBOOK
(Prentice-Hall, 1977) A very comprehensive one-volume manual.

Baker, Jerry
JERRY BAKER'S FLOWERING GARDEN (Collier Books, 1990) How to grow everything that flowers (annuals, perennials, bulbs, trees, shrubs and roses) without spending a lot of time or money.

Ball, Jeff and Liz
YARDENING: A GUIDE TO PLANT AND LANDSCAPE CARE FOR THE NONGARDENER (Macmillan, 1992) Covers lawn care, selecting, planting, and pruning trees and shrubs, use of flowers, high-yield vegetable gardens and more.

Better Homes and Gardens
COMPLETE GUIDE TO GARDENING (Meredith Books, 1979) Covers landscaping, lawns and ground covers, trees, shrubs, vines, perennials and biennials, annuals, bulbs, roses, special gardens, vegetables, fruits, nuts, houseplants, greenhouses, insects and diseases; 520 color photos and 550 drawings.

Blandford, Percy
GARDEN TOOLS AND GADGETS YOU CAN MAKE (TAB Books, 1989)

Brickell, Christopher (editor)
STEP-BY-STEP GARDENING TECHNIQUES (Crown, 1989) How to grow vegetables, fruits, lawns, and groundcovers, plus techniques of pruning, propagation, weed control, and greenhouse gardening; over 1,300 how-to illustrations.

Bubel, Nancy
52 WEEKEND GARDEN PROJECTS (Rodale Press, 1992) Describes projects for every season that can be completed in a weekend; includes planting a fast food garden, coaxing winter bulbs, creating a butterfly garden and getting a head start on tomatoes.

Buchanan, Rita
A WEAVER'S GARDEN (Interweave Press, 1987) How to grow plants for fiber, natural dyeing, soap and more.

Bush-Brown, James and Louise
AMERICA'S GARDEN BOOK (Scribner's, 1980) Originally published in 1939, this edition has been

revised and updated by the staff of the New York Botanical Garden; a new edition is planned for 1994.

Clevely, A.M.
THE TOTAL GARDEN: A COMPLETE GUIDE TO INTEGRATING FLOWERS, HERBS, FRUITS AND VEGETABLES (Harmony Books, 1988) How to have a garden that is both beautiful and productive.

Crockett, James Underwood
CROCKETT'S FLOWER GARDEN (Little, Brown, 1981) Month-by-month advice on growing annuals, perennials, biennials and bulbs.

Cruso, Thalassa
THE GARDENING YEAR (Lyons & Burford, 1990) Advice on what to do in the garden month-by-month.

Damrosch, Barbara
THE GARDEN PRIMER (Workman, 1988) Covers garden planning, techniques and 300 specific plants, all in a highly readable style for the beginner.

Dietz, Marjorie J.
THE ABC'S OF GARDENING: OUTDOOR AND INDOOR (Doubleday, 1985)

Evans, Hazel
GARDENING THROUGH THE YEAR: A MONTHLY GUIDE TO LOOKING AFTER YOUR GARDEN (Harper Perennial, 1987) How to design a garden and do the necessary monthly tasks.

Falk, Noel
THE PLANT DOCTOR'S PRESCRIPTION FOR A HEALTHY GARDEN (Stackpole, 1991) The host of "The Plant Doctor" on radio and TV answers frequently asked questions.

Faust, Joan (editor)
THE NEW YORK TIMES GARDEN BOOK (Lyons & Burford, 1991) Approximately 100 articles on a variety of how-to gardening topics.

Ferguson, John, and Mucke, Burkhard
THE GARDENER'S YEAR (Barron, 1991) Covers what to do in each season of the gardening year.

Goldbloom, Shelley
GARDEN SMARTS: A BOUNTY OF TIPS FROM AMERICA'S BEST GARDENERS (Globe Pequot, 1991) Nearly 1,200 tips on every aspect of gardening from 200 amateur and professional gardeners around the U.S.

Halpin, Anne M.
THE YEAR ROUND FLOWER GARDENER (Simon & Schuster, 1989) Step by-step guide to having indoor and outdoor flowers year-round, no matter where you live in the U.S.

Hessayon, Dr. D. G.
THE BEDDING PLANT EXPERT (Sterling, 1990) Covers the plants that do well in beds, borders, containers and hanging baskets.
THE FLOWER EXPERT (Sterling, 1990) Growing information on 1,500 flower varieties.
THE GARDEN EXPERT (Sterling, 1990) Tips and advice on techniques, plants, soil, and other gardening basics.

James, John
FLOWERS WHEN YOU WANT THEM: A GROWER'S GUIDE TO OUT-OF-SEASON BLOOM (Hawthorn Books, 1977) How to force a variety of bulbs, cut flowers, branches and pot plants indoors and in a greenhouse.

Jones, Pamela
HOW DOES YOUR GARDEN GROW?: THE ESSENTIAL HOME GARDEN BOOK (Viking Penguin, 1991)

Loewer, Peter
PETER LOEWER'S MONTH-BY-MONTH GARDEN ALMANAC FOR INDOOR AND OUTDOOR GARDENING (Putnam, 1983) This record of a year in his garden covers things to do each month for or in your garden.
A YEAR OF FLOWERS (Rodale Press, 1989) Covers 150 annuals, perennials, bulbs, wildflowers, everlastings, and houseplants that will provide flowers from January to December.

Loewer, Peter, and Halpin, Anne
SECRETS OF GREAT GARDENERS: HOW TO MAKE YOUR GARDEN AS BEAUTIFUL AS

THEIRS (Summit, 1991) Tips from the professionals at the Brooklyn Botanic Garden.

MacCaskey, Michael (editor)
COMPLETE GUIDE TO BASIC GARDENING (HP Books, 1986) Advice on selecting, growing, and caring for ornamental and edible plants; includes information on soil preparation, pruning, propagation and pest and disease control.

Mackey, Betty et al.
THE GARDENER'S HOME COMPANION: HOW TO RAISE AND PROPAGATE OVER 350 FLOWERS, SHRUBS, VINES, HERBS, VEGETABLES, BERRIES, AND LAWN AND ORNAMENTAL GRASSES (Macmillan, 1991) Plant descriptions and step-by-step instructions on cultivating, fertilizing, watering, pruning, mulching, propagating and harvesting, plus information on tools and equipment; includes regional gardening calendars.

Ortho
THE ORTHO BOOK OF GARDENING BASICS (Ortho, 1991) Covers garden styles and design, plus growing flowers, lawns, shrubs and trees; includes information on watering, feeding and pest and weed control and an encyclopedia of 1,700 plants.
SUCCESSFUL FLOWER GARDENING (Ortho, 1990) Describes over 500 species of flowering plants and various garden designs using these plants; includes 450 color photos.
THE EASIEST FLOWERS TO GROW (Ortho, 1990) Covers 100 varieties of easy-to-grow annuals, perennials, shrubs, vines and trees; includes design ideas.

Paul, Tessa
NEW FLOWERS: GROWING THE NEW GARDEN VARIETIES (Abrams, 1990) Describes the best of the newly developed garden plants (including roses); includes 200 color photos, 8 garden plans and list of sources.

Pearson, Robert (editor)
THE WISLEY BOOK OF GARDENING: A GUIDE FOR ENTHUSIASTS (Norton, 1983) Written by top English gardening experts.

Pettingill, Amos (pen name for William Harris)
THE WHITE-FLOWER-FARM GARDEN BOOK (Knopf, 1971) An alphabetized listing of plants and gardening techniques, plus how he and his wife started their famous Litchfield, Connecticut, nursery in 1947.

Ray, Richard; Fell, Derek; and MacCaskey, Michael
THE COMPLETE BOOK OF GARDENING (Oracle Books, 1987) Includes gardening techniques, garden layouts, plant selection according to site and use, plant descriptions and more; includes 600+ color photos.

Reader's Digest
READER'S DIGEST ILLUSTRATED GUIDE TO GARDENING (RD Association, 1981) The numerous illustrations make this a very helpful how-to manual; covers gardening outdoors and indoors, food and ornamental gardening, plant selection and much more.

Squire, David
THE GARDENER'S GUIDE (Crescent, 1991) Growing information on 500+ varieties of flowers, trees and shrubs.

Stewart, Martha
MARTHA STEWART'S GARDENING MONTH-BY-MONTH (Clarkson Potter, 1991) Describes her gardening agenda for each month, plus information on plant varieties, seed sources, natural pesticides, and recipes; includes 700 color photos of her six-acre suburban garden.

Sunset
BASIC GARDENING ILLUSTRATED (Sunset Books, 1981) A beginner's guide to gardening; includes 850 color drawings and plant selection charts.

Taloumis, George
WINTERIZE YOUR YARD AND GARDEN (Lippincott, 1976) How to care for your plants during the winter and get ready for spring.

Taylor's
GUIDE TO GARDENING TECHNIQUES (Houghton Mifflin, 1991) Based on *Taylor's Encyclopedia of Gardening* by Norman Taylor, it covers planting and transplanting, fertilizing, watering, making a new flower bed, preparing and maintaining a lawn, propa-

gation, pruning and pest control; includes source lists, regional information and the new USDA plant hardiness map.

Time-Life
COMPLETE GUIDE TO GARDENING AND LANDSCAPING (Prentice-Hall, 1991) Techniques

for planning, cultivating, and maintaining a garden; includes an encyclopedia of 700 plants.

Wright, Michael
THE COMPLETE BOOK OF GARDENING (Warner Books, 1989) A good general guide.

SOIL

Bear, Firman, et al.
EARTH: THE STUFF OF LIFE (University of Oklahoma Press, 1990, revised 2nd edition) An introduction to soil science; covers ecological issues, climate, soil conservation and more.

Brooklyn Botanic Garden
SOILS (BBG #110) Covers the basics of soil testing, organic composting, mulching, fertilizing and techniques for improving the soil.

Campbell, Stu
LET IT ROT! THE GARDENER'S GUIDE TO COMPOSTING (Storey, 1990, updated and revised edition) Covers what can and what cannot be composted, how to build a compost bin, and artificial and natural activators.
THE MULCH BOOK (Storey, 1991, revised and updated) In-depth descriptions of 50 mulches, plus the advantages and disadvantages of each.

Gershuny, Grace, and Martin, Deborah (editors)
THE RODALE BOOK OF COMPOSTING: EASY METHODS FOR EVERY GARDENER (Rodale Press, 1992, revised and updated) How to improve your soil, recycle kitchen and yard wastes, grow healthier plants, and create an earth-safe garden.

Handreck, K. A., and Black, N. D.
GROWING MEDIA FOR ORNAMENTAL PLANTS AND TURF (ISBS, 1989) Covers potting mixes, fertilizers, drainage, salinity, disease prevention and preparation of the soil for landscape planting.

Kitto, D.
COMPOSTING: THE ORGANIC NATURAL WAY (Sterling, 1988) Describes a variety of composting bins, when to turn, best materials for compost, how to use compost and more.

Lloyd, Gordon
DON'T CALL IT "DIRT"! IMPROVING YOUR GARDEN SOIL (Bookworm Publishing, 1976)

Logsdon, Gene
THE GARDENER'S GUIDE TO BETTER SOIL (Rodale Press, 1975) Covers improving the soil with mulching, composting, natural fertilizers and green manures.

Mather, Jim
SOIL CARE FOR GARDENERS: A PRACTICAL GUIDE (Trafalgar Square, 1990) How to understand and improve the soil in your garden; includes garden design for particular soils, drainage, composting, soil nutrition and more.

Ogden, Scott
GARDENING SUCCESS WITH DIFFICULT SOILS: LIMESTONE, ALKALINE CLAY AND CALICHE (Taylor, 1992) Covers growing roses, fruits and vegetables in difficult soils, plus informa-tion on heat-tolerant, lime-loving and wildlife-attract-ing plants.

Ortho
IMPROVING YOUR GARDEN SOIL (Ortho, 1992) How to solve problems with your soil.

Tompkins, Peter, and Bird, Christopher
SECRETS OF THE SOIL (HarperCollins, 1990) Covers alternatives to the use of synthetic chemicals for enriching the soil.

WATERING METHODS

Austin, Richard L.
LAWN SPRINKLERS: A DO-IT-YOURSELF GUIDE (TAB Books, 1990) Instructions for designing, installing, maintaining and repairing a sprinkling system for a variety of different lawn sizes and shapes.

Kramer, Jack
DRIP SYSTEM WATERING FOR BIGGER AND BETTER PLANTS (Norton, 1980) How to set up a drip system in flower, fruit, vegetable and container gardens.

Melby, P.
SIMPLIFIED IRRIGATION DESIGN (PDA Publications, no date) In-depth coverage of designing and installing both drip and sprinkler systems.

Raindrip, Inc.
DRIP WATERING MADE EASY: EVERYTHING YOU NEED TO KNOW TO PLAN, INSTALL, OPERATE AND MAINTAIN YOUR LOW VOLUME WATERING SYSTEM (2nd edition, 1992) A colorful 96-page booklet available free from Raindrip, Inc. Call 800-544-3747 outside California or 800-225-3747 inside California.

Young, Virgil E.
SPRINKLER IRRIGATION SYSTEMS (Mist'er Rain, 1976, 3rd edition) How to design, install and maintain an underground sprinkler system.

LANDSCAPE DESIGN

Appleton, Bonnie Lee
LANDSCAPE REJUVENATION: REMODEL-
ING THE HOME LANDSCAPE (Storey, 1988) De-
scribes what to do when an existing landscape needs help.

Better Homes and Gardens
STEP-BY-STEP LANDSCAPING (Meredith Books,
1991)

Binetti, Marianne
TIPS FOR CAREFREE LANDSCAPES: OVER 500
SURE-FIRE WAYS TO BEAUTIFY YOUR YARD
AND GARDEN (Garden Way, 1990) Which bulbs,
flowering shrubs, easy-care roses, annuals, perennials, groundcovers and container plants make for the
minimum amount of work and the best results.

Bisgrove, Richard
THE FLOWER GARDEN (Viking Penguin,
1989) How to design and combine plants to produce
an interesting flower garden; includes 7 plans.

Boisset, Caroline
TOWN GARDENS (Little, Brown, 1990) How to
create a garden that harmonizes with the style of
your house and turns site problems (narrow lot,
sunless patios, backyards that face north, etc.) into
assets; examples from expert garden designers plus a
selection guide of 120 plants.
VERTICAL GARDENING: CLIMBING
PLANTS, HANGING PLANTS, TRELLISES,
WALL PLANTING, TERRACES, WINDOW
BOXES (Grove Weidenfeld, 1988) How to use
climbers, hanging plants, and other items to enhance
a garden; includes 200-plant directory.

Breskend, J.
BACKYARD DESIGN: MAKING THE MOST
OF THE SPACE AROUND YOUR HOME (Little,
Brown, 1991) Examines the problems of backyards
that are different in size and location (city, country,
etc.) and offers solutions.

Brookes, John
THE BOOK OF GARDEN DESIGN (Macmillan, 1991) Describes exactly how to design a garden considering colors and textures of the plants, plus the garden site and use; over 500 color photos and illustrations.
THE COUNTRY GARDEN: A SEASONAL GUIDE TO DESIGNING AND PLANTING GARDENS WITH NATURAL STYLE (Crown, 1987) How to create a casual garden of massed and mixed plantings; over 500 color photos.
THE GARDEN BOOK (Crown, 1984) Over 1,000 plans and diagrams, plus 400 color photos make this a very useful book for design ideas for every size of garden.

Carley, Rachel
THE BACKYARD BOOK: IDEAS AND RESOURCES FOR OUTDOOR LIVING (Viking Penguin, 1988) Covers design ideas for decks, patios, pools and privacy; 300+ color photos.

Church, Thomas; Hall, Grace; and Laurie, Michael
GARDENS ARE FOR PEOPLE (McGraw-Hill, 1983, 2nd revised edition) The designs of the late American landscape architect, Thomas Church, illustrate how to use design principles in planning a landscape.

Cox, Jeff
LANDSCAPING WITH NATURE: USING NATURE'S DESIGNS TO PLAN YOUR YARD (Rodale Press, 1990) How to incorporate natural wilderness into your yard by using certain trees, shrubs, grasses, and ground covers, plus how to include water, wildlife and stone in your landscape.

Crockett, James Underwood, and Editors of Time-Life Books
LANDSCAPE GARDENING (Time-Life Books, 1971) Includes an encyclopedia of plants he feels are best for landscaping (deciduous trees and shrubs, evergreen trees and shrubs, ground covers, vines and palms).

Davies, Rosemary
THE CREATIVE GARDENER'S COMPANION (ISBS, 1987) Details on planning, designing, selecting plants, planting and caring for a personalized landscape.

Douglas, William Lake
HILLSIDE GARDENING: PLANTING, PROCEDURES AND DESIGN PRINCIPLES (Simon & Schuster, 1987) Describes various methods of handling a sloping site, which plants are appropriate, watering systems and more.

Douglas, William Lake, et al.
GARDEN DESIGN: HISTORY, PRINCIPLES, ELEMENTS, PRACTICE (Simon & Schuster, 1984) Examines many different styles of gardens and explains how to use ideas from them in today's gardens.

Druse, Ken
THE NATURAL GARDEN (Crown, 1988) How to combine native plants, ornamental grasses and wildflowers with other low-maintenance plants such as hardy perennials and bulbs to create a personal and informal garden anywhere; over 400 color photos and a directory of sources.

Eckbo, Garrett
HOME LANDSCAPING: THE ART OF HOME LANDSCAPING (McGraw-Hill, 1978, rev. edition) A good beginner's guide to the basics of landscape design.

Fell, Derek (editor)
THE COMPLETE GARDEN PLANNING MANUAL (HP Books, 1989) How to design an attractive and functional garden; includes photos of readily available plants with information on bloom period, soil and care requirements, and compatibility with other plants.

Fish, Margery
A FLOWER FOR EVERY DAY (Faber & Faber, 1981) Design ideas for producing a garden that provides monthly interest.

Fisher, Adrian
LABYRINTH: SOLVING THE RIDDLE OF THE MAZE (Crown, 1990) Covers the history of a variety of mazes—garden hedge, wooden, brick-path, courtyard and city; beautiful aerial photos.

Frederick Jr., William H.
THE EXUBERANT GARDEN AND THE CONTROLLING HAND: PLANT COMBINATIONS FOR NORTH AMERICAN GARDENS (Little, Brown, 1992) Contains plans, 235 color photos, and a 150-page appendix of characteristics of 600 ornamentals and ground covers with suggestions for combinations that do well in North American gardens.

Freeman, Kim, and Saft, Elizabeth
CULTIVATED PLEASURES: THE ART OF ROMANTIC GARDENING (Viking Penguin, 1989) Over 250 color photos convey the essence of a romantic garden.

Frieze, Charlotte
SOCIAL GARDENS: OUTDOOR SPACES FOR LIVING AND ENTERTAINING (Stewart, Tabori & Chang, 1988) An abundance of ideas from 95 American gardens for creating a variety of gardens; includes 250 color photos and a source list.

Grant, John and Carol
GARDEN DESIGN ILLUSTRATED (Timber Press, 1983) A reprint of the popular 1954 edition, it covers the basics of landscape design.

Greenoak, Francesca
GLORIOUS GARDENS: A PORTFOLIO OF IDEAS FOR PLANTING AND DESIGN (Congdon & Weed, 1989) How to design and plant an elegant garden; 225 color photos.

Hayward, Gordon
DESIGNING YOUR OWN LANDSCAPE: PLANTS AND WAYS TO USE THEM IN THE GARDEN (Whetstone Publishing, 1990) Emphasis is on gardening in U.S. zones 2 to 6.

Hobhouse, Penelope
BORDERS (HarperCollins, 1989) Advice from National Trust gardeners in England on planning, selecting plants, planting, staking and creating a pleasing overall design of borders of shrubs, annuals and perennials.
THE COUNTRY GARDENER (Little, Brown, 1989) How to plan a garden, either large or small, using a variety of options (ground covers, foliage, shrubs, trees, flowers, etc.); 800+ plants are grouped according to how they are used in the design.
FLOWER GARDENS (Little, Brown, 1991) How to select and place flowers for the best effect in an existing basic garden; covers island beds, borders, cottage groupings, formal schemes, etc.
GARDEN STYLE (Little, Brown, 1988) Describes and illustrates good garden design and explains how to achieve it through color, structural elements, site considerations and division of the garden into individual units.
PLANTING IN PATTERNS (HarperCollins, 1989) How to use the formal elements of garden design in permanent plantings of hedges, topiary, parterres, knots, mazes, and pergolas.

Ireys, Alice Recknagel
DESIGNS FOR AMERICAN GARDENS: A GUIDE WITH COMPLETE PLANS, GROWING INFORMATION AND HUNDREDS OF RECOMMENDED PLANTS (Prentice-Hall, 1991) Focuses on 14 plans designed for actual clients, and preparing the soil, selecting the plants and maintaining the resulting garden; Ms. Ireys is the designer of Burpee's gardens in a package and has been a landscape architect for over 50 years.
HOW TO PLAN AND PLANT YOUR OWN PROPERTY (Morrow, 1980) The many landscape plans included here provide a good starting point for design ideas.

James Jr., Theodore
LANDSCAPING: A FIVE YEAR PLAN (Macmillan, 1988) A step-by-step program for what to plant and what not to plant for an easy-care garden.
SPECIALTY GARDENS (Stewart, Tabori & Chang, 1992)

Jekyll, Gertrude
GARDENS FOR SMALL COUNTRY HOUSES (ISBS, 1981) How to design and create a garden for a country house.

Jensen, Jens
SIFTINGS (Johns Hopkins, 1990) Reprint of 1939 classic that focuses on the natural landscape.

Keen, Mary
THE GARDEN BORDER BOOK (Capability's, 1987) Photos, plans and plant lists for 30 borders of both amateurs and well-known gardeners (Graham Stuart Thomas, Rosemary Verey, Alvilde Lees-Milne, Christopher Lloyd, Lanning Roper, Russell Page, Peter Coats and others).

Leighton, Phoebe, and Simonds, Calvin
THE NEW AMERICAN LANDSCAPE GARDENER: A GUIDE TO BEAUTIFUL BACKYARDS AND SENSATIONAL SURROUNDINGS (Rodale Press, 1987) A step-by-step guide to designing, planting, and maintaining a personalized landscape; includes 10 special features to incorporate into a yard.

Lerner, Joel M.
THE COMPLETE HOME LANDSCAPE DESIGNER (St. Martin's, 1992)

Llewellyn, Roddy
BEAUTIFUL BACKYARDS (Sterling, 1991) Numerous design ideas and 44 color photos for handling tiny spaces, steep ravines, overgrown brush and other problems.

Lloyd, Christopher
THE MIXED BORDER (Wisley Handbook)(Sterling, 1991) How to mix shrubs, annuals, perennials, bulbs, ferns and grasses to achieve a visually pleasing result as well as controlling pests and diseases.
THE WELL-TEMPERED GARDEN (Random House, 1970) How he combines plants, colors, scents, etc. to create his beautiful gardens at Great Dixter.

Magill, Anne
LANDSCAPE DESIGN AND GARDENING PROCEDURES FOR THE NOT SO RICH (Melrose Garden Press, 1989) Essays on the theories, tools, techniques, mistakes and solutions to the problems of home landscape design.

Malitz, Jerome
PERSONAL LANDSCAPES (Timber Press, 1989) Ideas for creating a personalized landscape by not always following the rules.

Meyers, L. Donald
THE COMPLETE BACKYARD PLANNER (Scribner's, 1985) Covers drawing up a plan to suit your family's needs and doing the necessary improvements.

Murphy, Wendy B.
BEDS AND BORDERS: TRADITIONAL AND ORIGINAL GARDEN DESIGNS (Houghton Mifflin, 1990) Covers site, size, raised or flat beds, edging, spacing and using water, edible plants, rocks, etc. to create a variety of effects.

Murray, Elizabeth, and Fell, Derek
HOME LANDSCAPING: IDEAS, STYLES AND DESIGNS FOR CREATIVE OUTDOOR SPACES (Simon & Schuster, 1989) 250 color photos provide a multitude of ideas for the home owner.

Nuese, Josephine
THE COUNTRY GARDEN (Scribner's, 1970) Month-by-month ideas for landscaping, plus a wonderful read by the well-known garden columnist.

Oehme, Wolfgang, and Van Sweden, James
BOLD ROMANTIC GARDENS: THE NEW WORLD LANDSCAPES (Acropolis, 1990) How they create the American gardens that win prizes for them and bring year-round beauty and easy care to the owners; includes 275 color photos and 60 plans and plant lists.

Ortho
CREATIVE HOME LANDSCAPING (Ortho, 1987)

Ottesen, Carole
THE NEW AMERICAN GARDEN (Macmillan, 1988) How to achieve the natural look in landscaping with recommendations on specific plant varieties; includes source lists.

Page, Russell
THE EDUCATION OF A GARDENER (Random House, 1985) The experiences of a famous designer while creating landscapes both in America and abroad.

Paul, Anthony, and Rees, Yvonne
THE GARDEN DESIGN BOOK (Salem House, 1988) Surveys the work of 15 modern landscape de-

signers (Anthony Paul, Richard Haigh and Annie Wilkes, Gilles Clement, Roberto Burle Marx, Jacques Wirtz, Ivan Ruperti, Michael Balston, Rick Eckersley and Lisa Stafford, Henk Weijers, Wolfgang Oehme and James van Sweden, Beth Chatto, Takashi Sawano, Mien Ruys, Ulrich Timm and Hiroshi Makita); 350+ color photos.

Proctor, Rob
COUNTRY FLOWERS: WILD CLASSICS FOR THE CONTEMPORARY GARDEN (Harper-Collins, 1991) Describes 76 plants that moved from the wild into today's gardens; includes lilies, daisies, asters, poppies, anemones and more.

Reader's Digest
PRACTICAL GUIDE TO HOME LANDSCAPING (RD Association, 1977) Explains the design process and gives specific projects to incorporate into a home landscape.

Rose, Graham
THE CLASSIC GARDEN (Summit Books, 1989) The origins of and ideas for using pergolas, arbors, gazebos, fountains, herbs, water spouts, topiary, herbaceous borders, rose gardens, walled retreats and formal pools in creating a traditional garden.
THE ROMANTIC GARDEN: A GUIDE TO CREATING A BEAUTIFUL AND PRIVATE GARDEN PARADISE (Viking Penguin, 1988) Transforming an established shaded garden or woodland into a romantic retreat.

Rose, James C.
GARDENS MAKE ME LAUGH: A NEW EDITION (Johns Hopkins, 1990) Rose, a well-known landscape designer, tells it like he sees it in this exposé of his profession.

Scott-James, Anne
PERFECT PLANT, PERFECT GARDEN: 200 MOST REWARDING PLANTS FOR EVERY GARDEN (Summit Books, 1988) Descriptions, cultivation information and color photos for 200 plants for sun, shade and containers.

Smith, Mary Riley
THE FRONT GARDEN: NEW APPROACHES TO LANDSCAPE DESIGN (Houghton Mifflin, 1991)

Covers cottage gardens, edible landscapes, drought-tolerant gardens, formal gardens and other ways to liven up a large or small front yard.

Smyser, Carol A.
NATURE'S DESIGN: A PRACTICAL GUIDE TO NATURAL LANDSCAPING (Rodale Press, 1982) How to analyze your site, select the plants and prepare the area for a natural garden.

Stevens, David; Huntington, Lucy; and Key, Richard
THE COMPLETE BOOK OF GARDEN DESIGN, CONSTRUCTION AND PLANTING (Sterling, 1991) Covers initial planning, adding structural elements (paths, walls, etc.), and selecting and placing plants.

Strong, Roy
CREATING FORMAL GARDENS (Little, Brown, 1990) Describes the primary principles of formal gardens and presents examples using 18 period and private gardens of various sizes; includes rose-covered pergolas, topiary and apple tunnels.

Sunset
LANDSCAPING AND GARDEN REMODELING (Sunset Books, 1978) Garden planning and design ideas for all types of homes.
LANDSCAPING FOR PRIVACY: HEDGES, FENCES, ARBORS (Sunset Books, 1985) How to re-landscape existing gardens for increased privacy from the street, for pools, on roofs, etc.
LANDSCAPING ILLUSTRATED (Sunset Books, 1984) Covers planning guidelines, design and problem-solving ideas, how-to basics and information on selecting and combining plants and structural elements.

Sweetinburgh, Roger
DESIGNING YOUR GARDEN (Sterling, 1991) Covers the basics of landscape design, mistakes to avoid, handling problem spaces and more.

Taylor, Patrick
PLANTING IN PATTERNS (HarperCollins, 1989) How to create formal gardens with permanent plantings of hedges, topiary, knots, mazes, pergolas and parterres; includes the advice of the head gardeners of well-known English gardens.

Taylor's
GUIDE TO GARDEN DESIGN (Houghton Mifflin, 1988) Covers flower beds, food gardens, period gardens, city gardens, tree and shrub plantings, rock gardens, water gardens, winter gardens, shade areas, Japanese gardens, seaside gardens, dry sites and wildlife gardens; includes principles of landscaping, design plans and suggestions for which plants to use.

Thomas, Graham Stuart
THE ART OF PLANTING (Godine, 1984) Covers the various styles of gardens, what different plants do for a garden, how to select plants depending on their purpose, and much more.

Time-Life
DESIGNING YOUR GARDEN (Time-Life Books, 1988) Describes how to plan first on paper, use existing conditions to their best advantage, arrange the garden around focal points, use sun and shade, choose the right ground cover and much more.

Toogood, Alan
GARDEN ILLUSIONS: GARDENING BY DESIGN (Sterling, 1991) How to create depth and space by using different lawn shapes, plantings, structural screening, warm or cool colors and more.
SECRET GARDENS: CREATING ROMANTIC RETREATS (Trafalgar Square, 1988) How to use statuary, furniture, paths, walls, hedges, gateways, etc. to create secluded retreats within the garden.

Toogood, Alan, and Glover, John
THE SHELTERED GARDEN (Trafalgar Square, 1989) How to transform an existing sheltered area or create a new one; includes plant suggestions and ideas for a garden room or conservatory.

Verey, Rosemary
CLASSIC GARDEN DESIGN: HOW TO ADAPT AND RE-CREATE GARDEN FEATURES OF THE PAST (Random House, 1989) Describes the use of paths, knots, arbors, water and other elements in today's gardens; a reprint of her earlier work.

Walker, Theodore D.
PLANTING DESIGN (PDA Publications, 1985) Covers design principles and process, functional uses of plants, aesthetics, and preparation of planting plans and specifications.
RESIDENTIAL LANDSCAPING I: PLANNING, DESIGN, CONSTRUCTION (Van Nostrand Reinhold, 1990, 2nd edition) How to use professional techniques when landscaping your yard.

Williams, Robin
THE GARDEN PLANNER (Barron, 1990) A variety of garden shapes (i.e., small or large rectangle, L-shape, square, long narrow, triangle, etc.) are treated to different designs allowing you to select the type of garden you prefer for the space you have.

Wirth, Thomas
THE VICTORY GARDEN LANDSCAPE GUIDE (Little, Brown, 1984) Month-by-month suggestions for landscaping.

For related books, see:
GARDEN DESIGN WITH FOLIAGE by Glattstein (pag 71)
THE HOME LANDSCAPER and **THE BACKYARD LANDSCAPER** by Home Planners (page 45)
HOME LANDSCAPING IN THE NORTHEAST AND MIDWEST by Smith (page 192)
LANDSCAPING WITH HERBS by Adams (page 109)
MODERN LANDSCAPE ARCHITECTURE by Johnson (page 201)
A SMALL GARDEN DESIGNER'S HANDBOOK by Strong (page 176)
THE SMALL GARDEN PLANNER by Rose (page 176)
SOUTHERN HOME LANDSCAPING by Smith (page 194)
WESTERN HOME LANDSCAPING by Smith (page 199)

COMPANION PLANTING

Carr, Anna
GOOD NEIGHBORS: COMPANION PLANT-
ING FOR GARDENERS (Rodale Press, 1985) For
each plant listed, she gives the traditional thoughts
about its relationship with other plants plus what the
latest research has shown regarding this relationship;
includes designing the companion garden.

Flowerdew, Bob
GOOD COMPANIONS (Simon & Schuster, 1992)
How to combine flowers and vegetables in ways that
they help each other, plus plants that attract bees,
birds and butterflies.

Philbrick, Helen, and Gregg, Richard
COMPANION PLANTS AND HOW TO USE
THEM (Devin-Adair, 1990, revised edition)

Riotte, Louise
CARROTS LOVE TOMATOES: SECRETS OF
COMPANION PLANTING FOR SUCCESSFUL

GARDENING (Garden Way, 1976) Discusses which
vegetables, herbs and flowers profit from being planted
next to other plants.

ROSES LOVE GARLIC: SECRETS OF COM-
PANION PLANTING WITH FLOWERS (Gar-
den Way, 1983) Covers which flower and food plants
benefit by being placed next to each other.

SECRETS OF COMPANION PLANTING (Gar-
den Way, 1981) Describes which vegetables, herbs,
fruits and flowers go well together.

Verey, Rosemary
THE ART OF PLANTING (Little, Brown, 1990)
Covers companion planting ideas throughout the year;
includes a list of 130 popular garden plants and which
companion plants work best with them.

GARDEN PLANS

Addkison, Andrew, and Kramer, Jack
**50 GARDEN PLANS: A GUIDE TO DE-
SIGNING AND PLANTING YOUR IDEAL
GARDEN** (Harper Perennial, 1991) Plans for large
and small gardens; includes 150 drawings and 50 color
photos.

Coombs, Geoffrey
PLANS FOR SMALL GARDENS (Wisley Handbook) (Sterling, 1990) Sixteen plans for all shapes and
types of small gardens; includes suggestions for plants.

Damrosch, Barbara
**THEME GARDENS: HOW TO PLAN, PLANT
AND GROW 16 GLORIOUSLY DIFFERENT
GARDENS** (Workman, 1982) Covers fragrance, colonial, butterfly, secret, children's, old roses, Zen, Shakespeare, gray, seaside, Victorian, ornamental grasses and
white gardens and more; includes 400 color drawings,
photos and plans.

Gunn, Fenja
LOST GARDENS OF GERTRUDE JEKYLL
(Macmillan, 1991) A collection of watercolors and
detailed planting plans with contemporary plant lists

to use in recreating Jekyll designs from both sides of
the Atlantic; gardens have not been in print previously.

Ireland-Gannon Assoc. Staff (editors)
**THE HOME LANDSCAPER: FIFTY-FIVE PRO-
FESSIONAL LANDSCAPES YOU CAN DO**
(Home Planners, 1990) Landscapes specifically de-
signed to fit a house's architectural style (Cape Cod,
Colonials, Tudors, Ranch, Southwest, Georgian and
more); includes blueprints and plant lists.
THE BACKYARD LANDSCAPER (Home Plan-
ners, 1992) Forty plans for backyards.

Ireys, Alice R.
GARDEN DESIGN (Prentice-Hall, 1991) Contains
40 plans (annual, cutting, rose, bulbs, fragrance, container, herb, salad, etc.), each with plant list, planting
design grid and watercolor illustration.

Lerner, Joel M.
101 HOME LANDSCAPING IDEAS (Price Stern
Sloan, 1988) A wealth of ideas for all sizes and shapes
of property; includes zoned plant lists.

101 TOWNHOUSE GARDEN DESIGNS (Price Stern Sloan, 1987) Horticultural self-analysis helps you to create a landscape design to fit your personality.

Loewer, Peter
GARDENS BY DESIGN: STEP-BY-STEP PLANS FOR 12 IMAGINATIVE GARDENS (Rodale Press, 1986)

Ortho
LANDSCAPE PLANS (Ortho, 1989) Color photos and recommended plants keyed to the design of 33 plans.
FLOWER GARDEN PLANS (Ortho, 1991) Details for 42 flower gardens, many of which can be done on the weekend.

Oster, Maggie
35 GARDEN BLUEPRINTS: BEAUTIFUL POSSIBILITIES FOR DESIGNING YOUR GARDEN (Simon & Schuster, 1989) The plans are arranged according to plant types and themes; includes perennial gardens, Victorian garden, wildlife garden, herb garden, cutting gardens, cactus garden, ornamental grasses garden, Japanese garden, cottage garden, etc.

Phillips, Sue
THE WELL-PLANNED GARDEN (Grove Weidenfeld, 1988) Covers 60 designs for 12 types of gardens.

Stuart, David
PLANTING THE PERFECT GARDEN: BEAUTIFUL DESIGNS FOR POTS, BORDERS, TOWN AND COUNTRY GARDENS (Trafalgar Square, 1992) Describes 50 planting plans, each with a color photo and a photo-identification diagram, plus 30 additional plans for alternate layouts; includes details on plants used, planting seasons, siting, cost and degree of maintenance required; contains a glossary of plants and a list of U.S. mail order sources.

GARDEN DESIGN FIRMS

In addition to the above books, the following firms specialize in garden plans. This is not a complete list of all the companies out there, but it will get you started.

Anderson Horticultural Design Services
P.O. Box 5264, Minnetonka, MN 55343

Each design gives three different layouts that can be adapted to your yard. The plants used are hardy perennials, decorative shrubs and accent evergreens (primarily USDA zones 4 to 8/9). The plans include blueprints with a plant key, optional substitutions, descriptions and space requirements.

Border gardens: The three layouts compliment a sunny lawn and are for borders along a wall or property line, at the corner of the yard and an "island" border garden.

City gardens: The three layouts are for enclosed or walled, small-scale gardens; they include a green oasis, a vestpocket garden and a walled garden.

Concept gardens: The three layouts are for a garden of vertical spikes, a garden of feathery delights and a hillside garden for display of color.

Courtyard gardens: The three layouts are related to the city gardens in that they are for an enclosed space; they include a meandering entry, a backyard patio and an enclosed courtyard.

Drought resistant gardens: The three layouts are for a border garden, patio garden and a rock garden using plants that tolerate poor soil and dry conditions.

Foliage gardens: The three layouts are for foliage in the shade, a garden of ornamental grasses and foliage at the terrace.

Outdoor rooms: The three layouts are for gardens surrounding patios, decks and terraces.

Shade gardens: The three layouts are for a shaded viewing garden, a swirling shady border and a wooded pathway garden.

Waterside gardens: The three layouts are for a garden to frame a pond view, a garden to compliment a reflecting pool and garden color at the water's edge.

CompuGarden Inc.
1006 Highland Drive, Silver Spring, MD 20910

They will put together either a one- or two-year plan for a vegetable garden suited to your requirements, or you can order software for an IBM or IBM compatible PC; developed in collaboration with The New York Botanical Garden. (I've never wanted a vegetable garden, but after seeing their brochure, it's tempting.)

The Rosemary House
120 S. Market St., Mechanicsburg, PA 17055

They offer simple herb garden plans free, or for a $50 purchase of plants and your specifications (size, location, amount of sun, etc.), they will custom design an herb garden.

SeedScapes
P.O. Box 295, Edwardsburg, MI 49112

Plans include a semicircle herb garden, container and raised bed vegetable gardens, and five flower gardens (yellow, red, purple and pink for sunny areas, and a pink garden for shade); each plan includes layout, growing guidelines for each recommended plant, a general gardening manual, a monthly calendar and seed supply sources.

For related books, see:
BEHIND THOSE GARDEN WALLS IN HISTORIC SAVANNAH by Wood (page 204)
BOLD ROMANTIC GARDENS by Oehme and Van Sweden (page 41)
THE GARDEN ART OF CHINA by Lifang and Sianglin (page 150)
THE GARDEN BORDER BOOK by Keen (page 167)
GARDENING WITH COLOR by Keen (page 167)
HERB GARDEN DESIGN by Swanson and Rady (page 114)

LAWNS, GROUND COVERS, GRASSES

Baker, Jerry
JERRY BAKER'S LAWN BOOK (Ballantine, 1987)

Brooklyn Botanic Garden
GROUND COVERS AND VINES (BBG #86) How these low-maintenance plants add interest to a landscape.
HOME LAWN HANDBOOK (BBG #71) How to put in a new lawn using either seed or sod, plus growing grass in the shade and controlling diseases and weeds.
ORNAMENTAL GRASSES (BBG #117) Steps for site selection and growing grasses in all types of gardens.

Crockett, James Underwood, and Editors of Time-Life Books
LAWNS AND GROUND COVERS (Time-Life Books, 1971)

Fish, Margery
GROUND COVER PLANTS (Faber & Faber, 1980) Suggestions for which flowers, shrubs and conifers to use as ground covers.

Foley, Daniel J.
GROUND COVERS FOR EASIER GARDENING (Dover, 1972) A former editor of *Horticulture* magazine, Foley covers over 100 species of ground covers for different types of soil, light, climatic zones and landscapes.

Franklin, Stuart
BUILDING A HEALTHY LAWN: A SAFE AND NATURAL APPROACH (Storey, 1988) How to have a beautiful lawn without weedkillers, pesticides and fertilizers.

Garden Way Publishing Editors
LAWNS AND LANDSCAPING: 1001 QUES-
TIONS ANSWERED (Storey, 1989) Expert advice
in a question and answer format.

Grounds, Roger
ORNAMENTAL GRASSES (Trafalgar Square,
1990) An updated and enlarged edition of an out-of-
print definitive reference covering over 300 species.

Hessayon, Dr. D. G.
THE LAWN EXPERT (Sterling, 1990) Absolutely
everything you need to know to produce a perfect
lawn.

Knight, F. P.
HEATHS AND HEATHERS (Wisley Handbook)
(Sterling, 1991) Covers colors, uses and growing infor-
mation for heaths and heathers.

Lacey, Stephen
LAWNS AND GROUND COVER: THE NA-
TIONAL TRUST GUIDE (Trafalgar Square, 1991)
Using examples from Britain's National Trust gardens,
he discusses how the horizontal surface of a garden
(lawns and ground covers) contributes to the overall
style and atmosphere.

Loewer, Peter
GROWING AND DECORATING WITH
GRASSES (Walker, 1977) Where and how to grow
approximately 80 species of annual and perennial
grasses, sedges, rushes and bamboos, plus using dried
grasses for decoration.

MacCaskey, Michael
LAWNS AND GROUND COVERS: HOW TO
SELECT, GROW AND ENJOY (Price Stern Sloan,
1982) How to care for your traditional lawn or create
a low-maintenance one using one of the many ground
covers surveyed; includes planting from seed, sod or
sprigs, plus information on weeds, pests, diseases and
irrigation; 300+ color photos.

Mackenzie, David
COMPLETE MANUAL OF PERENNIAL
GROUND COVERS (Prentice-Hall, 1989) Com-
plete plant descriptions and planting and growing

information on bamboos, herbs, grasses, ferns, shrubs,
succulents and vines.

McHoy, Peter
OUTDOOR FLOORS: THE DESIGN AND
MAINTENANCE OF LAWNS, PATIOS AND
GROUND COVERS (Salem House, 1989) Covers
function and decorative possibilities of lawns, patios
and ground covers.

Meyer, Mary H., and Mower, Robert
ORNAMENTAL GRASSES FOR HOME AND
GARDEN (Scribner's, 1975) Covers 34 grasses for
zone 5 with information on propagation, fall color,
needs, etc.

Ortho
ALL ABOUT GROUND COVERS (Ortho Books,
1982)
ALL ABOUT LAWNS (Ortho Books, 1985)

Ottesen, Carole
ORNAMENTAL GRASSES: THE AMBER
WAVE (McGraw-Hill, 1989) Design ideas for using
ornamental grasses in borders, by the pool or pond, in
a rock garden or a meadow, as ground covers and more.

Proudley, Brian and Valerie
HEATHERS IN COLOR (Sterling, 1974) Covers
descriptions, cultivation and propagation of a variety
of heathers, landscape uses with three plans, flowering
periods and more.

**Reinhardt, Thomas and Martina; and
Moskowitz, Mark**
ORNAMENTAL GRASS GARDENING: DE-
SIGN IDEAS, FUNCTIONS AND EFFECTS
(Price Stern Sloan, 1989) The authors, landscape de-
signers who specialize in ornamental grasses, cover
how to plant and care for the 50 best grasses; includes
a list of suppliers.

Schultz, Warren
THE CHEMICAL-FREE LAWN: THE NEWEST
VARIETIES AND TECHNIQUES TO GROW
LUSH, HARDY GRASS (Rodale Press, 1989) How to
have a beautiful lawn without pesticides, herbicides or
chemical fertilizers.

Sunset
GROUND COVERS (Sunset Books, 1991) Covers plant selection, planting and care.
LAWNS AND GROUND COVERS (Sunset Books, 1989) How to choose, plant and maintain grasses and ground covers, plus detailed information on installing watering systems.

Taylor's
GUIDE TO GROUND COVERS, VINES AND GRASSES (Houghton Mifflin, 1987) Information on 316 plants (includes U.S. hardiness zones), plus care instructions, choosing the best plant for the site, and ideas for landscaping; 450+ color photos and 200 black- and-white drawings.
POCKET GUIDE TO GROUND COVERS FOR SHADE (Houghton Mifflin, 1990) Briefly describes the needs and uses of 79 species of ground covers that do well in shade.
POCKET GUIDE TO GROUND COVERS FOR SUN (Houghton Mifflin, 1990) Briefly describes the needs and uses of 79 species of ground covers that do well in the sun.

Thomas, Graham Stuart
PLANTS FOR GROUND COVER (Timber Press, 1990) A revised edition that includes information on U.S. hardiness zones and describes shrubs, climbers, herbaceous plants and grasses that do well as ground covers.

Time-Life
LAWNS AND GROUND COVERS: GARDENER'S GUIDE SERIES (Time-Life, 1989) How to sow, grow and maintain a beautiful grass lawn, or use shrubs, herbs, vines and other ground covers to create a low-maintenance lawn.

Underhill, Terry
HEATHS AND HEATHERS: THE GROWER'S ENCYCLOPEDIA (Trafalgar Square, 1991 new updated edition) Covers history, use, cultivation and propagation, plus descriptive lists of species, hybrids and cultivars.

Van de Laar, Harry
THE HEATHER GARDEN: DESIGN, MANAGEMENT, PROPAGATION, CULTIVARS (Collins, 1978) Descriptions and color photos of numerous species and cultivars, plus information on soil, pruning, propagation, pests and diseases and more.

Wyman, Donald
GROUND COVER PLANTS (Macmillan, 1970, 5th edition) Describes 250 plants that are less than three feet tall.

For related books, see:
HARROWSMITH GUIDE: GROUND COVERS by Bennett (page 190)
LANDSCAPE PLANTS OF THE SOUTHEAST by Halfacre and Shawcroft (page 193)

TREES, SHRUBS AND VINES

GENERAL REFERENCES

Bartels, Andreas
GARDENING WITH DWARF TREES AND SHRUBS (Timber Press, 1986) How dwarf, slow-growing plants can solve the problem of limited space; includes an encyclopedia of these plants and their cultural requirements.

Beckett, Kenneth
CLIMBING PLANTS (Timber Press, 1983) Covers climbing and trailing plants, garden uses, greenhouse climbers; includes an A to Z encyclopedia of genera and species.
EVERGREENS (Wisley Handbook) (Sterling, 1991) Covers selecting and growing trees, shrubs and climbers.

Bloom, Adrian
CONIFERS FOR YOUR GARDEN (Scribner's, 1972) Description and cultivation tips for all kinds of conifers plus 200 color photos.

Brooklyn Botanic Garden
FLOWERING SHRUBS (BBG #94) Covers camellias, viburnums, azaleas, roses and more.

FLOWERING TREES (BBG #102) How to select and grow and what time of year you can expect the trees to flower.
NURSERY SOURCE MANUAL (BBG #99) Gives botanical name, and retail and wholesale sources for 1,200 trees and shrubs.

Carr, David
FLOWERING SHRUBS: STEP BY STEP TO GROWING SUCCESS (Trafalgar Square, 1992) Surveys 75 of the most attractive shrubs available, and covers selecting the best shrub for the site and the soil, training, pruning and propagation.
GARDEN TREES: STEP BY STEP TO GROWING SUCCESS (Trafalgar Square, 1992) Covers selecting, siting, planting, pruning, staking, routine care, treating old or neglected trees; includes a guide to 50 popular broad-leaved and coniferous trees suitable for the garden.

Chalk, Douglas
HEBES AND PARAHEBES (Timber Press, 1988) Describes species and varieties, plus information on cultivation, propagation and landscape uses.

Chamberlin, Susan
HEDGES, SCREENS AND ESPALIERS: HOW TO SELECT, GROW AND ENJOY (HP Books, 1982) Describes 200 plants suitable for use as hedges, screens and espaliers; includes over 400 color photos, plus information on training and pruning.

Coats, Alice M.
GARDEN SHRUBS AND THEIR HISTORIES (Simon & Schuster, 1992, updated edition of the 1964 classic) Describes how familiar shrubs such as lilacs, roses, forsythia, etc. were discovered and introduced in America; includes 112 four-color botanical illustrations.

Courtright, Gordon
TREES AND SHRUBS FOR TEMPERATE CLIMATES (Timber Press, 1988, 3rd edition) Over 750 color photos of mature plants shown in landscape setting; for zones 6 to 10.

Cox, Jeff and Marilyn
FLOWERS FOR ALL SEASONS: A GUIDE TO COLORFUL TREES, SHRUBS AND VINES (Rodale Press, 1987) Covers 300 flowering woody plants, when they bloom, companion perennial plantings and more.

Cravens, Richard
VINES (Time-Life Books, 1979) Describes annual, perennial and tropical vines.

Crockett, James Underwood, and Editors of Time-Life Books
EVERGREENS (Time-Life Books, 1971) How to choose, plant and care for, plus descriptions, growing requirements and color photos of 29 genera of narrow-leaved evergreens and 71 genera of broad-leaved evergreens.
FLOWERING SHRUBS (Henry Holt, 1987) Reprint of 1972 edition; descriptions and growing information on the most common flowering shrubs.
TREES (Time-Life Books, 1972) How to choose, plant, feed, prune and spray, plus descriptions, growing requirements and color photos of 75 genera of deciduous trees.

Davis, Brian
FLOWERING TREES AND SHRUBS (Rodale Press, 1988) Cultivation requirements for over 450 varieties of foliage, flowers and fruits.
THE GARDENER'S ILLUSTRATED ENCYCLOPEDIA OF TREES AND SHRUBS (Rodale Press, 1987) Describes over 2,000 varieties of trees and shrubs giving origin, minimum winter temperature, soil and light requirements, pruning and propagating information, average height and spread, landscape use, etc.; 600+ color photos.

Dirr, Michael
ALL ABOUT EVERGREENS (Ortho, 1985) Selection guide and landscaping information on over 200 evergreens.
A MANUAL OF WOODY LANDSCAPE PLANTS: THEIR IDENTIFICATION, ORNAMENTAL CHARACTERISTICS, CULTURE, PROPAGATION AND USES (Stipes Publishing, 1990, 4th edition) Covers thousands of cultivars and hundreds of species in 300 genera of trees, shrubs and vines giving the Latin and common name, pronunciation, culture, diseases and pests, landscape value, propagation, size and zone.
PHOTOGRAPHIC MANUAL OF WOODY LANDSCAPE PLANTS: FORM AND FUNCTION IN THE LANDSCAPE (Stipes Publishing, 1978) Contains 1,295 black-and-white photos of mature plants and a brief description of each plant; a companion volume to the above book.

Druse, Ken
FLOWERING SHRUBS (Prentice-Hall, 1992) Detailed descriptions of over 130 flowering shrubs and how to use them in a landscape design.

Fell, Derek
TREES AND SHRUBS (HP Books, 1986) Covers 200 species and varieties with suggestions for use in the landscape; includes U.S. hardiness zones and 300+ color photos.

Frederick Jr., William H.
100 GREAT GARDEN PLANTS (Timber Press, 1986, updated edition) Trees, shrubs and ground covers suitable for the mid-Atlantic section of the U.S.

Gelderen, D. M. van, and Hoey Smith, J. R. P. van
CONIFERS (Timber Press, 1989, 2nd edition) Pictorial companion (1,180 color photos) to Krussmann's *Manual of Cultivated Conifers*; includes supplement of detailed drawings of cones.

Giono, Jean
THE MAN WHO PLANTED TREES (Chelsea Green, 1985) A fable about a man who reclaims a desolate area of southern France by planting 100 acorns a day.

Grace, Julie (editor)
ORNAMENTAL CONIFERS (Timber Press, 1983) Over 550 color photos and brief descriptions.

Haller, John M.
TREE CARE: A COMPREHENSIVE GUIDE TO PLANTING, NURTURING AND PROTECTING TREES (Macmillan, 1986, rev. ed.) Covers planting, pruning, fertilizing, bracing and cabling, wound repair, grafting, spraying, and controlling problems.

Harris, Cyril C. (editor)
AN ILLUSTRATED GUIDE TO FLOWERING TREES AND SHRUBS (Black Cat, 1988) Covers origin, cultivation and propagation of familiar and rare plants with recommendations on particular cultivars.

Harrison, Richmond E.
TREES AND SHRUBS (Timber Press, 1984) Brief descriptions and cultivation information, plus 582 color photos.

Hessayon, Dr. D. G.
THE TREE AND SHRUB EXPERT (Sterling, 1990) Describes and gives growing information for over 1,000 flowering shrubs, deciduous trees, climbers and conifers.

Hillier Nurseries
THE HILLIER COLOUR DICTIONARY OF TREES AND SHRUBS (Trafalgar Square, 1981) Descriptions of 3,500 woody plants; 600 color photos.
THE HILLIER MANUAL OF TREES AND SHRUBS (Trafalgar Square, 1992, revised and updated edition) Information on selecting and cultivating over 9,000 trees, shrubs, conifers, climbers and bamboos from 650+ genera.

Hudak, Joseph
SHRUBS IN THE LANDSCAPE (McGraw-Hill, 1984) Describes 285 species and 1,000 varieties of shrubs that are attractive, readily available and adapt well in the landscape.
TREES FOR EVERY PURPOSE (McGraw-Hill, 1980) Describes 257 trees for zones 2 to 10.

Johnson, Hugh
HUGH JOHNSON'S ENCYCLOPEDIA OF TREES (Portland House, 1990) Covers 600 species of deciduous trees and conifers; 1,000 color photos and drawings.

Kinahan, Sonia
GARDENING WITH TREES (Trafalgar Square, 1990) Covers the author's favorite trees that can be grown in the average-sized garden, plus planting and design information.

Krussmann, Gerd
MANUAL OF CULTIVATED BROAD-LEAVED TREES AND SHRUBS: VOLUMES I, II and III (Timber Press, 1986) Encompasses 5,000 species and over 6,000 cultivars in almost 800 genera; superb reference.
MANUAL OF CULTIVATED CONIFERS (Timber Press, 1985) Describes over 600 species and nearly 2,100 cultivars giving information on distribution, cultivation and recommended uses.

Lancaster, Roy
TREES FOR YOUR GARDEN (Scribner's, 1974) A to Z by genus with many color photos, plus suggestions for landscape use.

Lipkis, Andy and Katie
THE SIMPLE ACT OF PLANTING A TREE: THE TREE PEOPLE GUIDE TO HEALING YOUR NEIGHBORHOOD, YOUR CITY, AND YOUR WORLD (Jeremy Tarcher, 1990) How volunteers planted one million trees in Los Angeles in three years; specific details for any group that wishes to follow suit.

Lunardi, Constanza
SIMON & SCHUSTER'S GUIDE TO SHRUBS AND VINES (Simon & Schuster, 1989) Covers 160 plants, mostly for zones 6 to 9.

Macoboy, Stirling
WHAT SHRUB IS THAT? (Portland House, 1990)
Color photo, description, and growing information on
1,250 shrubs.
WHAT TREE IS THAT? (Crescent Books, 1991)
Identifies and gives cultivation data on over 300 gen-
era and 1,500 species from all over the world; 1,050
color photos.

Martin, Laura
FOLKLORE OF TREES AND SHRUBS (Globe
Pequot, 1992) Factual information, lore and anecdotes
on 100 trees and shrubs; entries include description,
native range, origin and how to cultivate.

Menninger, Edwin A.
FLOWERING VINES OF THE WORLD (Hearth-
side Press, 1970) Describes 2,000 vines and includes
600 photos.

Mitchell, Alan
THE TREES OF NORTH AMERICA (Facts On
File, 1987) An identification guide of native and introduced trees; covers approximately 500 species and
250 varieties and cultivars.

Mohlenbrock, Robert H., and Thieret, John
TREES: A QUICK REFERENCE GUIDE TO
TREES OF NORTH AMERICA (Collier Books,
1987) Illustrations of 236 common species arranged by
color and shape to make identification easy.

Obrizok, Bob
DWARF CONIFER: SELECTION GUIDE AND
CHECKLIST (1991, Dutchess County Conifers, 12
Miller Hill Drive, La Grangeville, NY 12540) A
pocket guide with brief descriptions of 1,105 dwarf
varieties and cultivars.

Patrick, John
TREES FOR TOWN AND CITY GARDENS
(ISBS, 1990) Covers over 150 suitable trees, plus in-
formation on feeding, pruning and general care.

Paul, Anthony, and Rees, Yvonne
DESIGNING WITH TREES (Salem House, 1989)
How to use the shape, size, color and scent of trees to
add design interest to a landscape; includes descriptions of 350 trees and selection recommendations.

Peattie, Donald C.
A NATURAL HISTORY OF TREES OF EAST-
ERN AND CENTRAL NORTH AMERICA
(Houghton Mifflin, 1991) Describes and gives histor-
ical information for all trees native to the region;
approximately 350 wood engravings.
A NATURAL HISTORY OF WESTERN TREES
(Houghton Mifflin, 1991) Companion volume and
same format as above.

Phillips, Roger
TREES OF NORTH AMERICA AND EUROPE
(Random House, 1978) With over 1,000 color photos,
this is an excellent guide for identifying 500 trees.

Phillips, Roger, and Rix, Martyn
THE RANDOM HOUSE BOOK OF SHRUBS
(Random House, 1989) Describes and gives color photos of over 1,900 flowering and evergreen shrubs; includes U.S. sources.

Pierot, Suzanne
THE IVY BOOK: THE GROWING AND CARE
OF IVY AND IVY TOPIARY (Macmillan, 1974)
How to grow ivy indoors and outdoors, plus character-
istics of the many different ivies.

Pirone, Pascal P.
TREE MAINTENANCE (Oxford University Press,
1988, 6th edition) Covers problems, symptoms, treatments, maintenance techniques and the use of pesticides; very comprehensive.

Platt, Rutherford
1001 QUESTIONS ANSWERED ABOUT TREES
(Dover, 1992) How to identify various species, determine age and weight, decide what trees to plant,
handle pests and diseases, and much more.

Poor, Janet M. (editor)
PLANTS THAT MERIT ATTENTION: VOL-
UME 1—TREES (Timber Press, 1984) Describes 143
trees, and, for each tree, three color photos show habit
and details of leaf, bark, flowers, fruit or cones; includes nursery sources and public gardens where trees
can be seen.

Preston, George
CLIMBING AND WALL PLANTS (Wisley Handbook) (Sterling, 1989) Covers preparing the soil, planting, necessary supports and pruning perennial, annual and fruit-bearing vines.

Rehder, Alfred and Harald
MANUAL OF CULTIVATED TREES AND SHRUBS HARDY IN NORTH AMERICA, EXCLUSIVE OF THE SUBTROPICAL AND TROPICAL REGIONS (Timber Press, 1987) Originally published in 1927 and revised and enlarged in 1940, this reprint remains a standard reference on woody plant material suitable for North American gardens.

Rose, Peter
CLIMBERS AND WALL PLANTS INCLUDING CLEMATIS, ROSES AND WISTERIA (Sterling, 1990) Covers zones, origin, care and propagation, and suggestions for using 110 genera.
IVIES (Sterling, 1990) Describes 125 varieties of indoor and outdoor ivies giving information on propagation, cultivation, ways to use as ground cover, in rock gardens, on pillars, etc.

Rupp, Rebecca
RED OAKS AND BLACK BIRCHES: THE SCIENCE AND LORE OF TREES (Storey, 1990) Unusual and fascinating facts (for example, the oak is the most lightning prone), plus down-to-earth specifics on 20 of the most important North American trees.

Rushforth, Keith
CONIFERS (Facts On File, 1987) Describes 600 species giving origin, needs, noted cultivars and zones.

Sargent, Charles S.
MANUAL OF THE TREES OF NORTH AMERICA (Dover, 1961) Complete descriptions on every native tree and tree-like shrub (717 species); a two-volume set with 783 illustrations.

Selsam, Millicent
TREE FLOWERS (Morrow, 1984) Descriptions and illustrations of the growth cycle of 12 common flowering trees (pussywillow, white oak, sugar maple, elm, apple, horse chestnut, flowering dogwood, magnolia, witch hazel, black walnut, black locust and tulip tree).

Symonds, George W. D.
THE SHRUB IDENTIFICATION BOOK (Morrow, 1963) Over 3,500 illustrations to aid in his "visual method" of identifying shrubs, vines and ground covers.
THE TREE IDENTIFICATION BOOK (Morrow, 1973) Over 1,500 illustrations for use in identifying and recognizing trees.

Taffler, Stephen
CLIMBING PLANTS AND WALL SHRUBS (Trafalgar Square, 1991) Which climbers to use and how to use them to create year-round color and interest in a garden.

Taylor, Jane
CLIMBING PLANTS: KEW GARDENING GUIDE (Timber Press, 1987) Introduction with 56 color photos and 36 line drawings.
CREATIVE PLANTING WITH CLIMBERS (Sterling, 1991) How to plant, grow, train and maintain climbers in a variety of ways.

Taylor's Guides
POCKET GUIDE TO FLOWERING SHRUBS (Houghton Mifflin, 1990) How to choose, plant and maintain 79 popular and less well-known flowering shrubs.
SHRUBS (Houghton Mifflin, 1987) Describes and gives growing information on 323 deciduous and broad-leaved evergreen shrubs.
TREES (Houghton Mifflin, 1988) Groups 200 trees by type (deciduous, coniferous, broadleaf evergreen) with descriptions and two color photos and one line drawing per tree.

Time-Life
EVERGREEN SHRUBS: GARDENER'S GUIDE SERIES (Time-Life, 1989)
TREES: GARDENER'S GUIDE SERIES (Time-Life, 1988) Covers planting, caring for, pruning and propagating; includes descriptions and illustrations of over 100 species and varieties.

Toogood, Alan
CONIFERS AND HEATHERS (Tiger, 1989) Covers planting, cultivation, propagation and care.

THE GARDEN TREES HANDBOOK: A COMPLETE GUIDE TO CHOOSING, PLANTING AND CARING FOR GARDEN TREES (Facts On File, 1990) Details on choosing, planting and caring for every species of tree grown in the U.S. and the United Kingdom.
SHRUBS AND DECORATIVE EVERGREENS (Gallery, 1990) Explains how to choose the best shrubs for your soil and climate with advice on planting, growing and pruning,

Trelease, William
WINTER BOTANY: AN IDENTIFICATION GUIDE TO NATIVE AND CULTIVATED TREES AND SHRUBS (Dover, 1967) Identifies 1,000 species of native trees and shrubs by twig, bark, leaf-scar, bud, berry and other winter characteristics.

Tykac, Jan
THE ILLUSTRATED GUIDE TO ORNAMENTAL SHRUBS (Chartwell Books, 1990) Morphology, origin, needs, propagation and flowering time of 96 species; includes drawings of their flower, twig or fruit.

Whitehead, Jeffrey
THE HEDGE BOOK: HOW TO SELECT, PLANT AND GROW A LIVING FENCE (Storey, 1991) Covers a variety of hedges, both evergreen and flowering, formal and informal, short and tall with information on the pluses and minuses, hardiness and maintenance requirements of each type of plant.

Wyman, Donald
DWARF SHRUBS: MAINTENANCE-FREE WOODY PLANTS FOR TODAY'S GARDEN (Macmillan, 1974) Includes lists of which plants to use for specific purposes (color, type of soil, seaside, etc.)
SHRUBS AND VINES FOR AMERICAN GARDENS (Macmillan, 1969) Describes over 1,700 species and cultivars.
TREES FOR AMERICAN GARDENS (Macmillan, 1990, updated and expanded 3rd edition) Detailed descriptions of the hardiness, habit, foliage, blossom-producing and fruit-bearing characteristics of over 1,500 species; includes lists of flowering trees, ornamental fruit trees, trees of a certain height, trees for the seashore, trees for the city, trees as wind screens and trees to avoid.

Zucker, Isabel
FLOWERING SHRUBS AND SMALL TREES (Grove Weidenfeld, 1990, revised and expanded edition) How to select and care for the flowering shrub best suited to your zone.

AZALEAS & RHODODENDRONS

The American Rhododendron Society (P.O. Box 1380, Gloucester, VA 23061, 804-693-4433) publishes a quarterly journal and offers a variety of other publications at discounts to members.

Clarke, J. Harold
GETTING STARTED WITH RHODODENDRONS AND AZALEAS (Timber Press, 1982) How to grow rhododendrons even in areas not usually considered suitable; includes soil preparation, maintenance, winter protection and fertilizing.

Cox, Kenneth
A PLANTSMAN'S GUIDE TO RHODODENDRONS (Sterling, 1991) A good introduction that covers selection, cultivation, propagation and problems.

Cox, Peter
THE LARGER RHODODENDRONS SPECIES (Timber Press, 1990, revised and enlarged edition) Covers all aspects of cultivation plus the latest botanical classifications; includes an addendum of newly described species and 82 color photos.
RHODODENDRONS (Wisley Handbook) (Sterling, 1989) How to plant and care for rhododendrons.
THE SMALLER RHODODENDRONS (Timber Press, 1985) Covers plants under five feet tall at maturity, with detailed cultural information and lists of recommended species and hybrids.

Cox, Peter and Kenneth
COX'S GUIDE TO CHOOSING RHODODENDRONS (Timber Press, 1990) Covers 100 species and 200 hybrids of rhododendrons chosen for moderate climates, plus a range of both deciduous and evergreen azaleas; includes lists of rhododendrons recommended for particular characteristics.

ENCYCLOPEDIA OF RHODODENDRON HYBRIDS (Timber Press, 1988) Describes and evaluates over 1,400 hybrids; information on hardiness, parentage, flowering time, awards, commercial availability and more.

Darden, Jim
GREAT AMERICAN AZALEAS: A GUIDE TO THE FINEST AZALEA VARIETIES (Greenhouse Press, 1986) Information on 400 varieties with 140 color photos of the best ones.

Davidian, H. H.
Each of the following volumes is an in-depth study based on the author's lifelong research and contains thorough species descriptions, historical background and much more.
RHODODENDRON SPECIES: VOLUME I—LEPIDOTES (Timber Press, 1982)
RHODODENDRON SPECIES: VOLUME II—ELEPIDOTES: ARBOREUM-LACTEUM (Timber Press, 1989)
RHODODENDRON SPECIES: VOLUME III—ELEPIDOTES: NERIIFLORUM-THOMSONII, AZALEASTRUM AND CAMTSCHATICUM (Timber Press, 1991)

Fairweather, Christopher
AZALEAS (Globe Pequot, 1988) Covers selection, planting, pruning and fertilizing.

Galle, Fred
AZALEAS (Timber Press, 1987, revised and enlarged edition) Describes over 6,000 cultivars with information on planting, care, propagation, pests and diseases, and suggestions for the best varieties for each region.

Gelderen, D. M. van, and Hoey Smith, J. R. P. van
RHODODENDRON PORTRAITS (Timber Press, 1992) Pictorial coverage of rhododendron species, varieties and cultivars; 1,150 color photos.

Greer, Harold
GREER'S GUIDE TO AVAILABLE RHODODENDRONS (Offshoot Publications, 1987) Describes 600 species and 1,200 hybrids.

Kessell, Mervyn
RHODODENDRONS AND AZALEAS (Sterling, 1990) Covers all aspects of care, cultivation and propagation of 70 types of rhododendrons and azaleas, plus choosing the best plants, U.S. hardiness ratings, companion planting and more.

Leach, David
RHODODENDRONS OF THE WORLD (Scribner's, 1961) Very comprehensive reference work covering planting, care, disease, propagation, forcing, greenhouse culture and hardiness; includes information on history and anatomy, suitability for a variety of gardens and worldwide distribution.

Livingston, Philip, and West, Franklin (editors)
HYBRIDS AND HYBRIDIZERS: RHODODENDRONS AND AZALEAS FOR EASTERN NORTH AMERICA (Timber Press, 1978) Evaluates over 1,400 varieties.

Ortho
ALL ABOUT AZALEAS, CAMELLIAS AND RHODODENDRONS (Ortho Books, 1985) Good full-color introduction with information on 400 varieties and general care.

Reiley, Edward
SUCCESS WITH RHODODENDRONS AND AZALEAS (Timber Press, 1992) Gives specific details and successful techniques from his many years of personal experience growing these plants; includes lists of recommended species and cultivars for a wide range of climates.

Salley, Homer, and Greer, Harold
RHODODENDRON HYBRIDS (Timber Press, 1992, 2nd edition, revised and enlarged) A guide to the parentage of approximately 5,000 registered rhododendron hybrids; 600 color photos that are different from those of the first edition.

Street, John
RHODODENDRONS (Globe Pequot, 1988) Covers history of species, cultivation, care, recommended varieties, U.S. and foreign gardens to visit, societies, suppliers and more.

Sunset
AZALEAS, RHODODENDRONS, CAMELLIAS
(Sunset Books, 1982) Growing directions and color photos for 98 varieties.

Van Veen, Ted
RHODODENDRONS IN AMERICA (Binford, 1986, 2nd edition)

CLEMATIS

The only clematis group is the International Clematis Society located in the Channel Islands (Clematis Nursery, Domarie Vin., Les Sauvages, St. Sampson's, Guernsey, Channel Islands). It publishes two newsletters a year.

Evison, Raymond J.
MAKING THE MOST OF CLEMATIS (Floraprint, 1991) Covers selection and cultivation, plus using clematis in a variety of ways; includes chart of 100 clematis. Evison founded the International Clematis Society.

Fair, Keith and Carol
CLEMATIS FOR COLOUR AND VERSATILITY (Trafalgar Square, 1991) Details on cultivation, pest and disease control, care, and numerous ways to use clematis in the garden; A to Z list of over 50 varieties.

Fisk, Jim
CLEMATIS (Wisley Handbook) (Sterling, 1991) Complete growing information for dozens of varieties, including hybrids that flower in the spring, summer and autumn.
CLEMATIS: THE QUEEN OF CLIMBERS (Sterling, 1991 revised and expanded edition) Covers planting, pruning, training, propagating, hybridizing and garden uses of 150 clematis.

Fretwell, Barry
CLEMATIS (Capability's, 1989) Describes 190 species, varieties and hybrids, plus information on cultivation and 120 color photos.

Howells, Dr. John
A PLANTSMAN'S GUIDE TO CLEMATIS (Sterling, 1991) Recommendations and growing advice from the director of the International Clematis Society.

Lloyd, Christopher, and Bennett, Tom
CLEMATIS (Capability's, 1989, revised and expanded edition) Details on over 280 species, varieties and hybrids that are grouped by color, plus cultivation and design ideas.

FUCHSIAS

The American Fuchsia Society (San Francisco County Fair Building, 9th Avenue and Lincoln Way, San Francisco, CA 94122) publishes a bimonthly bulletin and a variety of booklets and books. One of the books is *Fuchsia Culture* which includes descriptions of species and information on cultivation, pruning and controlling pests and diseases.

Bartlett, George
FUCHSIAS: THE COMPLETE GUIDE TO CULTIVATION, PROPAGATION AND EXHIBITION (Trafalgar Square, 1989) Includes recommendations of varieties that are easy to grow.
FUCHSIAS FOR HOUSE AND GARDEN (Trafalgar Square, 1991) Covers the basics of good growing, including watering, feeding, propagation, shaping, control of pests and diseases and exhibiting.

Boullemier, Leo
A CHECKLIST OF THE SPECIES, HYBRIDS AND CULTIVARS OF THE GENUS FUCHSIA (Sterling, 1991) Cultivation and propagation information on over 2,000 varieties with tips on hybrids, rousers, introducers, award winners, geographical availabilities and more.
FUCHSIAS (Trafalgar Square, 1989) Covers history, cultivation, propagation, pests and diseases and exhibiting.
A PLANTSMAN'S GUIDE TO FUCHSIAS (Sterling, 1991) Covers planting schemes, care, propagation and the most popular varieties.

Clapham, Sidney
FUCHSIAS FOR HOUSE AND GARDEN (David & Charles, 1982)

Clark, David
FUCHSIAS FOR GREENHOUSE AND GARDEN: A KEW GARDENING GUIDE (Timber Press, 1987) Introduction to fuchsias.

Clark, Jill
FUCHSIAS (Globe Pequot, 1988) All the basic information on selecting and growing fuchsias in the open garden, as espaliers, as bedding plants or in hanging baskets, plus hardiness zone chart and lists of suppliers, societies and gardens.

Ewart, Ron
THE FUCHSIA GROWER'S HANDBOOK (Sterling, 1990) Covers growing fuchsias in containers and beds, as hedges, plus information on propagation, hybridization, exhibition, and pests and diseases; includes a month-by-month guide.

Jennings, K., and Miller, V.
GROWING FUCHSIAS (Timber Press, 1983) Introduction on growing fuchsias that includes plant descriptions, training and shaping, and recipes for compost and fertilizer.

Law, Deborah
GROWING FUCHSIAS (ISBS, 1985) Instructions and illustrations on selection, propagation, care and maintenance.

Manthey, Gerda
FUCHSIAS (Timber, 1991) Details of species, hybrids and cultivars, plus discovery and history of the genus in cultivation and practical growing information.

Proudley, Brian and Valerie
HOW TO GROW FUCHSIAS (Sterling, 1983) Growing information for the garden, greenhouse or as houseplants, plus information on composts, propagation, training, winter care and pest control.

Waddington, Allan, and Swindells, Philip
THE FUCHSIA BOOK: BORDERS, BEDDING, CONTAINERS, HOUSEPLANTS, EXHIBITING (Trafalgar Square, 1992) Introduction to the cultivation and propagation of fuchsias.

Wells, George
FUCHSIAS (Wisley Handbook) (Sterling, 1990) Covers descriptions of approximately 160 cultivars and information on potting, watering, feeding, propagating, training and overwintering.

Wilson, Stanley J.
FUCHSIAS: A COMPLETE GUIDE TO THEIR PROPAGATION AND CULTIVATION FOR HOUSE AND GARDEN (Faber & Faber, 1976) How to grow indoors and outdoors, plus which varieties are suitable for various uses (window sill, greenhouse, permanent bedding, espalier, summer bedding, hanging baskets, exhibiting, etc.)

CAMELLIAS

The American Camellia Society (One Massee Lane, Fort Valley, GA 31030, 912-967-2722) publishes a quarterly journal and a yearbook.

Chang, Hung Ta, and Bartholomew, Bruce
CAMELLIAS (Timber Press, 1987) Taxonomic descriptions translated from the original Chinese.

Edgar, Logan A.
CAMELLIAS: THE COMPLETE GUIDE (Trafalgar Square, 1992) Covers every aspect of cultivation, from buying and planting to showing.

Feathers, David, and Brown, Milton (editors)
THE CAMELLIA (R. L. Bryan Co., 1978) Information from numerous contributors on all phases of camellia culture; recommended by the American Camellia Society.

Macoboy, Stirling
THE COLOUR DICTIONARY OF CAMELLIAS (Merrimack Publ., 1983) Contains over 200 color plates of camellias; another reference recommended by the American Camellia Society.

Noble, Mary, and Graham, Blanche
YOU CAN GROW CAMELLIAS (Dover, 1976) How to grow camellias outdoors or in a greenhouse; includes landscape uses.

Savell, Robert
GROWING CAMELLIAS (ISBS, 1985) Illustrations and instructions on selection, propagation, care and maintenance.

Trehane, David
CAMELLIAS (Wisley Handbook) (Sterling, 1991) Descriptions plus recommended species and cultivars and problems with pests and diseases.
A PLANTSMAN'S GUIDE TO CAMELLIAS (Sterling, 1990) Covers siting, species and cultivars, selection, outdoor cultivation and propagation.

BAMBOO

Dajun, Wang
THE BAMBOOS OF CHINA (Timber Press, 1987) Covers growing requirements and landscape uses for a large variety of Chinese bamboos; includes bamboos that are noninvasive, hardy and not overly large.

Farrelly, David
THE BOOK OF BAMBOO (Sierra Club Books, 1984) A good introduction to bamboo and the many ways it can be used.

Shou-liang, Chen, and Liang-chi, Chia
CHINESE BAMBOOS (Timber Press, 1988) Color photos and brief descriptions of 23 genera, 90 species, 8 varieties and 6 forms.

Takama, Shinji (photographer)
BAMBOOS: 100 PATHS TO BEAUTY (Books Nippan, 2nd edition, date not set) Eighty color photos from a premier bamboo photographer.

MISCELLANEOUS TREES, SHRUBS & VINES

American Hibiscus Society
HIBISCUS CATALOGUE (1984) Color photos and descriptions of 144 varieties.
HIBISCUS CATALOGUE (1991) Color photos and descriptions of varieties since the 1984 edition.
THE HIBISCUS HANDBOOK (1990 revised edition) Detailed information on hibiscus culture.

Beers, Les
GROWING HIBISCUS (ISBS, 1990, 2nd edition) Illustrations and instructions on selection, propagation, care and maintenance.

Blombery, Alec, and Rodd, Tony
PALMS (Salem House, 1983) Describes palms from around the world, plus cultivation and propagation information.

Brooker, M. I., and Kleinig, D. A.
FIELD GUIDE TO EUCALYPTS—VOLUME 1: SOUTHEASTERN AUSTRALIA (ISBS, 1983) Contains 1,000 descriptions with color photos and 240 maps.

Egolf, Donald R., and Andrick, Anne
THE LAGERSTROEMIA HANDBOOK/CHECKLIST: A GUIDE TO CRAPEMYRTLE CULTIVARS (American Assoc. of Botanical Gardens and Arboreta, 1978) Includes descriptions of known cultivars, information on hardiness and resistance to disease, plus a list of gardens with the best specimens.

Fearnley-Whittingstall, Jane
IVIES (Random House, date not set) Covers history and mythology of ivies, plus step-by-step instructions for growing both indoors and out; includes a list of American suppliers.

Fiala, Fr. John L.
LILACS (Timber Press, 1988) Everything you need to know about growing lilacs from the founding director of the International Lilac Society.

Gardiner, James M.
MAGNOLIAS (Globe Pequot, 1989) Cultivation, care and propagation information, plus 100 color photos and a list of American and British gardens to visit.

Jacobs, M. R.
GROWTH HABITS OF THE EUCALYPTS (ISBS, reprint of 1955 edition) Includes 140 black-and-white photos.

Jaynes, Richard
KALMIA: THE LAUREL BOOK II (Timber Press, 1988, revised and expanded 2nd edition) The standard reference on mountain laurel with information on

cultivation and propagation, plus descriptions of all the known cultivars.

McCurrach, James
PALMS OF THE WORLD (Harper, 1960) Describes 140 genera. A supplement adding 100 genera was written in 1976 by Arthur Langlois and published by University Presses of Florida.

McKelvey, Susan
THE LILAC (Macmillan, 1928) A classic monograph on lilacs.

Miller, Howard, and Lamb, Samuel
OAKS OF NORTH AMERICA (Naturegraph Publishers, 1985) Describes over 75 species and varieties; includes zone maps and 300+ photos.

Swartley, John C.
THE CULTIVATED HEMLOCKS (Timber Press, 1984, expanded and revised edition) A complete guide to hemlock species and cultivars.

Vertrees, J. D.
JAPANESE MAPLES (Timber Press, 1987, 2nd edition) Covers new cultivars introduced since the first edition, plus updated information on culture and propagation and a new section on landscape uses.

For related books, see:
CLIMBERS AND TRAILERS by Grace (page 180)
DISEASES OF TREES AND SHRUBS by Sinclair, Lyon and Johnson (page 74)
FLOWERING TREES OF THE WORLD FOR TROPICS AND WARM CLIMATES by Menninger (page 181)
GROUND COVERS AND VINES by Brooklyn Botanic Garden (page 48)
INSECTS THAT FEED ON TREES AND SHRUBS by Johnson and Lyon (page 73)

LANDSCAPE PLANTS FOR THE SOUTHEAST by Batson (page 192)
LANDSCAPE PLANTS OF THE SOUTHEAST by Halfacre and Shawcroft (page 193)
NATIVE SHRUBS AND WOODY VINES OF THE SOUTHEAST by Foote and Jones (page 193)
THE NATURAL HISTORY OF WILD SHRUBS AND VINES by Stokes (page 98)
THE PRUNING OF TREES, SHRUBS AND CONIFERS by Brown (page 75)
SHADE TREES FOR THE CENTRAL AND NORTHERN U.S. AND CANADA by Yiesla and Giles (page 192)
SHRUBS AND VINES FOR SOUTHERN LANDSCAPES by Adams (page 192)
TREES AND SHRUBS FOR DRY CALIFORNIA LANDSCAPES by Perry (page 198)
TREES AND SHRUBS FOR NORTHERN GARDENS by Snyder (page 192)
TREES AND SHRUBS FOR PACIFIC NORTHWEST GARDENS by Grant (page 197)
TREES AND SHRUBS HARDY IN THE BRITISH ISLES by Bean (page 204)
TREES FOR SMALL GARDENS by Davis (page 175)
TREES FOR SOUTHERN LANDSCAPES by Adams (page 192)
TREES OF GEORGIA AND ADJACENT STATES by Brown and Kirkman (page 193)
TREES OF SEATTLE by Jacobsen (page 197)
TREES OF THE SOUTH by Robinette (page 194)
TREES, SHRUBS AND WOODY VINES OF THE SOUTHWEST by Vines (page 196)
TROPICALS by Courtright (page 180)
WOODY ORNAMENTALS FOR DEEP SOUTH GARDENS by Rogers (page 194)

ROSES

The American Rose Society (P.O. Box 30000, Shreveport, LA 71130-0030) publishes the *Handbook for Selecting Roses*, an annual listing of their ratings on commercially available roses (organized by horticultural classification and color), the *American Rose Annual* which covers each new rose grown in different areas of the U.S., *Modern Roses 9*, a checklist of registered rose names, and *The American Rose*, a magazine that comes out eleven times a year (January-November). A library list is also available ($2).

Alcosser, Murray
THE ROMANTIC ROSE (Rizzoli International, 1990) Photographs of all types of roses in various forms—single bloom, bouquets and large gardens.

Austin, David
THE HERITAGE OF THE ROSE (Antique Collector's Club, 1988) A world-renowned rosarian examines 950 varieties of roses.

Barash, Cathy W.
ROSES (Chartwell, 1991) Discusses history, methods of planting, layering, pruning, budding, hybridizing and preserving for 120 different types of roses.

Beales, Peter
ROSES: AN ILLUSTRATED ENCYCLOPEDIA AND GROWER'S HANDBOOK OF SPECIES ROSES, OLD ROSES AND MODERN ROSES, SHRUB ROSES AND CLIMBERS (Henry Holt, 1992) Contains over 1,000 color illustrations, maps and charts.

TWENTIETH-CENTURY ROSES (Harper & Row, 1989) Comprehensive reference work on planting and cultivation of over 850 hybrids; includes 400+ color photographs.

Brooklyn Botanic Garden
ROSES (BBG #92) A guide to planting, pruning, hybridizing, propagating, and insect and disease control.

Browne, Roland A.
THE ROSE-LOVERS GUIDE: A PRACTICAL HANDBOOK ON ROSE GROWING (Atheneum, 1983) All the basics, plus his choices for best hybrid teas, grandifloras, floribundas and climbers and a chapter on "hybridizing for fun." Nice, chatty style.

Charlton, Don
GROWING AND SHOWING ROSES (Trafalgar Square, 1984) Proven methods for growing and showing roses.

Coggiatti, Stelvio
SIMON & SCHUSTER'S GUIDE TO ROSES (Simon & Schuster, 1987) Categorizes 200 varieties of roses by type and whether pre-1910 or post-1910.

Crockett, James Underwood, and Editors of Time-Life Books
ROSES (Time-Life Books, 1971) History, planting, pruning, protecting, propagating and flower arranging, plus color illustrations and descriptions of 344 varieties.

Dobson, Beverly
COMBINED ROSE LIST (Beverly Dobson, Irvington, NY) Annual list of hybrid rose cultivars giving the name, breeder, color and nurseries where the rose can be bought. She also publishes *Bev Dobson's Rose Letter* bimonthly which updates the *Combined Rose List*. Write to her at 215 Harriman Road, Irvington, New York 10533.

Fearnley-Whittingstall, Jane
ROSE GARDENS (Henry Holt, 1989) Formal and informal designs for rose gardens.

Fisher, John
THE COMPANION TO ROSES (Salem House, 1987) Mini-essays on all kinds of rose-related topics. (Did you know that Redoute's first commission was for flower portraits for Empress Josephine's bedroom at La Malmaison?)

Fitch, Charles M.
THE COMPLETE BOOK OF MINIATURE ROSES (Hawthorn Books, 1977) Information on growing both indoors and outdoor.

Garden Way Publishing Editors
ROSES: 1001 GARDENING QUESTIONS ANSWERED (Garden Way, 1989) Answers the most often asked questions about roses and rose growing.

Gault, S. Millar, and Synge, Patrick
DICTIONARY OF ROSES IN COLOUR (Royal Horticultural Society and British National Rose Society, 1971) Describes over 800 varieties in 18 major categories; over 500 color photographs.

Genders, Roy
THE ROSE: A COMPLETE HANDBOOK (Bobbs-Merrill, 1966) With an English slant, but does include such tidbits as the perfume of a rose, greenhouse growing and recipes.

Gibson, Michael
THE BOOK OF THE ROSE (Methuen, 1980) Contains history and growing information, plus descriptions of the world's most famous exhibition rose gardens.
GROWING ROSES (Timber Press, 1984) A good introduction for the novice that includes all of the popular groups and gives suggestions for the best varieties in each category plus advice on cultivation and garden uses.
GROWING ROSES FOR SMALL GARDENS (Timber Press, 1991) Examines patio, miniature shrub, climbers and roses suitable for use as ground covers.
ROSES (Wisley handbook) (Sterling, 1990) Basic information from the Royal Horticultural Society.
SHRUB ROSES, CLIMBERS AND RAMBLERS (Collins, 1981)

Hamilton, Beatrix
CONCISE ILLUSTRATED BOOK OF ROSES (Smithmark, 1989)

Harkness, Jack
THE MAKERS OF HEAVENLY ROSES (Souvenir Press, 1985)
THE WORLD'S FAVORITE ROSES AND HOW TO GROW THEM (McGraw-Hill, 1979) Color photos and descriptions of 123 of the most beautiful and growable roses in the world; includes information on the major breeders plus a chart giving vital statistics on 300 additional rose varieties.

Harkness, Peter
MODERN GARDEN ROSES (Globe Pequot, 1988)
Discusses 108 modern bush and shrub roses, including
the "Graham Thomas."
THE PHOTOGRAPHIC ENCYCLOPEDIA OF
ROSES (Smithmark, 1991) The qualities, size, color,
habit and how to use for almost 700 varieties of roses;
400 color photos.

Harris, Cyril
ILLUSTRATED GUIDE TO ROSES (Treasure
Press, 1989) Covers choosing roses, preparing the soil,
planting, pruning, pest control, propagating, exhibiting and cutting.

Hessayon, Dr. D. G.
THE ROSE EXPERT (Sterling, 1990) Full-color
photographs and detailed information on 330 roses.

Krussmann, Gerd
THE COMPLETE BOOK OF ROSES (Timber
Press, 1981) A mammoth 90 chapters covering an
immense amount of information; highly recommended by the American Rose Society and the American Horticultural Society.

Lacy, Allen
THE GLORY OF ROSES (Stewart, Tabori &
Chang, 1990) With text by Allen Lacy and more than
250 color photos by Christopher Baker, this book
conveys the mystery and beauty of roses.

Malins, Peter, and Graff, M. M.
PETER MALINS' ROSE BOOK (Dodd, Mead,
1979) Basic techniques, plus critical appraisal of the
most beautiful and durable roses of the previous 40
years and how to predict a variety's success or failure.

McCann, Sean
MINIATURE ROSES FOR HOME AND GAR-
DEN (Arco, 1985) Basics, plus propagating, pruning,
exhibiting and hybridizing; includes a list of the "Top
30" miniature roses for the novice.
MINIATURE ROSES: THEIR CARE AND CUL-
TIVATION (Stackpole, 1991) Describes how to
grow miniature roses in borders, hanging baskets, as
topiary and as houseplants; includes color photos of
the best 100 miniatures.

McGredy, Sam, and Jennett, S.
A FAMILY OF ROSES (Cassell, 1971)

Meilland, Alain
MEILLAND: A LIFE IN ROSES (Illinois University Press, 1984)

Nicolas, Dr. Jean Henri
A ROSE ODYSSEY (Doubleday Doran, 1937) Rem-
iniscences of his many trips to European rose centers.
A YEAR IN THE ROSE GARDEN (Doubleday
Doran, 1936)

Nisbet, Fred J.
GROWING BETTER ROSES (Knopf, 1974) Basics,
plus container and greenhouse growing.

Ortho
ALL ABOUT ROSES (Ortho Books, 1990 revised
edition) Good introduction to rose growing; recommended by the American Rose Society.

Osborne, Robert
HARDY ROSES: AN ORGANIC GUIDE TO
GROWING FROST- AND DISEASE-RESIS-
TANT VARIETIES (Storey, 1991) Discusses winter-
ing, cultivating and propagating, plus the top 49 hardy
roses.

Phillips, Roger, and Rix, Martyn
THE RANDOM HOUSE GUIDE TO ROSES
(Random House, 1988) Full color photos with detailed
descriptions of over 1,400 roses from all over the
world—old roses, species roses, hybrid teas, floribundas, climbers, ramblers and miniatures. Luscious!

Ray, Richard, and MacCaskey, Michael
ROSES: HOW TO SELECT, GROW AND
ENJOY (HP Books, 1984) Great beginning book de-
scribing over 200 varieties and giving the American
Rose Society's rating and fragrance rating. Over 500
color photos.

Reddell, Rayford Clayton
GROWING GOOD ROSES (Harper & Row, 1988)
Expert advice from a professional rose grower on selecting, buying, planting, maintaining, spraying, cutting, pruning and exhibiting.

Reilly, Ann
THE ROSE (Outlet Book Co., 1989) Color photographs of numerous species and some beautiful rose gardens, plus history of the rose in art, literature, religion, myth, music and legends; includes award-winning roses and creating new roses and hybrids.

Ridge, Antonia
FOR THE LOVE OF A ROSE: STORY OF THE CREATION OF THE FAMOUS PEACE ROSE (Faber & Faber, 1972) A true story of how two families, both besotted by roses, are united by marriage.

Rohde, Eleanour Sinclair
ROSE RECIPES (Dover, 1973) Century old recipes for sauces, jellies, tarts, salads, potpourris, sweet bags, pomanders and perfumes.

Sala, Orietta
THE WORLD'S BEST ROSES (Prentice-Hall, 1991) Over 1,000 color photos and descriptions of teas, hybrid teas, polyanthas, floribundas, miniatures, climbers and shrubs.

Scanniello, Steve, and Bayard, Tanya
ROSES OF AMERICA (Henry Holt, 1990) Expert advice from the rosarian at the Brooklyn Botanic Garden's Cranford Rose Garden; includes 300+ color photos of over 200 roses.

Shepherd, Roy E.
HISTORY OF THE ROSE (Earl M. Coleman, 1978) Reprint of 1954 edition; title is misleading since only the first chapter deals with history, and the remaining 11 chapters cover the main botanical divisions giving a general description of the group followed by details on the species; extensive bibliography.

Squire, David, and Newdick, Jane
THE BOOK OF THE ROSE (Crescent, 1991) Covers 250 varieties of species roses, hybrid tea, floribunda, climbing and rambling, and miniature roses with information on size, parentage, foliage and characteristics; 300 color photos.

Sunset
ROSES (Sunset Books, 1989) How to choose and grow healthy roses; includes a rose encyclopedia.

Swain, Bill
ROSES: QUESTIONS AND ANSWERS (Sterling, 1990) Answers to the 100 most frequently asked questions on how to grow, care for and propagate roses.

Swim, Herb
ROSES: FROM DREAMS TO REALITY (Stump Publishing, 1988)

Taylor's
GUIDE TO ROSES (Houghton Mifflin, 1986) Encyclopedia of 396 roses with color photos and information on the flowers, foliage and history of each; includes list of nurseries and articles by experts on every phase of growing roses.
POCKET GUIDE TO MODERN ROSES (Houghton Mifflin, 1989) Full color photos and descriptions of 79 floribundas, grandifloras, hybrid teas and miniatures.

Thomas, Graham Stuart
THE ART OF GARDENING WITH ROSES (Henry Holt, 1991) How to combine roses with other plants for a unique garden design.
CLIMBING ROSES OLD AND NEW (Dent, 1983, rev. ed.) Classifications, history, parentage, habit, structure, color and size of hundreds of climbers and ramblers.
SHRUB ROSES OF TODAY (Dent, 1980, rev. ed.) Encompasses 350 species, hybrids and the best modern varieties.

Tillotson, Will
ROSES OF YESTERDAY AND TODAY (Sweetbrier, 1980) Reprint of his 1959 catalogue.

Time-Life Books
ROSES: GARDENER'S GUIDE SERIES (Time-Life, 1989)

Toogood, Alan
ROSES IN GARDENS: GARDENING BY DESIGN (Sterling, 1990) Describes various ways to use roses: as a hedge, in a container, on a trellis, mixed with other flowers, etc.

Verrier, Suzanne
ROSA RUGOSA (Capability's, 1991) Describes over 200 varieties of shrub roses that are cold-hardy and practically pest-free (without chemicals); source list.

Warner, Christopher
CLIMBING ROSES (Globe Pequot, 1988) How to grow various varieties of climbing roses with an emphasis on color and fragrance.

Welch, David
ROSES (Timber Press, 1988) (Kew Gardening Guide) An introduction to growing roses.

Wheatcroft, Harry
MY LIFE WITH ROSES (Odhams, 1959)

OLD ROSES

Beales, Peter
CLASSIC ROSES: AN ILLUSTRATED ENCY-CLOPEDIA AND GROWER'S MANUAL OF OLD ROSES, SHRUB ROSES, AND CLIMBERS (Holt, Reinhart & Winston, 1985) History and culture of old roses, shrub roses and climbers; over 500 color photos.

Buist, Robert
THE ROSE MANUAL (E. M. Coleman, 1978) Reprint of the 1844 classic with updated foreword by Edith Schurr.

Bunyard, Edward A.
OLD GARDEN ROSES (E. M. Coleman, 1978) Reprint of 1936 edition with updated foreword by Bev Dobson.

Christopher, Thomas
IN SEARCH OF LOST ROSES (Summit Books, 1989) His adventurous search through various parts of the U.S. and Great Britain for the "great old roses of the past" with their unusual colors and headier fragrance.

Clarke, Ethne
MAKING A ROSE GARDEN (Grove Weidenfeld, 1992) How to use old roses to create cottage, formal Victorian, scented and other types of gardens.

Culpepper, Elizabeth
HERITAGE ROSES AND OLD FASHIONED CRAFTS (ISBS, 1989) Includes over 170 heritage roses with information on making potpourris, candles, stationery, toiletries and edibles from their petals.

Dickerson, Brent C.
THE OLD ROSE ADVISOR (Timber Press, 1992) Concentrating on roses developed before 1920, the author researched original material from France, Britain and the U.S. to compile a book of in-depth descriptions, cultural directions and complete history of the development of each rose group; includes extensive appendices on 2,332 cultivars.

Dierauff, E., and Jacob, A.
OLD GARDEN ROSES AND SELECTED MODERN HYBRIDS (Thames & Hudson, 1988) The origins of Damask, Bourbon, Alba, Moss and other varieties of old roses.

Druitt, Liz, and Shoup, G. Michael
LANDSCAPING WITH ANTIQUE ROSES
(Taunton Press, 1992)

Earle, Alice Morse
SUN DIALS AND ROSES OF YESTERDAY
(Macmillan, 1902)

Ellwanger, Henry B.
THE ROSE (E. M. Coleman, 1978) Reprint of 1882
classic on Hybrid Perpetuals; new foreword by Edith
Schurr.

Gore, Catherine
THE BOOK OF ROSES (E. M. Coleman, 1978)
Reprint of the 1838 book on French roses; new fore-
word by Leonie Bell.

Griffiths, Trevor
THE BOOK OF OLD ROSES (Michael Joseph,
1984) Divided into chapters by type of old rose; over
400 color photos and almost 600 descriptions.
THE BOOK OF CLASSIC OLD ROSES (Viking
Penguin, 1988) A continuation of *The Book of Old
Roses*; an additional 600 varieties.
A CELEBRATION OF OLD ROSES (Viking Pen-
guin, 1991) Another 600 varieties and 400 color photos.
MY WORLD OF OLD ROSES (Whitcoulls Pub-
lishers, 1983) His love of old roses is evident in this
lovely book.

Jekyll, Gertrude and Mawley, Edward
ROSES FOR ENGLISH GARDENS (Antique
Collector's Club, 1982) About old roses, especially
ramblers and early climbers; originally published in
1902. (In 1984, the Ayer Co. published an edition
revised by Graham Stuart Thomas and entitled *Roses*.)

Keays, Ethelyn
OLD ROSES (E. M. Coleman, 1978) Reprint of 1935
book telling how she studied and searched for old roses
to plant on her property in Calvert County, Maryland;
new foreword by Leonie Bell.

LeRougetel, Hazel
A HERITAGE OF ROSES (Stemmer House, 1988)
How roses first arrived in England, the United States,
China, Australia, New Zealand, India and Europe,
were propagated and redistributed internationally.

Lindley, John
ROSARIUM MONOGRAPHIA (E. M. Coleman,
1978) Reprint of 1820 edition with new foreword by
Lily Shohan.

McLeod, Judyth
OUR HERITAGE OF OLD ROSES (ISBS, 1987)
Growing, landscaping, and maintenance information,
plus using these roses for cosmetics, medicine and food.

Nottle, Trevor
GROWING OLD FASHIONED ROSES (ISBS,
1985) How to select, care for and propagate.

Parsons, Samuel
PARSONS ON THE ROSE (E. M. Coleman, 1979)
Reprint of 1882 edition with new foreword by Helen
L. Blake.

Paul, William
THE ROSE GARDEN (E. M. Coleman, 1978) Re-
print of 1848 edition with new foreword by Richard
Thomson.

Prince, William R.
PRINCE'S MANUAL OF ROSES (E. M. Coleman,
1979) Reprint of 1846 edition listing 1,600 roses including Hybrid Perpetuals and Noisette Roses; new
foreword by Leonie Bell.

Rivers, Thomas
ROSE AMATEUR'S GUIDE (E. M. Coleman,
1979) Reprint of the 4th edition of the 1846 guide to
rose cultivation; new foreword by Leonie Bell.

Steen, Nancy
THE CHARM OF OLD ROSES (Milldale Press,
1987) Reprint of the 1966 classic by a woman who spent
much of her life collecting, cultivating and studying
old roses.

Taylor's
POCKET GUIDE TO OLD-FASHIONED ROSES
(Houghton Mifflin, 1989) Color photos and descriptions of 79 old garden roses, shrub roses, climbers and
species roses.

Thomas, Graham Stuart
THE OLD SHRUB ROSES (Dent/RHS, 1983) Cov-
ers over 200 varieties of roses dating back to Victorian,

medieval and Roman times; foreword by Vita Sack-ville-West.

Welch, William C.
ANTIQUE ROSES FOR THE SOUTH (Taylor Publishing, 1990) All the basics for growing old roses in the South, plus craft ideas, floral arrangements and sources for antique roses.

Westrich, Josh (photographer)
OLD GARDEN ROSES AND SELECTED MODERN HYBRIDS (Thames & Hudson, 1988) Over 80 color photographs; foreword by Helene von Stein-Zeppelin and descriptions by Dierauff and Amy Jacob.

For related books, see:
THE BOOK OF ROSE ARRANGEMENTS by Clements (page 133)
THE COMPLETE BOOK OF 169 REDOUTE ROSES by Anderson (page 219)
A GARDEN OF ROSES by Parsons (page 220)
PAPA FLORIBUNDA by Wells (page 13)
THE ROSE GARDENS OF ENGLAND by Gibson (page 205)
THE ROSES by Redouté (page 220)

FOLIAGE

Aden, Paul (editor and compiler)
THE HOSTA BOOK (Timber Press, 1990, 2nd edition) All aspects of hosta culture and use are covered by hosta experts from three continents; includes some new cultivars since the first edition.

Billington, Jill
ARCHITECTURAL FOLIAGE (Sterling, 1991) How to use the shape of the plant and its position in the garden to create interest.

de Bray, Lys
THE GREEN GARDEN: THE ART OF FOLIAGE PLANTING (Sterling, 1991) Describes a variety of foliage plants and includes eight garden plans for using foliage.

Glattstein, Judy
GARDEN DESIGN WITH FOLIAGE: FERNS AND GRASSES, VINES AND GROUND COVERS, ANNUALS AND PERENNIALS, TREES AND SHRUBS (Storey, 1991) How to use leaf color and texture in the home landscape.

Grenfell, Diana
HOSTA: THE FLOWERING FOLIAGE PLANT (Timber Press, 1991) Written from an historical perspective, it traces the hosta's journey from Japan through Macao to Europe; includes lists of the species and recommended cultivars.

Jefferson-Brown, Michael, and Glover, John
LEAVES: FOR ALL-YEAR ROUND COLOUR AND INTEREST IN THE GARDEN (Trafalgar Square, 1989) How to make the most of foliage in your garden; includes plans and groupings for trees, shrubs, climbers, herbaceous and water plants.

Kelly, John
FOLIAGE IN YOUR GARDEN (Penguin, 1989) Describes ways to use a variety of foliage and gives suggestions for which plants to try.

Lloyd, Christopher
FOLIAGE PLANTS (Penguin, 1988) How to choose and care for foliage plants.

Pavord, Anna (editor)
FOLIAGE: PLANNING AND PLANTING
(HarperCollins, 1990) Covers the cultivation of foliage plants, how to combine foliage plants and flowers, and advice on using ferns, bamboos and grasses.

Schmid, W. George
THE GENUS HOSTA (Timber Press, 1992) Detailed descriptions of all species, varieties, forms and registered cultivars, as well as almost all of the non-registered classic hostas of historic and garden interest; lists nearly 3,500 names and synonyms, including non-English names.

Spencer, Roger
GROWING SILVER, GREY AND BLUE FOLIAGE PLANTS (ISBS, 1987) Illustrations and instructions on selection, propagation, care and maintenance.

For related books, see:
THE NATURAL SHADE GARDEN by Druse
(page172)

PESTS, WEEDS AND DISEASES

Ball, Jeff
RODALE'S GARDEN PROBLEM SOLVER:
VEGETABLES, FRUITS AND HERBS (Rodale
Press, 1988) Describes the symptoms and causes of over
700 problems, offers an organic solution and ways to avoid
any future problems.

Ball, Jeff and Liz
RODALE'S LANDSCAPE PROBLEM SOLVER:
A PLANT-BY-PLANT GUIDE (Rodale Press,
1989) Symptons of malaise and how to organically
control diseases and insect and animal pests on trees,
shrubs, roses, ground covers, vines, foliage plants and
lawns.
RODALE'S FLOWER GARDEN PROBLEM
SOLVER: ANNUALS, PERENNIALS, BULBS,
AND ROSES (Rodale Press, 1990) How to avoid
over 600 problems, but should they occur, how to
handle them organically.

Berenbaum, May
NINETY-NINE GNATS, NITS AND NIBBLERS
(University of Illinois Press, 1989) Interesting, funny
and educational account of the world of insects.

Bonar, Ann
THE GARDEN PLANT SURVIVAL MANUAL
(Gallery Books, 1989) How to identify and solve problems with ornamental trees, shrubs, perennials and
bulbs.

Brooklyn Botanic Garden
GARDENING WITHOUT PESTS (BBG #89)
Covers the primary garden insects and diseases and
how to control them.

Carr, Anna
RODALE'S COLOR HANDBOOK OF GARDEN
INSECTS (Rodale Press, 1983) A guide for identifying orchard or vegetable garden insects; 300+ color
photos of the egg, larval, pupal and adult stages.

Davidson, Ralph, and Lyon, William
INSECT PESTS OF FARM, GARDEN AND OR-
CHARD (John Wiley, 1987, 8th edition)

Ellis, Barbara, and Bradley, Fern (editors)
THE ORGANIC GARDENER'S HANDBOOK OF
NATURAL INSECT AND DISEASE CONTROL:
A COMPLETE PROBLEM SOLVING GUIDE TO

KEEPING YOUR GARDEN AND YARD HEALTHY WITHOUT CHEMICALS (Rodale Press, 1992 revised edition) Nonchemical ways to control pests and diseases on vegetables, fruits, flowers, trees and lawns; arranged alphabetically by plant and contains almost 600 color photos and illustrations.

Erickson, Jonathan
GARDENING FOR A GREENER PLANET: A CHEMICAL-FREE APPROACH (TAB Books, 1992) How to protect plants from bugs by using beneficial insects, companion planting, minerals and soaps and nonchemical pesticides; arranged by plant.

Gillespie, Janet
PEACOCK MANURE AND MARIGOLDS: A NO-POISON GUIDE TO A BEAUTIFUL GARDEN (Viking, 1964)

Hart, Rhonda M.
BUGS, SLUGS, AND OTHER THUGS (Storey, 1991) Covers their life cycle and habits and how to organically deter them.

Johnson, Warren, and Lyon, Howard
INSECTS THAT FEED ON TREES AND SHRUBS (Cornell University Press, 1988, 2nd edition revised and expanded) Covers over 900 insects, mites, and animals that damage trees and shrubs in the U.S. and Canada.

Kramer, Jack
FIRST AID FOR PLANTS (Plume, 1989) How to diagnose symptoms, plus techniques and unusual remedies such as aspirin, paprika, chili powder and ice cubes for keeping plants healthy.

Levy, Charles K.
A GUIDE TO HOME AND GARDEN PESTS (Viking Penguin, 1985) How to identify and eliminate them safely.

Lorenzi, Harri J., and Jeffrey, Larry S.
WEEDS OF THE UNITED STATES AND THEIR CONTROL (Van Nostrand Reinhold, 1987) Descriptions, locations and ways to control weeds.

Mother Earth News (editors)
THE HEALTHY GARDEN HANDBOOK: AN ILLUSTRATED GUIDE TO COMBATING INSECTS, GARDEN PESTS AND PLANT DISEASES (Simon & Schuster, 1989) Includes homemade fertilizers and selecting insect-resistant plants; organic approach.

Muenscher, Walter C.
WEEDS (Cornell University Press, 1980, 2nd edition) Descriptions of 571 North American weeds.

Olkowski, William; Daar, Sheila; and Olkowski, Helga
COMMON-SENSE PEST CONTROL: LEAST-TOXIC SOLUTIONS FOR YOUR HOME, GARDEN, PETS AND COMMUNITY (Taunton Press, 1991) A very complete reference on the least-toxic pest controls being sold today; details how to control yellow jackets, grubs, mosquitoes, termites, rats, weeds, roaches, ticks and many more creatures.

Ortho
CONTROLLING LAWN AND GARDEN INSECTS (Ortho, 1987) How to recognize and control, chemically and organically, over 60 common garden insects.
CONTROLLING WEEDS (Ortho, 1989) How to recognize and control over 100 common lawn, food and flower garden weeds; includes chemical and nonchemical methods.
ENVIRONMENTALLY FRIENDLY GARDENING: CONTROLLING VEGETABLE PESTS (Ortho, 1991) Covers various methods of handling 200 diseases and problems with pests.
THE ORTHO PROBLEM SOLVER (Ortho, 1984, 2nd edition) Covers pest and diseases, what causes the problem and how to solve it; arranged according to the plants affected.

Philbrick, Helen and John
THE BUG BOOK: HARMLESS INSECT CONTROLS (Garden Way, 1974) Describes over 100 insects, how to recognize their damage and what to do to control it; includes recipes for making insecticides and repellants and suggestions for companion plants.

Pirone, Pascal P.
DISEASES AND PESTS OF ORNAMENTAL PLANTS (John Wiley, 1978, 5th edition) Diagnosing and treating the problems of approximately 500

genera of indoor, outdoor and greenhouse-grown ornamentals.

Rice, Robert
NURSERY AND LANDSCAPE WEED CONTROL MANUAL (Thomson Publications, 1987) How to use chemicals properly when controlling weeds; includes tradenames, toxicity, application, reactions, storage and cleanup of herbicides.

Sinclair, Wayne; Lyon, Howard; and
Johnson, Warren
DISEASES OF TREES AND SHRUBS (Cornell University Press, 1987) Surveys 350 diseases affecting over 250 plant species and documents the information with 1,759 photos.

Smith, Miranda, and Carr, Anna
RODALE'S GARDEN INSECT, DISEASE, AND WEED IDENTIFICATION GUIDE (Rodale Press, 1988) Illustrates and describes over 200 insects, diseases and weeds that affect food gardens and covers organic ways to prevent and control them.

Spencer, Edwin Rollin
ALL ABOUT WEEDS (Dover, 1974) Profiles hundreds of weeds in various habitats (lawns, gardens, meadows, fields, etc.)

Stein, Sara
MY WEEDS: A GARDENER'S BOTANY (Harper Perennial, 1990) A new way to look at weeds, their anatomy and methods of propagation, germination and evolution.

U.S. Department of Agriculture
COMMON WEEDS OF THE UNITED STATES (Dover, 1970) An identification guide to 220 weeds with a drawing for each, plus range, appearance and habitat information.

Westcott, Cynthia
THE GARDENER'S BUG BOOK (Doubleday, 1973, 4th revised edition)
WESTCOTT'S PLANT DISEASE HANDBOOK (Van Nostrand Reinhold, 1990, 5th edition revised by Kenneth Horst) A guide to diagnosing and controlling diseases on hundreds of plants; for home gardeners and commercial growers.

Yepsen, Roger B.
THE ENCYCLOPEDIA OF NATURAL INSECT AND DISEASE CONTROL (Rodale Press, 1984) Nonchemical ways to control pests and diseases on vegetables, fruits, flowers, trees and lawns; handy reference as it is arranged alphabetically by plant.

For related books, see:
DISEASES OF GREENHOUSE PLANTS by Fletcher (page 121)
A FIELD GUIDE TO FLORIDA CRITTERS by Zak (page 195)
A FIELD GUIDE TO TEXAS CRITTERS by Zak (page 197)
HERBACEOUS PERENNIALS: DISEASES AND INSECT PESTS by Daughtrey (page 83)
IDENTIFYING DISEASES OF VEGETABLES by MacNab et al. (page 102)
RX FOR YOUR VEGETABLE GARDEN by Newcomb (page 103)

PRUNING

Allen, Oliver E.
PRUNING AND GRAFTING (Henry Holt, 1986)
Illustrates the three stages of pruning and various pruning techniques including espalier and topiary; reprint of 1978 Time-Life book.

Brickell, Christopher
PRUNING (Simon & Schuster, 1988) Diagrams and how-to information on pruning roses, flowering shrubs, vines, hedges, espaliers, and fruit trees and bushes.

Bridgeman, Peter H.
TREE SURGERY: THE COMPLETE GUIDE (Trafalgar Square, 1976)

Brooklyn Botanic Garden
PRUNING (BBG #126) Techniques for pruning trees, shrubs and herbaceous plants; includes topiary, bonsai, espalier and other special techniques.

Brown, George
THE PRUNING OF TREES, SHRUBS AND CONIFERS (Faber & Faber, 1977) Covers general pruning principles plus pruning information for specific plants.

Clarke, Graham
PRACTICAL PRUNING (Gallery, 1990) An introduction covering training young trees and shrubs and pruning mature plants.

Elliot, Rodger
PRUNING: A PRACTICAL GUIDE (ISBS, 1987) Explains the effectiveness of pruning and when and how to prune ground covers, shrubs, trees and climbers.

Halliwell, Brian; Turpin, John; and Wright, John
THE COMPLETE BOOK OF PRUNING (Trafalgar Square, 1988) Revised edition of *The Complete Handbook of Pruning* by Rodger Grounds.

Hill, Lewis
PRUNING SIMPLIFIED (Storey, 1986 update) Discusses and illustrates how to prune ornamentals, evergreens, hedges, fruit and nut trees, vines, topiary, ground covers, houseplants, bonsai and Christmas trees.

Johns, Patrick
AN INTRODUCTION TO PRUNING (Smithmark, 1991) Surveys various pruning methods including root pruning, shaping, retraining, pruning to encourage fruiting and more.

Ortho
ALL ABOUT PRUNING (Ortho, 1978)

Shigo, Alex L.
TREE PRUNING: A WORLDWIDE PHOTO GUIDE (Shigo & Trees Associates, 1989)

Stebbins, Robert L., and MacCaskey, Michael
PRUNING: HOW-TO GUIDE FOR GARDENERS (HP Books, 1983) How to prune over 350 plants; 300+ color photos.

Steffek, Edwin
THE PRUNING MANUAL (Van Nostrand Reinhold, 1982, 2nd revised edition) How to prune trees, shrubs, vines, roses, grapes and fruits.

Sunset
PRUNING HANDBOOK (Sunset Books, 1983) Color photos and step-by-step directions for pruning trees, shrubs, vines, fruits, nuts and berries.

Woodward, Jack
PRUNING HARDY FRUITS (Wisley Handbook) (Sterling, 1991) How to prune in order to improve fruit production, beauty and life span of these plants; includes tips on training various forms such as bush trees, espaliers and fans.

SEEDS/PROPAGATION

Bittman, Sam
SEEDS: THE ULTIMATE GUIDE TO GROW-ING VEGETABLES, HERBS AND FLOWERS (Bantam, 1989) Covers sowing and growing 250 different plants from seed; includes color photo of each plant and drawing of each seedling.

Brooklyn Botanic Garden
PROPAGATION (BBG #103) Describes the latest techniques, and gives a list of suppliers and a bibliography.

Browse, Phillip M.
PLANT PROPAGATION (Simon & Schuster, 1988) How to propagate seeds, roots, and bulbs by layering, stem and leaf cuttings, budding and grafting.

Bubel, Nancy
THE NEW SEED-STARTERS HANDBOOK (Rodale Press, 1988) All the techniques needed for growing over 200 vegetables, ornamental plants and wildflowers from seeds.

Clarke, Graham, and Toogood, Alan
THE COMPLETE BOOK OF PLANT PROPA-GATION (Sterling, 1990) Thoroughly describes the major propagating techniques then gives specifics for alpines, grasses, herbs, aquatics, conifers, carnivorous plants, climbers, bulbs, corms, ferns, perennials, fruits, trees, shrubs and greenhouse plants.

Derrick, Tony
GARDEN PLANTS FOR FREE (Smithmark, 1990) Explains the basic techniques, then discusses various examples including ground covers.

Dirr, Michael A., and Heuser Jr., Charles W.
THE REFERENCE MANUAL OF WOODY PLANT PROPAGATION: FROM SEED TO TIS-SUE CULTURE (Timber Press, 1987) How-to propagating information on 1,100 species and cultivars of deciduous and evergreen trees, shrubs and vines.

Foster, Catharine O.
PLANTS-A-PLENTY: HOW TO MULTIPLY OUTDOOR AND INDOOR PLANTS THROUGH CUTTINGS, CROWN AND ROOT

DIVISIONS, GRAFTING, LAYERING AND SEEDS (Rodale Press, 1977) Covers basic propagation techniques, plus information on handling specific plants.

Gardiner, Allan
MODERN PLANT PROPAGATION (ISBS, 1988) Step-by-step diagrams of all techniques, plus propagation details on a comprehensive alphabetical list of plants.

Garner, R. J.
THE GRAFTER'S HANDBOOK (Sterling, 1989, 5th edition) Instructions and illustrations for propagating plants by grafting.

Genders, Roy
GREENHOUSE PLANTS FROM SEED (Magna Print Books, 1974)
HARDY PERENNIALS FROM SEED (Magna Print Books, 1974)

Gorer, Richard
GROWING PLANTS FROM SEEDS (Faber & Faber, 1978)

Halpin, Anne M.
FOOLPROOF PLANTING: HOW TO SUCCESSFULLY START AND PROPAGATE MORE THAN 250 VEGETABLES, FLOWERS, TREES AND SHRUBS (Rodale Press, 1990) A complete A to Z planting guide with step-by-step instructions and numerous illustrations.

Hartmann, Hudson, et al.
PLANT PROPAGATION: PRINCIPLES & PRACTICES (Prentice-Hall, 1990, 5th edition) Intended as a university textbook, it covers all the basics of propagation techniques and tissue culture plus plant-by-plant methods.

Hill, Lewis
SECRETS OF PLANT PROPAGATION: STARTING YOUR OWN FLOWERS, VEGETABLES, FRUITS, BERRIES, SHRUBS, TREES AND HOUSEPLANTS (Storey, 1985) Explains and diagrams all types of propagation, the supplies needed and which methods to use for specific plants.

Jabs, Carolyn
THE HEIRLOOM GARDENER (Sierra Club Books, 1984) Covers growing, saving and locating sources of heirloom seeds of fruits and vegetables.

Kelly, John
SOWING A BETTER GARDEN (Unwin Hyman, 1988) Information on growing hundreds of trees, shrubs, perennials, bulbs and alpines from seed; includes many unusual ones not often found in nurseries.

Kyte, Lydiane
PLANTS FROM TEST TUBES: AN INTRODUCTION TO MICROPROPAGATION (Timber Press, 1987, 2nd revised edition) Explains and evaluates the process of tissue culture, describes how to set up a lab and gives 50 recipes for nutrient solutions.

Loewer, Peter
SEEDS AND CUTTINGS (Walker, 1975) Covers the basics, plus appendix has interesting lists (best ways to reproduce 179 different houseplants, month-by-month propagation projects, seeds that can be started any time of the year, etc.).

Macdonald, Bruce
PRACTICAL WOODY PLANT PROPAGATION FOR NURSERY GROWERS: VOLUME I (Timber Press, 1986) Macdonald, the director of the University of British Columbia Botanic Garden, details every facet of woody plant propagation (facilities, tools, materials and methodology).

McDonald, Elvin
HOW TO GROW FLOWERS FROM SEEDS (Van Nostrand Reinhold, 1979) How to start seeds indoors and outdoors with instructions on growing numerous annuals, biennials, perennials and bulbs from seeds. Also, his *How to Grow Houseplants from Seeds* and *How to Grow Vegetables and Herbs from Seeds* are similar treatments; good beginning guides.

Plumridge, Jack
HOW TO PROPAGATE PLANTS (ISBS, 1989, 2nd edition) Describes and gives examples for each method of propagation and discusses the advantages and disadvantages of each.

Reilly, Ann
PARK'S SUCCESS WITH SEEDS (Park Seed Co., 1978) Specifics on growing all kinds of indoor and outdoor plants from seeds; 1,000 color photos of seedlings and mature plants.

Rogers, Marc
SAVING SEEDS: THE GARDENER'S GUIDE TO GROWING AND STORING VEGETABLE AND FLOWER SEEDS (Storey, 1990) Information on when and how to store and test the seeds of over 40 vegetables and 60 flowers.

Seddon, George, and Bicknell, Andrew
PLANTS PLUS: A COMPREHENSIVE GUIDE TO SUCCESSFUL PROPAGATION OF HOUSE AND GARDEN PLANTS (Rodale Press, 1987) Covers 30 propagation methods for garden plants and houseplants; includes materials needed and a propagator's calendar.

Thompson, Peter
CREATIVE PROPAGATION: A GROWER'S GUIDE (Timber Press, 1989) Covers simple propagation techniques for approximately 600 garden plants.

Toogood, Alan
THE FLOWER GARDEN: SUMMER FLOWERS FROM SEED (Crown, 1987) A colorful catalogue of annuals with information on cultivation and using them for the best effect.
PROPAGATION (Scarbrough House, 1982) Illustrates and discusses cuttings, grafting, budding, division and layering methods of propagation for hundreds of plants.

Whealy, Kent (editor)
FRUIT, BERRY AND NUT INVENTORY (Seed Saver Publications, 1989) Describes 4,140 varieties of fruits, berries and nuts and where to buy them (248 mail order nurseries are listed).
THE GARDEN SEED INVENTORY (Seed Saver Publications, 1988, 2nd edition) Descriptions and sources for over 5,000 varieties of vegetable seeds; includes a listing of 215 U.S. and Canadian mail order seed companies.
SEED SAVERS EXCHANGE: THE FIRST TEN YEARS 1975-1985 (Seed Saver Publications, 1986) A variety of articles selected from their 1975 to 1985 yearbooks.

Young, James and Cheryl
SEEDS OF WOODY PLANTS IN NORTH AMERICA (Timber Press, 1992) A sourcebook that includes 386 genera and over 1,000 literature citations; revised edition of *Agriculture Handbook 450* from the U.S. Forest Service.

For related books, see:
COLLECTING, PROCESSING AND GERMINATING SEEDS OF WILDLAND PLANTS by Young (page 98)
DIRECTORY TO RESOURCES ON WILDFLOWER PROPAGATION by Sullivan and Daley (page 97)
SEED PROPAGATION OF NATIVE CALIFORNIA PLANTS by Emery (page 197)

ANNUALS AND BIENNIALS

Bales, Suzanne
ANNUALS (Prentice-Hall, 1991) Descriptions, color photos, cultural information and design ideas for 100+ annuals.

Beckett, Kenneth A.
ANNUALS AND BIENNIALS (Ballantine, 1984)

Consumer Guide editors
ANNUALS (Outlet Books, 1990) How to plan, prepare the soil, water, weed and feed, and control pests in a garden of annuals; includes a month-by-month maintenance calendar.

Crockett, James Underwood, and Editors of Time-Life Books
ANNUALS (Henry Holt, 1986) Reprint of 1973 Time-Life edition.

Fell, Derek
ANNUALS: HOW TO SELECT, GROW AND ENJOY (HP Books, 1983) Covers growing over 100 flowering annuals and which are best for cutting, drying, flower beds and borders; includes creating flower arrangements.

Garden Way Publishing editors
ANNUALS: 1001 GARDENING QUESTIONS ANSWERED (Storey, 1989) How to design, plant and maintain a variety of annual gardens (intricate flower beds, borders, container gardens, etc.).

Huxley, Anthony (editor)
GARDEN ANNUALS AND BULBS (Macmillan, 1971) Describes and illustrates 540 annuals and bulbs; alphabetized by botanical name.

Kilmer, John
THE ANNUAL ENCYCLOPEDIA (Crescent, 1989) Design ideas plus general care information.

Loewer, Peter
THE ANNUAL GARDEN: FLOWERS, FOLIAGE, FRUITS AND GRASSES FOR ONE SUMMER SEASON (Rodale Press, 1988) Describes and gives growing information on 300 annuals, from abelmoschus to zinnias.

Murray, Elizabeth
ESSENTIAL ANNUALS: THE 100 BEST FOR DESIGN AND CULTIVATION (Crescent, 1989) Covers basic growing information plus four methods of growing from seed.

Murray, Ian
BEDDING PLANTS: STEP BY STEP TO GROWING SUCCESS (Trafalgar Square, 1992) How to create a successful bedding display at modest cost using both popular and lesser known plants.

Nehrling, Arno and Irene
THE PICTURE BOOK OF ANNUALS (Arco, 1977) Covers growing annuals from seeds, caring for the plants and ways of using annuals in the garden and as houseplants.

Ortho
COLOR WITH ANNUALS (Ortho, 1987)

Proctor, Rob
ANTIQUE FLOWERS: ANNUALS—ENDURING CLASSICS FOR THE CONTEMPORARY GARDEN (HarperCollins, 1991) Describes the pleasure of gardening with annuals that have been around for at least 100 years (Poor Man's Orchid, Night-scented Stock, Loves-lies-bleeding, to name a few).

Reilly, Ann
HOW TO PLANT AND GROW ANNUALS (Smithmark, 1991) Describes and gives growing information and site suggestions for 100 varieties of annuals.

Rice, Graham
A HANDBOOK OF ANNUALS AND BEDDING PLANTS (Timber Press, 1986) An A to Z encyclopedia of ornamental annuals with propagating and growing information.

Simpson, A. G. W.
GROWING ANNUALS (ISBS, 1989) Illustrations and instructions on selection, propagation, care and maintenance.

Sunset
ANNUALS (Sunset Books, 1992) A color photo of over 100 flowering annuals, plus ways to use them in the garden.

Taylor's
GUIDE TO ANNUALS (Houghton Mifflin, 1986) Descriptions, color photos and growing advice for approximately 300 annuals; arranged by color to make planning easy.
POCKET GUIDE TO ANNUALS (Houghton Mifflin, 1990) Color photos and descriptions of 79 annuals.

Time-Life
ANNUALS: GARDENER'S GUIDE SERIES (Time-Life Books, 1988)

For related books, see:
THE FLOWER GARDEN by Toogood (page 79)
THE HARROWSMITH ANNUAL GARDEN by Bennett and Forsyth (page 190)

PERENNIALS

GENERAL REFERENCES

Armitage, Allan M.
HERBACEOUS PERENNIAL PLANTS: A TREATISE ON THEIR IDENTIFICATION, CULTURE AND GARDEN ATTRIBUTES (Timber Press, 1989) Extensive descriptions of approximately 3,000 perennials (height, color, blooming season, hardiness zones, growing needs, etc.), plus information on propagation, keys to species and cultivar recommendations.

Bales, Suzanne
PERENNIALS (Prentice-Hall, 1991) Detailed descriptions and color photos of over 100 perennials, plus cultural advice, design ideas and suggestions for companion plantings.

Beckett, Kenneth
GROWING HARDY PERENNIALS (Timber Press, 1981) A brief encyclopedia of the main genera and species, plus a selection of some of the best cultivars.

Bloom, Alan
ALAN BLOOM'S HARDY PERENNIALS (Trafalgar Square, 1992) How he was inspired to raise new varieties of alpines and hardy perennials, plus details on the 170 new varieties he introduced.
PERENNIALS FOR YOUR GARDEN (ISBS, 1981) Advice based on his personal experiences in growing perennials.

Brooklyn Botanic Garden
PERENNIALS: A GARDENER'S GUIDE (BBG #128) Fifteen articles on perennial borders, ornamental herbs, cottage and rock gardens, growing perennials in containers and more.
PERENNIALS: A NURSERY SOURCE MANUAL (BBG #118) Wholesale and retail sources for thousands of perennials, ferns, ornamental grasses, bamboos, herbs, aquatic and bulbous plants.
PERENNIALS AND THEIR USES (BBG #87) How to select, plant and care for perennials.

Brown, Emily
LANDSCAPING WITH PERENNIALS (Timber Press, 1986) The perennials are organized according to the type of landscaping site (sloping, shady, boggy, etc.) and how they will be used (cutting garden, beds, borders, strips, containers); includes 14 sample layouts.

Chatto, Beth
THE GREEN TAPESTRY: CHOOSING AND GROWING THE BEST PERENNIAL PLANTS

FOR YOUR GARDEN (Simon & Schuster, 1989) From the personal experience of creating her gardens at White Barn House in England, she describes how to select and group perennials for waterside, dry and shade gardens; includes U.S. hardiness zones.

Clausen, Ruth Rogers, and Ekstrom, Nicolas H.
PERENNIALS FOR AMERICAN GARDENS (Random House, 1989) Information on over 400 genera and 3,000 species arranged alphabetically; includes appendices of plant sources, listing of display gardens and an extensive bibliography.

Cox, Jeff and Marilyn
THE PERENNIAL GARDEN: COLOR HARMONIES THROUGH THE SEASONS (Rodale Press, 1985) Covers 300 perennials to use in creating beds and borders that provide maximum color year round.

Crockett, James Underwood
PERENNIALS (Henry Holt, 1986) Reprint of 1972 Time-Life book.

Daughtrey, Margery, and Semel, Maurie
HERBACEOUS PERENNIALS: DISEASES AND INSECT PESTS (Cornell University Media Services, 1987) How to identify and control problems with perennials.

Fell, Derek
ESSENTIAL PERENNIALS: THE 100 BEST FOR DESIGN AND CULTIVATION (Crown, 1989) How to achieve the best color results with perennials; includes rock and water gardens, meadows and fern gardens.

Free, Montague
ALL ABOUT THE PERENNIAL GARDEN: THE AMATEUR GARDENER'S HANDBOOK OF HARDY FLOWERS, HERBACEOUS AND WOODY PERENNIALS, INCLUDING BULBS AND SHRUBS, BIENNIALS AND ANNUALS (Doubleday, 1955) Contains still useful design ideas and lists of perennials for specific uses; includes an interesting chapter on a year in the life of a perennial garden.

Garden Way Publishing
PERENNIALS: 1001 GARDENING QUESTIONS ANSWERED (Doubleday, 1989) Covers plant selection; attracting birds and butterflies; creating rock, fragrance and cutting gardens; and more.

Giles, F. A.; Keith, Rebecca; and Saupe, Donald C.
HERBACEOUS PERENNIALS (Reston Publishing, 1980) A reference book alphabetized by botanical name with an index to common names.

Harper, Pamela
DESIGNING WITH PERENNIALS (Macmillan, 1991) Covers design principles, combining perennials with each other and with annuals, trees, shrubs and vines, using perennials as ground covers; and more; includes over 300 color photos.

Harper, Pamela, and McGourty, Frederick
PERENNIALS: HOW TO SELECT, GROW AND ENJOY (HP Books, 1985) Describes and gives growing information for over 350 plants; includes 240 color photos and a nursery source list.

Hill, Lewis and Nancy
SUCCESSFUL PERENNIAL GARDENING: A PRACTICAL GUIDE (Garden Way, 1988) Descriptions of over 150 species and suggestions for 16 theme gardens (rock, wild, shade, cutting, hummingbird and butterfly garden, etc.) plus information on dividing and propagating, and pest and disease control.

Hudak, Joseph
GARDENING WITH PERENNIALS MONTH BY MONTH (Timber Press, 1992, expanded edition) Covers March to September with lists of flowers available for each month; includes a section on hardy ferns and information on perennials that bloom for eight weeks or more, perennials suitable for areas of deep shade or constant moistness, and other specific garden requirements.

Jelitto, Leo, and Schacht, Wilhelm
HARDY HERBACEOUS PERENNIALS (Timber Press, 1990) A two-volume encyclopedia describing 4,200 species and 3,600 cultivars in 800 genera; 690 color photos and 352 black-and-white illustrations.

Lovejoy, Ann (editor)
PERENNIALS: TOWARD CONTINUOUS
BLOOM (Capability's, 1991) Interviews with 32 gardeners from around the U.S. on how they use perennials in their gardens.

McGourty, Frederick
THE PERENNIAL GARDENER (Houghton Mifflin, 1989) Covers long-flowering perennials, unusual perennials, combining perennials, moving and dividing perennials, mixing annuals and perennials, hostas, alliums, ornamental grasses, and kitchen herbs; includes seven border plans, two of which are for the famous borders at Hillside Gardens, his Connecticut nursery that specializes in perennials.

Nottle, Trevor
GROWING PERENNIALS (ISBS, 1985) Illustrations and instructions on selection, propagation, care and maintenance.

Ortho
ALL ABOUT PERENNIALS (Ortho Books, 1981) Descriptions and growing advice; the color photos are a plus in the selection and design process.

Oster, Maggie
HOW TO PLANT AND GROW PERENNIALS (Smithmark, 1991) Describes how to plant, grow, fertilize and propagate 100 perennials.

Phillips, Roger, and Rix, Martyn
THE RANDOM HOUSE BOOK OF PERENNIALS: VOLUME 1—EARLY PERENNIALS (Random House, 1991) Describes 1,250 plants with color photos of each—includes geraniums, primula, iris, viola, helleborus, paeonia, etc.
THE RANDOM HOUSE BOOK OF PERENNIALS: VOLUME 2—LATE PERENNIALS (Random House, 1991) Another 1,250 plants with color photos of each—includes ornamental grasses, ferns, delphiniums, dianthus, hosta, hemerocallis, aster, etc.

Proctor, Rob
ANTIQUE FLOWERS: PERENNIALS—ENDURING CLASSICS FOR THE CONTEMPORARY GARDEN (HarperCollins, 1990) A guide and sourcebook to historic perennial gardening; includes 140 color photos.

Sheldon, Elisabeth
THE PROPER GARDEN: ON PERENNIALS IN THE BORDER (Stackpole, 1989) From her gardening experiences in upstate New York, she shares her ideas for creating a mixed perennial border.

Still, Steven
MANUAL OF HERBACEOUS ORNAMENTAL PLANTS (Stipes, 1988, 3rd edition) Describes and gives growing information on 500 perennials, bulbs, ornamental grasses and hardy ferns.

Sunset
PERENNIALS (Sunset Books, 1992) Planting, caring for, and propagating over 120 perennials.

Taylor, Patricia
EASY CARE PERENNIALS: HOW TO PLAN AND CULTIVATE A GARDEN THAT BLOOMS FOR NINE MONTHS OF THE YEAR—WITH PRACTICALLY NO MAINTENANCE (Simon & Schuster, 1989) Covers 50 easy-to-find, easy-to-grow, relatively inexpensive and disease and pest resistant perennials that provide flowers from March through November; includes plant sources and charts of plants for shaded, semishaded, and sunny areas.

Taylor's
GUIDE TO PERENNIALS (Houghton Mifflin, 1986) Detailed descriptions of 387 perennials plus information on garden design, pests and diseases, how and where to buy the plants, what to do and when to do it in different parts of the country; 417 color photos arranged by color.
POCKET GUIDE: PERENNIALS FOR SHADE (Houghton Mifflin, 1989) Description and color photo for 79 perennials suitable for shady areas.
POCKET GUIDE: PERENNIALS FOR SUN (Houghton Mifflin, 1989) Description and color photo for 79 perennials suitable for sunny areas.

Thomas, Graham Stuart
PERENNIAL GARDEN PLANTS OR THE MODERN FLORILEGIUM (Timber Press, 1990, 3rd edition) Alphabetized descriptions of 2,000 species of plants, grasses, sedges, rushes and ferns with information on U.S. hardiness zones.

Time-Life
PERENNIALS: GARDENER'S GUIDE SERIES
(Time-Life Books, 1988) Covers growing perennials in the garden and in containers, planting and transplanting, propagating, pinching, deadheading, combining with other plants and much more.

Trehane, Piers (editor)
INDEX HORTENSIS—VOLUME I: PERENNIALS (Timber Press, 1990) Covers the correct names of 140 plant families, 1,060 generic names, 5,700 species names, 800 infra-specific names, 14,300 cultivar names, 2,700 synonyms and 390 herbs; alphabetized by genus.

Williamson, John
PERENNIAL GARDENS: A PRACTICAL GUIDE TO HOME LANDSCAPING (Globe Pequot, 1992) How to create over 40 perennial gardens including an Elizabethan knot garden, secret wildflower garden, fragrant garden, silver-and-gold garden or a low-maintenace garden; includes lists of plants needed, illustrations showing plant placement and growing information for each garden.

Wilson, Helen V.
THE NEW PERENNIALS PREFERRED (Collier Books, 1992) First issued in 1945 and revised and updated in 1961, it covers designing perennial borders and includes sample plans; contains a list of her favorite perennials and how to use and care for them, plus lists of perennials according to their purpose (fragrance, shade, cutting, drought-, heat-, pollution-, salt-resistant).
SUCCESSFUL GARDENING WITH PERENNIALS: HOW TO SELECT AND GROW MORE THAN 500 KINDS FOR TODAY'S YARD AND GARDEN (Doubleday, 1976) How to design, select the plants, grow and maintain a perennial garden.

Woods, Chris
ENCYCLOPEDIA OF PERENNIALS: A GARDENER'S GUIDE (Facts On File, 1992) Describes and gives information on cultivation, landscape use and propagation for over 450 genera (3,000 species) of herbaceous perennials; includes a list of horticultural societies, a complete bibliography and 300+ color photos.

SPECIFIC PERENNIALS

Chrysanthemums

The National Chrysanthemum Society, Inc. USA (10107 Homar Pond Drive, Fairfax Station, VA 22039) publishes a quarterly journal and a variety of handbooks and pamphlets.

Ackerson, Cornelius
THE COMPLETE BOOK OF CHRYSANTHEMUMS (Doubleday, 1957) Covers growing chrysanthemums in greenhouses and outdoors in North America.

Brook, Wallace
GROWING AND SHOWING CHRYSANTHEMUMS (Trafalgar Square, 1984) Successful ways of growing and exhibiting chrysanthemums.

Locke, Baden
CHRYSANTHEMUMS: THE COMPLETE GUIDE (Trafalgar Square, 1990) Details for growing award-winning chrysanthemums: buying the new plant, planting, caring for, protecting the blooms, increasing stock, controlling pests and diseases and complex methods for creating new cultivars.

Machin, Barrie, and Scopes, Nigel
CHRYSANTHEMUMS: THE YEAR ROUND (Blandford Press, 1978) In-depth coverage of growing chrysanthemums in a greenhouse.

Randall, Harry, and Wren, Alan
GROWING CHRYSANTHEMUMS (Timber Press, 1983) Information for growing all kinds of chrysanthemums, early to late flowering, garden and greenhouse.

Skeen, Bruce
GROWING CHRYSANTHEMUMS (ISBS, 1985) Illustrations and instructions on selection, propagation, care and maintenance.

Woolman, Jack
A PLANTSMAN'S GUIDE TO CHRYSANTHEMUMS (Sterling, 1991) A good introduction that includes growing information, design plans and descriptions of all types of chrysanthemums.

Lilies

The North American Lily Society (P.O. Box 272, Owatonna, MN 55060) publishes quarterly bulletins and two illustrated handbooks —*Let's Grow Lilies* by Virginia Howie and the *Lily Disease Handbook* by Edward A. McRae. It also publishes *Named Lily Hybrids and Their Origins* by Eunice Fisher, which lists over 1,300 lilies and gives hybridizer, color, registration date, parentage, height and time of bloom.

Bird, Richard
LILIES (Chartwell, 1991) Covers the size, habit and preferences of 45 species and 60 hybrids, plus general information on cultivation, propagation and pests and diseases.

Fox, Derek
GROWING LILIES (Croom Helm, 1985) Covers all the basics and includes ways to use lilies in various types of gardens.

Haw, Stephen G.
LILIES OF CHINA: LILIUM, CARDIOCRINUM, NOMOCHARIS AND NOTHOLIRION (Timber Press, 1986) Covers distribution, habitat, propagation and cultivation.

Jefferson-Brown, Michael
THE LILY: FOR GARDEN, PATIO AND DISPLAY (Trafalgar Square, 1988) Covers wild lilies and modern hybrids with information on seed germination, height, flower form and pose.
A PLANTSMAN'S GUIDE TO LILIES (Sterling, 1991) How to select the best ones, where to plant them and how to maintain them.

Jekyll, Gertrude
LILIES FOR ENGLISH GARDENS (Antique Collector's Club, 1982) Reprint; 68 black-and-white and 8 color illustrations.

Daylilies

The American Hemerocallis Society (1454 Rebel Drive, Jackson, MS 39211) publishes a quarterly journal and *Daylilies: Everything You've Always Wanted to Know About Daylilies.*

Grosvenor, Graeme
GROWING DAYLILIES (ISBS, 1990, 2nd edition) How to plant, grow and maintain daylilies; includes 100 color photos.

Hill, Lewis and Nancy
DAYLILIES: THE PERFECT PERENNIAL (Garden Way, 1991) Describes over 200 popular cultivars and how to use them in your northern or southern garden; includes a list of sources.

Munson Jr., R. W.
HEMEROCALLIS: THE DAYLILY (Timber Press, 1989) An annotated listing, grouped by color, of the best modern cultivars; also includes hybridizing, landscaping, growing needs and standards of judging; Munson, a well-known daylily breeder, covers what has happened with daylilies since A. B. Stout's book.

Stout, A. B.
DAYLILIES (Timber Press, 1986) The 1934 classic updated by American daylily authority, Dr. Darrel Apps, with a foreword by Graham Stuart Thomas.

Webber, Steve (editor)
THE DAYLILY ENCYCLOPEDIA (Webber Gardens, 1988) Alphabetized descriptions of over 1,150 daylilies from a specialist in the field.

Iris

The American Iris Society (7414 East 60th Street, Tulsa, OK 74145) publishes a quarterly bulletin and *The World of Irises* (1978), which contains articles by 34 contributors including international authorities on irises.

Caillet, Marie, and Mertzweiller, Joseph K. (editors)
THE LOUISIANA IRIS: THE HISTORY AND CULTURE OF FIVE NATIVE AMERICAN SPECIES AND THEIR HYBRIDS (Texas Gardener Press, 1988) Covers cultivation, history and hybridization of beardless irises that do best in Southern wetlands but can be grown into zone 4.

Cassidy, G. E., and Linnegar, Sidney
GROWING IRISES (Timber Press, 1987) A good introduction to the variety and many uses of irises.

Dykes, William R.
THE GENUS IRIS (Dover, 1974) Reprint of the classic 1913 work that established the modern classifications of irises and described them completely.

Grosvenor, Graeme
GROWING IRISES (ISBS, 1985) Illustrations and instructions on selection, propagation, care and maintenance.

Kohlein, Fritz
IRIS (Timber Press, 1987) This first completely modern treatment of irises covers over 200 species plus subspecies, varieties, natural hybrids and cultivars; includes habitat, cultivation, seed germination, breeding and reproductive physiology.

Linnegar, Sidney, and Hewitt, Jennifer
IRISES (Wisley Handbook) (Sterling, 1991) Covers bearded, beardless, crested and bulbous irises, plus information on propagation and problems.

Mathew, Brian
THE IRIS (Timber Press, 1989, 2nd edition) A guide to the wild species of genus *Iris*, with descriptions of the plants, their classification, distribution and habitat, and cultivation hints.

McEwen, Currier
THE JAPANESE IRIS (University Press of New England, 1990) Covers the history and cultivation.
SIBERIAN IRISES (Timber Press, 1981) Covers growing the Siberian iris in many different climates, plus hybridization, how to judge show irises and a list of buying sources.

Price, Molly
THE IRIS BOOK (Dover, 1973, 2nd edition) Describes all the important varieties, both hybrid and species, plus information on planting, bloom schedules, diseases and more.

Waddick, James, and Yu-tang, Zhao
IRIS OF CHINA (Timber Press, 1992) From Waddick's 7,500-mile collecting trip in 1989 comes this description of new species, plus information on the distribution, ecology and environment of Chinese iris in their natural habitats throughout China.

Westrich, Josh
THE IRIS: THE RAINBOW FLOWER (Thames & Hudson, 1989) A book of 80 color photos of irises.

Primroses

The American Primrose Society (Route 5, Box 93, Hillsboro, OR 97124) has a quarterly journal.

Bellis, Florence
GARDENING AND BEYOND (Timber Press, 1986) Bellis developed the famous Barnhaven primroses, but this is more than a book about primroses; it is her reflections on gardening and her seaside garden.

Fenderson, G. K.
A SYNOPTIC GUIDE TO THE GENUS PRIMULA (ISBS, 1986) Very thorough reference work on the genus *Primula*.

Hyatt, Brenda
AURICULAS (Globe Pequot, 1989) How to feed, cultivate and train primroses, plus solutions for housing a collection.

Klaber, Doretta
PRIMROSES AND SPRING (Barrows, 1966) Descriptions and growing information for the major species and cultivars grown in the U.S.

Robinson, Mary A.
PRIMULAS: THE COMPLETE GUIDE (Trafalgar Square, 1991) Descriptions of hundreds of plants with advice on cultivation, propagation, and pest and disease control.

Shaw, Barbara
THE BOOK OF PRIMROSES (Timber Press, 1991) From many years' experience growing and painting primroses, she offers practical advice on cultivation and botanical painting; 64 beautiful color illustrations.

Swindells, Philip
A PLANTSMAN'S GUIDE TO PRIMULAS (Sterling, 1991) An introduction to growing primulas that includes an A to Z list of the best species.

Wemyss-Cooke, Jack
PRIMULAS OLD AND NEW (Trafalgar Square, 1986) Covers auriculas, primroses, primulas, and poly-

anthus with information on cultivation, propagation, hybridizers and the most popular varieties.

Geraniums

The International Geranium Society (P.O. Box 92734, Pasadena, CA 91109) publishes a quarterly journal, *Geraniums Around the World.*

Armitage, Allan M.
SEED PROPAGATED GERANIUMS (Timber Press, 1986)

Bagust, Harold
MINIATURE AND DWARF GERANIUMS (Timber Press, 1988, expanded edition) Complete cultivation and propagation information for approximately 500 small varieties of geraniums; Bagust operated one of the world's largest geranium nurseries for many years.

Clark, David
PELARGONIUMS: A KEW GARDENING GUIDE (Timber Press, 1988) Describes and give cultivation and propagation information on 200 species and cultivars.

Conder, Susan
COMPLETE GERANIUM: CULTIVATION, COOKING, CRAFTS (Crown, 1992) Gardening tips; recipes for desserts, bath oils and face creams; ideas for dried arrangements; and more.

Llewellyn, J.
GROWING GERANIUMS AND PELARGONIUMS (ISBS, 1985) Illustrations and instructions on selection, propagation, care and maintenance.

Shellard, Alan
GERANIUMS FOR HOME AND GARDEN (Trafalgar Square, 1981) Covers selecting, propagating, potting, shaping, feeding, hybridizing and pests and diseases; includes greenhouse growing.

Taylor, Jan
GERANIUMS AND PELARGONIUMS: THE COMPLETE GUIDE TO CULTIVATION, PROPAGATION AND EXHIBITION (Trafalgar Square, 1989) A thorough coverage with emphasis on the Pelargoniums (Regal, Zonal and Ivy-Leaved).

PELARGONIUMS FOR COLOUR AND VARIETY (Trafalgar Square, 1991) Explains geranium cultivation, propagation, and hybridization with advice on soils, watering, feeding, pruning, over-wintering, and pest and disease control; includes extensive lists of recommended plants.

Wilson, Helen V.
THE JOY OF GERANIUMS: THE STANDARD GUIDE TO THE SELECTION, CULTURE AND USE OF THE PELARGONIUM (Quill, 1980) Reprint of the 1946 edition.

Yeo, Peter
HARDY GERANIUMS (Timber Press, 1985) How to select, care for and propagate 100 species and botanical varieties plus cultivars and hybrids.

MISCELLANEOUS PERENNIALS

Bailey, Steven
CARNATIONS: PERPETUAL-FLOWERING CARNATIONS, BORDERS AND PINKS (Sterling, 1990) Covers growing in the garden, greenhouse or on the windowsill; includes information on American-spray carnations.

Bartlett, Mary
GENTIANS (Hippocrene Books, 1976) Growing information and illustrations of many species.

Cobb, James
MECONOPSIS (Timber Press, 1989) Describes the discovery of the plant, the challenges of cultivating them, habitat problems and how to overcome them; includes a descriptive A to Z listing of the species with advantages and disadvantages of each species.

Coon, Nelson
THE COMPLETE BOOK OF VIOLETS (Barnes, 1977) Includes information on outdoor cultivated violets, indoor Parma violets and pansies.

Cooper, Leslie
A PLANTSMAN'S GUIDE TO DELPHINIUMS (Sterling, 1990) Describes species, varieties and hybrids and gives cultivation and propagation information, plus ideas for planting schemes and companion plants.

Edwards, Colin
DELPHINIUMS: THE COMPLETE GUIDE
(Trafalgar Square, 1990) Details on growing, propagating through seeds, cuttings and hybridization, exhibiting, arranging and drying; includes species list and recommended cultivars.

Farrar, Elizabeth
PANSIES, VIOLAS AND SWEET VIOLETS
(Hurst, 1989) Covers history, cultivation, propagation and garden design; the book has a charming old-fashioned quality.

Fuller, Rodney
PANSIES, VIOLAS AND VIOLETTAS: THE
COMPLETE GUIDE (Trafalgar Square, 1991) Covers history, cultivation, propagation through cuttings or seed harvesting, breeding new varieties, exhibiting and descriptions.

Harding, Alice H.
THE PEONY (Sagapress, 1985) Reprint of 1917 work covering history, mythology, soil preparation, seed setting and her personal ratings of different varieties.

Haworth-Booth, Michael
THE MOUTAN, OR TREE PEONY (St. Martin's, 1963) Covers history and propagation, plus a checklist of tree peony varieties.

Jarratt, Joy
GROWING CARNATIONS (ISBS, 1987) Covers soil and site, watering, feeding, staking, propagating, exhibiting and handling pests and diseases.

Klaber, Doretta
GENTIANS FOR YOUR GARDEN (Barrows, 1964) Describes nearly 100 species and hybrids, divided by spring, summer and fall, and tells how to grow them.
VIOLETS OF THE UNITED STATES (Barnes, 1976) An identification guide with botanical illustrations for North American violet species.

Kohlein, Fritz
GENTIANS (Timber Press, 1991) A comprehensive guide to the genus and its related genera; includes propagation, cultivation, pests and diseases and uses in the garden or rock garden.

Lewis, Peter, and Lynch, Margaret
CAMPANULAS (Timber Press, 1989) Describes over 300 species, important hybrids and cultivars; includes information on using campanulas in the landscape and which other plants go well with them.

Nehrling, Arno and Irene
PEONIES: OUTDOORS AND IN (Dover, 1975 edition of 1960 work) Includes cultural information for herbaceous and tree peonies and lists of older cultivars.

Smith, Fred C.
A PLANTSMAN'S GUIDE TO CARNATIONS AND PINKS (Sterling, 1990) How to choose the best site and varieties, propagating, fighting pests and diseases, plus A to Z descriptive lists of the best species and varieties.

For related books, see:
BULBS AND PERENNIALS by Grace (page 90)
BULBS AND PERENNIALS by Harrison (page 90)
CANADIAN GARDEN PERENNIALS by Buckley (page 190)
COLOR IN MY GARDEN by Wilder (page 167)
HARDY PERENNIALS FROM SEED by Genders (page 78)
THE HARROWSMITH PERENNIAL GARDEN by Lima (page 191)
A MANUAL OF SAXIFRAGES by Webb and Gornall (page 157)
PERENNIAL GARDEN COLOR by Welch (page 195)

BULBS

GENERAL REFERENCES

Bales, Suzanne
BULBS (Prentice-Hall, 1992) Cultural information and descriptions of over 115 kinds of bulbs, plus planning and designing with bulbs.

Brooklyn Botanic Garden
BULBS (BBG #96) How to select spring-blooming and other seasonal bulbs, plus hints on forcing and special landscape uses.
THE GARDENER'S WORLD OF BULBS (BBG #127) How to use bulbs in formal borders, casual gardens, lawns and colorful mixed plantings that bloom from early spring until autumn.

Bryan, John
BULBS (Timber Press, 1989) Two-volume reference work encompassing 230 genera and thousands of species and cultivars; 754 color photos and 110 botanical paintings in color.

Crockett, James Underwood and Editors of Time-Life Books
BULBS (Henry Holt, 1987) Reprint of 1971 edition; covers history of bulbs and contains an illustrated encyclopedia with photos and descriptions of 85 genera of bulbs.

Fell, Derek
ESSENTIAL BULBS: THE 100 BEST FOR DESIGN AND CULTIVATION (Crescent, 1989) Describes when and how deep to plant, naturalizing, forcing bulbs indoors and more.

Genders, Roy
BULBS: A COMPLETE HANDBOOK OF BULBS, CORMS, AND TUBERS (Bobbs-Merrill, 1973) Reference work with an English slant.
MINIATURE BULBS (St. Martin's, 1963)

Grace, Julie (editor)
BULBS AND PERENNIALS (Timber Press, 1984)

Harrison, Richmond E.
BULBS AND PERENNIALS (Timber Press, 1988) A product of New Zealand, it is abundantly illustrated with 643 color photos.

James Jr., Theodore
FLOWERING BULBS INDOORS AND OUT (Macmillan, 1991) Covers over 80 types of bulbs arranged in seasonal order; includes preparing the soil, ideas for landscaping and forcing spring bulbs for blooming indoors in winter.

Lawrence, Elizabeth
THE LITTLE BULBS: A TALE OF TWO GAR-DENS (Duke University Press, 1985 reprint, introduction by Allen Lacy) The charming story of her small city garden in North Carolina and the enormous rural garden of a friend in Ohio.

Mathew, Brian
DWARF BULBS (Arco, 1973) Details unusual bulbs that grow under six inches tall.
THE LARGER BULBS (Trafalgar Square, 1978) Companion book for *Dwarf Bulbs*.
THE SMALLER BULBS (Trafalgar Square, 1988) A thorough treatment that goes beyond his *Dwarf Bulbs*.
THE YEAR ROUND BULB GARDEN (Batsford, 1978)

Miles, Bebe
BULBS FOR THE HOME GARDENER (Grosset & Dunlap, 1976) Covers cultural and growing information on both hardy and tender bulbs; includes forcing and propagation.
THE WONDERFUL WORLD OF BULBS (Van Nostrand, 1963)

Ortho
ALL ABOUT BULBS (Ortho Books, 1986) Descriptions, color photos and growing advice on Dutch and species bulbs.

Pate, John, and Dixon, Kingsley
TUBEROUS, CORMOUS AND BULBOUS PLANTS (Timber Press, 1982)

Phillips, Roger, and Rix, Martyn
THE RANDOM HOUSE BOOK OF BULBS (Random House, 1989) A new edition of *The Bulb Book*; information on more than 1,000 bulbs and bulb-like plants arranged in bloom sequence with 300+ color photos showing plant from bulb to bloom.

Reynolds, Marc, and Meachem, William
THE COMPLETE BOOK OF GARDEN BULBS (Funk & Wagnalls, 1971) A good introduction that also includes such topics as bulb growing in warmer climates, companion plants for bulbs and bulbs as cut flowers.

Rix, Martyn
GROWING BULBS (Timber Press, 1989) Good introduction to the subject.

Rockwell, F. F., and Grayson, Esther C.
THE COMPLETE BOOK OF BULBS (Doubleday, 1953) Revised and edited by Marjorie Dietz and reissued by Lippincott in 1977.

Rossi, Rosella
SIMON & SCHUSTER'S GUIDE TO BULBS (Simon & Schuster, 1989) Basic information on choosing and cultivating over 200 varieties of bulbs with color photos of each.

Scheider, Alfred
PARK'S SUCCESS WITH BULBS (Park Seed Co., 1981) Surveys 200 genera of bulbs, corms, tubers, rhizomes and tuberous roots; 350+ color illustrations.

Scott, George
BULBS: HOW TO SELECT, GROW AND ENJOY (HP Books, 1982) Covers bloom season, colors, height, propagation and storage tips for over 250 bulbs.

Simpson, A. G. W.
GROWING BULBS (ISBS, 1985) Illustrations and instructions on selection, propagation, care and maintenance.

Stites, William, et al.
PARADISE CONTAINED (Doubleday, 1990) How to force and grow bulbs indoors with unusual ideas for containers to use; includes sources for bulbs and containers.

Sunset
BULBS FOR ALL SEASONS (Sunset Books, 1985) Descriptions, color photos and growing information for 77 bulbs, plus ideas for use in the landscape and in containers.

Swindells, Philip
BULBS FOR ALL SEASONS: GARDENING BY DESIGN (Sterling, 1990) Step-by-step instructions and how-to drawings.

Taylor's Guides
BULBS (Houghton Mifflin, 1986) Describes 300 bulbs, plus information on zones and growing.
POCKET GUIDE TO BULBS FOR SPRING (Houghton Mifflin, 1989) Descriptions, color photos and growing information for 79 spring bulbs.
POCKET GUIDE TO BULBS FOR SUMMER (Houghton Mifflin, 1989) Descriptions, color photos and growing information for 79 summer bulbs.

Time-Life
BULBS: THE GARDENER'S GUIDE SERIES (Time-Life Books, 1989)

Whiteside, Katherine, and Hales, Mick
CLASSIC BULBS: HIDDEN TREASURES FOR THE MODERN GARDEN (Villard Books, 1992) Describes and gives cultivation advice on antique flowering bulbs; 200 color photos and mail order sources.

Wilder, Louise Beebe
ADVENTURES WITH HARDY BULBS (Macmillan, 1990, foreword by Allen Lacy) Reprint of the 1936 classic; detailed information and her personal observations on 350 bulbs, rhizomes, tubers and corms.

SPECIFIC BULBS

Dahlias

"My advice to the Women's Club of America is to raise more hell and fewer dahlias."
William Allen White

The American Dahlia Society (159 Pine Street, New Hyde Park, NY 11040) issues a quarterly bulletin.

Damp, Philip
DAHLIAS: THE COMPLETE GUIDE (Trafalgar Square, 1990) Covers all aspects of cultivating dahlias, plus 150 of the best dahlias to grow.
DAHLIAS (Globe Pequot, 1988) Covers history and development, selecting the best plants, preparing the soil, planting and cultivating, handling pests and diseases, gardens to visit, societies and plant supply sources.

GROWING DAHLIAS (Timber Press, 1986) Good introduction covering growing, propagating, storing and exhibiting dahlias.
A PLANTSMAN'S GUIDE TO DAHLIAS (Sterling, 1991) Covers planting schemes, year-round care, propagation tips, essential tools and all the popular varieties.

Hammett, Keith
THE WORLD OF DAHLIAS (Tuttle, 1980) Guide on classifying, growing, propagating, showing and storing dahlias.

Parker, Gayner W.
GROWING DAHLIAS (ISBS, 1987) How to select, propagate, care for and maintain dahlias.

Narcissus (Daffodils)

The American Daffodil Society (1686 Grey Fox Trails, Milford, OH 45150, 513-248-9137) publishes a quarterly magazine, *The Daffodil Journal*. It also publishes *Daffodils to Show and Grow* (1989), a listing of daffodils usually found in gardens and a *Handbook for Growing, Exhibiting, and Judging Daffodils* (1990).

Barnes, Don
DAFFODILS: FOR HOME, GARDEN AND SHOW (Timber Press, 1987) One of the most thorough treatments on growing daffodils in the garden or in pots; with complete descriptions of all species.

Blanchard, John
NARCISSUS, A GUIDE TO WILD DAFFODILS (Alpine Garden Society, Surrey, England, 1990)

Bowles, E. A.
A HANDBOOK OF NARCISSUS (Timber Press, 1985) Reprint of the 1934 classic.

Jefferson-Brown, Michael
NARCISSUS (Timber Press, 1991) History and cultivation, hybridizing, pests and diseases, propagation and exhibiting information for all forms of currently available daffodils.

Quinn, Carey E.
DAFFODILS, OUTDOORS AND IN (Hearthside Press, 1959)

Wells, James S.
MODERN MINIATURE DAFFODILS: SPECIES AND HYBRIDS (Timber Press, 1989) Covers indoor and outdoor culture with in-depth descriptions of species and hybrids.

Begonias

The American Begonia Society (8922 Conway Drive, Riverside, CA 92503) publishes "The Begonian" bimonthly and has publications for sale.

Catterall, Eric
GROWING BEGONIAS (Timber Press, 1984) Describes tuberous and non-tuberous begonias and how to care for them in the garden, indoors or in a greenhouse.

Hopkinson, Judith and Simon
BEGONIAS: CLASSIC GARDEN PLANTS (Globe Pequot, 1989) How to select and grow tuberous begonias.

Kramer, Jack
BEGONIAS AS HOUSE PLANTS (Van Nostrand Reinhold, 1976) Covers starting a begonia collection, basic cultural requirements, propagation for indoor and outdoor growing and brief descriptions of 300 begonias; includes information on exhibiting and photographing.

Thompson, Mildred and Edward
BEGONIAS: THE COMPLETE REFERENCE (Times Books, 1981) Describes and gives growing information on over 2,450 species and cultivars.

Wall, Bill
BEGONIAS (Wisley Handbook)(Sterling, 1990) Good introduction to the various types of begonias; includes a list of recommended plants.

MISCELLANEOUS BULBS

Anderton, Eric, and Park, Ron
GROWING GLADIOLI (Timber Press, 1989) Details on classification, cultivation and distribution; covers modern hybrids and offers propagation advice and a complete list of cultivars.

Bowles, E. A.
A HANDBOOK OF CROCUS AND COLCHICUM FOR GARDENERS (Timber Press, 1985) Reprint of the 1924 classic with a new foreword by Brian Mathew and color photos to supplement the original illustrations.

Bown, Deni
AROIDS: PLANTS OF THE ARUM FAMILY (Timber Press, 1988) Covers the familiar ones (philodendrons, calla lilies, anthuriums, etc.), plus the unusual like the *Titan arum* of Sumatra.

Grey-Wilson, Christopher
THE GENUS CYCLAMEN: A KEW MAGAZINE MONOGRAPH (Timber Press, 1988) Describes all species and many of the new cultivars.

Killingbeck, Stanley
TULIPS (Chartwell, 1991) Covers all of the major groups with information on breeding, cultivating, forcing, etc.

Lodewijk, Tom
THE BOOK OF TULIPS (Vendome Press, 1979) A history of tulips, plus how to select, plant and grow.

Mathew, Brian
THE CROCUS: A REVISION OF THE GENUS CROCUS (Timber Press, 1983) A description and botanical illustration for each species.

Nightingale, Gay
GROWING CYCLAMEN (Timber Press, 1987) A good introduction covering history, descriptions, propagation, cultivation, disease control and more.

North American Gladiolus Council
HOW TO GROW GLORIOUS GLADIOLUS (North American Gladiolus Council, c/o Peter Welcenbach, 11102 W. Calumet Road, Milwaukee, WI 53224) How to select, plant, grow, store, propagate, hybridize, handle pests/diseases and exhibit.

For related books, see:
BULB MAGIC IN YOUR WINDOW by Peter (page 117)
FLOWERING BULBS FOR WINTER WINDOWS by Walker (page 117)

WILDFLOWERS AND WILD PLANTS

It's spring as I write this, and the Texas wildflowers are at their peak. Nature, unhampered by humans, is giving its best. If you love wildflowers, try to visit us some spring.

Andrews, Jonathan
COUNTRY DIARY BOOK OF CREATING A WILD FLOWER GARDEN (Henry Holt, 1987) A beautifully illustrated guide to producing a wildflower garden.

Art, Henry
GARDEN OF WILDFLOWERS: 101 NATIVE SPECIES AND HOW TO GROW THEM (Storey, 1986) For use in any part of the U.S., it covers culture and propagation, and includes sources, societies and botanical gardens of interest to wildflower enthusiasts.

Each of the following guides covers wildflowers native to a specific region, and gives growing and blooming information along with landscaping ideas:
THE WILDFLOWER GARDENER'S GUIDE (CALIFORNIA, DESERT SOUTHWEST, NORTHERN MEXICO) (Storey, 1990)
THE WILDFLOWER GARDENER'S GUIDE (MIDWEST, GREAT PLAINS, CANADIAN PRAIRIES) (Storey, 1991)
THE WILDFLOWER GARDENER'S GUIDE (NORTHEAST, MID-ATLANTIC, GREAT LAKES, EASTERN CANADA) (Storey, 1987)
THE WILDFLOWER GARDENER'S GUIDE (PACIFIC NORTHWEST, ROCKY MOUNTAIN, WESTERN CANADA) (Storey, 1990)

Austin, Richard L.
WILD GARDENING: STRATEGIES AND PROCEDURES USING NATIVE PLANTINGS (Simon & Schuster, 1986) How to choose the best plants and what to do to make them flourish.

Barre, Claude
JEWELS OF THE PLAIN: WILDFLOWERS OF THE GREAT PLAINS GRASSLANDS AND HILLS (University of Minnesota, 1983) Emphasis is on wildflowers of the northern Great Plains.

Birdseye, Clarence and Eleanor
GROWING WOODLAND PLANTS (Dover, 1972) Describes soil and light requirements, propagation techniques and care required on 200+ wildflowers and ferns native to the northern U.S. and southern Canada.

Brooklyn Botanic Garden
GARDENING WITH WILDFLOWERS (BBG #38) Discusses wildflowers by regions, plus gives information on growing and propagating.

GARDENING WITH WILDFLOWERS AND NATIVE PLANTS (BBG #119) How to grow and propagate wildflowers, native flowering trees, shrubs and ferns.

Bruce, Hal
HOW TO GROW WILDFLOWERS AND WILD SHRUBS AND TREES IN YOUR OWN GARDEN (Knopf, 1976) Primarily deals with wild plants of the eastern part of North America.

Courtenay, Booth
WILDFLOWERS AND WEEDS (Prentice-Hall, 1990) Similar plants from 11 families are grouped together to make identification easier; intended for the Midwest; 650 color photos.

Crockett, James U., and Allen, Oliver E.
WILDFLOWER GARDENING (Henry Holt, 1986; reprint of the 1977 Time-Life edition) A good introduction to this subject.

Dana, Mrs. William Starr
ACCORDING TO SEASON: A CELEBRATION OF NATURE (Houghton Mifflin, 1990) A collection of essays about wildflowers; a reprint of the 1894 edition and sequel to the book below.
HOW TO KNOW THE WILD FLOWERS: A GUIDE TO THE NAMES, HAUNTS AND HABITS OF OUR COMMON WILD FLOWERS (Houghton Mifflin, 1989 gift edition with 24 exquisite new color paintings) This new edition of the 1893 book has updated botanical information and covers 500+ plants categorized by color and season.

Durant, Mary
WHO NAMED THE DAISY? WHO NAMED THE ROSE?: A ROVING DICTIONARY OF NORTH AMERICAN WILD FLOWERS (Congdon & Weed, 1976) Origins of the names of over 100 common wildflowers, plus cultivation tips and cooking suggestions.

Elias, Thomas S., and Dykeman, Peter A.
EDIBLE WILD PLANTS: A NORTH AMERICAN FIELD GUIDE (Sterling, 1990) How to identify, harvest and prepare over 200 common wild plants; arranged by season.

Ferguson, Mary
WILDFLOWERS THROUGH THE SEASONS (Arrowood Press, 1989)

Fichter, George S.
WILDFLOWERS OF NORTH AMERICA (Random House, 1982) Audubon Society Beginners Guide Series.

Fisher, John
WILDFLOWERS IN DANGER (Trafalgar Square, 1989)

Genders, Roy
THE WILDFLOWER GARDEN (Dufour, 1977) How to grow wildflowers from seed and use in borders, small beds, rock gardens, along walks and in water gardens; includes creating a wild herb garden.

Hitchcock, Susan
WILDFLOWERS ON THE WINDOWSILL: A GUIDE TO GROWING WILD PLANTS INDOORS (Crown, 1984) How to grow 48 species of wild plants, flowers, herbs and ferns.

Houk, Rose
EASTERN WILDFLOWERS: A PHOTOGRAPHIC CELEBRATION FROM NEW ENGLAND TO THE HEARTLAND (Chronicle Books, 1989) Photos and descriptive information.

Imes, Rick
WILDFLOWERS: HOW TO IDENTIFY THEM AND GROW THEM IN YOUR GARDEN (Rodale Press, 1992) Describes and illustrates over 250 common North American species arranged by habitat.

Jefferson-Brown, Michael
WILD FLOWER GARDENING (Wisley Handbook) (Sterling, 1991) Color photos and expert advice.

Johnson, C. Pierpoint
A CONCISE ENCYCLOPEDIA OF WILDFLOWERS (Gallery, 1989) Originally published in 1860, it contains a description and full color drawing for each of 1,600 species.

Johnson, Lady Bird, and Lees, Carlton B.
WILDFLOWERS ACROSS AMERICA (Abbeville Press, 1988) Photographic tour, region by region, of America's wildflowers; 200 color photos.

Jones, Samuel B., Jr., and Foote, Leonard E.
GARDENING WITH NATIVE WILD FLOW-ERS (Timber Press, 1990) Intended for the eastern and midwestern U.S., it covers which wildflowers and hardy ferns to use and how to use them in shady, sunny or wetland areas; also instructions for creating a wildflower meadow.

Kenfield, Warren G.
THE WILD GARDENER IN THE WILD LAND-SCAPE (Connecticut College Arboretum, 1989) A new edition of the 1966 classic that examines how to modify "wild" landscapes without destroying the naturalness.

Loewer, Peter
THE WILD GARDENER: ON FLOWERS AND FOLIAGE FOR THE NATURAL BORDER (Stackpole Press, 1991) Cultivation, propagation, historical and botanical information.

Martin, Laura
WILDFLOWER FOLKLORE (Globe Pequot, 1984) Botanical information, legends, myths and stories about 105 North American wildflowers, plus medicinal, pioneer and Indian uses.
THE WILDFLOWER MEADOW BOOK: A GARDENER'S GUIDE (Globe Pequot, 1990, 2nd ed.) How-to information on creating a wildflower meadow, plus sources, regional bibliography and tips from the experts.

Miles, Bebe
WILDFLOWER PERENNIALS FOR YOUR GARDEN: A DETAILED GUIDE TO YEARS OF BLOOM FROM AMERICA'S LONG-NE-GLECTED NATIVE HERITAGE (Hawthorn Books, 1976) Categorizes 100 wildflowers by the area best suited for them: sun, shade or damp; line drawings by H. Peter Loewer.

Mohlenbrock, Robert H.
WILDFLOWERS: A MACMILLAN FIELD GUIDE (Macmillan, 1987)

National Wildflower Research Center
WILDFLOWER HANDBOOK (Pacesetter Press, 1989) A resource guide of planting information plus organizations, societies, seed and plant sources, and extensive bibliography.

Newcomb, Laurence
NEWCOMB'S WILDFLOWER GUIDE: AN IN-GENIOUS NEW KEY SYSTEM FOR QUICK, POSITIVE FIELD IDENTIFICATION OF WILDFLOWERS, FLOWERING SHRUBS AND VINES (Little, Brown, 1989)

Niering, William, and Spellenberg, Richard
FAMILIAR WILDFLOWERS OF NORTH AMERICA (Knopf, forthcoming, 6 volumes)

Ortho
LANDSCAPING WITH WILDFLOWERS AND NATIVE PLANTS (Ortho, 1985)

Peterson, Roger Tory
PETERSON'S FIRST GUIDE TO WILDFLOW-ERS (Houghton Mifflin, 1986) A simplified field guide to the common wildflowers of northeastern and north-central North America.

Phillips, Harry
GROWING AND PROPAGATING WILD-FLOWERS (University of North Carolina Press, 1985) Ten years of research produced this invaluable guide to almost 100 genera of primarily eastern U.S. wildflowers and ferns, but the propagating techniques are applicable anywhere.

Phillips, Norma
ADVENTURES OF A 'WILD' PLANTS WOMAN: IN PURSUIT OF NATIVE PLANT PRESERVATION (Little Bridge, 1988) Written from the personal experience of owning a wildflower nursery, she details how to propagate and preserve native plants.
THE ROOT BOOK: A CONCISE GUIDE TO PLANTING AND GROWING WILDFLOWERS AND HARDY FERNS (Little Bridge, 1983) Covers wildflowers, ferns, wild orchids, violets and mosses.

Rees, Yvonne
WILDFLOWER GARDENING: STEP BY STEP TO GROWING SUCCESS (Trafalgar Square, 1992) Advice on using wildflowers in gardens, meadows, lawns, ponds, marshes and woodlands; includes list of recommended plants.

Reynolds, William
WILDFLOWERS OF AMERICA (Smithmark, 1988)

Rickett, Harold W.
WILD FLOWERS OF THE USA (McGraw-Hill, 1966, six volumes)

Robinson, William
THE WILD GARDEN (Trafalgar Square, 1986) Reprint of the British classic originally published in 1870 and full of planting ideas.

Rose, Graham
THE SUNDAY TIMES BOOK OF WOODLAND AND WILDFLOWER GARDENING (Trafalgar Square, 1988) The winners of various London competitions on designs for woodland gardens; includes the winning design from the Chelsea Flower Show and tips from professionals.

Smith, Richard M.
WILD PLANTS OF AMERICA: A SELECT GUIDE FOR THE NATURALIST AND TRAVELER (John Wiley, 1989) A guide to national forests, parks and preserves where wildflowers abound.

Smyser, Carol A.
A NATURE'S DESIGN: A PRACTICAL GUIDE TO NATURAL LANDSCAPING (Rodale Press, 1982)

Sperka, Marie
GROWING WILDFLOWERS (Macmillan, 1984) Instructions for planting and propagating over 200 species of wildflowers that grow in the temperate zone of North America; includes information on preparing the garden bed and the plants, plus lists of nurseries.

Steffek, Edwin
THE NEW WILD FLOWERS AND HOW TO GROW THEM (Timber Press, 1983) Covers descriptions, native habitat and growing information arranged by common name.

Stevenson, Violet
THE WILD GARDEN: MAKING NATURAL GARDENS USING NATIVE PLANTS (Viking Penguin, 1985) Design ideas for wildflower lawns, water gardens, meadows, woodlands and more.

Stokes, Donald
THE NATURAL HISTORY OF WILD SHRUBS AND VINES (Globe Pequot, 1981) Identifies and describes the natural history of 49 genera found in eastern and central North America.

Stokes, Donald and Lillian
A GUIDE TO ENJOYING WILDFLOWERS (Little, Brown, 1986)

Strickler, Dee
ALPINE WILDFLOWERS (Falcon Press, 1990)
FOREST WILDFLOWERS (Falcon Press, 1988)
PRAIRIE WILDFLOWERS (Falcon Press, 1986)

Sullivan, Gene, and Daley, Richard
DIRECTORY TO RESOURCES ON WILDFLOWER PROPAGATION (National Council of State Garden Clubs, 1981) Covers which propagation methods to use for which wildflowers.

Taylor, Kathryn, and Hambin, Stephen
HANDBOOK OF WILD FLOWER CULTIVATION (Collier Books, 1976) Cultural requirements and propagation methods for a large variety of wildflowers.

Tenenbaum, Frances
GARDENING WITH WILDFLOWERS (Ballantine, 1986) Writing from personal experience, she covers how to introduce wildflowers to your garden, plus ground covers, ferns, woodland gardens, seashore gardens, making a meadow, collecting wildflowers and buying wildflowers.

Time-Life
WILDFLOWERS: GARDENER'S GUIDE SERIES (Time-Life Books, 1990)

Tull, Delena
A PRACTICAL GUIDE TO EDIBLE AND USE-
FUL PLANTS (Gulf Publishing, 1987) Includes recipes and information on harmful plants, natural dyes
and textile fibers.

Wilson, Jim
LANDSCAPING WITH WILDFLOWERS: AN
ENVIRONMENTAL APPROACH TO GAR-
DENING (Houghton Mifflin, 1992) Covers the
major types of wildflower gardens (woodland, meadow,
prairie-style, specialized western and southwestern,
high-altitude), how to attract birds and butterflies,
plants for specific regions of the U.S., lists of wildflower
nurseries and societies, and a description of his South
Carolina wildflower garden.

Young, Andrew
A PROSPECT OF FLOWERS: A BOOK ABOUT
WILD FLOWERS (Viking Penguin, 1986)

Young, James and Cheryl
COLLECTING, PROCESSING AND GERMI-
NATING SEEDS OF WILDLAND PLANTS
(Timber Press, 1986) Divided into two sections, the
first covers the basics of native plant gardening, and
the second section offers specifics on germination.

For related books, see:
THE AUDUBON SOCIETY FIELD GUIDE TO
NORTH AMERICAN WILDFLOWERS: EAST-
ERN REGION by Niering and Olmstead (page 192)
THE AUDUBON SOCIETY FIELD GUIDE TO
NORTH AMERICAN WILDFLOWERS: WEST-
ERN REGION by Niering and Olmstead (page 198)
COUNTRY FLOWERS by Proctor (page 42)
A FIELD GUIDE TO PACIFIC STATES WILD-
FLOWERS by Niehaus and Ripper (page 198)
A FIELD GUIDE TO ROCKY MOUNTAIN
WILDFLOWERS by Craighead (page 197)

A FIELD GUIDE TO SOUTHWESTERN AND
TEXAS WILDFLOWERS by Niehaus and Ripper
(page 196)
GARDEN IN THE WOODS CULTIVATION
GUIDE and NURSERY SOURCES: NATIVE
PLANTS AND WILDFLOWERS by New England
Wildflower Society (pages 191, 192)
THE GUIDE TO FLORIDA WILDFLOWERS by
Taylor (page 195)
THE NATIONAL TRUST BOOK OF WILD-
FLOWER GARDENING by Stevens (page 208)
NORTHLAND WILD FLOWERS by Moyle (page
218)
PHOTOGRAPHING WILDFLOWERS by Black-
lock (page 218)
SOUTHERN WILDFLOWERS by Martin (page
194)
SPRING WILDFLOWERS OF NEW ENGLAND
and SUMMER WILDFLOWERS OF NEW EN-
GLAND by Dwelley (page 191)
TEXAS WILDFLOWERS by Meier and Reid (page
196)
TEXAS WILDFLOWERS PORTRAITS by
O'Kennon (page 196)
WILD AND WONDERFUL FLOWERS FOR
YOUR HOME by Fleck and Stevens (page 133)
WILD EDIBLE PLANTS OF NEW ENGLAND by
Richardson (page 192)
WILDFLOWERS FOR ALL SEASONS by Vojtech
and Prance (page 220)
WILDFLOWERS IN THE CAROLINAS by Bat-
son (page 193)
WILD FLOWERS OF BRITAIN by Phillips (page
207)
WILDFLOWERS OF NORTH CAROLINA by
Justice and Bell (page 193)
WILDFLOWERS OF THE AMERICAN WEST by
Houk (page 197)
WILDFLOWERS OF THE WESTERN CAS-
CADES by Ross et al. (page 198)

FOOD GARDENS

GENERAL REFERENCES

The National Gardening Association (180 Flynn Avenue, Burlington, VT 05401, 802-863-1308) is for people interested in growing food. It publishes a monthly magazine and offers discounts on books. In addition, the association has authored *Gardening: The Complete Guide to Growing America's Favorite Fruits and Vebetables* (Addison-Wesley, 1986), which is a basic introduction to food gardening.

It also publishes a series of step-by-step growing guides on various vegetables. Each 36-page book covers germination, sowing, cultivating, caring for, harvesting, storing and cooking.

Adams, John F.
GROW FRUITS AND VEGETABLES THE WAY THEY USED TO TASTE (Wynwood Press, 1989)

Arkin, Frieda
THE ESSENTIAL KITCHEN GARDENER (Henry Holt, 1990) An A to Z encyclopedia of when, where and how to plant and care for a large number of vegetables, herbs and berries; includes pest and disease control, harvesting, storage and kitchen tips.

Berg, Donald J.
THE KITCHEN GARDENER'S GUIDE (Ten Speed Press, 1987)

Bittman, Sam
THE SALAD LOVER'S GARDEN (Doubleday, 1992) Covers growing greens, herbs and salad vegetables; includes when and where to plant, preparing the soil, plant selection, successive planting, companion planting, container planting, controlling pests, recipes and a list of suppliers.

Creasy, Rosalind
THE COMPLETE BOOK OF EDIBLE LANDSCAPING: HOME LANDSCAPING WITH FOOD-BEARING PLANTS AND RESOURCE-SAVING TECHNIQUES (Sierra Club Books, 1982) Suggestions for which edible plants are best for the garden, plus descriptions and mixing food and decorative plants.

THE GARDENER'S HANDBOOK OF EDIBLE PLANTS (Sierra Club Books, 1986)

Crockett, James Underwood, and Editors of Time-Life
VEGETABLES AND FRUITS (Henry Holt, 1986) Reprint of 1972 edition.

DeSaulles, Denys
HOME GROWN (Houghton Mifflin, 1988) How to grow fruits and vegetables organically; plan an herb garden; preserve by freezing, drying or canning; and more.

Garden Way Publishing Editors
FRUITS AND VEGETABLES: 1001 GARDENING QUESTIONS ANSWERED (Storey, 1990) Question and answer format with expert advice.

Gessert, Kate R.
THE BEAUTIFUL FOOD GARDEN: CREATIVE LANDSCAPING WITH VEGETABLES, HERBS, FRUITS AND FLOWERS (Storey, 1987) Covers ornamental characteristics, drawbacks, adaptability, pests and more.

Hagy, Fred
THE PRACTICAL GARDEN OF EDEN (Overlook Press, 1990) How to landscape with fruits and vegetables; includes garden design, selecting the plants best suited to the climate, pest control and supplier sources.

Heinerman, John
ENCYCLOPEDIA OF FRUITS, VEGETABLES AND HERBS (Prentice-Hall, 1988)

Holt, Geraldene
THE GOURMET GARDENER: THE FRUITS OF THE GARDEN TRANSPORTED TO THE TABLE (Little, Brown, 1990) Surveys the kitchen gardens (fruits, vegetables, herbs) of well-known chefs; includes tips and recipes.

Kourik, Robert
DESIGNING AND MAINTAINING YOUR EDIBLE LANDSCAPE NATURALLY (Metamorphic Press, 1986) How to have an attractive food garden.

Lee, Hollis
NUTS, BERRIES AND GRAPES (Countryside Books, 1978) Covers planting, growing and care of walnuts, pecans, chestnuts, almonds, blackberries, strawberries, blueberries and grapes.

Mittlieder, J. R.
MORE FOOD FROM YOUR GARDEN (Woodbridge Press, 1975) Describes his method of growbox gardening which combines soil gardening and hydroponic gardening.

Newcomb, Duane
THE POSTAGE STAMP GARDEN BOOK: HOW TO GROW ALL THE FOOD YOU CAN EAT IN VERY LITTLE SPACE (Jeremy Tarcher, 1975) Covers planning, preparing the soil, and when and how to plant and care for 29 vegetables and 13 herbs.

Proulx, Annie
THE GOURMET GARDENER: GROWING CHOICE FRUITS AND VEGETABLES WITH SPECTACULAR RESULTS (Fawcett Columbine, 1987)

Riemer, Jan
THE BEGINNER'S KITCHEN GARDEN (Morrow, 1975)

Seymour, John
THE SELF-SUFFICIENT GARDENER: A COMPLETE GUIDE TO GROWING AND PRESERVING ALL YOUR OWN FOOD (Doubleday, 1979)

Smith, W. S.
GARDENING FOR FOOD (Macmillan, 1972)

For related books, see:
FRUIT AND VEGETABLE GARDENS by Greenoak (page 205)
GARDENING AT A GLANCE by Denckla (page 143)
GARDENING IN THE SOUTH: VEGETABLES AND FRUITS by Hastings (page 193)
GROWING AND USING EXOTIC FOODS by Van Atta (page 182)
THE HEIRLOOM GARDENER by Jabs (page 78)

PACIFIC NORTHWEST GUIDE TO HOME GARDENING by McNeilan and Ronningen (page 198)

THE VICTORIAN KITCHEN GARDEN by Davies (page 205)

VEGETABLES

Baker, Jerry
JERRY BAKER'S FAST, EASY VEGETABLE GARDEN (Plume, 1985)

Bales, Suzanne
VEGETABLES (Prentice-Hall, 1991) Details on growing and color photos of over 70 veggies; includes pest control information.

Ball, Jeff
JEFF BALL'S 60 MINUTE VEGETABLE GARDEN (Collier Books, 1992) How to grow 400 pounds of vegetables in a 200 square foot garden with only 60 minutes of work each week; includes designs for 20 unique devices (vertical trellises, boxed raised beds, growing tunnels, etc.) that gardeners can build to aid them in producing this garden.

THE SELF-SUFFICIENT SUBURBAN GARDENER (Ballantine, 1986) How to make the best use of a small space to produce a high yield vegetable garden.

Bartholomew, Mel
SQUARE FOOT GARDENING: A NEW WAY TO GARDEN IN LESS SPACE WITH LESS WORK (Rodale Press, 1981) How to get big crops from a small space and with less work.

Brooklyn Botanic Garden
THE HOME VEGETABLE GARDEN (BBG #69) Covers plant selection, planting and harvesting.

Bubel, Nancy
THE COUNTRY JOURNAL BOOK OF VEGETABLE GARDENING (National Historical Society, 1983)

Burr, Fearing
FIELD AND GARDEN VEGETABLES OF AMERICA (American Botanist, 1988) Facsimile of 1865 edition with descriptions of almost 1,100 herbs and vegetables, many of which disappeared long ago.

Chan, Peter
BETTER VEGETABLE GARDENS THE CHINESE WAY: PETER CHAN'S RAISED BED SYSTEM (Storey, 1985)

PETER CHAN'S MAGICAL LANDSCAPE (Storey, 1988)

Clarke, Ethne
THE ART OF THE KITCHEN GARDEN (Knopf, 1987) How to plant, cook, and preserve food for your table.

Cox, Jeff
HOW TO GROW VEGETABLES ORGANICALLY (Rodale Press, 1988) A comprehensive guide to growing vegetables successfully without chemicals.

Crockett, James Underwood
CROCKETT'S VICTORY GARDEN (Little, Brown, 1977) Preparing the garden, plus detailed month-by-month instructions for growing vegetables.

Cruso, Thalassa
MAKING VEGETABLES GROW (Lyons & Burford, 1990) A reprint of the 1975 classic.

Faust, Joan
THE NEW YORK TIMES BOOK OF VEGETABLE GARDENING (Quadrangle Books, 1975) How to plan, plant and care for numerous vegetables and 12 herbs.

Fell, Derek
VEGETABLES: HOW TO SELECT, GROW AND ENJOY (HP Books, 1982) Covers seed starting, preparing the soil, planting, fertilizing and controlling pests and diseases for over 80 vegetables and 30 herbs.

Fenton, Tom
GROWING AND SHOWING VEGETABLES (Trafalgar Square, 1984) Proven methods for growing and showing vegetables.

Gilbertie, Sal
HOME GARDENING AT ITS BEST: PRODUCTIVE WAYS TO GROW YOUR OWN FRESH VEGETABLES (Macmillan, 1977)

Harrington, Geri
GROW YOUR OWN CHINESE VEGETABLES
(Storey, 1984) How to find the seeds, grow, harvest
and cook Chinese vegetables.

Heiser, Charles B.
THE GOURD BOOK (University of Oklahoma
Press, 1979) Covers history and the various uses of
gourds.

Hendrickson, Robert
THE GREAT TOMATO BOOK: THE ONE COM-
PLETE GUIDE TO GROWING AND USING TO-
MATOES EVERYWHERE (Stein & Day, 1984)

Hessayon, Dr. D. G.
THE VEGETABLE EXPERT (Sterling, 1990) Detailed information on seed, soil, growth, problem prevention and harvesting.

Jeavons, John
HOW TO GROW MORE VEGETABLES THAN
YOU EVER THOUGHT POSSIBLE ON LESS
LAND THAN YOU CAN IMAGINE (Ten Speed
Press, 1982) Covers the French intensive method,
which requires less space and time and produces 4 to 6
times as much as the average American garden.

Kline, Roger A.
THE HEIRLOOM VEGETABLE GARDEN (Cor-
nell Cooperative Extension, revised edition, 1986)

Larkcom, Joy
ORIENTAL VEGETABLES: THE COMPLETE
GUIDE FOR GARDEN AND KITCHEN
(Kodansha, 1991) Organic growing information and
sources for over 100 oriental vegetables.
THE SALAD GARDEN: SALADS FROM SEED
TO TABLE—A COMPLETE, ILLUSTRATED
YEAR ROUND GUIDE (Viking Penguin, 1984)
How to grow a variety of salad greens, including edible
flowers and herbs.
VEGETABLES FROM SMALL GARDENS: A
GUIDE TO INTENSIVE CULTIVATION (Faber
& Faber, 1986)

Lau, Joy
VEGETABLES FOR THE HOME GARDENER
(ISBS, 1987) Discusses growing over 70 types of vege-
tables.

Lorenz, Oscar, and Maynard, Donald
KNOTT'S HANDBOOK FOR VEGETABLE
GROWERS (John Wiley, 1988)

Lyte, Charles
THE KITCHEN GARDEN (Oxford Illustrated
Press, 1984)

MacNab, Alan; Sherf, Arden; and Springer, J. K.
IDENTIFYING DISEASES OF VEGETABLES
(Pennsylvania State University, 1983) Covers symptoms, spreading, unfavorable weather conditions and
the reoccurrence of common diseases of popular vegetables.

Men's Garden Clubs of America Staff
A–Z HINTS FOR THE VEGETABLE GAR-
DENER: FROM THE 10,000 MEMBERS OF THE
MEN'S GARDEN CLUBS OF AMERICA (Storey,
1977) Hundreds of alphabetized hints and tips from
the members' personal experiences.

Meyers, Perla
THE EARLY SUMMER GARDEN (Simon &
Schuster, 1988) Vegetable gardening.

Mother Earth News Editors
THE ABUNDANT VEGETABLE GARDEN: A
HANDBOOK FOR SUCCESS (Mother Earth
News, 1985)

Newcomb, Duane
THE APARTMENT FARMER: THE HASSLE-
FREE WAY TO GROW VEGETABLES IN-
DOORS, ON BALCONIES, PATIOS, ROOFS,
AND IN SMALL YARDS (Hawthorn, 1977) Grow-
ing veggies in containers.
THE BACKYARD VEGETABLE FACTORY:
SUPER YIELDS FROM SMALL SPACES (Rodale
Press, 1988) How to get the largest crops from gardens
that are 10' x 10' or smaller by utilizing zone planting,
plant groupings, containers and vertical gardening.
GROWING VEGETABLES THE BIG YIELD-
SMALL SPACE WAY (Jeremy Tarcher, 1981)

**THE NEW COMPLETE VEGETABLE GAR-
DENER'S SOURCEBOOK** (Prentice-Hall, 1989)
Compiled with his wife, Karen, this provides a wealth of
sources, charts, lists and how-to information.
Rx FOR YOUR VEGETABLE GARDEN (Jeremy
Tarcher, 1982)

Ogden, Shepherd
**STEP-BY-STEP TO ORGANIC VEGETABLE
GROWING** (HarperCollins, 1992) An updated revi-
sion of the classic by his grandfather, Sam Ogden.

Ogden, Shepherd and Ellen
**THE COOK'S GARDEN: GROWING AND
USING THE BEST TASTING VEGETABLE
VARIETIES** (Rodale, 1989) Surveys many types of
seeds, where to obtain them, growing and harvesting
them, plus 56 recipes.

Ortho
ALL ABOUT VEGETABLES (Ortho, 1981)

Raymond, Dick
DICK RAYMOND'S GARDENING YEAR
(Simon & Schuster, 1985)
**DOWN-TO-EARTH GARDENING KNOW-
HOW FOR THE 90'S: VEGETABLES AND
HERBS** (Storey, 1991) A classic that has been up-
dated with detailed advice for the beginner.
GARDEN WAY'S JOY OF GARDENING (Gar-
den Way, 1983) How to turn any piece of land into a
vegetable garden; over 600 color photos.

Raymond, Dick and Jan
HOME GARDENING WISDOM (Garden Way,
1982)

Robbins, Ann Roe
25 VEGETABLES ANYONE CAN GROW
(Dover, 1974) Planting directions for asparagus, beans,
beets, broccoli, celery, etc.

Rossant, Colette, and Melendez, Marianne
**VEGETABLES: THE ART OF GROWING,
COOKING, AND KEEPING THE NEW AMER-
ICAN HARVEST** (Viking, 1991)

Rupp, Rebecca
**BLUE CORN AND SQUARE TOMATOES: UN-
USUAL FACTS ABOUT COMMON GARDEN
VEGETABLES** (Storey, 1987) Answers hundreds of
questions about the history and origin of 20 everyday
vegetables; includes recipes, bibliography and a seed
source list.

Spoczynska, Joy
THE INDOOR VEGETABLE GARDEN
(Trafalgar Square, 1986)

Sunset
VEGETABLE GARDENING ILLUSTRATED
(Sunset Books, 1987) Descriptions and instructions
on growing and harvesting a variety of vegetables
and berries.

Taylor's
GUIDE TO VEGETABLES AND HERBS
(Houghton Mifflin, 1987) Describes all the basic information needed on 135 vegetables and 75 herbs;
includes over 400 color photos and 200 black-and-
white drawings.
POCKET GUIDE TO VEGETABLES (Houghton
Mifflin, 1990) One page on each of 79 different vegetables giving basic information (selecting, hardiness,
planting, care) plus a color photo.

Thomson, Bob
THE NEW VICTORY GARDEN (Little, Brown,
1987) Filled with time-saving tips from his TV show,
this updated and expanded version of *Crockett's Victory
Garden* arranges gardening tasks month-by-month.

Time-Life
**SUMMER VEGETABLES: GARDENER'S
GUIDE SERIES** (Time-Life Books, 1988)

Tokuno, Gajin
**LET NATURE DO THE GROWING: THE FER-
TILIZER-FREE VEGETABLE GARDEN** (Japan
Publications USA, 1986) How to grow 78 American
and Japanese vegetables without chemicals of any
kind; includes over 900 illustrations.

Van Patten, George F.
ORGANIC GARDEN VEGETABLES (Van Patten Publishing, 1992, 2nd edition) How to select,
plant, care for and harvest over 300 vegetables.

Vilmorin-Andrieux, M. M.
THE VEGETABLE GARDEN (Ten Speed Press, 1981) First published in 1885, this book describes a very large number of vegetables, many no longer available, and discusses various cultivation methods; hundreds of lovely engravings.

Walls, Ian G.
GROWING TOMATOES (Trafalgar Square, 1989) Detailed information for both the professional and home gardener on growing tomatoes in a greenhouse.
SIMPLE VEGETABLE GROWING (Trafalgar Square, 1989)

Whealy, Kent (editor)
THE GARDEN SEED INVENTORY: 2ND EDITION (Seed Savers Publications, 1988) Descriptions and sources for 5,291 varieties of vegetables from 215 U.S. and Canadian seed companies.

For related books, see:
BACKYARD ORGANIC GARDENER by Smith (page 144)
CASH FROM SQUARE FOOT GARDENING by Bartholomew (page 185)
CONTAINER VEGETABLES by Cotner (page 163)
CONTROLLING VEGETABLE PESTS by Ortho (page 73)
COOKING FROM THE GARDEN by Creasy (page 107)
THE GARDEN SEED INVENTORY by Whealy (page 79)
GROWING VEGETABLES AND HERBS WITH RECIPES FOR THE FRESH HARVEST by *Southern Living* (page 194)
GROWING VEGETABLES WEST OF THE CASCADES by Solomon (page 199)
A GUIDE TO TROPICAL AND SUBTROPICAL VEGETABLES by Acrivos (page 180)
HARROWSMITH SALAD GARDEN by Forsyth and Simonds (page 191)
THE NEW SEED-STARTERS HANDBOOK by Bubel (page 77)
ORIENTAL HERBS AND VEGETABLES by Brooklyn Botanic Garden (page 150)
THE PACIFIC NORTHWEST GARDENER'S ALMANAC by Kenady (page 198)

PARSNIPS IN THE SNOW by Staw and Swander (page 199)
THE VEGETABLE BOOK: A TEXAN'S GUIDE TO GARDENING by Cotner (page 195)
VEGETABLE GARDENING by Esmonde-White (page 191)
VEGETABLE GROWING FOR SOUTHERN GARDENS by Adams (page 192)
VEGETABLES (cookbook) by Famularo and Imperiale (page 106)
THE VICTORY GARDEN COOKBOOK by Morash (page 107)

FRUITS

Cox, Jeff
FROM VINES TO WINES: THE COMPLETE GUIDE TO GROWING GRAPES AND MAKING YOUR OWN WINE (Storey, 1989) Detailed information on growing grapes and making wine; includes sources.

Forsell, Mary
BERRIES: CULTIVATION, DECORATION AND RECIPES (Bantam, 1989) Growing and cooking information for a variety of edible berries, plus decorating ideas using nonedible berries; excellent listing of sources plus over 200 color photos.

Gardner, Jo Ann
THE OLD-FASHIONED FRUIT GARDEN: THE BEST WAY TO GROW, PRESERVE AND BAKE WITH SMALL FRUIT (Chelsea Green Publishing, 1991) Includes growing information on elderberries, rhubarb, strawberries, raspberries, currants, gooseberries and citron, with 175 recipes for these and other fruits.

Godden, Geoff
GROWING CITRUS TREES (ISBS, 1988) How to grow oranges, lemons, grapefruit, mandarins, tangelos, limes and more.

Hendrickson, Robert
THE BERRY BOOK: THE ILLUSTRATED HOME GARDENER'S GUIDE TO GROWING AND USING OVER 50 KINDS AND 500 VARIETIES OF BERRIES (Doubleday, 1981) How to prepare the

ground, plant, grow and control pests and diseases; includes recipes.

Hessayon, Dr. D. G.
THE FRUIT EXPERT (Sterling, 1991) Growing, training, feeding, pruning, problem control and propagating information for all kinds of fruit trees and berries.

Hill, Lewis
FRUITS AND BERRIES FOR THE HOME GARDEN (Storey, 1992, updated edition) Suggests the best varieties, and how to grow, prune, harvest and propagate them.

Johns, Leslie, and Stevenson, Violet
FRUIT FOR THE HOME AND GARDEN (Angus & Robertson, 1985) Covers growing both cold and milder climate fruits outdoors or in greenhouses; includes recipes.

McPhee, John
ORANGES (Farrar, Straus & Giroux, 1967) Covers botany, history and myths about oranges, plus the worldwide orange industry.

Ortho
CITRUS AND TROPICAL FRUIT (Ortho Books, 1985)
FRUITS, BERRIES AND NUTS (Ortho Books, 1987)

Ray, Richard, and Walheim, Lance
CITRUS: HOW TO SELECT, GROW AND ENJOY (HP Books, 1980) Information on growing and using over 100 varieties of citrus with details on tree size, growth, fruit size and color; includes 400+ color photos.

Reich, Lee
UNCOMMON FRUITS WORTHY OF ATTENTION: A GARDENER'S GUIDE (Addison-Wesley, 1992) History, growing and propagating information on 19 easy-to-grow exotic fruits.

Sanders, Rosanne
THE APPLE BOOK (Philosophical Library, 1988) Descriptions, stories, legends, and beautiful watercolors of 122 varieties of apples.

Sunset
HOW TO GROW FRUITS, NUTS AND BERRIES (Sunset Books, 1984) Growing information and charts on the most common berries, fruits and nuts.

Tukey, Harold B.
DWARFED FRUIT TREES FOR ORCHARD, GARDEN AND HOME (Cornell University Press, 1978) Encompasses everything needed to successfully grow these trees.

For related books, see:
FRUIT, BERRY AND NUT INVENTORY by Whealy (page 79)
GROWING FRUIT IN THE UPPER MIDWEST by Gordon (page 197)
GROWING FRUITS, BERRIES AND NUTS IN THE SOUTHWEST and SOUTHEAST by McEachern (page 194)
HARROWSMITH BOOK OF FRUIT TREES by Bennett (page 190)
A HARROWSMITH GARDENER'S GUIDE: BERRIES by Bennett (page 190)
PRUNING HARDY FRUITS by Woodward (page 76)
WESTERN FRUITS, BERRIES AND NUTS by Stebbins (page 199)

GARDENING AND COOKING

Ballantyne, Janet
JOY OF GARDENING COOKBOOK (Garden Way, 1984)

Barrett, Judith
FROM AN ITALIAN GARDEN (Macmillan, 1992) Over 200 recipes for Italian dishes using fruits and vegetables.

Belsinger, Susan
FLOWERS IN THE KITCHEN (Interweave, 1991) Recipes for cooking with edible flowers such as daylily buds and scented geraniums.

Belsinger, Susan, and Dille, Carolyn
COOKING WITH HERBS (Van Nostrand Reinhold, 1984)

Benenson, Sharen
THE NEW YORK BOTANICAL GARDEN
COOKBOOK (Hastings, 1983)

Berkley, Robert
APPLES: A COOKBOOK (Simon & Schuster,
1991) Over 50 recipes for using numerous varieties of
apples, plus mail order sources.
BERRIES: A COOKBOOK (Simon & Schuster,
1990) Fifty recipes for main courses, desserts and bev-
erages, plus mail order sources for a variety of berries
and berry products.
PEPPERS: A COOKBOOK (Simon & Schuster,
1992) Fifty recipes arranged according to the hotness
of the pepper; includes information on the varieties of
peppers available and mail order sources.

Birchfield, Jane
GREAT AUNT JANE'S COOK AND GARDEN
BOOK (Lippincott, 1976) Over 220 recipes grouped
according to season, along with gardening tips, household hints, folk wisdom and entertaining anecdotes.

Blanchard, Marjorie
HOME GARDENER'S MONTH-BY-MONTH
COOKBOOK (Storey, 1985)

Carlman, Susan F.
FARMER'S MARKET COOKBOOK (Chicago Re-
view Press, 1988) Easy to prepare fruit and vegetable
recipes for salads, main dishes, breads, desserts and
more.

Creasy, Rosalind
COOKING FROM THE GARDEN (Sierra Club
Books, 1989) Tells how gardeners from all over the
U.S. planted vegetable gardens she designed (for example, a Cajun garden in Louisiana) then amateur and
professional cooks fixed the produce; includes 180
recipes, suppliers and resources.

De Witt, Dave, and Gerlach, Nancy
THE WHOLE CHILE PEPPER BOOK (Little,
Brown, 1990) Covers growing and using different types
of pepper, how hot the peppers are, and their history;
includes 150+ recipes and seed and pepper sources.

Famularo, Joseph, and Imperiale, Louise
VEGETABLES: THE NEW MAIN COURSE
COOKBOOK (Barron, 1985)

Giobbi, Edward
PLEASURES OF THE GOOD EARTH: A COOK-
BOOK (Knopf, 1991)

Hirsch, David
THE MOOSEWOOD RESTAURANT KITCHEN
GARDEN: CREATIVE GARDENING FOR THE
ADVENTUROUS COOK (Simon & Schuster,
1992) How to plant and use over 35 herbs and 30
vegetables.

Holt, Geraldene
RECIPES FROM A FRENCH HERB GARDEN
(Simon & Schuster, 1989) Wonderful recipes, plus 60
color photos of the food and of French gardens.

Hurley, Judith B.
RODALE'S GARDEN-FRESH COOKING (Rodale
Press, 1987) Salt-free recipes using produce from every
season, plus how to select fruits and vegetables at their
peak, how to save time in preparation and how to ripen
produce in the kitchen.

Hutson, Lucinda
THE HERB GARDEN COOKBOOK (Gulf Pub-
lishing, 1992) Intended for herb growers in the Southwest and lovers of Mexican and Southwestern food;
includes growing information for culinary herbs that
do well in bright sun; also recipes and source list.

Klein, Erica L.
SKINNY SPICES (Surrey Books, 1991) Fifty recipes
for seasoning mixes of herbs and spices, plus two recipes for each of the mixes and a list of sources.

Kluger, Marilyn
WILD FLAVOR: DELECTABLE WILD FOODS
TO BE FOUND IN FIELD AND FOREST AND
COOKED IN COUNTRY KITCHENS (Henry Holt,
1990) How to cook wild foods.

Leggatt, Jenny
COOKING WITH FLOWERS (Ballantine, 1988)
Over 150 recipes covering appetizers to desserts.

Lo, Kenneth
NEW CHINESE VEGETARIAN COOKING
(Pantheon, 1987) Main dishes and side dishes using common and Chinese vegetables.

Mahnken, Jan
A COOK'S GARDEN (Countryman Press, 1985) Recipes for those who like to eat what they grow.

Marcin, Marietta M.
COMPLETE BOOK OF HERBAL TEAS: GROWING, HARVESTING, BREWING (Congdon & Weed, 1985) Covers 70 herbs and how to make the perfect cup of tea using them.

Marton, Beryl
OUT OF THE GARDEN INTO THE KITCHEN (McKay, 1977) Growing and preparing fruits, vegetables and grains.

Matson, Ruth A.
GARDENING FOR GOURMETS: GOOD EATING FROM A SMALL BACKYARD (Doubleday, 1959) Includes 50 recipes. She also wrote *Cooking By the Garden Calendar* (Doubleday, 1955).

Morash, Marian
THE VICTORY GARDEN COOKBOOK (Knopf, 1982) Contains 800 vegetable recipes, plus growing, harvesting, storing and preparation tips.

Nazzaro, Lovel
PESTO MANIFESTO (Chicago Review Press, 1987) Describes how to grow basil organically, plus her basic recipe for pesto and the numerous ways to use it.

Norris, Dorry B.
THE SAGE COTTAGE HERB GARDEN COOKBOOK: CELEBRATIONS, RECIPES AND HERB GARDENING TIPS FOR EVERY MONTH OF THE YEAR (Globe Pequot, 1991) Covers a month-by-month use of herbs; she ran an herbal shop and bed and breakfast in Trumansburg, New York.

Owen, Millie
A COOK'S GUIDE TO GROWING HERBS, GREENS AND AROMATICS (Knopf, 1978)

Rago, Linda
DOORYARD HERB COOKBOOK (Pictorial Histories, 1988) A month-by-month guide to growing and cooking with herbs.

Ralston, Nancy, and Jordan, Marynor
THE NEW ZUCCHINI COOKBOOK: AND OTHER SQUASH (Storey, 1990, revised edition) Covers a wide variety of recipes, plus directions for canning, freezing, storing and drying.

Rankin, Dorothy
PESTOS! COOKING WITH HERB PASTES (Crossing Press, 1985) How to create and use a variety of herb pastes.

Richardson, Noel
SUMMER HERBAL DELIGHTS: GROWING AND COOKING WITH FRESH HERBS (Sterling, 1991) An introduction to herb gardening and cookery with over 170 recipes and 19 different herbs; he is the owner of Raven Hill Herb Farm on Vancouver Island.
WINTER HERBAL PLEASURES: PRESERVING AND COOKING WITH HERBS (Sterling, 1991) How to preserve summer and winter herbs to maintain their flavor and freshness, plus recipes for using them.

Rohde, Eleanour Sinclair
CULINARY AND SALAD HERBS (Dover, 1972) Recipes for using the major culinary and salad herbs in salads, teas, butters, etc.

Schmidt, R. Marilyn
FLAVORED VINEGARS: HERB AND FRUIT (Barnegat, 1988) Recipes for 32 vinegars, plus recipes for using them; also which vinegars make the best base, how long to let them stand before using and information on vinegar facials and hair rinses.

Schneider, Elizabeth
UNCOMMON FRUITS AND VEGETABLES: A COMMONSENSE GUIDE (HarperCollins, 1990) An encyclopedic cookbook using a variety of new types of produce from arugula to yucca.

Shepherd, Renee
RECIPES FROM A KITCHEN GARDEN: VOL-
UME I (Shepherds Garden Pub., 1987) Features a
wide range of recipes using fresh vegetables and herbs
and illustrated with Mimi Osborne's beautiful drawings.
RECIPES FROM A KITCHEN GARDEN: VOL-
UME II (Shepherds Garden Pub., 1990) More wonderful things to eat and drawings to fall in love with.

Smith, Leona W.
THE FORGOTTEN ART OF FLOWER COOK-
ERY (Pelican, 1985 reprint of 1973 edition) Covers
26 flowers and includes numerous recipes for using
them.

Tatum, Billy Joe
WILD FOODS FIELD GUIDE AND COOK-
BOOK (Workman, 1985, 2nd edition) Covers 70 wild
plants and over 350 recipes for using them.

Tolley, Emelie, and Mead, Chris
COOKING WITH HERBS (Crown, 1989) Over
200 recipes and stories from the U.S. and around the
world; 350+ color photos.

Trewby, Mary
A GOURMET'S GUIDE TO HERBS AND SPICES
(HP Books, 1989) Color photos of each herb, plus over
50 recipes.

For related books, see:
THE ART OF THE KITCHEN GARDEN by
Clarke (page 101)
THE COOK'S GARDEN by Ogden (page 103)
THE GOURMET GARDEN by Holt (page 100)
THE FORGOTTEN ARTS: GROWING, GAR-
DENING AND COOKING WITH HERBS by
Bacon (page 109)
GROWING HERBS IN POTS by Brimer (page 110)
GROWING VEGETABLES AND HERBS WITH
RECIPES FOR THE FRESH HARVEST by *South-
ern Living* (page 194)
HERBS: A CONNOISSEUR'S GUIDE by Fleming
(page 111)
PRACTICAL HERB GARDENING WITH REC-
IPES by Bunch (page 110)

HERBS

The Herb Society of America, Inc. (9019 Kirtland-Chardon Road, Mentor, OH 44060) has an annual publication, *The Herbarist*. Sixty-one illustrated articles originally printed in *The Herbarist* were selected by the society staff for inclusion in *Herbs for Use and for Delight* (Dover, 1974). The society also issues a quarterly newsletter and offers book lists and library privileges.

The American Herb Association (P.O. Box 1673, Nevada City, CA 95959) offers a list of recommended herb books for $2. The director, Kathi Keville, is the author of *The Illustrated Encyclopedia of Herbs* (Bantam, 1991) and *American Country Living: Herbs* (Crescent Books, 1991).

Adams, James
LANDSCAPING WITH HERBS (Timber Press, 1987) More than 30 plans for incorporating herbs into a variety of gardens.

Andrews, Theodora
A BIBLIOGRAPHY ON HERBS, HERBAL MEDICINE, "NATURAL" FOODS, AND UNCON- **VENTIONAL MEDICAL TREATMENT** (Libraries Unlimited, 1982) Covers 749 general reference works, books and periodicals on specific topics such as growing cooking, medicinal, cosmetics, etc.

Bacon, Richard M.
THE FORGOTTEN ARTS: GROWING, GARDENING AND COOKING WITH HERBS (Yankee Books, 1972) Covers planting, growing and uses for over 35 herbs; includes numerous recipes.

Bayard, Tanya
SWEET HERBS AND SUNDRY FLOWERS: MEDIEVAL GARDENS AND THE GARDENS OF THE CLOISTERS (Godine, 1986)

Beale, Galen, and Boswell, Mary Rose
THE EARTH SHALL BLOSSOM: SHAKER HERBS AND GARDENING (The Countryman Press, 1991) How to create a Shaker garden of flowering herbs, tea herbs, fragrance herbs and culinary

herbs; includes descriptions of restored Shaker gardens.

Beston, Henry
HERBS AND THE EARTH: AN EVOCATIVE EXCURSION INTO THE LORE AND LEGEND OF OUR COMMON HERBS (Godine, 1990) Reprint of a 1935 classic book on herbs filled with how-to information, folklore and history.

Bonar, Ann
THE MACMILLAN TREASURY OF HERBS: A COMPLETE GUIDE TO THE CULTIVATION AND USE OF WILD AND DOMESTICATED HERBS (Macmillan, 1985) Describes and illustrates 59 herbs with history, cultivation, medicinal and cooking information.

Bonar, Ann, and MacCarthy, Daphne
HOW TO GROW AND USE HERBS (Beekman Publishing, 1980) Introduction to herbs with basic information on planning, cultivating, harvesting, preserving, storing and using.

Bremness, Lesley
THE COMPLETE BOOK OF HERBS: A PRACTICAL GUIDE TO GROWING AND USING HERBS (Viking, 1988) Over 250 full color photos with growing information covering over 100 herbs; advice on garden design, craft ideas, recipes, health use and much more.
HERBS (RD Association, 1990) Growing, harvesting, preserving; culinary, cosmetic and medicinal uses for 90 herbs.
WORLD OF HERBS: RECIPES, REMEDIES AND DECORATIVE IDEAS (Trafalgar Square, 1990) Examines history, folklore and getting good results from an herb garden, plus how to use the herbs' seeds, leaves, flowers, roots and essential oils in a variety of ways.

Brimer, John Burton
GROWING HERBS IN POTS (Simon & Schuster, 1976) In-depth planting information and numerous recipes for basil, chives, dill, sweet marjoram, mint, oregano, parsley, rosemary, sage, tarragon and thyme.

Brooklyn Botanic Garden
CULINARY HERBS (BBG #98) How to select, grow, propagate, harvest, freeze and dry culinary herbs.
HERBS AND COOKING (BBG #122) Placement and ornamental uses of herbs; includes recipes.
HERBS AND THEIR ORNAMENTAL USES (BBG #68) A guide to using herbs to provide color, texture and interest (e.g., as border plants).

Bunch, Bryan H.
PRACTICAL HERB GARDENING WITH RECIPES (TAB Books, 1984) History and advice on organically growing and using the 25 most useful herbs.

Clarkson, Rosetta
GREEN ENCHANTMENT: THE MAGIC AND HISTORY OF HERBS AND GARDEN MAKING (Macmillan, 1991) Covers medicinal and magical herbs, witches and monastery gardens, cooking with herbs and early gardening tools; a reprint of the 1940 classic.
HERBS: THEIR CULTURE AND USES (Macmillan, 1990) New edition of a 1942 classic on growing 101 herbs, plus information on garden design, growing herbs indoors and using herbs in a variety of ways.
MAGIC GARDENS: A MODERN CHRONICLE OF HERBS AND SAVORY SEEDS (Collier Books, 1992) First issued in 1939, it covers herbal medicine and magic, garden mazes, directions for making lavender, rosemary and mint sachets, and a list of her 20 favorite culinary herbs and their uses.

Courtier, Jane
HERBS: GARDENING BY DESIGN (Sterling, 1987) General advice on gardening with herbs, plus specifics on 40 of the best herbs to grow; includes cooking, medicinal and cosmetic recipes.

Crockett, James U.; Tanner, Ogden; and Editors of Time-Life Books
HERBS (Time-Life Books, 1977)

Cullum, Elizabeth
A COTTAGE HERBAL (David & Charles, 1975) Covers making an herb garden, harvesting and drying, culinary herbs, country wines and herbal teas, natural dyes from herbs, and medicinal and cosmetic uses.

D'Andrea, Jeanne
ANCIENT HERBS IN THE J. PAUL GETTY
MUSEUM (J. P. Getty Trust, 1989)

Elbert, Virginie and George A.
FUN WITH GROWING HERBS INDOORS
(Crown, 1974) A good book for those without yard
space or who prefer indoor gardening.

Fell, Derek
ESSENTIAL HERBS: THE 100 BEST FOR DE-
SIGN AND CULTIVATION (Crescent, 1989)
Plant descriptions, uses, growing information and
planning an herb garden.

Felton, Elise
ARTISTICALLY CULTIVATED HERBS
(Woodbridge Press, 1990) How to make a herbal topiary, bonsai, windowbox, hanging basket, strawberry jar
and more.

Fleming, Susan
HERBS: A CONNOISSEUR'S GUIDE (Crown,
1990) Covers growing, harvesting, identifying, cooking with herbs (129 recipes), herbal remedies and
cosmetics.

Forsell, Mary
HEIRLOOM HERBS: USING OLD-FASH-
IONED HERBS IN GARDENS, RECIPES, AND
DECORATIONS (Random House, 1991) Covers
the planting of 45 antique herbs, plus a history of herb
gardens, and past and present uses of herbs in cooking,
cleaning, scents and medicine.

Foster, Gertrude B.
HERBS FOR EVERY GARDEN (Dutton, 1966)
Includes growing information, cooking with herbs and
projects using herbs; she and her husband developed
the Laurel Hill Herb Farm in New Jersey and started
The Herb Grower Magazine.

Foster, Gertrude B., and Louden, Rosemary F.
PARK'S SUCCESS WITH HERBS (Park Seed Co.,
1980) This mother-daughter team have compiled one
of the best books on growing herbs from seeds; includes
color photos of both the seedlings and the mature
plants.

Fox, Helen Morgenthau
GARDENING WITH HERBS FOR FLAVOR
AND FRAGRANCE (Dover, 1972) Reprint of the
1933 edition; how to prepare the soil, grow 68 herbs,
harvest, and store; includes over 60 recipes, legends,
more.
THE YEARS IN MY HERB GARDEN (Macmillan,
1953)

Freeman, Sally
HERBS FOR ALL SEASONS: GROWING AND
GATHERING HERBS FOR FLAVOR, HEALTH
AND BEAUTY (Penguin, 1991) How to set up a
kitchen pharmacy, cooking with herbs, herbal cosmetics, herbal fragrance and information on growing
herbs.

Garden Way Publishing Editors
HERBS: 1001 QUESTIONS ANSWERED (Sto-
rey, 1990) Expert advice in a question and answer
format.

Garland, Sarah
THE COMPLETE BOOK OF HERBS AND
SPICES (Viking, 1979) Covers approximately 300
herbs and spices.
THE HERB GARDEN: A COMPLETE ILLUS-
TRATED GUIDE TO GROWING AND USING
SCENTED, CULINARY AND MEDICINAL
HERBS (Penguin, 1984) Includes garden design
ideas.

Genders, Roy
GROWING HERBS AS AROMATICS: POMAN-
DERS, POTPOURRIS AND PERFUMES (Keats,
1977) Covers growing, propagating, harvesting, drying
and storing fragrant herbs.

Gerard, John
THE HERBAL OR GENERAL HISTORY OF
PLANTS (Dover, 1975) A revised and enlarged edition of the 1633 book from which modern English
herbals are derived; a huge work.

Gibbons, Euell
STALKING THE HEALTHFUL HERBS (Hood,
1989) How to find wild plants; this is a reprint of an
earlier edition.

Gilbertie, Sal
HERB GARDENING AT ITS BEST: EVERY-THING YOU NEED TO KNOW ABOUT GROWING 200 HERBS (Macmillan, 1978) A good introduction by the owner of Gilbertie's Herb Farm in Connecticut; for the person just getting started growing herbs.
KITCHEN HERBS: THE ART AND ENJOY-MENT OF GROWING HERBS AND COOKING WITH THEM (Bantam, 1988) How to create a kitchen herb garden, plus recipes for using fresh and dried herbs.

Greig, Denise
THE BOOK OF MINT (ISBS, 1989) Covers a variety of mints with information on growing, preserving, drying and extracting the oil; includes recipes for using mint as a flavoring and a fragrance and for medicinal purposes.

Grieve, Margaret
A MODERN HERBAL (Dover, 1971, two volumes) An alphabetized encyclopedia giving botanical data, medical properties, folklore, etc.; originally published in 1931.

Hale, Beatrice, and Hinds, Elizabeth
THE TWENTY-FIVE HERB BOOK (ISBS, no date) Information on and recipes using the 25 most popular culinary herbs.

Hemphill, John and Rosemary
HERBS: THEIR CULTIVATION AND USAGE (Sterling, 1984) Includes herbal remedies, recipes and information on growing herbs.

Holt, Geraldene
GERALDENE HOLT'S COMPLETE BOOK OF HERBS (Henry Holt, 1992) Covers the history, cultivation and use of herbs in seasonings, cosmetics and medicines.

Hopkinson, Simon and Judith
HERBS (Globe Pequot, 1989) A variety of designs for herb gardens, plus using herbs in cooking and medicine.

Houdret, Jessica
HERB GARDENING: STEP BY STEP TO GROWING SUCCESS (Trafalgar Square, 1992) Guide to growing a wide variety of common and exotic herbs.

Jacobs, Betty E. M.
GROWING AND USING HERBS SUCCESS-FULLY (Garden Way, 1981) How to grow, harvest and use herbs; includes marketing tips for selling herbs and herbal products (this is an updated version of her *Profitable Herb Growing At Home*).

Kirkpatrick, Debra
USING HERBS IN THE LANDSCAPE: HOW TO DESIGN AND GROW GARDENS OF HERBAL ANNUALS, PERENNIALS, SHRUBS AND TREES (Stackpole, 1992) Growing information and culinary and medicinal uses for a variety of herbs, plus lists of herbs arranged by climate and site, and over 20 plans with emphasis on incorporating an herb garden into a total landscape plan.

Kowalchik, Claire, and Hylton, William (editors)
RODALE'S ILLUSTRATED ENCYCLOPEDIA OF HERBS (Rodale Press, 1987) A great A to Z reference book covering over 150 herbs, plus history, lore, growing, uses and storage.

Kraska, Martha E.
HERBS (Prentice-Hall, 1992) Descriptions, culinary uses and cultural requirements of over 65 herb varieties; includes information on companion planting and herb garden design.

Kreuter, Marie-Luise
THE MACMILLAN BOOK OF NATURAL HERB GARDENING (Macmillan, 1985) How to plant, care for, harvest and preserve almost 70 herbs; includes herbal history and recipes.

Lathrop, Norma Jean
HERBS: HOW TO SELECT, GROW AND ENJOY (HP Books, 1981) A great introduction to growing, harvesting, storing, and using over 200 herbs; includes over 400 color photos.

Leyel, Mrs. C. F.
HERBAL DELIGHTS: TISANES, SYRUPS, CONFECTIONS, ELECTUARIES, ROBS, JULEPS, VINEGARS AND CONSERVES (Faber & Faber, 1987) Originally issued in 1937, and revised in 1947, this is a reprint of the later edition.

Loewenfeld, Claire
HERB GARDENING: WHY AND HOW TO GROW HERBS (Faber & Faber, 1989) Complete information on 47 varieties; covers indoor and outdoor growing and using herbs.

Loewenfeld, Claire, and Back, Philippa
THE COMPLETE BOOK OF HERBS AND SPICES (David & Charles, 1978, revised edition) Detailed descriptions of over 100 herbs and spices.

Lust, John (editor)
THE HERB BOOK (Bantam, 1983) Information on a large variety of medicinal herbs.

Lyte, Charles
HERB GARDEN (Oxford Illustrated, 1986) Encyclopedia of medicinal and culinary herbs.

Mabey, Richard, and McIntyre, Michael (editors)
THE NEW AGE HERBALIST (Macmillan, 1988) Using herbs for body care, relaxation, house care, nutrition and healing; over 200 herbs are illustrated in the glossary.

McLeod, Judyth
LAVENDER, SWEET LAVENDER (ISBS, 1989) Covers botanical information along with culinary, fragrance and craft uses.

McRae, Bobbi A.
THE HERB COMPANION WISHBOOK AND RESOURCE GUIDE (Interweave Press, 1992) Over 1,000 herbal mail-order sources for plants, seeds, magazines, books and newsletters; plus information on classes, festivals, public gardens with herb collections, organizations and much more.

Miloradovich, Milo
GROWING AND USING HERBS AND SPICES (Dover, 1986) A handbook of growing and using all the herbs and spices common to North America.

Moos, Elayne
HERB GARDENER'S MAIL ORDER SOURCE BOOK (Woodsong Graphics, 1987) An annotated list of over 150 sources.

Oliver, Paula
HERB RESOURCE DIRECTORY (Northwind Farm Publications, Rt 2, Box 246, Shevlin, MN 56676, 218-657-2478) The 1990–91 edition is a source book of over 800 herb sources and resources for hobbyists and businesses; includes resources in Canada, Australia, Great Britain and New Zealand.

Oster, Maggie
FLOWERING HERBS: FRESH HERBS FOR THE GARDEN AND HOME (Longmeadow Press, 1991)

Parkinson, John
A GARDEN OF PLEASANT FLOWERS: PARADISI IN SOLE PARADISUS (Dover, 1991) Complete and unabridged edition of the famous 1629 English herbal.

Paterson, Allen
HERBS IN THE GARDEN (Dent, 1985) A large amount of cultural information, garden design and culinary uses.

Phillips, Roger, and Foy, Nicky
THE RANDOM HOUSE BOOK OF HERBS (Random House, 1990) Covers over 400 species of herbs (culinary, scented, medicinal, etc.)

Prenis, John
THE WINDOWSILL HERB GARDEN (Running Press, 1990) Twenty-five culinary herbs and recipes.

Reid, Shirley
HERBS FOR THE HOME AND GARDEN: A PRACTICAL STEP-BY-STEP GUIDE (HarperCollins, 1991) A beginner's guide covering all the well-known herbs plus the less known but available ones.

Reppert, Bertha
A HERITAGE OF HERBS: HISTORY, EARLY GARDENING AND OLD RECIPES (Stackpole Books, 1976) Describes over 230 native American herbs plus information on five types of colonial herb gardens (kitchen, bee, apothecary, dyer, sentimental); includes recipes.

Rinzler, Carol Ann
THE COMPLETE BOOK OF HERBS, SPICES AND CONDIMENTS: FROM GARDEN TO KITCHEN TO MEDICINE CHEST (Facts On File, 1990) Nutritional value, chemical constituents, medicinal benefits, various uses and possible side effects of over 100 entries.

Rogers, Barbara R.
FRESH HERBS: OVER 100 USES FOR GROW-ING, COOKING, COSMETICS, AND GARDEN DESIGN (Gallery Books, 1990) Includes hydroponic and indoor gardening.

Rohde, Eleanour Sinclair
A GARDEN OF HERBS (Dover, 1969) Includes instructions for making teas, pies, syrups, conserves, wines and perfumes.
HERBS AND HERB GARDENING (Gale Re-search, 1976) A good beginner's guide from the En-glish herb authority.
THE OLD ENGLISH HERBALS (Dover, 1989) Herbal information culled from numerous rare sources.

Rose, Jeanne
JEANNE ROSE'S HERBAL STUDIES COURSE: A COMPLETE HOME STUDY HERB COURSE (Jeanne Rose, 1988) Divided into three volumes: me-dicinal, seasonal and reference herbals.
JEANNE ROSE'S MODERN HERBAL (Putnam, 1987)

Shaudys, Phyllis V.
THE PLEASURE OF HERBS: A MONTH-BY-MONTH GUIDE TO GROWING, USING, AND ENJOYING HERBS (Garden Way, 1986) Perfect for the beginner; includes over 165 recipes and 150 craft ideas.

Silverman, Maida
CITY HERBAL (Godine, 1990)

Simmons, Adelma Grenier
HERB GARDENING IN FIVE SEASONS (Dutton, 1977) Winter, spring, summer, autumn and Christmas herbs are covered.
HERB GARDENS OF DELIGHT: WITH PLANTS FOR EVERY MOOD AND PURPOSE (Hawthorn Books, 1974) Covers the basics of making an herb garden, then details gardens that emphasize fragrance, culinary,

decorative, Shakespearean, medicinal uses, dyes and religion; includes plans for each type.
HERBS THROUGH THE SEASONS AT CAPRILANDS (Rodale Press, 1987) Based on her many years of experience of growing and using herbs at her herb farm in Coventry, Connecticut.
A MERRY CHRISTMAS HERBAL (Morrow, 1976) Filled with legend, ideas for decorations, recipes, and gifts and planting instructions for your Christmas garden of 36 herbs; also a description of Caprilands at Christmas.

Simon, James E.; Chadwick, Alena F; and Croker, Lyle E.
HERBS: AN INDEXED BIBLIOGRAPHY 1971-1980 (Archon Books, 1984) An in-depth tool for further study and research by serious herbalists.

Stevenson, Violet
GROWING HERBS SUCCESSFULLY (Tiger, 1989) Covers cultivation, propagation, harvesting, drying and preserving 50 herbs.

Streep, Peg
A GIFT OF HERBS: AN ILLUSTRATED GAR-DEN IN MINIATURE (Viking, 1991) History, lore and use for 60 herbs.

Stuart, Malcolm (editor)
THE ENCYCLOPEDIA OF HERBS AND HERBALISM (Grosset & Dunlap, 1979) Describes 420 herbs with botanical profiles, habitats, methods of culti-vation and uses in medicine, cooking, cosmetics, etc.

Sunset
HERBS: AN ILLUSTRATED GUIDE (Sunset Books, 1972) Describes the different varieties of herbs, and how to landscape and cook with them.

Swanson, Faith H., and Rady, Virginia B.
HERB GARDEN DESIGN (University Press of New England, 1984) Plans and installation information for 51 herb gardens.

Swindells, Philip
HARLOW CAR BOOK OF HERB GARDENING (Trafalgar Square, 1988) How to grow a wide variety of herbs.

Taylor's
POCKET GUIDE TO HERBS AND EDIBLE FLOWERS (Houghton Mifflin, 1990) Color photos and descriptions of 79 of the most popular herbs and edible flowers.

Titterington, Rosemary
GROWING HERBS: A GUIDE TO MANAGEMENT (Trafalgar Square, 1991) How to create an herb garden as well as set up a small herb business.

Tolley, Emelie, and Mead, Chris
HERBS: GARDENS, DECORATIONS AND RECIPES (Clarkson Potter, 1985) A best-seller with over 400 color photographs on all types of herb gardens and the wonderful products that come from them; includes sources.

Vickers, Lois, and Norfolk Lavender Co. Staff
THE SCENTED LAVENDER BOOK (Little, Brown, 1991) Choosing the plants, growing, extracting the oil, drying and using lavender, plus the book itself is scented. Note: You can receive a catalogue of Norfolk Lavender's many products (excluding plants) by calling 800-886-0050.

Weiss, Gaea and Shandor
GROWING AND USING THE HEALING HERBS (Rodale Press, 1985) How to grow and use herbs for simple medicinal purposes.

Woodward, Marcus (editor)
LEAVES FROM GERARD'S HERBAL (Dover, 1969) Selections from the most famous of English herbals.

Zabar, Abbie
THE POTTED HERB (Stewart, Tabori & Chang, 1988) Growing herbs in containers, herbal topiary, recipes and ideas for unusual ways to use herbs (e.g. herb-scented ink and herbal incense).

For related books, see:
THE BUSINESS OF HERBS by Northwind Farm (page 186)
COOKING WITH HERBS by Tolley and Mead (page 108)

COUNTRY WREATHS FROM CAPRILANDS by Simmons (page 140)
CULINARY AND SALAD HERBS by Rohde (page 107)
ENGLISH HERB GARDENS by Cooper and Taylor (page 205)
GIFTS FROM THE HERB GARDEN by Tolley and Mead (page 132)
THE HARROWSMITH ILLUSTRATED BOOK OF HERBS by Lima (page 191)
HERBAL GIFTS by Sheen (page 132)
HERBAL TREASURES by Shaudys (page 132)
THE HERB GARDEN COOKBOOK by Hutson (page 106)
HERB GARDENING IN TEXAS by Meltzer (page 196)
HERBS AND FLOWERS OF THE COTTAGE GARDEN by Wilkinson (page 162)
HERBS AND HERB GARDENS OF BRITAIN by Peplow (page 207)
IN AN HERB GARDEN by Carter (page 2)
THE NEW ENGLAND HERB GARDENER by Turcotte (page 192)
ODENA'S TEXAS HERB BOOK by Conrad and Murray (page 195)
OLD TIME HERBS FOR NORTHERN GARDENS by Kamm (page 191)
ORIENTAL HERBS AND VEGETABLES by the Brooklyn Botanic Garden (page150)
PROFITS FROM YOUR BACKYARD HERB GARDEN by Sturdivant (page 186)
RECIPES FROM A FRENCH HERB GARDEN by Holt (page 106)
THE SAGE COTTAGE HERB GARDEN COOKBOOK by Norris (page 107)
SOUTHERN HERB GROWING by Hill and Barclay (page 193)
SPEAKING OF HERBS by Wold (page 186)
SUMMER HERBAL DELIGHTS by Richardson (page 107)
TEXAS GARDENER'S GUIDE TO GROWING AND USING HERBS by Sitton (page 196)

INDOOR GARDENING

GENERAL REFERENCES

The Indoor Gardening Society of America (5305 S.W. Hamilton Street, Portland, OR 97221) is for people interested in growing plants on windowsills, under lights or in greenhouses. It publishes a bimonthly newsletter.

Brookes, John
THE INDOOR GARDEN BOOK (Crown, 1986) Covers how to use houseplants, cut and dried flowers, containers and much more to enhance a home's interior; 750 color photos and illustrations.

Cervantes, George
GARDENING INDOORS WITH HIGH INTENSITY DISCHARGE LAMPS (Interport USA, 1986) How to grow plants, flowers and vegetables year-round using high-intensity discharge lamps.

Cruso, Thalassa
MAKING THINGS GROW: A PRACTICAL GUIDE FOR THE INDOOR GARDENER (Lyons & Burford, 1989) An excellent how-to book for succeeding with all types of indoor plants and herbs.

Dale, John
THE NEW INDOOR LIGHT GARDEN (Hartley & Marks, 1992) How to grow plants and flowers year-round under ordinary lights.

Elbert, Virginie and George A.
FUN WITH TERRARIUM GARDENING (Crown, 1973) Construction of different types of terrariums, selection of plants and care for the terrarium.

Fitch, Charles M.
THE COMPLETE BOOK OF TERRARIUMS (Hawthorn Books, 1974) How to construct a terrarium and select the plants to create a miniature garden.

Halpin, Anne M. (editor)
RODALE'S ENCYCLOPEDIA OF INDOOR GARDENING (Rodale Press, 1980) Presenting organic methods, this book focuses on houseplants, herbs, bulbs, bonsai, terrariums, greenhouses and more.

Heitz, Halina
INDOOR PLANTS (Barron, 1991) Advice and 500 color photos.

Kayatta, Ken, and Schmidt, Steven
SUCCESSFUL TERRARIUMS: A STEP-BY-STEP
GUIDE (Houghton Mifflin, 1975) Covers construction basics, plus information on animals and terrariums for children.

Loewer, Peter
BRINGING THE OUTDOORS IN: HOW TO DO
WONDERS WITH VINES, WILDFLOWERS,
FERNS, MOSSES, BULBS, CACTI, AND DOZ-
ENS OF OTHER PLANTS MOST PEOPLE OVER-
LOOK (Walker, 1974) Also includes information on building a window greenhouse and sources of supply.

Maddocks, Cheryl
GROWING INDOOR PLANTS (ISBS, 1987)
Color photos and instructions on selection, propagation, care and maintenance.

Martin, Tovah
THE ESSENCE OF PARADISE: FRAGRANT
PLANTS FOR INDOOR GARDENING (Little,
Brown, 1991) If the plant has a scent (not all are pleasant), you will learn how to grow and care for it.

Murphy, Wendy B., and Editors of Time-Life Books
GARDENING UNDER LIGHTS (Time-Life
Books, 1978) Basic information on how to garden under lights, propagation, plus descriptions, color photos and growing information on a wide variety of plants suitable for light gardening.

Peter, Ruth M.
BULB MAGIC IN YOUR WINDOW (Morrow,
1975) How to force bulbs.

Simmons, Marion H.
GROWING ACACIAS (ISBS, 1988) Describes over 350 species with information on selecting, planting and propagating.

Simpson, Norman D.
THE INSTANT GUIDE TO HEALTHY INDOOR
BULBS AND ANNUALS (Times Books, 1985)
Covers caring for 33 popular plants, what can go wrong and how to make the plants healthy again.

Spoczynska, Joy
THE INDOOR KITCHEN GARDEN (Harper-
Collins, 1989)

Walker, Marian C.
FLOWERING BULBS FOR WINTER WINDOWS
(Van Nostrand, 1965) How to force tulips, narcissi, hyacinths, and a variety of other bulbs into bloom.

Wright, Michael, and Brown, Dennis (editors)
THE COMPLETE INDOOR GARDENER (Random House, 1979) Fourteen experts cover 110 topics on all phases of indoor gardening.

For related books, see:
FUN WITH GROWING HERBS INDOORS by
Elbert and Elbert (page 111)
THE INDOOR VEGETABLE GARDEN by
Spoczynska (page 103)
PARADISE CONTAINED by Stites et al. (page 91)
WILDFLOWERS ON THE WINDOWSILL by
Hitchcock (page 95)
THE WINDOWSILL HERB GARDEN by Prenis
(page 113)

HOUSEPLANTS

Baker, Jerry
JERRY BAKER'S HAPPY, HEALTHY HOUSE-
PLANTS (Plume, 1985) Covers growing requirements for 130 of the most popular houseplants and includes information on greenhouse growing, holiday plants, African violets, orchids, terrariums and more.

Beckett, Kenneth
THE HOUSEPLANT LIBRARY SERIES (Salem
House, 1989) Each volume contains a description, growing information and a color photo for 80 unusual plants:
  FRAGRANT PLANTS—Describes jasmine, freesia, heliotrope, hyacinth and many others.
  PLANTS FOR SHADY CORNERS—Flowering and foliage plants that do best away from windows.
  PLANTS FOR SUNNY WINDOWS—Flowering plants that do best in direct sunlight.
  PLANTS FOR WARM ROOMS—Plants from the tropics and subtropics.
THE RHS ENCYCLOPEDIA OF HOUSE PLANTS
INCLUDING GREENHOUSE PLANTS (Salem
House, 1987) Alphabetized descriptions, flowering season, temperature and other needs for 4,000 houseplants; 1,000 color photos.

Better Homes and Gardens Editors
THE NEW HOUSEPLANTS BOOK (Meredith Books, 1990)

Bromeliad Society of Australia
GROWING BROMELIADS (ISBS, 1989) Basic information on the cultivation of bromeliads.

Brookes, John (editor)
HOUSEPLANTS (RD Home Handbook) (RD Association, 1990) Excellent resource covering 120 flowering and foliage houseplants, cacti and bulbs; 152 detailed diagrams and 284 color photos.

Brooklyn Botanic Garden
INDOOR GARDENING (BBG #112) How to select, maintain and arrange houseplants in a home or office.

Chvisoli, Alessandro, and Boriani, Maria
SIMON & SCHUSTER'S GUIDE TO HOUSEPLANTS (Simon & Schuster, 1987)

Conder, Susan
TERENCE CONRAN'S DECORATING WITH PLANTS (Little, Brown, 1986) How to use plants to enhance an attractive room, add a focal point to dull rooms or downplay a room's unattractive features.

Crockett, James Underwood
CROCKETT'S INDOOR GARDEN (Little, Brown, 1978) Month-by-month coverage on growing houseplants.

Crockett, James Underwood, and Editors of Time-Life Books
FLOWERING HOUSEPLANTS (Henry Holt, 1986) How to choose, care for, and decorate with 145 flowering houseplants; reprint of 1971 edition.
FOLIAGE HOUSEPLANTS (Henry Holt, 1986) How to choose, care for, and decorate with over 250 foliage houseplants; reprint of 1972 edition.

Davidson, William
EXOTIC FLOWERING HOUSEPLANTS (HP Books, 1990) General information and blooming tips for 75 plants grouped by difficulty of care (easy, moderate, difficult).

EXOTIC FOLIAGE HOUSEPLANTS (HP Books, 1990) General care information on 75 foliage houseplants grouped as easy, moderate or difficult to grow.
THE HOUSEPLANT SURVIVAL MANUAL (Ward Lock, 1988) Covers care, enviroment, climate control, areas of risk, treatment and cures for over 50 popular houseplants.
AN ILLUSTRATED GUIDE TO FOLIAGE HOUSEPLANTS (Arco, 1982) How to grow 150 easy-care foliage houseplants.
AN ILLUSTRATED GUIDE TO FLOWERING HOUSEPLANTS (Arco, 1981) Features 150 plants to grow for year–round color in your home.

Derrick, Tony
HARDY HOUSEPLANTS (Chartwell, 1988) Emphasizes houseplants that are interesting and beautiful but do not need pampering; covers care, pest control, environment, self-watering pots and more.

Elbert, George and Virginie
FOLIAGE PLANTS FOR DECORATING INDOORS: PLANTS, DESIGN, MAINTENANCE FOR HOMES, OFFICES AND INTERIOR GARDENS (Timber Press, 1989) Discusses the plants' needs and how to best use them decoratively.
THE MIRACLE HOUSEPLANTS: THE GESNERIAD FAMILY (Crown, 1984) Excellent introduction to identifying and growing the numerous plants in this family that includes African violets and gloxinias.
PLANTS THAT REALLY BLOOM INDOORS (Simon & Schuster, 1974) Descriptions, illustrations and detailed growing information on all kinds of flowering tropicals.

Everett, Thomas H.
ONE HUNDRED AND ONE FLOWERING HOUSE PLANTS ANYONE CAN GROW (Fawcett, 1975)

Faust, Joan
THE N.Y. TIMES BOOK OF HOUSE PLANTS (Random House, 1983) A good introductory manual covering over 100 houseplants.

Fitch, Charles M.
THE COMPLETE BOOK OF HOUSEPLANTS
(Hawthorn Books, 1972) Information on over 1,000
plants, plus the basics of caring for houseplants.

Garden Way Editors
FLOWERING HOUSEPLANTS (Longmeadow
Press, 1990)

Gilbert, Richard
200 HOUSEPLANTS ANYONE CAN GROW:
HOW TO GROW AND WHERE TO PLACE THE
BEST OF TODAY'S FOOLPROOF HOUSE-
PLANTS (HP Books, 1988) Includes guides to selecting, growing and watering, plus a color photo of
each plant.

Gough, Tom
THE INSTANT GUIDE TO HEALTHY FLOW-
ERING HOUSEPLANTS: VOLUME II (Times
Books, 1985) Covers 33 popular species, what goes
wrong and how to fix it.

Graf, Dr. Alfred B.
EXOTIC HOUSEPLANTS (Macmillan, 1976, 10th
edition)

Hamilton, David L.
THE ART OF HIGH-TECH WATERING
(Hamilton's Publishing, 1986) How to determine a
plant's water requirements based on its age and height,
the size of the container and the amount of light it
receives.
MAINTENANCE TECHNIQUES FOR INTE-
RIOR PLANTS (Hamilton's Publishing, 1986) Pre-
cise information on when to water, how much to water
and how to tell when a plant is either over- or under-
watered.

Hamilton, Patricia
THE ABC'S OF INDOOR FICUS TREES (New
Leaf, 1991) Small pamphlet with detailed information on light, air, water and nutrient needs, plus signs
of trouble.

Hay, Roy; McQuown, F. R.; and Beckett, G. K.
THE DICTIONARY OF HOUSE PLANTS (Mc-
Graw-Hill, 1974) Description, color photo and infor-
mation on the care of approximately 500 plants.

Herwig, Rob
THE GOOD HOUSEKEEPING ENCYCLOPEDIA
OF HOUSE PLANTS (Hearst Books, 1990)
GROWING BEAUTIFUL HOUSEPLANTS: AN
ILLUSTRATED GUIDE TO THE SELECTION
AND CARE OF MORE THAN 1,000 VARIETIES
(Facts On File, 1992) A total reference describing the
characteristics of each plant and its needs for light, tem-
perature, water, humidity and soil; includes information
on ideal location, propagation and selecting the ideal
plant and contains over 1,200 color photos.
HOW TO GROW HEALTHY HOUSEPLANTS
(HP Books, 1979) Describes and gives growing infor-
mation for over 600 common and exotic houseplants;
over 350 color photos.

Herwig, Rob, and Schubert, Margot
THE TREASURY OF HOUSEPLANTS (Macmillan, 1979)

Hessayon, Dr. D. G.
THE GOLD PLATED HOUSE PLANT EXPERT
(Century, 1989) An enlarged edition of *The New
Houseplant Expert*, this details growing information for
over 1,000 houseplants.
THE INDOOR PLANT SPOTTER (Sterling,
1990) How to identify a plant when you don't know
what it is; over 400 color photos and over 700 color
drawings.
THE NEW HOUSEPLANT EXPERT (Sterling,
1990) Best-seller covering the care of flowering and
foliage houseplants and cacti.

James, Ross
GROWING HOUSEPLANTS IN TEMPERATE
AND COOL CLIMATES (ISBS, 1988) Covers plant
selection; watering; feeding; requirements for light,
heat and humidity; repotting; propagation; pests and
diseases; and flowering times.

Kramer, Jack
BROMELIADS (Harper & Row, 1981) Illustrations
and general growing information, plus specifics on the
different genera.
AN ILLUSTRATED GUIDE TO FLOWERING
HOUSEPLANTS: HOW TO ENJOY YEAR-
ROUND COLOUR IN YOUR HOME, FEATUR-
ING 150 PLANTS (Routledge Press, 1981)

Loewer, Peter
THE INDOOR WINDOW GARDEN (Contemporary Books, 1990) A selection of 50 unusual plants to grow indoors with cultivation information on each.

Martin, Tovah
ONCE UPON A WINDOWSILL: A HISTORY OF INDOOR PLANTS (Timber Press, 1989) How and why plants moved indoors during the Victorian age, plus practical information on houseplants.

McDonald, Elvin (editor)
THE COLOR HANDBOOK OF HOUSE PLANTS (Hawthorn Books, 1975) Describes and gives growing requirements for 250 houseplants.

Mott, Russell
THE TOTAL BOOK OF HOUSE PLANTS (Delacorte Press, 1975) Cultural information plus paintings for 350 indoor plants.

Ortho
ALL ABOUT HOUSEPLANTS (Ortho, 1982)
ORTHO'S COMPLETE GUIDE TO SUCCESSFUL HOUSEPLANTS (Ortho, 1984)

Padilla, Victoria
BROMELIADS (Crown, 1986) A standard reference work covering the various genera and species most often found in cultivation.

Rapp, Joel
MR. MOTHER EARTH'S MOST REWARDING HOUSEPLANTS (Ballantine, 1989) Discusses needs and care requirements for hundreds of exotic foliage and flowering plants.

Rapp, Lynn and Joel
MOTHER EARTH'S HASSLE-FREE INDOOR PLANT BOOK (Fawcett, 1990)

Rauh, Werner
THE BROMELIAD LEXICON (Sterling, 1991) One of the world's leading authorities on bromeliads describes cultivation, propagation, pest and disease control for every type of bromeliad; includes a special section on forcing blooms, plus over 300 photos and illustrations.

Reader's Digest
SUCCESS WITH HOUSE PLANTS (RD Association, 1979) A comprehensive manual examining most of the plants that do well indoors.

Seddon, George
THE ESSENTIAL GUIDE TO PERFECT HOUSE PLANTS (Summit Books, 1985)

Solit, Karen and Jim
KEEP YOUR GIFT PLANTS THRIVING: A COMPLETE GUIDE TO PLANT SURVIVAL (Storey, 1985) Covers light, moisture, fertilizer and temperature requirements, plus pruning, propagation and planting the gift plant outdoors.

Stevenson, Violet
INDOOR PLANTS (Arco, 1980) Covers over 150 foliage and flowering plants, ferns, palms, cacti and succulents and indoor bulbs.
PLANTS AND FLOWERS IN THE HOME (Longmeadow Press, 1975) How to choose and care for houseplants, plus flower arranging, dish and bottle gardens and more.

Sunset
DECORATING WITH HOUSE PLANTS (Sunset Books, 1988) Display ideas, tips on plant care and a guide for choosing the best plants.
HOUSE PLANTS A-Z: HOW TO CHOOSE, GROW AND DISPLAY (Sunset, 1983, 4th edition) Over 130 color photos of popular houseplants with information on caring for and displaying the plants.

Taloumis, George
HOUSEPLANTS FOR FIVE EXPOSURES (Signet Books, 1975)

Taylor's
GUIDE TO HOUSEPLANTS (Houghton Mifflin, 1987) Description, color photos, and growing information for 322 houseplants divided into seven categories: hanging plants, small foliage plants, orchids, bromeliads and flowering plants, showy foliage, lacy leaves and cacti/succulents.

Time-Life
FLOWERING HOUSEPLANTS: GARDENER'S GUIDE SERIES (Time-Life Books, 1990)

FOLIAGE HOUSEPLANTS: GARDENER'S GUIDE SERIES (Time-Life Books, 1988)

Titchmarsh, Alan
THE LAROUSSE GUIDE TO HOUSE PLANTS (Larousse, 1982) Arranges the most common houseplants by family in order to simplify identification; includes 350 colored drawings.

Toogood, Alan
DESIGNING WITH HOUSEPLANTS (Smithmark, 1990) General information on choosing and caring for houseplants, plus how to develop a color scheme encompassing both flowering and foliage plants.

Wall, Bill
BROMELIADS (Wisley Handbook) (Sterling, 1990) General care information plus detailed advice for specifically recommended plants.

Williams, Barry E., and Hodgson, Ian (editors)
GROWING BROMELIADS (Timber Press, 1990) Discusses appearance, habitat, growing requirements and care needed for all the major genera.

For related books, see:
BEGONIAS AS HOUSE PLANTS by Kramer (page 93)
ORCHIDS AS HOUSE PLANTS by Northen (page 128)
ORCHIDS AS HOUSE PLANTS by Ritterhausen (page 128)
PLANTS PLUS by Seddon and Bicknell (page 79)

GREENHOUSES

Bartholomew, Alexander
CONSERVATORIES, GREENHOUSES AND GARDEN ROOMS (Holt, Rinehart & Winston, 1985) A complete step-by-step guide to design, construction, planting and maintenance.

Brooklyn Botanic Garden
GREENHOUSES AND GARDEN ROOMS (BBG #116) How to control temperature, humidity, air circulation; how to shade your plants in a freestanding greenhouse, window greenhouse, conservatory or solar greenhouse; includes information on orchid greenhouses.

Eaton, Jerome
GARDENING UNDER GLASS: AN ILLUSTRATED GUIDE TO THE GREENHOUSE (Macmillan, 1973) Guide for the beginner covering types, construction and management of greenhouses.

Edwards, Jonathan
GREENHOUSE GARDENING: STEP BY STEP TO GROWING SUCCESS (Trafalgar Square, 1992) Covers what to do and when to do it in an easy-to-follow calendar of progress.

Fletcher, J. T.
DISEASES OF GREENHOUSE PLANTS (John Wiley, 1986)

Head, William
GARDENING UNDER COVER: A NORTHWEST GUIDE TO SOLAR GREENHOUSES, COLD FRAMES AND CLOCHES (Sasquatch Books, 1989) Information gleaned from experimental gardens in Oregon and 100+ under cover gardeners; covers design, building and using greenhouses, cold frames and cloches to grow vegetables, herbs and ornamental plants; only the planting timetables are geared to the Pacific Northwest, the rest is applicable anywhere.

Hessayon, Dr. D. G.
BE YOUR OWN GREENHOUSE EXPERT (Sterling, 1991) A beginner's guide covering growing both food and decorative plants; includes choosing the right size and type of greenhouse and step-by-step instructions on building a variety of greenhouses from a simple window box all the way up to a separate, elaborate, all-season building.

Hussey, N. W., and Scopes, N. (editors)
BIOLOGICAL PEST CONTROL: THE GLASSHOUSE EXPERIENCE (Cornell University Press, 1985) How to control pests through natural means.

McCullagh, James C. (editor)
THE SOLAR GREENHOUSE BOOK (Rodale Press, 1978) Written by a variety of experts in the field,

it covers building and growing vegetables in a solar greenhouse.

McDonald, Elvin
THE FLOWERING GREENHOUSE DAY BY DAY (Van Nostrand, 1966) Covers routine maintenance and seasonal plantings throughout the year.

Menage, Ronald
THE PRACTICAL BOOK OF GREENHOUSE GARDENING (Sterling, 1991) A beginnner's guide with suggestions and advice on growing unusual plants in the greenhouse.

Nearing, Helen and Scott
BUILDING AND USING OUR SUN-HEATED GREENHOUSE: GROW VEGETABLES ALL YEAR ROUND (Garden Way, 1977)

Northen, Henry and Rebecca T.
GREENHOUSE GARDENING (Ronald Press, 1973, 2nd edition) Good introduction to the numerous types of plants that can be grown under glass.

Ortho
GREENHOUSE PLANTS (Ortho, 1990) Covers growing information for over 500 plants.
GREENHOUSES: PLANNING, INSTALLING AND USING GREENHOUSES (Ortho, 1991) Information on building a solar or conventional greenhouse, using one of the nine plans and instructions, or selecting a kit; includes advice on temperature, light, and humidity control, and starting plants from seeds or cuttings.

Porter, Wes
THE GARDEN BOOK AND THE GREENHOUSE (Workman, 1989)

Rees, Yvonne, and Palliser, David
CONSERVATORY GARDENING: CREATING AN INDOOR GARDEN (Trafalgar Square, 1990) Covers every stage of making an indoor garden.

Shapiro, Andrew M.
THE HOMEOWNER'S COMPLETE HANDBOOK FOR ADD-ON SOLAR GREENHOUSES AND SUNSPACES (Rodale Press, 1985) How to build or buy the latest greenhouse.

Smith, Miranda
GREENHOUSE GARDENING (Rodale Press, 1985)

Stone, Robert
GARDEN ROOMS (Sterling, 1990) Color photos, drawings and instructions on producing garden rooms.

Sunset
GREENHOUSE GARDENING (Sunset Books, 1976) Covers materials, equipment and design, plus growing techniques.

Swithinbank, Anne
A HANDBOOK OF GREENHOUSE AND CONSERVATORY PLANTS (Trafalgar Square, 1990) Details temperature and light needs, propagating methods, pruning guidelines and pest control for ornamentals grown in a greenhouse.

Time-Life
GREENHOUSE GARDENING: GARDENER'S GUIDE SERIES (Time-Life, 1989)

Toogood, Alan
THE CONSERVATORY: PLANNING, PLANTING, FURNISHING (Sterling, 1991) Covers design, planning, construction, equipment and furnishings, plus tips for choosing and growing a large variety of plants.
GREENHOUSE GARDENER (Prentice-Hall, 1986) Covers heating, watering and ventilating, plus what to grow; includes monthly guide for controlling pests and diseases.

Tresidder, Jane, and Cliff, Stafford
LIVING UNDER GLASS (Crown, 1986) Over 200 color photos of ideas for sunrooms, greenhouses, conservatories and other rooms where glass, light and plants work together.

Walls, Ian G.
THE COMPLETE BOOK OF THE GREENHOUSE (Sterling, 1991, revised and updated 4th edition) A comprehensive guide covering construction and techniques of greenhouse growing, plus specific information for food and ornamental plants.
MAKING THE MOST OF YOUR GREENHOUSE (Barron, 1978) Describes heating, cooling, watering

and feeding systems for a greenhouse, plus mist propagation, lighting, growing mixes and more.

Woods, May, and Warren, Arete
GLASS HOUSES (Rizzoli, 1988) The history of conservatories and greenhouses from early Roman times to their popularity in England and America.

For related books, see:
BALL RED BOOK: GREENHOUSE GROWING by Ball (page 185)
CHRYSANTHEMUMS: THE YEAR ROUND by Machin and Scopes (page 86)
GREENHOUSE GARDENING IN THE SOUTH by Minar (page 194)
GREENHOUSE OPERATION AND MANAGEMENT by Nelson (page 186)
GREENHOUSE PLANTS FROM SEED by Genders (page 78)
ORGANIC GARDENING UNDER GLASS by Abraham (page 142)
SECRETS TO A SUCCESSFUL GREENHOUSE BUSINESS . . . by Taylor (page 186)
WHEN DOES IT FLOWER? by Hamilton (page 126)

AFRICAN VIOLETS

The African Violet Society of America (P.O. Box 3609, Beaumont, TX 77704) publishes a bimonthly magazine and has a library from which members can borrow.

Clements, Tony
AFRICAN VIOLETS (Trafalgar Square, 1992) Covers care, tips for a long flowering season, pest and disease control, and propagating through cuttings and seeds; he is England's leading African violet authority with 20 years' experience in commercial violet growing.

Coulson, Ruth
GROWING AFRICAN VIOLETS (ISBS, 1987) Covers water, light, temperature, food, humidity and grooming needs, plus potting and propagating.

Elbert, Virginie and George
THE MIRACLE HOUSE PLANTS: AFRICAN VIOLETS AND OTHER EASY-TO-BLOOM PLANTS IN THE GESNERIAD FAMILY (Crown, 1976)

Free, Montague
ALL ABOUT AFRICAN VIOLETS: THE COMPLETE GUIDE TO SUCCESS WITH SAINT-PAULIAS (Doubleday, 1979, revised and updated edition) Complete growing information—potting, soils, watering, handling problems, etc.

James, Theodore Jr.
AFRICAN VIOLETS AND OTHER GESNERIADS: HOW TO SELECT AND GROW (HP Books, 1983) How to grow, care for and display over 100 varieties.

Ortho
AFRICAN VIOLETS AND FLOWERING HOUSEPLANTS (Ortho Books, 1985)

Robey, Melvin
AFRICAN VIOLETS: GIFTS FROM NATURE (Associated University Presses, 1988)
AFRICAN VIOLETS, QUEENS OF THE INDOOR GARDENING KINGDOM (A. S. Barnes, 1982)

Sunset
HOW TO GROW AFRICAN VIOLETS (Sunset Books, 1977) Growing information, plus color photos of 200 varieties.

Wall, Bill
AFRICAN VIOLETS AND RELATED PLANTS (Wisley Handbook) (Sterling, 1991) Advice on the basics of growing these plants.

CACTI & SUCCULENTS

The Cactus and Succulent Society of America (P.O. Box 3010, Santa Barbara, CA 93130) publishes the bimonthly *Cactus and Succulent Journal* and a bimonthly newsletter. It also has a lending library.

Andersohn, Gunter
CACTI AND SUCCULENTS (Sterling, 1983) Covers plant requirements and propagation for the most important and generally available cacti.

Backeberg, Curt
CACTUS LEXICON (Blandford, 1976) A reference book for identification purposes.

Bash, Barbara
DESERT GIANT: THE WORLD OF THE SA-
GUARO CACTUS (Little, Brown, 1990)

Benson, Lyman
THE CACTI OF THE UNITED STATES AND
CANADA (Stanford University Press, 1982) A huge
taxonomic study containing every native or introduced species, variety and hybrid; includes 977 photos.

Britton, Nathaniel, and Rose, John
THE CACTACEAE: DESCRIPTIONS AND IL-
LUSTRATIONS OF PLANTS OF THE CACTUS
FAMILY (Dover, 1937, 2nd edition, two volumes)
Full botanical descriptions for every cactus in the
world; includes over 1,275 illustrations.

Chapman, Peter R., and Martin, Margaret J.
EXOTIC CACTI (HP Books, 1989) Descriptions and
growing information for over 75 exotic cactus varieties; includes requirements for light, food, water, temperature and soil.

Chidamian, Claude
THE BOOK OF CACTI AND OTHER SUCCU-
LENTS (Timber Press, 1984) Reprint of 1958 book.

Cullmann, Willy; Gotz, Erich; and Groner, Gerhard
ENCYCLOPEDIA OF CACTI (Timber Press, 1986)
Translated from the German, it contains information
on 750 species and 400+ color photos.

Gentry, Howard Scott
AGAVES OF CONTINENTAL NORTH AMER-
ICA (University of Arizona Press, 1982) Gives taxonomic descriptions, distribution, and habitat for 136
native species grouped in 20 genera.

Gibson, Arthur, and Nobel, Park
CACTUS PRIMER (Harvard University Press,
1986)

Graham, Victor
GROWING SUCCULENT PLANTS (Timber
Press, 1987) Where and how to grow succulents, prop-
agation, vegetative reproduction, pests and diseases.

Harland, W. and S.
GROWING CACTI AND SUCCULENTS (ISBS,
1985) Instructions and illustrations on selection, propagation, care and maintenance.

Innes, Clive
CACTI (Wisley Handbook) (Sterling, 1989) Growing advice and color photos.
THE HANDBOOK OF CACTI AND SUCCU-
LENTS (Chartwell, 1988) Growth habit, place of
origin, and characteristics of hundreds of plants; includes greenhouse growing and propagation.

Innes, Clive, and Glass, Charles
CACTI (Portland House, 1991) Requirements for
each genus of cacti (1,300 varieties) is covered along
with 1,200 color photos.

Jacobsen, Hermann
LEXICON OF SUCCULENT PLANTS: SHORT
DESCRIPTIONS, HABITS AND SYNONYMY
OF SUCCULENT PLANTS OTHER THAN
CACTACEAE (Blandford, 1974) Describes 366 gen-
era and 8,600 species; includes 1,200 black-and-white
photos.

Keen, Bill
CACTI AND SUCCULENTS: STEP-BY-STEP
TO GROWING SUCCESS (Trafalgar Square,
1991) An introductory guide on selecting, caring for
and propagating cacti and succulents that provide the
best results for the least amount of work.

Kramer, Jack
CACTI AND OTHER SUCCULENTS (Abrams,
1977) Covers starting a collection, growing information, propagating, repotting and indoor uses; includes
growing under lights and in greenhouses.

Lamb, Edgar and Brian
POCKET ENCYCLOPEDIA OF CACTI IN COL-
OUR (Sterling, revised 1981 edition) Contains 326
color photos with descriptions and cultural notes.

Martin, Margaret J., and Chapman, Peter R.
SUCCULENTS AND THEIR CULTIVATION
(Scribner's, 1977) Detailed information on six major
succulent families and more general information on
other succulents.

Martin, Margaret J.; Chapman, Peter R.; and Auger, H. A.
CACTI AND THEIR CULTIVATION (Scribner's, 1971) A good introduction.

Perl, Philip, and Ferorelli, Enrico
CACTI AND SUCCULENTS (Time-Life Books, 1978)

Pilbeam, John
CACTI FOR THE CONNOISSEUR: A GUIDE FOR GROWERS AND COLLECTORS (Timber Press, 1987) Alphabetized listing of over 90 genera naming all valid species within each genera and recommending the best species.
THE INSTANT GUIDE TO HEALTHY CACTI (Times Books, 1985) How to care for, detect and solve problems.

Pizzetti, Mariella
SIMON & SCHUSTER'S GUIDE TO CACTI AND SUCCULENTS (Simon & Schuster, 1985) Color photos plus place of origin, method for propagation, temperature requirements and more for over 300 species.

Preston-Mafham, Rod and Ken
CACTI: THE ILLUSTRATED DICTIONARY (Sterling, 1991) Describes and illustrates in color photos over 1,100 species and varieties of globe-shaped cacti.

Rauh, Werner
THE WONDERFUL WORLD OF SUCCULENTS (Smithsonian Press, 1984, 2nd revised edition) Descriptions of genera and species arranged by family.

Rowley, Gordon
THE ILLUSTRATED ENCYCLOPEDIA OF SUCCULENTS: A GUIDE TO THE NATURAL HISTORY AND CULTIVATION OF CACTUS AND CACTUS-LIKE PLANTS (Crown, 1978) Good introduction to succulents.

Schuster, Danny
THE WORLD OF CACTI: HOW TO SELECT AND CARE FOR OVER 1,000 SPECIES (Facts On File, 1990) How to grow cacti indoors, outdoors and in solariums; how to handle disease and propagation; includes a list of suppliers.

Stover, Hermine
THE SANSEVIERIA BOOK (Endangered Species Press, 1983) An identification guide to a large variety of "mother-in-law tongue."

Sunset
CACTUS AND SUCCULENTS (Sunset Books, 1978) Growing requirements for 150 cacti and succulents.

Taylor, Nigel
GENUS ECHINOCEREUS: A KEW MAGAZINE MONOGRAPH (Timber Press, 1985) Includes 12 excellent botanical illustrations.

For related books, see:
CACTI OF TEXAS AND NEIGHBORING STATES by Weniger (page197)
THE NATIVE CACTI OF CALIFORNIA by Benson (page 197)

ORCHIDS

The American Orchid Society (6000 South Olive Avenue, West Palm Beach, FL 33405-4159) offers an extensive list of books and some videos. In addition, they publish several books on orchids, such as the *Handbook on Orchid Culture* (1988), which is written by experts and covers growing popular orchid genera. AOS also issues a monthly magazine of over 110 pages plus two quarterly magazines.

Baker, Margaret and Charles
ORCHID SPECIES CULTURE: PESCATOREA-PLEIONE (Timber Press, 1991) How to provide an environment similar to that of the species's native country; covers six genera (*Pescatorea, Phaius, Phalaenopsis, Pholidota, Phragmipedium, Pleione*).

Bechtel, Helmut; Cribb, Phillip; and Launert, Edmund
THE MANUAL OF CULTIVATED ORCHID SPECIES (MIT Press, 1986 revised edition) Covers the special features, habitat, taxonomic history, name derivation and cultural requirements of 217 genera; lists of over 1,200 species that do best in greenhouses; 720 color photos.

Black, Peter McKenzie
COMPLETE BOOK OF ORCHID GROWING
(Trafalgar Square, 1988, new edition revised by Wilma
Rittershausen) Covers the characteristics, culture,
care and flowering times of orchids that are easily
obtained commercially.

Bristow, Alec
ORCHIDS (Wisley Handbook) (Sterling, 1989)
Covers potting, watering, fertilizing, pest and disease
control of over 100 of the easiest species to cultivate.

Brooklyn Botanic Garden
ORCHIDS FOR THE HOME AND GREEN-
HOUSE (BBG #107) Handbook of articles on choosing
orchids, which varieties are the best, soil preparation,
pots, watering, fertilizing, pests, diseases, etc.

Cash, Catherine
THE SLIPPER ORCHIDS (Timber Press, 1991)
Complete description, historical information, culture
and hybridization of four genera (*Cypripedium,
Paphiopedilum, Selenpedium* and *Phragmipedium*). This
is not a revision of her *A Survey of the Slipper Orchids*
(1973), but is a new work.

Correll, Donovan S.
NATIVE ORCHIDS OF NORTH AMERICA
(Stanford University Press, 1950) A classic taxonomic
book on 200 species and varieties of orchids.

Cribb, Phillip
THE GENUS PAPHIOPEDILUM: A KEW MAG-
AZINE MONOGRAPH (Timber Press, 1987) Comprehensive coverage of the history, description,
cultivation, distribution and taxonomy of this genus;
includes 56 lovely watercolors by the Kew staff.

Cribb, Phillip, and Bailes, Christopher
THE HARDY ORCHIDS: A KEW MAGAZINE
MONOGRAPH (Timber Press, 1989) Covers orchids
that can be grown outdoors in most of Europe and
North America, and those that will live in certain
areas if they are given some protection.

Cribb, Phillip, and Butterfield, Ian
THE GENUS PLEIONE: A KEW MAGAZINE
MONOGRAPH (Timber Press, 1988) Complete in-

formation on this easy-to-grow small orchid; 14 watercolors.

Davies, Paul, and Huxley, Jenne and Anthony
WILD ORCHIDS OF BRITAIN AND EUROPE
(Trafalgar Square, 1990) Covers 36 European orchid
genera; includes 328 color photos.

Dressler, Robert L.
THE ORCHIDS: NATURAL HISTORY AND
CLASSIFICATION (Harvard University Press,
1990) Covers the structures, classification, evolution
and ecology of orchids.

DuPuy, David, and Cribb, Phillip
THE GENUS CYMBIDIUM (Timber Press, 1988)
Complete taxonomy on the 44 species, plus history,
anatomy, pollination, cultivation and more; 28 watercolors.

Fanfani, Alberto
SIMON & SCHUSTER'S GUIDE TO ORCHIDS
(Simon & Schuster, 1989) Guide to 160 cultivated
species, morphology, ecology, classification and cultivation.

Fitch, Charles M.
ALL ABOUT ORCHIDS (Doubleday, 1981) Covers
starting a collection, temperature, light and humidity
requirements, growing in a greenhouse, outdoors or in
a window, propagating, pests and diseases; plus exhibiting and photographing.

Hamilton, Robert
THE NEW ORCHID DOCTOR (1988, available
from the American Orchid Society) Sequel to *The
Orchid Doctor*; includes appendices on potting mixes,
insecticides and fungicides.
THE ORCHID DOCTOR (1980, available from the
American Orchid Society) Reference book of common problems and suggested cures.
WHEN DOES IT FLOWER?: ORCHID SPECIES
IN THE GREENHOUSE SINCE 1881 (1986,
available from the American Orchid Society) Gives
peak flowering times for 7,100 orchid species and
natural hybrids.

Hawkes, Alex
ENCYCLOPEDIA OF CULTIVATED ORCHIDS: ILLUSTRATED, DESCRIPTIVE MANUAL OF THE MEMBERS OF THE ORCHIDACEAE CURRENTLY IN CULTIVATION (Faber & Faber, 1987 reprint of 1965 edition) Cultural and taxonomic information on nearly 700 genera; a major work on orchids.

Hillerman, Fred, and Holst, Arthur
AN INTRODUCTION TO THE CULTIVATED ANGRAECOID ORCHIDS OF MADAGASCAR (Timber Press, 1986) Covers selecting and cultivating, plus descriptions of every currently known species.

Hollingsworth, Albert
GROWING ORCHIDS IS FUN (Sun Bulb Co. Inc., 1989) Excellent for beginners as it takes a step-by-step approach to orchid growing.

Hunt, P. Francis
THE ORCHID (Smithmark, 1987) Takashi Kijima's photographs with botanical information on 170 species of orchids growing in North and South America, Europe, Australia, Africa, Malaysia, Indonesia, Hawaii and other areas.

James, I. D.
THE ORCHID GROWERS HANDBOOK (Sterling, 1988) Good introduction covering buying the plants, seed germination, pests and diseases, etc. with specific advice on the most popular varieties.

Kijima, Takashi
ORCHIDS (Mallards, 1990) A collection of photographs commemorating the 12th World Orchid Conference in 1987; contains over 200 species with botanical name, history, geographic range and time of bloom.
THE ORCHID: THE WILD SPECIES (Gallery, 1987) A book of magnificent photographs with very brief notes giving country of origin, magnification ratio, hybridization information and/or relative rarity.

Kramer, Jack
GROWING HYBRID ORCHIDS INDOORS (Universe, 1985) Examines advances in hybridization and meristem culture in addition to information on varieties and how to buy, grow and propagate.

THE WORLD WILDLIFE FUND BOOK OF ORCHIDS (Abbeville Press, 1989) The legend, history, botany and cultivation of orchids.

Leroy-Terquem, Gerald, and Parisot, Jean
ORCHIDS: CARE AND CULTIVATION (Sterling, 1991) Covers 30 different species with information on heating, lighting, ventilation, watering, fertilizing, repotting, controlling pests and diseases and propagating.

Luer, Carlyle A.
THE NATIVE ORCHIDS OF THE U.S. AND CANADA EXCLUDING FLORIDA (New York Botanical Garden, 1975) Comprehensive coverage and a companion volume to *The Native Orchids of Florida* (p. 193).

Morrison, Gordon
GROWING ORCHIDS (ISBS, 1985) Illustrations and instructions on selection, propagation, care and maintenance.
GROWING ORCHIDS IN AUSTRALIA AND NEW ZEALAND (ISBS, 1985) Despite the title, this book is a general introduction for anyone interested in orchid growing; also includes topics on orchid biology for the more advanced grower.
THE ORCHID GROWER'S MANUAL (ISBS, 1989) Part textbook and part reference, it covers how a plant grows and what it needs, plus physiology, ecology, anatomy, taxonomy and culture of orchids.

Noble, Mary
YOU CAN GROW ORCHIDS (McQuerry Orchid, 1987, 5th revised edition) A basic, illustrated book especially good for beginners.
YOU CAN GROW PHALAENOPSIS ORCHIDS (McQuerry Orchid, 1989) Covers potting, pests, diseases, species and hybrids.
YOU CAN GROW CATTLEYA ORCHIDS (McQuerry Orchid, 1991, 2nd edition) Similiar to the 1989 book in coverage of cattleya orchids.

Northen, Rebecca T.
HOME ORCHID GROWING (Prentice-Hall, 1990, 4th edition) A classic in the field with descriptions of 650 species; suitable for beginners and experienced growers; this 4th edition reflects the many changes in orchid names in the past 20 years.

ORCHIDS AS HOUSEPLANTS (Dover, 1976, 2nd edition) How to produce flowering orchids in windows, orchid cases or under artificial light.

MINIATURE ORCHIDS (Van Nostrand Reinhold, 1980) Covers 600+ species of tiny orchids with information on their habitat, culture, ecology and history.

Ortho
ALL ABOUT GROWING ORCHIDS (Ortho, 1988) Covers the basics of growing orchids indoors and under lights; includes an encyclopedia of the most common species and hybrids.

Rentoul, J. N.
GROWING ORCHIDS I (Timber Press, 1980) Covers cymbidiums and slippers.

GROWING ORCHIDS II (Timber Press, 1982) Covers the cattleyas and other epiphytes.

GROWING ORCHIDS III (Timber Press, 1982) Covers vandas and dendrobiums.

GROWING ORCHIDS IV (Timber Press, 1985) Covers the australasian families.

GROWING ORCHIDS: EXPANDING YOUR ORCHID COLLECTION (ISBS, 1990) When you're ready to start growing the less common orchid genera, this book is for you.

THE HYBRID STORY (Timber Press, 1991) Covers hybrids in all the major orchid genera since the 1850s; includes 167 color photos.

THE SPECIALIST ORCHID GROWER (Timber Press, 1987) Advice for the orchidist who wants to specialize in certain genera or species.

Rhodehamel, William
A MASDEVALLIA CULTURAL GUIDE (1988, available from the American Orchid Society) A comprehensive guide to growing and flowering masdevallias in greenhouses or under lights in all climates.

Rittershausen, Brian and Wilma
ORCHIDS AS HOUSEPLANTS (Sterling, 1990) Advice on which orchids make the best houseplants and how to grow them; includes monthly calendar notes.

ORCHID GROWING ILLUSTRATED (Sterling, 1985) Covers types of orchids, equipment needed, potting, propagating and caring for; close-up photos show the techniques well.

ORCHIDS IN COLOR (Sterling, 1984) Cultural information and color photographs for over 100 of the most commonly grown species and hybrids.

Rittershausen, Wilma
EXOTIC ORCHIDS (HP Books, 1989) Growing instructions and descriptions for 75 orchids, arranged according to ease of cultivation.

Sessler, Gloria Jean
ORCHIDS AND HOW TO GROW THEM (Prentice-Hall, 1978) Covers history, culture, pests, diseases, exhibiting and judging orchids.

Sheehan, Thomas and Marion
ORCHID GENERA ILLUSTRATED (Van Nostrand Reinhold, 1979) Describes 60 genera.

Shuttleworth, F.S.; Zim, H.S.; and Dillon, G.W.
GOLDEN GUIDE TO ORCHIDS (Golden Press, 1989, revised edition) An excellent beginner's book, plus a reference book for the more knowledgeable; updated taxonomy.

Skelsey, Alice F., and Editors of Time-Life Books
ORCHIDS (Time-Life Books, 1978) Covers history and growing orchids indoors and outdoors, plus descriptions and color illustrations of 82 orchid genera.

Stewart, Joyce
ORCHIDS: A KEW GARDENING GUIDE (Timber Press, 1988) An excellent introduction to the most important genera, species and hybrids.

Sunset
ORCHIDS (Sunset Books, 1977) Advice on growing 250 varieties of orchids either in the house, a greenhouse, or the garden.

Tibbs, Mike, and Bilton, Ray
ORCHIDS: AN ILLUSTRATED IDENTIFIER AND GUIDE TO CULTIVATION (Smithmark, 1990) This survey of the major groups of orchids is written by the staff of McBean's Orchids; includes information on care and common problems, and cultural tables for six major genera.

Upton, Walter T.
DENDROBIUM ORCHIDS OF AUSTRALIA (Timber Press, 1989) Detailed description, flowering

period, geographic distribution, habitat and cultural requirements for each species and natural hybrid; includes a line drawing and color photo of each entry, plus information on the use of each plant in hybridization, dominant traits and a list of hybrids resulting from crosses with that plant.

Wisler, Gail
HOW TO CONTROL ORCHID VIRUSES: THE COMPLETE GUIDEBOOK (Maupin House, 1989) How to identify the major orchid viruses, and, although they are not currently curable, ensure a virus-free collection.

Withner, Dr. Carl L.
THE CATTLEYAS AND THEIR RELATIVES— VOLUME I: THE CATTLEYAS (Timber Press, 1988) and **VOLUME II: THE LAELIAS** (Timber Press, 1990) These are the first of six planned volumes on the culture, hybridization and descriptions of this species by the former curator of the orchid collections at the New York Botanic Garden and the Brooklyn Botanic Garden.

For related books, see:
THE NATIVE ORCHIDS OF FLORIDA by Luer (page 193)
ORCHIDS AT KEW by Stewart (page 208)
ORCHIDS FROM "CURTIS'S BOTANICAL MAGAZINE" by Sprunger (page 220)
THE ORCHIDS OF MAINE by Cameron (page 190)

FERNS

The American Fern Society (Dept. of Botany, University of Tennessee, Knoxville, TN 37996) publishes a quarterly journal and a bimonthly newsletter.

Abbe, Elfriede
THE FERN HERBAL: INCLUDING THE FERNS, THE HORSETAILS AND THE CLUB MOSSES (Cornell University Press, 1985)

Foster, F. Gordon
FERNS TO KNOW AND GROW (Timber Press, 1984, 3rd edition, revised and enlarged) Culture and propagation information gained through 40 years of experience with ferns.

Goudey, Christopher J.
MAIDENHAIR FERNS: IN CULTIVATION (ISBS, 1985) Describes natural habitat, best growing conditions, propagation techniques, and pest and disease data for 140 species; 400 color photos.

Hoshizaki, Barbara Joe
FERN GROWERS MANUAL (Knopf, 1979) Describes fern genera and species throughout the world, plus growing information.

Jones, David
ENCYCLOPEDIA OF FERNS: AN INTRODUCTION TO FERNS, THEIR STRUCTURE, BIOLOGY, ECONOMIC IMPORTANCE, CULTIVATION AND PROPAGATION (Timber Press, 1987) Covers over 700 temperate and tropical ferns growing all around the world.

Lellinger, David B.
A FIELD MANUAL TO THE FERNS AND FERN-ALLIES OF THE U.S. AND CANADA (Smithsonian, 1985) An identification guide for 406 native and naturalized species of ferns with information on classification, range, habitat, ecology, structure and life cycle.

Mason, John
GROWING FERNS (ISBS, 1990) Covers growing and propagating over 100 genera of worldwide cultivated ferns.

Mickel, John, and Fiore, Evelyn
THE HOME GARDENER'S BOOK OF FERNS (Holt, Rinehart & Winston, 1979) For growing ferns indoors and outdoors.

Parsons, Frances T.
HOW TO KNOW THE FERNS: A GUIDE TO THE NAMES, HAUNTS AND HABITS OF OUR COMMON FERNS (Dover, 1899, 2nd edition) A classic on ferns of the eastern and central U.S.

Streams, John (editor)
TREASURES OF NATURE: FERNS (Crossing Press, 1987)

Time-Life
FERNS (Time-Life Books, 1977)

Vail, Roy
PLATYCERIUM HOBBYIST'S HANDBOOK
(Desert Biological Publications, 1984)

For related books, see:
THE FERNS OF BRITAIN AND IRELAND by
Page (page 207)

FERNS OF THE NORTHEASTERN U.S. by
Wiley (page 192)
**A FIELD GUIDE TO FERNS AND THEIR RE-
LATED FAMILIES: NORTHEASTERN AND
CENTRAL NORTH AMERICA** by Cobb (page 190)

GIFTS AND CRAFTS FROM THE GARDEN

GENERAL REFERENCES

Black, Penny
THE BOOK OF POTPOURRI: FRAGRANT FLOWER MIXES FOR SCENTING AND DECO-RATING THE HOME (Simon & Schuster, 1989) Forty potpourri recipes, plus information on drying flowers.
A PASSION FOR FLOWERS (Simon & Schuster, 1992) Describes over 40 original uses for fresh, dried and pressed flowers; projects are divided by seasons and photographed in and around her cottage in Cornwall, England.
THE SCENTED HOUSE (Simon & Schuster, 1991)

Cusick, Dawn
THE BOOK OF COUNTRY HERBAL CRAFTS: A STEP-BY-STEP GUIDE TO MAKING OVER 100 BEAUTIFUL WREATHS, GARLANDS, BOUQUETS—AND MUCH MORE (Rodale Press, 1991) Detailed directions, complete material lists and step-by-step illustrations.

Diamond, Denise
THE COMPLETE BOOK OF FLOWERS (North Atlantic Books, 1990) Growing information, plus numerous ways to use flowers and herbs.

LIVING WITH THE FLOWERS: A GUIDE TO BRINGING FLOWERS INTO YOUR DAILY LIFE (Morrow, 1982) Covers the basics of flower botany and flower gardening, plus numerous ways to use flowers (fresh arrangements, dried, pressed, pot-pourris, cooking, lotions and for health).

Duff, Gail
NATURAL FRAGRANCES: OUTDOOR SCENTS FOR INDOOR USES (Storey, 1991) One hundred recipes using flowers and herbs to make pot-pourri, bath herbs, sachets, scented candles, furniture polish, etc.

Ehrman, Hugh (compiler)
FRUITS OF THE EARTH: FLOWERS AND FRUIT IN NEEDLEPOINT (Simon & Schuster, 1991) Over 40 designs from some of the best contemporary designers. (Note: There are many needlework books with flower and fruit patterns and charts. I included only one, but I hope it starts you thinking about creating a piece of needlework inspired by your garden.)

Lane, Mary
POT POURRI: A PRACTICAL GUIDE (ISBS, 1985) Covers which flowers and herbs are most used,

how to grow and dry them, plus old and new recipes for mixing the flowers and herbs and how to use the resulting potpourri.

McRae, Bobbi A.
NATURE'S DYEPOT: A RESOURCE GUIDE FOR SPINNERS, WEAVERS AND DYERS (Fiberworks Publications, 1991) Includes sources for plants and seeds for dyes, an extensive bibliography of books and articles on natural dyeing, an A to Z chart of potential dye plants and sources for miscellaneous supplies. Available from P.O. Box 49770, Austin, TX 78765.

Oster, Maggie
GIFTS AND CRAFTS FROM THE GARDEN (Rodale Press, 1988) Over 100 easy-to-make projects including baskets, potpourris and holiday decorations.

Puckett, Sandy
FRAGILE BEAUTY: THE VICTORIAN ART OF PRESSED FLOWERS (Little, Brown, 1992) How to create a "pressing" garden (what to grow and when to harvest), plus instructions on creating pressed flower designs.

Scobey, Joan, and Myers, Norma
GIFTS FROM YOUR GARDEN (Bobbs-Merrill, 1975) Covers drying and pressing flowers, plus preparing potpourris, bath sachets and culinary items (vinegars, jellies, jams, teas).

Shaudys, Phyllis V.
HERBAL TREASURES: INSPIRING MONTH-BY-MONTH PROJECTS FOR GARDENING, COOKING AND CRAFTS (Storey, 1990) Projects for every month of the year, plus information on beginning an herb business and teaching classes.

Sheen, Joanna
HERBAL GIFTS (Sterling, 1991) Instructions and photos on growing, drying and preparing a wide variety of herbs; includes wreaths, dried arrangements, potpourris, sachets and recipes for jams, jellies, oils, etc.

Tolley, Emelie, and Mead, Chris
GIFTS FROM THE HERB GARDEN (Clarkson Potter, 1991) How to use fresh and dried herbs to add beauty and fragrance to your home.

For related books, see:
HERITAGE ROSES AND OLD-FASHIONED CRAFTS by Culpepper (page 67)

FLOWER ARRANGING

Ascher, Amalie A.
THE COMPLETE FLOWER ARRANGER (Simon & Schuster, 1977) An introduction covering design basics and various types of arrangements.

Bailey, Lee
LEE BAILEY'S SMALL BOUQUETS: A GIFT FOR ALL SEASONS (Crown, 1990)

Barnett, Fiona
WEDDING FLOWERS (Simon & Schuster, 1991) Over 60 arrangements organized by season plus information on materials, techniques, figuring the number of flowers needed and working with a professional designer.

Bridges, Derek
THE CRAFTY FLOWER ARRANGER: A PRACTICAL SOURCEBOOK OF INVENTIVE IDEAS (Trafalgar Square, 1989) Instructions for using flowers in a variety of ways—unusual containers, windowboxes, collage, silk arrangements and more.
FLOWER ARRANGER'S BIBLE (Trafalgar Square, 1991) Ideas for all types of arrangements (wildflowers, dried flowers, Christmas, church, etc), suggestions for special occasions, preservation of flowers and greenery, plus preparing for shows and equipment needed.
A FLOWER ARRANGER'S WORLD (Trafalgar Square, 1990) Step-by-step photos and instruction for creating arrangements from around the world.
FLOWERS FOR CELEBRATIONS: BEAUTIFUL ARRANGEMENTS FOR SPECIAL OCCASIONS (Trafalgar Square, 1988) How to decorate every room in the house for holidays, anniversaries and weddings.

Brinton, Diana (editor)
THE COMPLETE GUIDE TO FLOWER ARRANGING (Sterling, 1991) How to choose the flowers, find the vases and prepare the arrangements for a multitude of occasions; over 200 color photos.

Clements, Julia
THE BOOK OF ROSE ARRANGEMENTS (Arco, 1984)
FLOWER ARRANGEMENTS: MONTH BY MONTH, STEP BY STEP (Trafalgar Square, 1984)
FLOWER ARRANGER'S BEDSIDE BOOK (Batsford, 1982) Her personal experiences and thoughts on flower arranging, plus practical advice, short stories and verse.

Coleman, Rona
THE SEASONAL FLORIST AND FLOWER ARRANGER (Trafalgar Square, 1990) Covers all the essentials of flower arranging: seasonal availability of flowers; choosing, conditioning and caring for flowers; wiring; and suggestions for special occasions.

Coleman, Rona, and Pepper, S.
THE ENCYCLOPEDIA OF FLOWER ARRANGING: DECORATING WITH FRESH, DRIED AND PRESSED FLOWERS (Wellfleet, 1989) Covers the basic design forms, flower conditioning, using flowers and leaves from each season, and more.

Conder, Susan; et al.
FLOWER ARRANGING: A STEP-BY-STEP GUIDE (Mallard Press, 1990)

Cook, Hal
ARRANGING: THE BASICS OF CONTEMPORARY FLORAL DESIGN (Morrow, 1985)

Cowles, Fleur
FLOWER DECORATIONS: A NEW APPROACH TO FLOWER ARRANGING (Gallery Books, 1989) Using pebbles, moss, fruits, vegetables, unusual containers and color combinations, and a variety of other techniques that can result in highly original arrangements.

Dale, John
THE FLOWER ARRANGER'S HANDBOOK: ONE THOUSAND VARIETIES OF FLOWER AND FOLIAGE ORGANIZED BY COLOR (Dutton, 1986)

Ferguson, Barry, and Cowan, Tom
LIVING WITH FLOWERS (Rizzoli, 1990)

Fleck, Irma, and Stevens, Marcia
WILD AND WONDERFUL FLOWERS FOR YOUR HOME (Timber Press, 1989) To illustrate the versatility of wildflowers, the authors have collected, preserved and arranged local (New York) wildflowers in many different types of homes.

Forsell, Mary
THE BOOK OF FLOWER ARRANGING: FOR FRESH, DRIED AND ARTIFICIAL FLOWERS (Running Press, 1989)

Gatrell, Anthony
DICTIONARY OF FLORISTS AND FLOWER ARRANGING (Trafalgar Square, 1989) An alphabetical compilation of all the terms likely to be used in floristry and flower arranging.

Guild, Tricia
DESIGNING WITH FLOWERS (Crown, 1986) Floral arrangements with the naturalness of a cottage garden; includes 180 beautiful color photos.

Hillier, Malcolm
THE BOOK OF FRESH FLOWERS: A COMPLETE GUIDE TO SELECTING AND ARRANGING (Simon & Schuster, 1988) Describes the principles and techniques for creating beautiful flower arrangements.
READERS DIGEST HOME HANDBOOK OF FLOWER ARRANGING (RD Association, 1990) Covers tools, techniques, various styles, materials used, advice from the experts, and step-by-step illustrations for arrangements of fresh, dried and pressed flowers.

Johnson, Marion
SMALL AND BEAUTIFUL FLOWER ARRANGEMENTS: AN IDEA BOOK FOR MINIATURE FLOWER ARRANGEMENTS (Crown, 1983)

Johnson, Norman K.
EVERYDAY FLOWERS: GROWING, ARRANGING AND LIVING WITH YOUR FLOWERS (Longstreet Press, 1990) How to grow and gather flowers, arrange them in ways that best suits their shape and then care for them in their vases.

Kawase, Toshiro
INSPIRED FLOWER ARRANGEMENTS
(Kodansha, 1990) Features 88 fantastic arrangements
from one of Japan's leading designers.

Lamancusa, Kathy
**KATHY LAMANCUSA'S GUIDE TO FLORAL
DESIGN** (TAB Books, 1990)

Madderlake (company name)
**FLOWERS REDISCOVERED: NEW IDEAS FOR
USING AND ENJOYING FLOWERS** (Stewart,
Tabori & Chang, 1985) Examples of using a variety of
flowers from the garden, from the field or from the
florist, plus fruits and vegetables to create unusual
arrangements.

Maia, Ronaldo
MORE DECORATING WITH FLOWERS
(Abrams, 1991) How to work with and arrange a
variety of flowers using only flowers or combining
flowers with unusual items.

Mann, Pauline
**FLOWER ARRANGER'S WORKBOOK: A CRE-
ATIVE AND PRACTICAL GUIDE TO COLOR-
BY-COLOR FLOWER ARRANGING THROUGHOUT
THE YEAR** (Trafalgar Square, 1989) Explains the
various aspects of color (hue, value, tint, tone, shade
and weakness) and how to use it in flower arranging.
WEDDING FLOWERS (Trafalgar Square, 1985)
Design ideas for weddings and receptions, including
church flowers, bridal bouquets and headdresses.

Maurice, Grizelda
A FLOWER ARRANGER'S GARDEN (Trafalgar
Square, 1988) An illustrated guide to planting and
growing flowers for both arranging and drying.

McDaniel, Gary M.
FLORAL DESIGN AND ARRANGEMENT
(Prentice-Hall, 1989, 2nd edition)

McNicol, Pamela
FLOWERS FOR WEDDINGS (Trafalgar Square,
1992) Surveys all types of weddings from very formal
to more casual affairs; covers selecting colors, conditioning blossoms, controlling costs and using flowers
in bouquets, pew ends, outdoor displays and table

decoration; includes a chapter on the Royal Wedding
flowers she did for Prince Andrew and Miss Sarah
Ferguson at Westminster Abbey.

Monckton, Shirley
ARRANGING FLOWERS (Sterling, 1989) Step-
by-step directions for creating spectacular floral arrangements for all types of occasions.

National Association of Flower Arranging
**STAFF BOOK OF FLOWER ARRANGING: A
STEP-BY-STEP GUIDE TO FLOWERS FOR
THE HOME** (Dutton, 1986)

Nehrling, Arno and Irene
**GARDENING FOR FLOWER ARRANGE-
MENT** (Dover, 1976) Cultivation information on
over 500 plants suitable for flower arrangements.

Newdick, Jane
BETTY CROCKER'S BOOK OF FLOWERS
(Prentice-Hall, 1989) How to use fresh and dried
flowers in arrangements and in ways you may not have
thought of.
THE 5-MINUTE CENTERPIECE (Crown, 1991)
How to use fruit or ordinary household items (coffee
mugs, sugar bowls, baskets, stemware, dishes, etc.) and
a few simple tools to make a quick centerpiece.
FIVE MINUTE FLOWER ARRANGER (Crown,
1989)
**PERIOD FLOWERS: DESIGNS FOR TODAY
INSPIRED BY CENTURIES OF FLORAL ART**
(Crown, 1991) Flower arrangements based on various
historical periods.

Ortho
ARRANGING CUT FLOWERS (Ortho, 1985) A
good introductory guide to modern design theories,
materials needed and techniques used.

Otis, Denise, and Maia, Ronaldo
DECORATING WITH FLOWERS (Abrams,
1978) A truly beautiful book of arrangements suitable
for every room in the house and for all occasions, from
the most formal to the simplest.

Packer, Jane
CELEBRATING WITH FLOWERS (Ballantine,
1988)

FLOWERS FOR ALL SEASONS: SPRING (Ballantine, 1989) Ideas for formal and informal spring arrangements to use in entertaining or as gifts.

FLOWERS FOR ALL SEASONS: SUMMER (Ballantine, 1989) Designs for the kitchen, living and dining rooms, weddings, parties and more.

FLOWERS FOR ALL SEASONS: FALL (Fawcett, 1989) Tips and techniques for fall arrangements.

FLOWERS FOR ALL SEASONS: WINTER (Fawcett, 1989) Includes designs for holiday garlands.

Pfahl, Peter, and Kalin, Elwood
AMERICAN STYLE FLOWER ARRANGING (Prentice-Hall, 1982)

Piercy, Harold
THE CONSTANCE SPRY BOOK OF FLOWER ARRANGING (Octopus Books, 1983)
CONSTANCE SPRY CREATIVE IDEAS IN FLORISTRY AND FLOWER ARRANGING (Trafalgar Square, 1989) Discusses various types of flower arrangements and gives advice on the best ways to prepare and display flowers.
THE CONSTANCE SPRY HANDBOOK OF FLORISTRY (Trafalgar Square, 1990) Through illustrations, takes both the amateur and the expert through progressively complicated arrangements for Christmas decorations, weddings, bouquets, funeral arrangements and the use of dried and silk flowers.

Ruffin, Lisa
LEONARD THARP: AN AMERICAN STYLE OF FLOWER ARRANGEMENT (Taylor Publishing, 1986) How to use anything from nature to create interesting and beautiful arrangements.

Sheen, Joanna
THE FLORAL DESIGNER: USING COLOR AND TEXTURE IN FLOWER ARRANGING (Sterling, 1990) Covers a variety of large, small, elaborate and simple centerpieces and vase arrangements.

Stevenson, Violet
CREATIVE FLOWER ARRANGING (Salem House, 1986) How to use unusual containers, flowers, fruits, foliage and everlastings to create distinctive arrangements.

Taylor, Jean
CREATIVE FLOWER ARRANGEMENT (Stanley Paul, 1973) A guide to preserving plants, making containers and preparing materials.

Time-Life
FLOWERS FOR CUTTING AND DRYING: GARDENER'S GUIDE SERIES (Time-Life Books, 1990) Covers design of a cutting garden, keeping cut flowers fresh, drying and preserving flowers, flower arranging and descriptions and color photos of more than 150 genera of plants suitable for cutting and drying.

Tonks, Diana
SPECTACULAR FLOWERS (Trafalgar Square, 1992) Sixty flower arrangements in close-up photographs at 15 of Britain's historic and stately homes (e.g., Glamis Castle, Warwick Castle, Blenheim Palace, Stoneleigh Abbey); advice on arranging flowers, color schemes, coordinating flowers and furnishings, and seasonal arrangements.

Tozer, Zibby
THE ART OF FLOWER ARRANGING (Warner Books, 1983)

Turner, Kenneth
KENNETH TURNER'S FLOWER STYLE: THE ART OF FLORAL DESIGN AND DECORATION (Grove Weidenfeld, 1989) Covers both his mammoth and simple arrangements; includes 160 color photos.

Vagg, Daphne
FLOWER ARRANGER'S A-Z: A PRACTICAL ALPHABETICAL GUIDE TO FLOWER ARRANGING, COMPETITIONS AND FLORAL TERMS (Trafalgar Square, 1989) Surveys themes, historical periods, color, symbolism, international styles, special occasions, competition arranging, materials and mechanics, and the artistic influences of flower arranging.
FLOWERS IN EVERY ROOM (Trafalgar Square, 1985) Covers basic arranging techniques, plus a guide for choosing the flowers best suited to a room's decor.

Vaughan, Mary Jane
THE COMPLETE BOOK OF CUT FLOWER
CARE (Timber Press, 1988) Covers seasonal availability, expected vase life and information on caring
for almost 250 kinds of cut flowers and foliage; intended for amateurs and professionals.

Veevers-Carter, Ming
CELEBRATION FLOWERS: DESIGNING AND
ARRANGING (Sterling, 1990) Illustrations and instructions for arrangements for all types of celebrations
(weddings, christenings, Christmas, Halloween, etc.).

Verey, Rosemary
THE FLOWER ARRANGER'S GARDEN (Little,
Brown, 1989) Ideas for seasonal borders and beds that
produce year-round flowers for indoor use.

Webb, Iris (editor)
THE COMPLETE GUIDE TO FLOWER AND
FOLIAGE ARRANGEMENT (Doubleday, 1979) A
variety of experts discuss design, color, ikebana, drying
and preserving flowers, and more.

Westland, Pamela
ARRANGING FLOWERS NATURALLY
(Chartwell, 1991) How to select the best flowers for
indoor floral arrangements, plus tips on using unusual
containers.
FLOWER ARRANGING FOR SPECIAL OCCA-
SIONS (Columbus Books, 1985) How to create arrangements for Christmas, weddings, christenings,
harvest festivals, special candlelit dinners and other
occasions using fresh, dried and wild flowers.

IKEBANA

Coe, Stella
IKEBANA: A PRACTICAL AND PHILOSOPH-
ICAL GUIDE TO FLOWER ARRANGEMENT
(Overlook Press, 1984)

Komoda, Shusui, and Pointer, Horst
IKEBANA: SPIRIT AND TECHNIQUE (Ster-
ling, 1987) Covers the traditions of the ancient Japanese art form of flower arranging; a good beginner's
guide.

Ohno, Noriko
POETRY OF IKEBANA (Kodansha, 1991)

Palmer, Elizabeth
IKEBANA: THE ART OF JAPANESE FLOWER
ARRANGING (Chartwell, 1989) An introduction
to arrangements in shallow containers and in tall
containers, plus floating arrangements and more.

Sato, Shozo
THE ART OF ARRANGING FLOWERS: A COM-
PLETE GUIDE TO JAPANESE IKEBANA
(Abrams, no date) Covers the various ikebana styles,
equipment needed and techniques; includes a basic
course in the Moribana style and advanced ikebana.

Steere, William
FLOWER ARRANGEMENT: THE IKEBANA
WAY (Madison Square Press, 1972) Covers the styles
and techniques of the Ikenobo, Ohara and Sogetsu
schools.

Teshigahara, Wafu
IKEBANA: A NEW ILLUSTRATED GUIDE TO
MASTERY (Kodansha, 1981)

DRIED FLOWERS

Beazley, Mary, and Scott, Margaret K.
PRESSED FLOWERS THROUGH THE SEA-
SONS (Trafalgar Square, 1983) A seasonal approach
to dried flower arranging.

Black, Penny
THE BOOK OF PRESSED FLOWERS: A COM-
PLETE GUIDE TO PRESSING, DRYING AND
ARRANGING (Simon & Schuster, 1988) Step-by-
step instructions for making pictures, cards, gifts,
frames, candles, pillows and more, all using pressed
flowers.

Brooklyn Botanic Garden
DRIED FLOWER DESIGNS (BBG #76) Describes
drying flowers and foliage; includes arranging tips and
craft ideas.

Bullivant, Elizabeth
DRIED FRESH FLOWERS FROM YOUR GAR-
DEN (Viking Penguin, 1990) Detailed information
on 200 plants which are suitable for drying.

Conder, Susan
DRIED FLOWERS: GROWING, DRYING AND ARRANGING (David R. Godine, 1988) Arranged by what is available at each season, it covers not only the usual flower arrangements, but also includes baskets, wreaths, pomanders and more.

Condon, Geneal
THE COMPLETE BOOK OF FLOWER PRESERVATION (Pruett, 1982) How to preserve a variety of plants.

Docker, Amanda
AN ENGLISH COUNTRY LADY'S BOOK OF DRIED FLOWERS (Doubleday, 1990) One of England's best known dried flower arrangers gives suggestions and advice for numerous types of arrangements for weddings, holidays, room decoration, outdoor events, etc.

Embertson, Jane
PODS: WILDFLOWERS AND WEEDS IN THEIR FINAL BEAUTY (Scribner's, 1979) Covers the bloom and pod stages of 150 Northeast and Midwest U.S. plants with suggested arrangements; includes 450 color photos.

Floyd, Harriet
PLANT IT NOW, DRY IT LATER (McGraw-Hill, 1973) Drying, storing and using techniques, all arranged according to season.

Foster, Maureen
THE FLOWER ARRANGER'S ENCYCLOPEDIA OF PRESERVING AND DRYING (Sterling, 1989) Covers harvesting and drying techniques on over 250 plants, including flowers, ferns, fruits, berries, mosses, lichens and more.

Hannemann, Cellestine
GLORIOUS PRESSED FLOWER PROJECTS (Sterling, 1991) Step-by-step directions for creating dozens of original projects, plus information on preserving "difficult" flowers.

Hillier, Malcolm
DECORATING WITH DRIED FLOWERS (Crown, 1988) Covers flower arranging principles and materials; includes a step-by-step guide and 123 color photos to inspire both the novice and the experienced flower arranger.

Hillier, Malcolm, and Hilton, Colin
THE BOOK OF DRIED FLOWERS: A COMPLETE GUIDE TO GROWING, DRYING AND ARRANGING (Simon & Schuster, 1987) Includes complete instructions and color illustrations for recreating the author's arrangements.

Jacobs, Betty E. M.
FLOWERS THAT LAST FOREVER: GROWING, HARVESTING AND PRESERVING (Storey, 1988) Perfect for the beginner, it covers 31 flowers and six ornamental grasses.

James Jr., Theodore
THE POTPOURRI GARDENER (Macmillan, 1990) Specifics on growing, harvesting and drying 100+ perennials, annuals, roses, flowering bulbs, herbs and shrubs, all of which keep their color and scent when dried; 20 recipes.

Joosten, Titia
FLOWER DRYING WITH A MICROWAVE (Sterling, 1988) How to use silica gel and a microwave (or conventional oven) to shorten the drying time of over 200 flowers, wildflowers and leaves.

Karel, Leonard
DRIED FLOWERS FROM ANTIQUITY TO THE PRESENT: A HISTORY AND PRACTICAL GUIDE TO FLOWER DRYING (Scarecrow Press, 1973)

Lindgren, Linda Lee
DECORATIONS FROM NATURE: GROWING, PRESERVING AND ARRANGING NATURALS (Chilton, 1986)

MacFarlane, Ruth
COLLECTING AND PRESERVING PLANTS FOR SCIENCE AND PLEASURE (Prentice-Hall, 1984) Covers how to identify, label, mount, package, store and display plants.

Mann, Pauline
FLOWERS THAT LAST: ARRANGING DRIED AND PRESERVED PLANTS AND FLOWERS (Batsford, 1984) Covers basic design principles, plus

pressing and drying flowers, preserving with glycerine and bleaching.

Mierhof, Annette
THE DRIED FLOWER BOOK: GROWING, PICKING, DRYING, ARRANGING (Dutton, 1981)

Mitchell, Ann L.
THE DRIED FLOWER GARDEN (Trafalgar Square, 1992) Instructions for growing and drying flowers, foliage, vegetable leaves, herbs, lichens and wildflowers; includes a detailed alphabetical guide of plants and how to dry and arrange them.

Ohrbach, Barbara
THE SCENTED ROOM: CHERCHEZ'S BOOK OF DRIED FLOWERS, FRAGRANCE AND POTPOURRI (Clarkson Potter, 1986) How to create and use dried flowers, fragrance and potpourri in the home.

Olson, Beverly, and Lazzara, Judy
COUNTRY FLOWER DRYING (Sterling, 1988) Instructions for air drying many flowers, wildflowers and grasses and using them in wreaths, potpourri and baskets.

O'Neil, Sunny
FLORAL KEEPSAKES (Meredith Books, 1990) Step-by-step directions for 65 projects (wreaths, table displays, weddings, etc.), plus flower drying techniques.

Penzner, Diana, and Forsell, Mary
EVERLASTING DESIGN: IDEAS AND TECHNIQUES FOR DRIED FLOWERS (Houghton Mifflin, 1988) Covers methods of preserving and arranging garden flowers.
EVERLASTING DESIGN: MORE IDEAS AND TECHNIQUES FOR DRIED FLOWERS (Facts On File, 1987) Additional ideas and techniques, plus over 100 color and black-and-white illustrations.

Petelin, Carol
THE COUNTRY DIARY BOOK OF FLOWERS: DRYING, PRESSING AND POTPOURRI (Henry Holt, 1991) Details on which garden flowers most successfully retain their color and fragrance when dried;

includes instructions for bouquets, wreaths, potpourri, sachets, etc. with additional information on sources.
THE CREATIVE GUIDE TO DRIED FLOWERS (Viking, 1989)

Pulleyn, Rob, and Mautor, Claudette
EVERLASTING FLORAL GIFTS (Sterling, 1991) Detailed step-by-step instructions for over 100 dried flower projects (wreaths, topiary, trees, paperweights, potpourri, Shaker sprigs, hearth bouquets, etc.).

Rogers, Barbara R.
THE ENCYCLOPEDIA OF EVERLASTINGS: THE COMPLETE GUIDE TO GROWING, PRESERVING AND ARRANGING DRIED FLOWERS (Weidenfeld & Nicolson, 1988) Covers which flowers and plants work best, the various drying methods, the necessary tools, list of sources and more.

Scott, Margaret Kennedy
PRESSED FLOWERS AND FLOWER PICTURES (Trafalgar Square, 1988) Covers all the steps for pressing flowers to use in cards, calendars and framed pictures.

Sheen, Joanna
DRIED FLOWER GARDENING (Sterling, 1991) How to grow over 100 different blooms, grasses, ferns and other plants suitable for drying, plus drying and arranging tips.
FLOWER PRESSING (Sterling, 1990) Which flowers are the most suitable candidates for pressing and how best to press and use them.
PRESSED FLOWERS: CREATING AND STYLING (Godine, 1988) Covers choosing the flowers, pressing them and making a variety of items (cards, calendars, doorplates, boxes, bouquets, etc.).

Silber, Mark and Terry
THE COMPLETE BOOK OF EVERLASTINGS: GROWING, DRYING AND DESIGNING WITH DRIED FLOWERS (Knopf, 1988) The Silbers, owners of Hedgehog Hill Farm in Maine where everlastings are the focus, have written a definitive book covering harvesting and hang drying 145 varieties of everlastings; includes 382 color photos.

Thorpe, Patricia
EVERLASTINGS: THE COMPLETE BOOK OF DRIED FLOWERS (Facts On File, 1985) Covers every aspect of growing, preserving and using everlastings.

Westland, Pamela
DECORATING WITH DRIED FLOWERS (Chartwell, 1991) Includes 20 step-by-step projects, plus instructions for drying and preserving flowers, foliage, vegetables and berries.
FLOWERCRAFTS: THE ENCHANTED GARDEN (Sedgewood Press, 1988) Ways to use fresh and dried flowers in home decoration, in beauty preparations, as gifts and more.

Whitlock, Sarah, and Rankin, Martha
DRIED FLOWERS: HOW TO PREPARE THEM (Dover, 1975) A "guide to dehydration, glycerinizing, pressing plant material, using silica gel" (Dover catalogue).

Wiita, Betty
DRIED FLOWERS FOR ALL SEASONS (Van Nostrand Reinhold, 1982) Various methods (air drying, silica gel, glycerin, microwaving and pressing) are covered along with ways to use the resulting dried flowers.

Wood, Rob and Lucy
THE ART OF DRIED FLOWERS (Running Press, 1991)

WREATHS

Cusick, Dawn, and Pulleyn, Rob
WREATHS 'ROUND THE YEAR (Sterling, 1990) Instructions for over 90 herbal, dried and evergreen wreaths; a wonderful introduction for the novice.

Kollath, Richard
WREATHS: CREATIVE IDEAS FOR THE YEAR ROUND (Houghton Mifflin, 1990) Specific instructions for making 75 traditional and unusual wreaths.

WREATHS: TECHNIQUES, MATERIALS, STEP-BY-STEP PROJECTS AND CREATIVE IDEAS FOR ALL THE YEAR ROUND (Facts On File, 1988) Fifty wreaths with either a straw, wire, grapevine or styrofoam base.
YEAR-ROUND WREATHS: CREATIVE IDEAS FOR EVERY SEASON (Facts On File, 1992) Sequel to the above book with another 50 innovative wreaths, plus new techniques and materials such as corn, straw flowers, gourds, lichen, moss, etc.

Lloyd, Elizabeth Jane
ENCHANTED CIRCLES: THE ART OF MAKING DECORATIVE WREATHS FOR ALL SEASONS AND SPECIAL OCCASIONS (Simon & Schuster, 1990) Covers designs from Scandinavia, England, France and North America; includes a variety of techniques.

Pulleyn, Rob
THE WREATH BOOK (Sterling, 1988) Instructions for over 100 wreaths using herbs, flowers, evergreens, fruits and vegetables, cones and toys.

Sherman, Steve
CHRISTMAS WREATHS (Viking Penguin, 1987) Instructions for 45 wreaths created by well-known florists from around the U.S.
WREATHS FOR ALL SEASONS (Viking Penguin, 1986) Covers 42 wreaths including ones made with cloth, candy, grapevines and bread.

Simmons, Adelma Grenier
COUNTRY WREATHS FROM CAPRILANDS: THE LEGEND, LORE AND DESIGN OF TRADITIONAL HERBAL WREATHS (Wieser & Wieser, 1989) Step-by-step instructions for making herbal wreaths and garlands.

Part III:

Specific
Gardening
Methods

ORGANIC GARDENING

Abraham, George and Katy
ORGANIC GARDENING UNDER GLASS: FRUITS, VEGETABLES, AND ORNAMENTALS IN THE GREENHOUSE (Van Nostrand Reinhold, 1984) Includes information on type of soil needed, herbs and greenhouse construction.

Ball, Jeff, and Cresson, Charles O.
THE 60 MINUTE FLOWER GARDEN: HAVE A YARD FULL OF DAZZLING FLOWERS IN ONE HOUR A WEEK (Rodale Press, 1987)

Barbarow, Peter
GIVE PEAS A CHANCE: ORGANIC GARDENING CARTOON-SCIENCE (Naturegraph, 1989) Through cartoons learn how to make compost, improve your soil, use organic fertilizers, propagate plants, control pests and more.

Bradley, Fern (editor)
RODALE'S CHEMICAL-FREE YARD AND GARDEN: THE ULTIMATE AUTHORITY ON SUCCESSFUL ORGANIC GARDENING (Rodale Press, 1991) Covers safe gardening products and techniques, recommendations for fertilizers and pest controls and a system for switching to chemical-free gardening.

Bradley, Fern, and Ellis, Barbara (editors)
RODALE'S ALL NEW ENCYCLOPEDIA OF ORGANIC GARDENING: THE INDISPENSABLE RESOURCE FOR EVERY GARDENER (Rodale Press, 1992) Covers techniques, design, growing food crops, herbs, bulbs, annuals, perennials, shrubs, trees, ground covers, vines, how to make and use compost, control pests and diseases organically, and more; includes over 420 A to Z entries.

California Action Network
ORGANIC WHOLESALERS DIRECTORY AND YEARBOOK: ORGANIC FOOD AND FARM SUPPLIES—Annual directory published by California Action Network, P.O. Box 464, Davis, CA 95617, 916-756-8518.

Carr, Anna
ADVANCED ORGANIC GARDENING (Rodale Press, 1982)

Coleman, Eliot
THE NEW ORGANIC GROWER: A MASTER'S MANUAL OF TOOLS AND TECHNIQUES

FOR THE HOME AND MARKET GARDENER
(Chelsea Green, 1989) Includes crop rotation, green manures, tillage, soil blocks, season extenders, cutting costs, marketing produce, an extensive bibliography and much more.

Conford, Philip (editor)
THE ORGANIC TRADITION (Green Books, 1988) Anthology of the writings of 10 British authors on organic gardening.

Denckla, Tanya
GARDENING AT A GLANCE: THE ORGANIC GARDENER'S HANDBOOK ON VEGETABLES, FRUITS, NUTS AND HERBS (Wooden Angel, 1991) Excellent reference on growing food without using chemicals; includes information on specific plants, charts on controlling pests and companion plantings.

Ellis, Barbara (editor)
RODALE'S ILLUSTRATED ENCYCLOPEDIA OF GARDENING AND LANDSCAPING TECHNIQUES: CHEMICAL FREE (Rodale Press, 1990) Everything you need to know to grow annuals, perennials, bulbs, herbs, roses, grasses, trees, shrubs and food gardens; includes recipes and projects.

Foster, Catharine O.
ORGANIC FLOWER GARDENING (Rodale Press, 1975) Surveys organic methods for growing perennials, annuals and bulbs.

Hamilton, Geoff
THE ORGANIC GARDEN BOOK (Crown, 1987)

Hay, Jim
GARDEN MATTERS: FEEDING PLANTS THE ORGANIC WAY (Sterling, 1991) Conditioning the soil with natural fertilizers and homemade plant food.

Hessayon, Dr. D. G.
THE BIO-FRIENDLY GARDENING GUIDE (Sterling, 1991) How to improve the soil and the plants without harming pets, wildlife, people and the environment.

Hills, Lawrence D.
FERTILITY WITHOUT FERTILIZERS: A BASIC APPROACH TO ORGANIC GARDENING (Universe, 1977) How to make and use organic fertilizers.

Hunt, Marjorie
BASIC ORGANIC GARDENING (Rodale Press, 1982)

Hunt, Marjorie, and Bortz, Brenda
HIGH-YIELD GARDENING: HOW TO GET MORE FROM YOUR GARDEN SPACE AND MORE FROM YOUR GARDENING SEASON (Rodale Press, 1986) Tips for intensive gardening using organic techniques.

Kreuter, Marie-Luise
THE MACMILLAN BOOK OF ORGANIC GARDENING (Collier Books, 1985)

Lacey, Roy
ORGANIC GARDENING (Trafalgar Square, 1988)

Pike, Dave
ORGANIC GARDENING: STEP-BY-STEP TO GROWING SUCCESS (Trafalgar Square, 1991) Techniques for organically growing flowers, grasses, water gardens, fruits and vegetables.

Poincelot, Raymond P.
NO-DIG, NO-WEED GARDENING (Rodale Press, 1986) How to grow flowers and vegetables in any size garden.

Powell, Thomas and Betty
YOUR GARDEN HOMESTEAD ON INCHES, YARDS, OR ACRES (Houghton Mifflin, 1977)

Riotte, Louise
ASTROLOGICAL GARDENING: THE ANCIENT WISDOM OF SUCCESSFUL PLANTING AND HARVESTING BY THE STARS (Garden Way, 1989) Details the ancient art of moon gardening. **IN NATURE'S HANDS: AN ORGANIC GARDENING POTPOURRI, FROM ARMADILLOS TO ZUCCHINI** (Taylor Publishing, 1992) A blend of organic gardening tips, folklore, astrological gardening guidelines, natural insect controls, garden recipes and much more.

SLEEPING WITH A SUNFLOWER: A TREA-SURY OF OLD-TIME GARDENING LORE (Garden Way, 1987) Covers folk wisdom, planting by the moon, organic planting tips and pest control, cooking, preserving and more.

Rodale, Jerome I.
THE ORGANIC FRONT (Rodale Press, 1948) The book that popularized the organic gardening movement.

Rodale, Robert, and Johns, Glenn F.
THE BASIC BOOK OF ORGANIC GARDEN-ING (Ballantine, 1981) All the information needed for becoming a successful organic gardener: soil preparation, composting, mulching, chemical-free pest control and more.

Smith, Keith
BACKYARD ORGANIC GARDENER (ISBS, 1990) How to grow organic vegetables.

Sunset
AN ILLUSTRATED GUIDE TO ORGANIC GAR-DENING (Sunset Books, 1991) The details on creating and maintaining a successful chemical-free garden.

Toogood, Alan
ENVIRONMENTALLY FRIENDLY GARDEN (Sterling, 1991) Advice on chemical-free plant care and how to include wildlife in the garden.

For related books, see:
THE BUG BOOK by Philbrick (page 73)
COMMON-SENSE PEST CONTROL by Olkowski et al. (page 73)
COMPOSTING: THE ORGANIC NATURAL WAY by Kitto (page 35)
DESIGNING AND MAINTAINING YOUR EDI-BLE LANDSCAPE NATURALLY by Kourik (page 100)
GARDENING WITHOUT WORK . . . by Stout (page 183)
GRANDMA'S GARDEN by Martin (page 162)
HARDY ROSES by Osborne (page 64)

HAWAIIAN ORGANIC GROWING GUIDE by James-Palmer (page 197)
HOME GROWN by De Saulles (page 100)
HOW TO GROW MORE VEGETABLES THAN YOU EVER THOUGHT POSSIBLE ON LESS LAND THAN YOU CAN IMAGINE by Jeavons (page 102)
HOW TO GROW VEGETABLES ORGANI-CALLY by Cox (page 101)
HOW TO HAVE A GREEN THUMB WITH-OUT AN ACHING BACK by Stout (page 183)
LET NATURE DO THE GROWING by Tokuno (page 103)
NATURAL GARDENING IN THE LOWER RIO GRANDE VALLEY by Coons (page 195)
THE ORGANIC GARDENER'S HANDBOOK OF NATURAL INSECT AND DISEASE CON-TROL by Ellis and Bradley (page 72)
ORGANIC GARDEN VEGETABLES by Van Patten (page 103)
ORIENTAL VEGETABLES by Larkcom (page 102)
PRACTICAL HERB GARDENING WITH REC-IPES by Bunch (page 110)
RODALE'S FLOWER GARDEN PROBLEM SOLVER by Ball (page 72)
RODALE'S GARDEN INSECT, DISEASE AND WEED IDENTIFICATION GUIDE by Smith and Carr (page 74)
RODALE'S GARDEN PROBLEM SOLVER by Ball (page 72)
RODALE'S LANDSCAPE PROBLEM SOLVER by Ball (page 72)
THE RUTH STOUT NO-WORK GARDEN BOOK by Stout and Clemence (page 184)
THE SELF-SUFFICIENT SUBURBAN GAR-DEN by Ball (page 101)
SLUGS, BUGS AND OTHER THUGS by Hart (page 73)
STEP-BY-STEP TO ORGANIC VEGETABLE GROWING by Ogden (page 103)

XERISCAPE

The National Xeriscape Council, Inc. (P.O. Box 163172, Austin, TX 78716, 512-392-6225) compiles information about water conservation techniques in landscaping and disseminates it through the bimonthly *National Xeriscape News* and how-to brochures.

Chatto, Beth
THE DRY GARDEN (Dent, 1981) How to conserve water and improve the soil; which plants work best in a dry garden.

DeFreitas, Stan
THE WATER-THRIFTY GARDEN (Taylor Publishing, 1992) Covers the seven principles of xeriscaping, water-efficient landscape plans that include color, the best lawn grasses and more; includes a dictionary of drought-tolerant plants and lists of mail order nurseries and support organizations.

Duffield, Mary Rose, and Jones, Warren D.
PLANTS FOR DRY CLIMATES: HOW TO SELECT, GROW AND ENJOY (HP Books, 1992, updated edition) Covers the advantages and disadvantages, plus soil, water, sun and temperature requirements of over 350 plants that are both decorative and drought-resistant; 500 color photos.

Ellefson, Connie; Stephens, Tom; and Welsh, Doug
XERISCAPE GARDENING: WATER CONSERVATION FOR THE AMERICAN LANDSCAPE (Macmillan, 1992) Covers the principles of low-water landscaping and how to create a xeriscape through changes in garden design, watering methods and plant selection.

Knopf, Jim
THE XERISCAPE FLOWER GARDENER: A WATERWISE GUIDE FOR THE ROCKY MOUN-

TAIN REGION (Johnson Books, 1991) How to garden in arid climates; includes edibles and gardening for wildlife, butterflies and hummingbirds.

Millard, Scott
GARDENING IN DRY CLIMATES (Ortho, 1989) Covers lawns, vegetable and flower gardens in the dry western part of the U.S.; growing information on 200 suitable plants.

Sunset
WATERWISE GARDENING: BEAUTIFUL GARDENS WITH LESS WATER (Sunset Books, 1989) How to conserve water and still have a beautiful garden through the proper use of soils, mulches, and irrigation; includes a list of appropriate plants.

Taylor's
GUIDE TO WATER-SAVING GARDENING (Houghton Mifflin, 1990) Surveys 259 flowers, ground covers, shrubs and trees that require less water; includes suggestions for all parts of the U.S., plus information on plant selection, improving the soil, water-saving methods of irrigation and maintenance.

Walters, James, and Backhaus, Balbir
SHADE AND COLOR WITH WATER-CONSERVING PLANTS (Timber Press, 1992) How to plan, develop, install and maintain low-water-use landscapes; describes 300+ species and cultivars of arid-adapted plants.

For related books:
See section on "Rock Gardens".
BEAUTIFUL GARDENS by Johnson and Millard (page 201)

HYDROPONICS

Hydroponic Society of America (P.O. Box 6067, Concord, CA 94524) publishes a directory of sources for hydroponics gardening, which includes a list of books on hydroponics and related subjects. They also issue a bimonthly newsletter of book reviews and articles by growers and researchers.

Bridwell, Raymond
HYDROPONIC GARDENING: THE MAGIC OF HYDROPONICS FOR THE HOME GARDENER (Woodbridge Press, 1990, revised edition) With a small amount of space and 15 to 20 minutes a day, you can grow fruits and vegetables year-round.

Dekorne, James B.
HYDROPONIC HOT HOUSE: LOW COST, HIGH-YIELD GREENHOUSE GARDENING (Loompanics Unlimited, 1992)

Douglas, James S.
BEGINNER'S GUIDE TO HYDROPONICS: SOILLESS GARDENING (Penguin, 1984) To get you started.
ADVANCED GUIDE TO HYDROPONICS: SOILLESS CULTIVATION (Pelham Books, 1985)

Detailed coverage of principles, unit design and construction, nutrients, deficiencies and more.

Hudson, Joel
HYDROPONIC GREENHOUSE GARDENING (National Graphics, 1976) An introduction to hydroponics giving the equipment needed plus how to plant, care for, feed, and detect problems.

Jones, Lem, with Beardsley, Paul and Cay
HOME HYDROPONICS . . . AND HOW TO DO IT (Crown, 1977) Covers the very simple to the more advanced methods of growing plants without soil; includes information on equipment needed, nutrient solutions, soil substitutes and complete directions for building a greenhouse.

Kenyon, Stewart
HYDROPONICS FOR THE HOME GARDENER (Van Nostrand Reinhold, 1979) How to build an easy-to-maintain hydroponic unit, plus how to plant, light, feed and care for vegetables and herbs indoors.

Loewer, Peter
THE INDOOR WATER GARDENER'S HOW-TO HANDBOOK (Walker, 1973) Describes the nec-

essary equipment and techniques for growing a variety of plants and bulbs in water.

Nicholls, R. E.
BEGINNING HYDROPONICS: SOILLESS GARDENING (Running Press, 1990, rev. edition) The basics of growing vegetables, houseplants, flowers and herbs without soil.

Resh, Howard
HYDROPONIC FOOD PRODUCTION: A DE-FINITIVE GUIDE TO SOILLESS CULTURE (Woodbridge Press, 1989, 4th edition revised and enlarged) For the more advanced and the commercial hydroponic gardener.
HYDROPONIC HOME FOOD GARDENS (Woodbridge Press, 1990) Discusses a variety of vegetables, systems, diseases, pests, nutrient formulas, etc.

Smith, Dennis L.
ROCKWOOL IN HORTICULTURE (Grower Books, 1987) Covers requirements for rockwool growing, sources and types of rockwool, equipment, watering, nutrition, growing food and flowers and more.

Sutherland, Dr. Struan
HYDROPONICS FOR EVERYONE (ISBS, 1987) Explains the simplest to the more complex set-ups for growing flowers, herbs and vegetables using natural or artificial light.

For related books, see:
MORE FOOD FROM YOUR GARDEN by Mittlieder (page 100)

Part IV:

Special
Types
of
Gardens

ORIENTAL GARDENS

GENERAL REFERENCES

Bring, Mitchell, and Wayemberg, Josse
JAPANESE GARDENS: DESIGN AND MEAN-ING (McGraw-Hill, 1988)

Brooklyn Botanic Garden
JAPANESE GARDENS (BBG #108) Surveys Japanese design, plants, Koi, basins, stones, etc.
ORIENTAL HERBS AND VEGETABLES (BBG #101) Learn how to grow Oriental herbs and vegetables.

Conder, Josiah
LANDSCAPE GARDENING IN JAPAN (Dover, 1990) Covers hill and water gardens, flat gardens, tea house gardens, passage gardens and elaborate gardens; reprint of the 1912 work that brought Japanese gardening ideas to the West.

Engel, David
CREATING A CHINESE GARDEN (Timber Press, 1986) Thirty-two excellent color photos and 160 black-and-white illustrations complement the landscaping ideas.

JAPANESE GARDENS FOR TODAY: A PRAC-TICAL HANDBOOK (C. E. Tuttle, 1959) Design ideas for entrances, stone groupings, walls, ornaments and using water in the garden.

Kenkyuijo, Tatsui T.
GARDEN VIEWS I: MODERN JAPANESE GARDENS (Books Nippan, 1990) How to create a small modern Japanese garden.
GARDEN VIEWS II: STONE AND SAND GAR-DENS (Books Nippan, 1990) How stone and sand is used in the Japanese garden.

Keswick, Maggie
THE CHINESE GARDEN (St. Martin's, 1986)

Lifang, Chen, and Sianglin, Yu
THE GARDEN ART OF CHINA (Timber Press, 1986) Over 100 garden plans for rockeries, trees, flowers and water.

Newsome, Samuel
JAPANESE GARDEN CONSTRUCTION (ISBS, 1988) Covers the origin and history of Japanese gardens, plus explores the design elements used in a Japanese garden; reprint of 1939 edition.

Ohashi, Haruzo
JAPANESE GARDENS OF THE MODERN ERA
(Japan Publications USA, 1987)

Ortho
CREATING JAPANESE GARDENS (Ortho, 1989) How to plan, design and build a Japanese garden using plants that are available in North America.

Richards, Betty, and Kaneko, Anne
JAPANESE PLANTS: KNOW THEM AND USE THEM (C. E. Tuttle, 1988) Covers description and history of the familiar (maples, irises, azaleas), plus the not-so-familiar.

Seike, Kiyoshi, and Kudo, Masanobu
A JAPANESE TOUCH FOR YOUR GARDEN (Kodansha, 1980) Details for including Japanese elements (water pools, sand patterns, stone groupings, etc.) in a small or large garden, plus suggestions for American plants and trees to use.

Slawson, David A.
SECRET TEACHINGS IN THE ART OF JAPANESE GARDENS: DESIGN PRINCIPLES, AESTHETIC VALUES (Kodansha, 1991) Understanding and using Japanese design ideas in your garden.

Takenosuke, Tatsui
GARDEN VIEWS IV: TREE AND MOSS GARDENS (Books Nippan, 1991) How to place trees and moss in a garden to achieve different effects.

Teien, Tatsui
GARDEN VIEWS III: WATER AND STREAM GARDENS (Books Nippan, 1990) Details and plans for using water in a variety of ways.

Tsu, F. Y.
LANDSCAPE DESIGN IN CHINESE GARDENS (McGraw-Hill, 1988)

Yoshikawa, Isao
ELEMENTS OF JAPANESE GARDENS (Books Nippan, 1991) Over 500 photos (413 in color) of gates, walls, fences, walkways, stone patterns, lanterns, water basins and others.

BONSAI

The American Bonsai Society (Box 358, Keene, NH 03431) publishes an in-depth journal and a newsletter, both four times a year. They also sell numerous books on bonsai and have an extensive library of slide and video programs demonstrating the techniques of bonsai.

Bonsai Clubs International (2636 West Mission Road, #277, Tallahassee, FL 32304) publishes *Bonsai Magazine*, has a slide lending program, a large lending library, a book selling service and a directory of suppliers.

Adams, Peter D.
THE ART OF BONSAI (Sterling, 1990) Geared to the intermediate level, it covers styles, techniques, when to prune, repotting and which containers are best, wiring and more.
BONSAI DESIGN: DECIDUOUS AND CONIFEROUS TREES (Sterling, 1990) Covers the first six years of growing bonsai from the hornbeam, elm, juniper, beech and others.
BONSAI DESIGN: JAPANESE MAPLES (Sterling, 1988) Surveys techniques and gives 13 examples of the variety of ways Japanese maples can be treated.
SUCCESSFUL BONSAI GROWING (Sterling, 1987) Introduction describing the basic styles, repotting, wiring branches, thinning, sources and more.

Ainsworth, John
THE ART OF INDOOR BONSAI: CULTIVATING TROPICAL, SUB-TROPICAL AND TENDER BONSAI (Trafalgar Square, 1988) Includes which plants are suitable and specific details on cultivating them.

Anderson, Charles and Ruth
CARE AND FEEDING OF BONSAI (Harbor Crest, 1988)

Barton, Dan
THE BONSAI BOOK: THE DEFINITIVE ILLUSTRATED GUIDE (Trafalgar Square, 1990) Contains step-by-step instructions and photographs for traditional as well as new techniques; includes a five-year plan.

Bester, John (translator)
CLASSIC BONSAI OF JAPAN (Kodansha, 1989) Color photographs of the best examples of bonsai in

Japan with notes on plant type, age, size, balance, style and harmony.

Bloomer, Mary H.
TIMELESS TREES: THE U.S. NATIONAL BONSAI COLLECTION (Horizons West, 1986) Examples of trees, miniature forests and viewing stones at the National Arboretum in Washington.

Brooklyn Botanic Garden
BONSAI FOR INDOORS (BBG #81) How to select the correct plants.
BONSAI: SPECIAL TECHNIQUES (BBG #51) Covers advanced techniques of cascade, stoneclasping and miniatures; includes information on pinching, pruning and wiring.
DWARFED POTTED TREES: THE BONSAI OF JAPAN (BBG #13) For beginners, includes repotting, root pruning, watering, wiring, winter care, containers; also Yeddo spruce, wisteria and Satsuki azalea bonsai.
INDOOR BONSAI (BBG #125) Describes the latest cultivation techniques for growing bonsai indoors.

Chan, Peter
BONSAI: THE ART OF GROWING AND KEEPING MINIATURE TREES (Chartwell, 1987) How to start a tree, the special care required, which trees are suitable and the various styles such as slanted trunk, multiple trunk and reclining.
BONSAI MASTER CLASS (Sterling, 1988) Step-by-step projects enable the reader to learn the necessary principles plus the skills necessary to produce bonsai.

Clark, Randy
OUTSTANDING AMERICAN BONSAI: A PHOTOGRAPHIC ESSAY ON THE WORKS OF FIFTY AMERICAN BONSAI ARTISTS (Timber Press, 1989) Sixty color photos plus descriptions of the trees and information about the creators who were selected by the directors of the National Bonsai Foundation as representative of the finest bonsai artists in America in 1987.

Daute, Horst
MACMILLAN BOOK OF BONSAI (Collier Books, 1986) Over 100 step-by-step color photos illustrate techniques for the care and cultivation of all types of bonsai; includes starting a plant or choosing and caring for a purchased one and special tools and equipment needed.

Giorgi, Gianfranco
SIMON & SCHUSTER'S GUIDE TO BONSAI (Simon & Schuster, 1991) Covers technique, styles, which plants are most suitable, plus how to care for 124 different plants.

Kawasumi, Masakuni
BONSAI WITH AMERICAN TREES (Kodansha, 1984, 2nd edition) Covers which American trees work best for bonsai and step-by-step illustrations on trimming, potting, wiring, cutting and grafting.

Koide, Nobukichi
THE MASTERS BOOK OF BONSAI (Collingridge Books, 1968) Instructions for evergreen and deciduous, flowering and fruiting trees.

Koreshoff, Deborah
BONSAI: ITS ART, SCIENCE, HISTORY AND PHILOSOPHY (Timber Press, 1984) One of the standard works on bonsai, it encompasses an enormous amount of information on growing and training techniques.

Lesniewicz, Ilona, and Zhimin, Li
CHINESE BONSAI: THE ART OF PENJING (Blandford Press, 1988)

Lesniewicz, Paul
BONSAI: THE COMPLETE GUIDE TO ART AND TECHNIQUE (Sterling, 1984) Surveys the various tree shapes and groupings, rock plantings and miniature landscapes; covers growing plants from seed, cuttings and the wild; plus gives information on training, pruning and caring for bonsai.
INDOOR BONSAI (Sterling, 1985) Covers the best plants for indoor bonsai plus light and soil needs, when to repot, feeding, watering, wiring and pruning.
THE WORLD OF BONSAI (Sterling, 1991) Over 100 full-page color photos evoking the spirit of bonsai and specific bonsai masterpieces.

Lesniewicz, Paul, and Kato, Hideo
PRACTICAL BONSAI (Avery Publishing Group, 1991)

Meyer, Jerome
THE BONSAI BOOK OF PRACTICAL FACTS (Purchase Publishing, 1988)

Murata, Kyuzo
FOUR SEASONS OF BONSAI (Kodansha, 1991) From the private collection of Japan's leading authority, 180 bonsai at their peak time of the year are shown; includes traditional trees plus perennials, wildflowers and grasses.

Naka, John Yoshio
BONSAI TECHNIQUES I (1975) and BONSAI TECHNIQUES II (1982) are available from the Bonsai Institute of California, P.O. Box 78211, Los Angeles, CA 90016.

Owen, Gordon
THE BONSAI IDENTIFIER (Chartwell, 1990) Covers 40+ species and their most common varieties, care and style for each, plus general information on branches, trunk, silhouette, etc.

Perl, Philip, and Editors of Time-Life Books
MINIATURES AND BONSAI (Time-Life Books, 1979)

Pike, Dave
BONSAI: STEP-BY-STEP TO GROWING SUCCESS (Trafalgar Square, 1990) Basics plus a five-year training plan for hardy bonsai, special techniques, rock plantings, and more.
INDOOR BONSAI: A BEGINNER'S STEP-BY-STEP GUIDE (Trafalgar Square, 1989) Covers growing, training and which plants do best indoors; includes creating multiple trunk bonsai from single seedlings and rock plantings.

Resnick, Susan M.
BONSAI (Little, Brown, 1992) Written in cooperation with the Brooklyn Botanic Garden.

Roger, Alan
BONSAI (Wisley Handbook) (Sterling, 1990) Advice plus 42 pages of color photos.

Samson, Isabelle and Remy
THE CREATIVE ART OF BONSAI (Sterling, 1991) Instructions for Chinese and Japanese styles, indoor and outdoor pieces, plus growing and landscaping ideas; 60 species are covered.

Shufunotomo Editors
THE ESSENTIALS OF BONSAI (Timber Press, 1982) A best-selling introduction for beginners that includes step-by-step photos plus all the basic information needed for getting started.

Stowell, Jerald P.
THE BEGINNER'S GUIDE TO AMERICAN BONSAI (Kodansha, 1978) Stowell, the first president of the American Bonsai Society, covers American trees and shrubs suitable for bonsai and gives regional timetables for potting, wiring and shaping.

Sunset
BONSAI (Sunset Books, 1976, 2nd edition) Step-by-step techniques for growing miniature trees.

Takayanagi, Yoshio
MASTERPIECES OF BONSAI (Kodansha, 1986)

Tomlinson, Harry
THE COMPLETE BOOK OF BONSAI: A PRACTICAL GUIDE TO ITS ART AND CULTIVATION (Abbeville Press, 1991) Gives cultivation and styling information for over 100 species of trees and shrubs; includes 700 color photos.

Webber, Leonard
BONSAI FOR THE HOME AND GARDEN: A PRACTICAL STEP-BY-STEP GUIDE (HarperCollins, 1985) He relates his experiences in creating bonsai.

Young, Dorothy S.
BONSAI: THE ART AND TECHNIQUE (Prentice-Hall, 1985) Introduction covering the basics for the beginner.

Yunhua, Hu
CHINESE PENJING: MINIATURE TREES AND LANDSCAPES (Timber Press, 1988) How to create penjing, plus photos of some plants that are over 500 years old. He is the director of the Penjing Research Center at the Shangai Botanical Garden.
PENJING: THE CHINESE ART OF MINIATURE GARDENS (Timber Press, 1982) Practical and historical information on penjing, the Chinese ancestor of bonsai.

For related books, see:
BETTER VEGETABLE GARDENS THE CHINESE WAY by Chan (page 101)

TOPIARY GARDENS

Brooklyn Botanic Garden
TRAINED AND SCULPTURED PLANTS (BBG #36) Covers topiary, espalier, pleaching, and which plants do best for these forms.

Carr, David
TOPIARY AND PLANT SCULPTURE: A BEGINNER'S STEP-BY-STEP GUIDE (Trafalgar Square, 1991) Covers various sculpting techniques, plus which plants to use, where and how to use them and how to keep them healthy.

Clevely, A. M.
TOPIARY: THE ART OF CLIPPING TREES AND ORNAMENTAL HEDGES (Salem House, 1988)

Curtis, Charles H., and Gibson, W.
THE BOOK OF TOPIARY (C. E. Tuttle Co., 1985) Reprint of 1904 classic that describes the creation of a topiary garden plus history, planting, fertilizing and training new plants.

Gallup, Barbara, and Reich, Deborah
THE COMPLETE BOOK OF TOPIARY (Workman Publishing, 1987) Detailed instructions for 75 indoor and outdoor projects using techniques from famous large (e.g., Versailles) and unknown small gardens; introduction by Rosemary Verey.

Hammer, Patricia Riley
THE NEW TOPIARY: IMAGINATIVE TECHNIQUES FROM LONGWOOD GARDENS (Antique Collector's Club, 1991) How to train flowers and ivies into large and small indoor and outdoor shapes in a matter of weeks.

Lacey, Geraldine
CREATING TOPIARY (ISBS, 1987) Explains how to choose, shape and train the most suitable plants for an outdoor whimsical or formal topiary garden; includes photos of the best examples of topiary from around the world.

For related books, see:
ENGLISH TOPIARY GARDENS by Clark and Wright (page 204)

ROCK GARDENS

The American Rock Garden Society (P.O. Box 67, Millwood, NY 10546) offers a quarterly bulletin, worldwide seed exchange, bookstore discounts, a book and slide library and garden tours. Their list of "All Time Favorite Rock Garden Books" is extensive and includes members' opinions about the books.

Ashberry, Anne
MINIATURE GARDENS (Van Nostrand, 1951)

Baxendale, Martin
GARDENING IN MINIATURE (Sterling, 1990) How-to information on using smaller plants in various gardening situations; includes alpines, dwarf conifers, bulbs, etc.

Bird, Richard
A GUIDE TO ROCK GARDENING (Trafalgar Square, 1990) How to design, create and maintain rock gardens, raised beds, alpine houses, dry stone walls, gravel beds and paving plantings.

Bissland, J. H.
COMMON SENSE IN THE ROCK GARDEN (de la Mare, 1938)

Bloom, Alan
ALPINES FOR TROUBLE-FREE GARDENING (Faber, 1961)
ALPINES FOR YOUR GARDEN (Floraprint, 1981) Covers over 750 species and varieties and includes ideas for landscaping.

Brooklyn Botanic Garden
ROCK GARDENING (BBG #91) Covers every aspect from beginning to advanced techniques.

Carl, Joachim
MINIATURE GARDENS (Timber Press, 1990) Explores the principles and techniques of a specialized form of alpine gardening that developed in England in the 1920s: gardening in troughs and on slabs; includes instructions for building artificial troughs and slabs.

Charlesworth, Geoffrey
THE OPINIONATED GARDENER: RANDOM OFFSHOOTS FROM AN ALPINE PARADISE (David Godine, 1988) His experiences in creating a four-acre alpine garden in Massachusetts.

Clay, Sampson
THE PRESENT DAY ROCK GARDEN, BEING A COMPLEMENTARY VOLUME TO FARRER'S

"ENGLISH ROCK GARDEN" (Theophrastus, 1976) A reprint of the 1937 edition.

Elliot, Roy
ALPINE GARDENING (Theophrastus, 1978)

Elliott, Jack
ALPINES IN THE OPEN GARDEN (Timber Press, 1991) Not all alpines require rock gardens or special soil conditions; how to use alpines in perennial borders or other ordinary garden areas.

Elliott, Joe
ALPINES THE EASY WAY (Wisley Handbook) (Sterling, 1991) An introductory guide covering raised beds, sinks and troughs and alpine houses.

Farrer, Reginald
ALPINES AND BOG PLANTS (Theophrastus, 1976) Reprint of the 1908 edition.
THE ENGLISH ROCK GARDEN (Theophrastus, 1976) (2 volumes) Reprint of the 1919 edition.
MY ROCK GARDEN (Theophrastus, 1971) Reprint of the 1907 edition.

Ferguson, Katherine (editor)
HARROWSMITH GARDENER'S GUIDE TO ROCK GARDENS (Camden House, 1988) Five experts advise how to plan and build a rock garden.

Foerster, Dr. Karl
ROCK GARDENS THROUGH THE YEAR: AN ILLUSTRATED GUIDE FOR BEGINNERS AND EXPERTS (Sterling, 1987) Covers perennials, bulbs, shrubs, small trees, dwarf conifers, ferns, grasses and water/marsh plants suitable for rock gardens.

Foster, H. Lincoln
ROCK GARDENING: A GUIDE TO GROWING ALPINES AND OTHER WILDFLOWERS IN THE AMERICAN GARDEN (Timber Press, 1982) A classic in the field for its wealth of information (examines 1,900 plants in 400 genera) and great readability.

Foster, H. Lincoln and Laura L.
CUTTINGS FROM A ROCK GARDEN: PLANT PORTRAITS AND OTHER ESSAYS (Atlantic Monthly Press, 1990) How they created a rock garden at Millstream House in northwest Connecticut, plus portraits of over 100 genera, and "Reflections on the Gardening Art."

Foster, Raymond
ROCK GARDEN AND ALPINE PLANTS (David & Charles, 1982) The plants discussed are arranged by cultural requirements; includes a helpful listing of the form, flower, height, soil and site needs of each plant.

Grey-Wilson, Christopher
THE ALPINE FLOWERS OF BRITAIN AND EUROPE (Collins, 1979)
A MANUAL OF ALPINE AND ROCK GARDEN PLANTS (Timber Press, 1989) Descriptions and cultivation requirements for the most readily available alpines with notations on which are easy to grow and which are more difficult.

Griffith, Anna
COLLINS GUIDE TO ALPINES AND ROCK GARDEN PLANTS (Collins, 1964)

Harkness, Mabel G., and D'Angelo, Deborah (compilers and updaters)
THE BERNARD E. HARKNESS SEEDLIST HANDBOOK (Timber Press, 1986) A guide to the seed exchanges of the American Rock Garden Society, Alpine Garden Society and Scottish Rock Garden Club giving species or cultivar description, habit and hardiness, plant height, outstanding characteristics, country of origin and key to references where more information can be found.

Heath, Royton
THE COLLINGRIDGE GUIDE TO COLLECTORS' ALPINES: THEIR CULTIVATION IN FRAMES AND ALPINE HOUSES (Timber Press, 1983) Describes the various types of alpine gardens and alpine plants, plus gives information on alpine houses and frames.
ROCK PLANTS FOR SMALL GARDENS (Collingridge, 1982) Covers how to select and care for rock garden plants.

Hill, Lawrence D.
THE PROPAGATION OF ALPINES (Theophrastus, 1976) A practical guide by an English nurseryman; reprint of 1950 edition.

Ingwersen, Will
ALPINES (Timber Press, 1991) A reference work, plus a very personal account of the favorite alpines of the best known English rock gardener. Ingwersen died in 1990.
ALPINES IN COLOUR (Sterling, 1991) Reissue; descriptions and cultivation information for over 200 alpines.
MANUAL OF ALPINE PLANTS (Sterling, 1991) Revised and updated edition of a standard reference on alpines; A to Z format with detailed descriptions of species, varieties and hybrids, plus cultivating advice and a growing-difficulty rating chart.

Joyce, David
ROCK GARDENS AND ALPINE PLANTS (Prentice-Hall, 1986)

Klaber, Doretta
ROCK GARDEN PLANTS: NEW WAYS TO USE THEM AROUND YOUR HOME (Bramhall House, 1959) Includes an A to Z listing (by botanical name) of approximately 400 plants giving description and growing information; written from her personal experience with Cloud Hill Nursery in Quakertown, Pennsylvania.

Kohlein, Fritz
SAXIFRAGES AND RELATED GENERA (Timber Press, 1984) Covers species, cultivars and hybrids, propagation, pests and diseases, and ways of using saxifrages in the garden.

Lawrence, Elizabeth
A ROCK GARDEN IN THE SOUTH (Duke University Press, 1990, edited and updated edition) Includes the principles of rock gardening, plus her personal experiences of what works and what doesn't work when creating a rock garden in the middle South.

Mathew, Brian
THE GENUS LEWISIA: A KEW MAGAZINE MONOGRAPH (Timber Press, 1989) Covers history, taxonomy, cultivation information and available cultivars.

Moggi, Guido
THE MACDONALD ENCYCLOPEDIA OF ALPINE FLOWERS (Macdonald, 1984)

Rolfe, Robert
THE ALPINE HOUSE (Timber Press, 1991) Covers site selection, construction, ventilation, lighting and cultivation methods of this popular method of alpine gardening in England.

Tanner, Ogden
ROCK AND WATER GARDENS (Time-Life Books, 1982) How to construct a rock or water garden, plus descriptions and growing information on plants to use.

Thomas, Graham Stuart
THE ROCK GARDEN AND ITS PLANTS: FROM GROTTO TO ALPINE HOUSE (Timber Press, 1989) A complete history of rock gardening plus advice on creating, restoring, and maintaining various types of rock gardens

Webb, D. A., and Gornall, R. J.
A MANUAL OF SAXIFRAGES (Timber Press, 1988) A comprehensive encyclopedia of botanic and cultivation information; includes maps showing the native habitats of various species.

Wilder, Louise Beebe
ADVENTURES IN MY GARDEN AND ROCK GARDEN (Doubleday, 1923)
PLEASURES AND PROBLEMS OF A ROCK GARDEN (Doubleday, 1928)
THE ROCK GARDEN (Doubleday, 1933)

Williams, Jean (editor)
ROCKY MOUNTAIN ALPINES (Timber Press, 1986) The proceedings of a 1986 Colorado symposium; includes cultivation, propagation and landscaping information on the native alpines of western North America.

For related books, see:
CAMPANULAS by Lewis and Lynch (page 89)
GARDENING WITH DWARF TREES AND SHRUBS by Bartels (page 51)
GENTIANS by Kohlein (page 89)
GENTIANS FOR YOUR GARDEN by Klaber (page 89)

WATER GARDENS

Allison, James
WATER IN THE GARDEN: A COMPLETE GUIDE TO THE DESIGN AND INSTALLATION OF PONDS, FOUNTAINS, STREAMS AND WATERFALLS (Little, Brown, 1991) Describes natural looking ponds, pools, streams, fountains and waterfalls that can be installed in all kinds of gardens.

Aslet, Ken; Warwich, John; and Bolders, Jan
WATER GARDENS (Wisley Handbook)(Sterling, 1990) An introduction covering design, construction, selection of plants and maintenance.

Brooklyn Botanic Garden
WATER GARDENING (BBG #106) Covers tropical water lilies and lotuses, pools, bog gardens, plants for pond and lake edges.

Chatto, Beth
THE DAMP GARDEN (Dent, 1986) A wealth of ideas and descriptive plant lists for the more advanced water gardener with details on a swamp garden and sunny and shady damp gardens; includes how she created her own damp garden.

Dawes, John
BOOK OF WATER GARDENS (TFH Publications, 1989) A complete guide that covers choosing the site, design ideas, types of construction and plant choices.

Fogg, H. G. Witham
THE WATER GARDEN (W & G Foyle, 1960) Covers aquatic, waterside, and bog plants for the outdoor and small indoor water garden.

Heritage, Bill
PONDS AND WATER GARDENS (Sterling, 1987) A step-by-step guide to design and construction, plus information on plant varieties.

Jekyll, Gertrude
WALL, WATER AND WOODLAND GARDENS (Ayer Co., 1983) A reprint with the added bonus of modern color photos.

Ledbetter, Gordon T.
WATER GARDENS (Norton, 1980) A good source of design ideas and also includes a diary for each day of the year in a water garden.

Leverett, Brian
WATER GARDENS: STEP BY STEP TO SUC-
CESS (Trafalgar Square, 1991) Basics on design (formal, cottage, rock, classical, ornamental, patio),
construction, plants and fish.

Llewellyn, Roddy
WATER GARDENS, THE CONNOISSEUR'S
CHOICE (Ward Lock, 1987) History of water garden-
ing plus a survey of 48 water gardens including Hidcote
Manor, Stourhead and Beth Chatto's garden.

Matson, Tim
EARTH PONDS: THE COUNTRY POND
MAKER'S GUIDE (Countryman Press, 1991 revised
and expanded) Complete information on building a
country pond and an aquadome, plus the story of his
own pond.

Muhlberg, Helmut
THE COMPLETE GUIDE TO WATER PLANTS:
A REFERENCE BOOK (Sterling, 1982) Genera and
species of numerous cultivated aquatic plants.

Ortho
GARDEN POOLS AND FOUNTAINS (Ortho,
1988) The basics, plus landscaping, bridge building,
adding a waterfall and ensuring the water quality.

Paul, Anthony, and Rees, Yvonne
THE WATER GARDEN: A GUIDE TO
DESIGNING, INSTALLING AND PLANTING
ORNAMENTAL AND NATURAL WATER
FEATURES (Viking Penguin, 1986) Ideas for bridges,
pavings, cascades, lighting and more.

Perry, Frances
THE WATER GARDEN (Van Nostrand Reinhold,
1981) Construction and complete information on
water lilies, aquatic plants, and bog garden plants; first
published in 1938 and has been revised and reissued
many times.

Robinson, Peter
POOL AND WATERSIDE GARDENING: A
KEW GARDENING GUIDE (Timber Press, 1987)
Includes 75 color photos and 50 black-and-white
illustrations.

WATERLILIES AND OTHER AQUATIC
PLANTS (Henry Holt, 1989) Examines which lilies
and other plants to choose and why.

Stadelmann, Peter
WATER GARDENS (Barron, 1992) Advice and
instructions for creating streams, pools, water wheels,
fountains, and large and small water gardens.

Sunset
GARDEN POOLS, FOUNTAINS AND WA-
TERFALLS (Sunset Books, 1989) Covers planning,
building and maintaining a water garden.

Swindells, Philip
AT THE WATER'S EDGE: GARDENING
WITH MOISTURE-LOVING PLANTS (Sterling,
1991) Design ideas, plus selecting plants for all types
of water gardens.
GARDEN MATTERS: SMALL GARDEN POOLS
(Sterling, 1991) Covers simple-to-build pools, plus advice on propagating water plants and keeping ornamental and scavenging fish, freshwater snails, mussels
and other species.
A GUIDE TO WATER GARDENING (Scribner's,
1975) Covers choosing a site and a design for both
indoor and outdoor water gardens, plants, pests and
diseases and stocking with fish.
THE WATER GARDEN: GARDENING BY DE-
SIGN (Sterling, 1990) Advice, color photos, how-to
drawings and step-by-step instructions.
WATERLILIES (Timber Press, 1983) Covers pool
construction and hardy day and night waterlilies.

Swindells, Philip, and Mason, David
THE COMPLETE BOOK OF THE WATER GAR-
DEN (Overlook Press, 1990) Examines natural water
gardens, bogs, waterfalls, fountains and streams; suggests appropriate plants.

Thomas, Charles B.
WATER GARDENS FOR PLANTS AND FISH
(TFH Publications, 1988) Written by the owner of
Lilypons Water Gardens in Maryland and Texas, it
includes planning and installing a water garden, and
information on the plants and fish to put in it.

Uber, William
WATER GARDENING BASICS (Dragonflyer Press, 1988) The author owns Van Ness Water Gardens in California; covers everything you need to know (building, plant and fish selection, maintaining water quality, etc.).

For related books, see:
ENGLISH WATER GARDENS by Cooper and Taylor (page 205)
HARROWSMITH GUIDE: WATER GARDENS by Archibald (page 190)

COTTAGE GARDENS

Brooklyn Botanic Garden
AMERICAN COTTAGE GARDENING (BBG #123, 1990) Covers the basics of creating a cottage garden with advice for different regions of the country.

Clark, Timothy
MARGERY FISH'S COUNTRY GARDENING (Trafalgar Square, 1989) Describes the gardening methods she used in her East Lambrook Manor cottage garden.

Fish, Margery
COTTAGE GARDEN FLOWERS (Faber & Faber, 1980) Discusses the best plants for a cottage garden, what they need and how they behave.

Gardner, Jo Ann
THE HEIRLOOM GARDEN: SELECTING AND GROWING OVER 300 OLD-FASHIONED OR-NAMENTALS (Storey, 1992) Covers flowers, herbs, shrubs and vines used in American gardens between 1600 and 1950; includes a directory of sources.

Genders, Roy
THE COTTAGE GARDEN AND OLD-FASH-IONED FLOWERS (Viking Penguin, 1987) History and cultivation of flowers in a cottage garden.

Guest, Sarah L.
FLOWERS FOR THE AUSTRALIAN COT-TAGE GARDEN (ISBS, 1989) Features over 300 annuals and perennials that are easy to grow and have long blooming periods; includes symbolic meanings and histories of each plant plus border design and maintenance.

Halliwell, Brian
OLD GARDEN FLOWERS (ISBS, 1987) History, origin and growing information on unusual and hard-to-find flowers often found in cottage gardens.

Lloyd, Christopher, and Bird, Richard
THE COTTAGE GARDEN (Prentice-Hall, 1990) Covers planning a cottage garden: the plants to use as well as the features such as gates, fences and paths which give such charm to a cottage garden; a beautiful book!

Martin, Laura
GRANDMA'S GARDEN: A CELEBRATION OF OLD-FASHIONED GARDENING (Longstreet Press, 1990) Covers ways to recapture yesterday's gardens; includes 40 period photographs.

Mitford, Mary R.
MY GARDEN: A NINETEENTH CENTURY WRITER ON HER ENGLISH COTTAGE GARDEN (Houghton Mifflin, 1990) A collection of her articles and letters about her garden to such friends as Elizabeth Barrett Browning.

Nottle, Trevor
COTTAGE GARDEN FLOWERS (ISBS, 1988) Describes the charms of cottage flowers.
THE COTTAGE GARDEN REVIVED (ISBS, 1985) Covers the history and technique of 19th century cottage gardening, plus ideas for re-creating such a garden.

Phillips, Sue
CREATING A COTTAGE GARDEN (Grove Weidenfeld, 1990) A how-to book covering the various seasons of a cottage garden.

Stuart, David, and Sutherland, James
PLANTS FROM THE PAST (Viking Penguin, 1990) The histories of the oldest herbaceous plants: when they were first used, when they were most popular and when hybrids were introduced.

Swindells, Philip
COTTAGE GARDENING IN TOWN AND COUNTRY (Sterling, 1991) A step-by-step guide for planning, creating and maintaining an English cottage garden.

Thompson, Peter
COUNTRY GARDENING, COUNTRY STYLE: A NATURAL APPROACH TO PLANNING AND PLANTING (Trafalgar Square, 1992) How to re-create the atmosphere and tranquility of a country garden by restoring lost features such as meadows, ponds and orchards and selecting the best trees, shrubs and perennials; includes 63 drawings and plans with before-and-after arrangements.

Whiten, Faith and Geoff
MAKING A COTTAGE GARDEN (Salem House, 1985)

Whiteside, Katherine
ANTIQUE FLOWERS: A GUIDE TO USING OLD-FASHIONED SPECIES IN CONTEMPORARY GARDENS (Random House, 1988) Describes 50 plants that are at least 100 years old; includes nursery sources.

Wilkinson, Jennifer
HERBS AND FLOWERS OF THE COTTAGE GARDEN (ISBS, 1990) Describes and illustrates over 1,000 cottage plants and herbs; information on border gardens, formal gardens, shady gardens, rock gardens and many other types.

For related books, see:
AMERICA'S COTTAGE GARDENS by Thorpe and Sonneman (page 203)
ENGLISH COTTAGE GARDENS by Clarke (page 204)

CONTAINER GARDENS

Baxendale, Martin
WINDOW BOXES (Sterling, 1991) How-to drawings and step-by-step instructions for creating window boxes.

Beckett, Kenneth; Carr, David; and Stevens, David
THE CONTAINED GARDEN: A COMPLETE ILLUSTRATED GUIDE TO GROWING PLANTS, FLOWERS, FRUITS AND VEGETABLES OUTDOORS IN POTS (Viking, 1983) Covers container size needed, selection and care of the best plants (annuals, perennials, herbs, roses, bulbs, climbers, conifers, shrubs, vegetables, fruits), combining plants in one container and more.

Brooklyn Botanic Garden
CONTAINER GARDENING (BBG #85) Ideas for windows, patios, terraces and rooftops.

Brown, Kathleen
SEASONAL CONTAINER GARDENING: WITH CREATIVE RECIPES FOR CONSERVATORY, EDIBLE AND HISTORICAL PLANTINGS (Michael Joseph, 1991) How to plant over 125 different containers for year-round color; features "recipes," with the number and type of plants used, type of

soil and suggested container; includes historical plantings in the Victorian and Edwardian styles.

Brown, Kathleen, and Romain, Effie
CREATIVE CONTAINER GARDENING: 150 RECIPES FOR BASKETS, TUBS AND WINDOW BOXES (Viking Penguin, 1988) Describes exactly how to produce 150 different container gardens using annuals, perennials, shrubs, bulbs, etc. A color photo of each project is included.

Colburn, Nigel
THE CONTAINER GARDEN (Little, Brown, 1990) Encompasses not only the use of containers alone, but also combining container plants with plants in garden beds; has suggestions for using annuals, perennials, fruits, vegetables, herbs, bulbs and trees in a variety of containers.

Cotner, Dr. Sam
CONTAINER VEGETABLES: THE EASY WAY TO GARDEN (Texas Gardener Press, 1987) Here's how to have a vegetable garden when space is at a premium.

Daley, Allen and Stella
MAKING AND USING TERRARIUMS AND
PLANTERS (Blandford Press, 1986) Covers history
of the terrarium, plus tools, materials and techniques
to construct eight different shapes and information on
planting and maintaining the terrarium.

DeLestrieux, Elisabeth, and Hageman, Kees
THE ART OF GARDENING IN POTS (Antique
Collector's Club, 1990) A wealth of ideas for creating unusual gardens in pots; 236 color photos will
stir your imagination.

Ernst, Ruth Shaw
THE MOVABLE GARDEN: HOW TO USE
POTTED PLANTS INDOORS AND OUT TO
CREATE A CAREFREE YEAR-ROUND GAR-
DEN (Globe Pequot, 1991) Complete information on
over 80 plants that thrive outside in summer, then suc-
cessfully move indoors when the weather turns cool.

Halpin, Anne M.
THE WINDOW BOX BOOK (Simon & Schuster,
1989) Describes the creation of Romantic, Formal or
Flight of Fancy window boxes.

Heitz, Halina
CONTAINER PLANTS (Barron, 1992) How to
turn a balcony, porch or patio into a garden using
container plants; 300+ color photos.

Hillier, Malcolm
THE BOOK OF CONTAINER GARDENING
(Simon & Schuster, 1991) Planting ideas for tubs,
pots, urns and hanging baskets with tips for plant care
and information on choosing, making and decorating containers.

Keeling, Jim
THE TERRACOTTA GARDENER (Trafalgar
Square, 1990) Well-known gardeners such as Rosemary
Verey and Penelope Hobhouse create beautiful gardens
using various forms of terracotta as the containers.

McDonald, Elvin
DECORATIVE GARDENING IN CONTAIN-
ERS (Doubleday, 1978)

McHoy, Peter
CONTAINER GARDENING (Blandford Press,
1986)

Nimmo, Derek
WONDERFUL WINDOWBOXES (Sterling, 1990)
Details for nearly 100 windowboxes emphasizing food,
fragrance and color.

Ortho
GARDENING IN CONTAINERS (Ortho, 1983)

Rees, Yvonne, and Palliser, David
CONTAINER GARDENING ALL YEAR
ROUND (Trafalgar Square, 1991) How to plant,
prune and control pests and diseases on flowers,
fruits, vegetables and foliage plants grown in every
type of container.

Simpson, Norman D.
THE INSTANT GUIDE TO HEALTHY
WINDOWBOX AND BALCONY PLANTS
(Times Books, 1986) Covers problems in container
grown shrubs and ornamentals, how to correct the
problems and details for daily care.

Skelsey, Alice F.
CUCUMBERS IN A FLOWERPOT (Workman
Publishing, 1984) Revised edition of *Farming in a
Flowerpot* (1975).

Stewart, Diana
THE WINDOW BOX: POT, TUB AND BASKET
BOOK (Hearst Books, 1985) Covers a variety of
window boxes (all-season, seasonal, alpine, cactus,
bonsai, scented, heather, herb, vegetable, fruit and
boxes for children).

Sunset
CONTAINER GARDENING (Sunset Books,
1984) Complete guide including detailed plant descriptions.

Toogood, Alan
CONTAINER GARDENING: FLOWERS AND
FOLIAGE IN POTS, TUBS, AND BASKETS
(Smithmark, 1991) Information on the year-round
needs and the care required for container-grown
plants.

CONTAINER GARDENING: GARDENING BY DESIGN (Sterling, 1991) Advice, color photos, how-to drawings and step-by-step instructions.

Waite, Ray
GARDENING IN ORNAMENTAL CONTAIN-ERS (Cassell/RHS, 1991, 2nd edition) Focuses on perennials and annuals that are salvaged through seeds or cuttings.

Whiten, Faith and Geoff
THE ART OF CONTAINER GARDENING (Dutton, 1987) How to create attractive potted plants by considering design, form, balance and color.

Wilson, Jim
LANDSCAPING WITH CONTAINER PLANTS (Houghton Mifflin, 1990) How to combine flower and foliage, ideas for a variety of possible containers, watering and fertilizing information and soil mixtures from the host of the Victory Garden show.

Yang, Linda
THE TERRACE GARDENER'S HANDBOOK: RAISING PLANTS ON A BALCONY, TERRACE, ROOFTOP, PENTHOUSE OR PATIO (Timber Press, 1982) Covers soil, container types, which plants are the most suitable and year-round maintenance.

For related books, see:
Section on "Houseplants"
THE APARTMENT FARMER by Newcomb (page 103)
THE COMPLETE BOOK OF PATIO AND CONTAINER GARDENING by Williams (page 176)
GROWING HERBS IN POTS by Brimer (page 110)
MINIATURE GARDENS by Carl (page 155)
PARADISE CONTAINED by Stites, George and Sears (page 91)
THE POTTED HERB by Zabar (page 115)

COLOR GARDENS

Bown, Deni
ALBA: THE BOOK OF WHITE FLOWERS (Timber Press, 1989) Over 1,000 species and forms (annuals, perennials, trees, shrubs, etc.); also information on flower arrangements and white greenhouse plants.

de Bray, Lys
BORDERS: A GUIDE TO SPRING, SUMMER AND AUTUMN COLORS (Ward Lock, 1987) Covers choosing the site, designing the border and suggested plants.

Clifton, Joan
MAKING A WHITE GARDEN (Grove Weidenfeld, 1990) Planning and planting a white spring garden, city garden, herbaceous garden, topiary garden, walled garden, water garden, window box and indoor garden; inspired by the white garden at Sissinghurst.

Dale, John, and Gunnell, Kevin
THE GARDENER'S PALETTE: THE COMPLETE GUIDE TO SELECTING PLANTS BY COLOR (Random House, 1992) Directory of over 1,000 flowers organized by color with information on planting, cultivation and propagation for each entry; includes ideas for cutting and preserving blooms, mixing and matching plantings, developing color schemes and more.

Grenfell, Diana, and Grounds, Roger
THE WHITE GARDEN (Trafalgar Square, 1990) Shows how to select and place white flowers in either a total white garden or in combination with other plants; includes 10 garden plans.

Haring, Elda
COLOR FOR YOUR YARD AND GARDEN (Hawthorn, 1971) Various types of plants (flowers, fruits, foliage) are grouped by color.

Hobhouse, Penelope
COLOR IN YOUR GARDEN (Little, Brown, 1985) Over 1,000 plants are categorized by color and season and plans are given for both large and small, monochromatic and mixed gardens.

Jekyll, Gertrude
COLOUR SCHEMES FOR THE FLOWER GARDEN (Ayer, 1984) Reprint of her 1908 book which gives formulas for color in the garden.

Keen, Mary
GARDENING WITH COLOR (Random House, 1991) Eighteen plans for borders are given along with suggestions for plants that work best together to form a harmonious color arrangement.

Kelly, John
THE ALL-SEASONS GARDEN: HOW TO CREATE COLOR AND INTEREST THROUGHOUT THE YEAR (Viking Penguin, 1987) Ideas for planning and planting a multicolored garden.

Lacey, Stephen
THE STARTLING JUNGLE: COLOUR AND SCENT IN THE ROMANTIC GARDEN (Godine, 1989) How to select and place plants using the principles of harmony and contrast.

Moody, Mary (editor)
FLOWERS BY COLOR: A COMPLETE GUIDE TO OVER 1,000 POPULAR GARDEN FLOWERS (Mallard, 1990) Flowers are divided into five color groups with photos and descriptions, plus how to use color in the garden as a background, an accent or a special effect.

Simmons, Adelma Grenier
THE SILVER GARDEN (available from Caprilands Herb Farm, Coventry, Connecticut) Information on the planning and building of the three silver gardens at Caprilands and the large assortment of plants in those gardens.

Squire, David
THE COMPLETE GUIDE TO USING COLOR IN YOUR GARDEN: HOW TO COMBINE PERENNIALS, ANNUALS, TREES AND SHRUBS FOR A MORE BEAUTIFUL LANDSCAPE (Rodale Press, 1991) Complete descriptions of over 400 plants divided by color groups, plus 12 plans for using the plants in beds and containers, on walls, etc.; adapted for American gardens.

Sunset
GARDEN COLOR: ANNUALS AND PERENNIALS (Sunset Books, 1981) One hundred thirty plants are described and ideas for using them are given.

Underwood, Mrs. Desmond
GREY AND SILVER PLANTS (Collins, 1971) The plants are alphabetized by genus and detailed information is given on each one.

Wilder, Louise Beebe
COLOR IN MY GARDEN: AN AMERICAN GARDENER'S PALETTE (Atlantic Monthly, 1990) Reprint of 1918 edition; gives specific combinations of plants to use with charts showing color and bloom week by week.

For related books, see:
GROWING SILVER, GREY AND BLUE FOLIAGE PLANTS by Spencer (page 72)

FRAGRANCE GARDENS

Bonar, Ann
GARDENING FOR FRAGRANCE (Sterling, 1991) Instructions for turning your yard into a source of year-round fragrance.

Brooklyn Botanic Garden
GARDENING FOR FRAGRANCE (BBG #121) How to use herbs, annuals, roses, houseplants and others for fragrance.

Genders, Roy
SCENTED FLORA OF THE WORLD (St. Martin's, 1977) A detailed coverage of scented plants (flowers, shrubs, trees, etc.).

Lacey, Stephen
SCENT IN YOUR GARDEN (Little, Brown, 1991) Describes ,000 fragrant plants and how to use them to best advantage.

Reddell, Rayford, and Galyean, Robert
GROWING FRAGRANT PLANTS (Harper-Collins, 1989) Contains information on all types of fragrant plants, including trailers, vines and ground covers, and explains how to plant, grow, harvest and utilize them in making potpourri and wreaths or extracting the oils.

Rohde, Eleanour Sinclair
THE SCENTED GARDEN (Medici Society, 1989, re-issue of 1931 edition) Includes recipes for potpourri, soaps and vinegars, and a 44-page plant list.

Sanecki, Kay
THE FRAGRANT GARDEN (Trafalgar Square, 1981) Covers the history of scent in gardens, plus classifies fragrant plants by their type (bulb, shrub, tree, greenhouse plant, etc.)

Squire, David, and Newdick, Jane
THE SCENTED GARDEN (Rodale Press, 1988) Features over 500 varieties of scented plants divided into daytime scents, night scents, scented patios, scented flower borders, etc.; 70 pages of charts cover various types of fragrances (sweet, musk, etc.).

Taylor, Jane
FRAGRANT GARDENS: GARDENING BY DE-SIGN (Sterling, 1987) Advice, color photos, how-to drawings and step-by-step instructions.

Verey, Rosemary
THE SCENTED GARDEN: CHOOSING, GROWING, USING THE PLANTS THAT BRING FRAGRANCE TO YOUR LIFE, YOUR HOME AND YOUR TABLE (Van Nostrand Reinhold, 1981) Encompasses the history of fragrance in the garden, plus how to select, grow and use 1,100 fragrant flowers, trees, shrubs, bulbs, roses, herbs, etc.

Wilder, Louise Beebe
THE FRAGRANT PATH: A BOOK ABOUT SWEET-SCENTED FLOWERS AND LEAVES (Macmillan, 1990, reprint of 1932 book) Describes over 1,000 fragrant plants (annuals, bulbs, shrubs, climbers, herbs, perennials, trees and roses); covers night-scented flowers, fragrant plants for rock and Southern gardens, summer and autumn scents and plants with unpleasant scents.

Wilson, Helen V., and Bell, Leonie
THE FRAGRANT YEAR: SCENTED PLANTS FOR YOUR GARDEN AND YOUR HOME (Barrows, 1967) Classifies fragrant plants by autumn, winter, early bulbs, small perennials, etc.

For related books, see:
FRAGRANT FLOWERS OF THE SOUTH by Miranda (page 194)
FRAGRANT PLANTS by Beckett (page 117)
GROWING HERBS AS AROMATICS by Genders (page 111)
THE STARTLING JUNGLE by Lacey (page 167)

SEASONAL GARDENS

Allen, Oliver E.
WINTER GARDENS (Time-Life Books, 1979) Description and cultural information on plants suitable for a winter garden and the garden chores that need to be performed in fall and winter.

Bowles, E. A.
MY GARDEN IN AUTUMN AND WINTER (Jack, 1915)
MY GARDEN IN SPRING (Theophrastus, 1971) Reprint of 1914 edition.
MY GARDEN IN SUMMER (Jack, 1914)
   The four-acre garden created by Edward Bowles can be seen at Myddelton House outside London. If you aren't able to find these books, they are quoted extensively in *A Bouquet of Garden Writing* by Ursula Buchan.

Brooklyn Botanic Garden
THE WINTER GARDEN (BBG #129) How bark, berries, bulbs, grasses, conifers and hollies add interest to the winter garden.

Foster, Raymond
THE GARDEN IN AUTUMN AND WINTER (David & Charles, 1983) Covers basic planning, plus bulbs, perennials, shrubs, trees and vines suitable for the fall and winter garden.

Kinahan, Sonia
OVERLOOK GUIDE TO WINTER GARDENS (Penguin, 1985)

Lacy, Allen
THE GARDEN IN AUTUMN (Atlantic Monthly, 1990) Details on almost 400 perennials, annuals, ornamental grasses, bulbs and woody plants that thrive in an autumn garden; includes mail order sources.

Lawrence, Elizabeth
GARDENS IN WINTER (Harper, 1961; reissued in 1973 by Claitor's Publishing) Primarily about her North Carolina garden, but it includes other gardens she has seen, read about or learned about from her many correspondents.

Pavord, Anna
THE FLOWERING YEAR (Abbeville Press, 1991) Plans for three different gardens for each month from March through October.

Thomas, Graham Stuart
COLOUR IN THE WINTER GARDEN (J. M. Dent, 1984, 3rd edition) Covers shrubs, trees, heathers, rhododendrons and bulbs.

Verey, Rosemary
THE GARDEN IN WINTER (Little, Brown, 1988) Covers designing a winter garden, plus information on 150 suitable plants; examples from both American and English gardens.

Wilson, Helen V.
COLOR FOR YOUR WINTER YARD AND GARDEN WITH FLOWERS, BERRIES, BIRDS AND TREES (Scribner's, 1978) Explores bulbs, perennials, trees, shrubs, lighting, attracting birds and more.

For related books, see:
THE COUNTRY GARDEN by Brookes (page 39)
WINTER GARDENING IN THE MARITIME NORTHWEST by Colebrook (page 197)

SHADE GARDENS

Allen, Oliver E., and Editors of Time-Life Books
SHADE GARDENS (Henry Holt, 1986, reprint of Time-Life 1979 edition) Describes and gives growing information on annuals, perennials, bulbs, ferns, shrubs, ground covers and small trees that do well in the shade.

Brooklyn Botanic Garden
GARDENING IN THE SHADE (BBG #61) Describes the use of shrubs, trees, annuals, bulbs, evergreens, vines and perennials in shaded areas.

Druse, Ken
THE NATURAL SHADE GARDEN (Clarkson Potter, 1992) How to arrange shade plants to make a lush, colorful garden even if you only have four hours or less of direct sunlight each day; includes suggestions for shade plants for rock, water, woodland and container gardens; 420 color photos.

Fish, Margery
GARDENING IN THE SHADE (Faber & Faber, 1984) Covers 1,600 plants which do well in all types of shade and soil; includes gold, silver and variegated-leaved plants.

Morse, Harriet K.
GARDENING IN THE SHADE (Timber Press, 1982) General information plus suggestions for planting schemes and a directory of plants suitable for shade gardening; first published in 1939, revised in 1962.

Ortho
SHADE GARDENING (Ortho, 1982) How to design and select and maintain the plants for a shade garden that's full of color.

Paterson, Allen
PLANTS FOR SHADE (Dent, 1981) Describes over 100 plants and how to use them to have year-round interest in the garden.

Pierot, Suzanne
WHAT CAN I GROW IN THE SHADE? (Liveright, 1977) Surveys plants that do well in areas of little sun, water and air circulation; appendix groups these shade plants by U.S. climatic region.

Reed, Virginia
SHADY GARDENS (ISBS, 1989) Describes the differences between shade and sun-loving plants, problems that can result when they are in competition, and

gives a selection of suitable and unusual plants that grow well in shade.

Schenk, George
THE COMPLETE SHADE GARDENER (Houghton Mifflin, 1991) Covers lawns, garden pests, trees, shrubs, ferns, perennials and edibles and gives an evaluation on each of the suggested plants; very thorough treatment.

Wilson, Helen Van Pelt
SUCCESSFUL GARDENING IN THE SHADE (Doubleday, 1975)

Zeman, Anne M.
SHADE GARDENING (Prentice-Hall, 1992) Descriptions of over 80 shade-loving plants.

For related books, see:
HOSTA by Grenfell (page 70)
THE HOSTA BOOK by Aden (page 70)
SHADE AND COLOR WITH WATER-CONSERVING PLANTS by Walters and Backhaus (page 146)
TAYLOR'S POCKET GUIDE TO GROUND COVERS FOR SHADE (page 50)
TAYLOR'S POCKET GUIDE: PERENNIALS FOR SHADE (page 84)

SEASIDE GARDENS

Foley, Daniel J.
GARDENING BY THE SEA FROM COAST TO COAST (Parnassus Imprints, 1982) Advice on using roses, heath and heather, rosemary, ornamental vines, ground covers, hardy perennials, flowering shrubs, annuals, bulbs and evergreens in areas that have special requirements because of wind, sand, salt spray and tide.

Huxley, Anthony, and Taylor, William
FLOWERS OF GREECE AND THE AEGEAN (Trafalgar Square, 1990) A field guide with color photos and descriptions of 452 species; includes information on hillside, island, mountain and seaside gardens.

Littlefield, Susan
SEASIDE GARDENING: PLANTINGS, PROCEDURES AND DESIGN PRINCIPLES (Simon & Schuster, 1987) Design ideas plus a selection of plants that do well near the sea.

Polunin, Oleg, and Huxley, Anthony
FLOWERS OF THE MEDITERRANEAN (Trafalgar Square, 1990) Describes over 700 plants and contains over 300 color photos.

Schmidt, R. Marilyn (editor)
GARDENING ON THE EASTERN SEASHORE (Barnegat, 1989, 2nd edition) Gives specific techniques for overcoming the rigors of sand, salt and wind, plus descriptions of over 300 plants that do well in this environment.

Thaxter, Celia
AN ISLAND GARDEN (Houghton Mifflin, 1988) A detailed description of her cottage garden on Appledore Island in the Gulf of Maine; this reprint of the 1894 edition includes the Childe Hassam paintings and chapter illuminations. (See the July 1990 issue of *Victoria* magazine for an interesting article about this garden.)

For related books, see:
GARDENING AND BEYOND by Bellis (page 87)
MARTHA'S VINEYARD: GARDENS AND HOUSES by Lewis (page 202)
NANTUCKET: GARDENS AND HOUSES by Lewis (page 202)

CITY AND SMALL GARDENS

Allen, Oliver E.
GARDENING WITH THE NEW SMALL
PLANTS: THE COMPLETE GUIDE TO GROW-
ING DWARF AND MINIATURE SHRUBS,
FLOWERS, TREES AND VEGETABLES
(Houghton Mifflin, 1987) Covers shrubs that never
outgrow their location, miniature roses, small vegeta-
ble plants that produce large crops, and other small
plants that are hardier and less disease prone than their
full-sized parents.

Baxendale, Martin
THE VERY SMALL GARDEN (ISBS, 1987) How
to plan a small garden to create an effect of year-round
profusion and an illusion of space.

Brookes, John
THE SMALL GARDEN BOOK (Crown, 1989)
How to design and plant small garden areas, whether
a backyard or a window box.

Colby, Deirdre
CITY GARDENING (Simon & Schuster, 1988)
Covers gardening on a rooftop, window ledge, alley-
way, terrace or backyard.

Davis, Brian
TREES FOR SMALL GARDENS (Rodale Press,
1988) Gives soil and sun requirements, planting, pruning and cultivation information for over 300 trees.

Evans, Hazel
THE PATIO GARDEN (Viking Penguin, 1986)
Choose the right trees, shrubs and plants for the
best effect in a patio; includes the use of water in
some designs.

Fawcett, Brian
THE COMPACT GARDEN: DISCOVERING
THE PLEASURES OF PLANTING IN A SMALL
SPACE (Camden House, 1992) How to create a small
garden.

Hart, Rhonda Massingham
TRELLISING: HOW TO GROW CLIMBING
VEGETABLES, FRUITS, FLOWERS, VINES
AND TREES (Storey, 1992) How to increase output
while saving time and space; includes design and construction information on different types of trellises, growing information on over 25 varieties of suitable plants,
how to espalier with fruit trees, and supplier lists.

Ireys, Alice Recknagel
SMALL GARDENS FOR CITY AND COUN-
TRY: A GUIDE TO DESIGNING AND PLANT-
ING YOUR GREEN SPACES (Prentice-Hall,
1978) Includes a list of her favorite plants.

King, Louisa
BEGINNER'S GARDEN (Scribner's, 1927) A compilation of her published articles on the small garden.
She also wrote *The Little Garden* (1921) and *Variety in
the Little Garden* (1923).

Kramer, Jack
PATIO GARDENING (HP Books, 1980) Plans and
instructions for planters and containers, plus how to
grow vertical gardens on trellises, posts and arbors.

Leverett, Brian
GARDEN DESIGN: PLANNING SMALLER
GARDENS (Trafalgar Square, 1989) Basic informa-
tion on designing and creating a small garden.

Miller, Michael
GARDENING IN SMALL SPACES (Putnam,
1984) Detailed plans for small front and side gardens,
balcony and roof gardens, even window boxes.

Page, Gill
TOWN GARDENS: GARDENING BY DESIGN
(Sterling, 1991) Advice, color photos, how-to draw-
ings and step-by-step instructions.

**Page, Gill; Toogood, Alan; Baxendale, Martin;
Stone, Robert**
SMALL GARDENS (Sterling, 1990) Covers the design and planting of town gardens, herb gardens, container gardens and window boxes.

Rees, Yvonne
THE ART OF BALCONY GARDENING (Sterling, 1991) Ideas for transforming a balcony.

Rees, Yvonne, and Palliser, David
PATIO GARDENING: STEP BY STEP TO
GROWING SUCCESS (Trafalgar Square, 1992)
Discusses the secrets of successful patio gardening;
includes many ideas for achieving dramatic results,
how to build a patio, pond and barbecue, and recommendations of plants for year-round color.

Rose, Graham
THE SMALL GARDEN PLANNER (Simon &
Schuster, 1991) Describes 60 different plans for small
gardens and patios.

Stevens, David
PRIVATE GARDENS: SUCCESSFUL GAR-
DENING IN ONE HOUR A WEEK (Henry Holt,
1990) How to use structures, ornaments and furnishings along with plants to create small private gardens.

Strong, Roy
CREATING SMALL GARDENS (Random House,
1987) Describes 24 small gardens (e.g., corridor herb
garden, tiny cottage garden, secluded garden) and
gives a list of plants for each.
A SMALL GARDEN DESIGNER'S HAND-
BOOK (Little, Brown, 1989) Covers the structural
elements (pavings, paths, steps, walls, fences, hedges,
archways, trellises, arbors, ornaments, benches and
containers) that make a small garden successful.
SMALL PERIOD GARDENS: PRACTICAL
GUIDE TO DESIGN AND PLANTING (Rizzoli,
1992)

Sunset
LANDSCAPING FOR SMALL SPACES (Sunset
Books, 1992) Design ideas and plant choices for small
spaces.

Tarrant, David
HIGHRISE HORTICULTURE: A GUIDE TO
GARDENING IN SMALL SPACES (Voyageur
Press, 1990) Gardening ideas for a balcony or indoor
room.

Time-Life
GARDENING IN SMALL PLACES: GARDEN-
ER'S GUIDE SERIES (Time-Life, 1989)

Wallach, Carla
GARDENING IN THE CITY: BACKYARDS,
BALCONIES, TERRACES AND PENTHOUSES
(Harcourt Brace Jovanovich, 1976) How to design,
plant and maintain a garden for these specific areas.

Williams, Robin
THE COMPLETE BOOK OF PATIO AND CON-
TAINER GARDENING (Sterling, 1991) How to

plan and build different types of patios, plus using hanging baskets, window boxes, various containers, lighting, etc. to furnish the patios.

Yang, Linda
THE CITY GARDENER'S HANDBOOK: FROM BALCONY TO BACKYARD (Random House, 1990) A very complete guide to gardening in small spaces and containers; covers designs, plant selection, pruning, pests, pollution and much more.

For related books, see:
BEHIND THOSE GARDEN WALLS IN HISTORIC SAVANNAH by Wood (page 204)

GARDENING WITH DWARF TREES AND SHRUBS by Bartels (page 51)
THE GARDENS OF SAN FRANCISCO by Hockaday (page 201)
GROWING ROSES FOR SMALL GARDENS by Gibson (page 63)
HIDDEN GARDENS OF BEACON HILL by Moore and Weener (page 202)
PLANS FOR SMALL GARDENS by Coombs (page 45)
TOWN GARDENS by Boisset (page 38)
TREES FOR TOWN AND CITY GARDENS by Patrick (page 54)

Papilio ajax.

Anosia plexippus
or Danais archippus.

WILDLIFE IN THE GARDEN

Ajilvsgi, Geyata
BUTTERFLY GARDENING FOR THE SOUTH
(Taylor Publishing, 1991) Describes butterflies native to the South and the creation of landscapes to attract them; includes information on photographing butterflies.

Brooklyn Botanic Garden
GARDENING FOR WILDLIFE (BBG #114) Ideas for attracting birds and butterflies to your garden; includes plant lists and sources.

Dennis, John V.
THE WILDLIFE GARDENER (Knopf, 1985) How to plant to attract birds, insects and even small mammals and reptiles.

Ernst, Ruth Shaw
THE NATURALIST'S GARDEN: BRING YOUR YARD TO LIFE WITH PLANTS THAT ATTRACT WILDLIFE (Rodale Press, 1987) How to plan and plant a garden that attracts birds, butterflies and other insects and wildlife.

Logsdon, Gene
WILDLIFE IN YOUR GARDEN (Rodale Press, 1983) How to get rid of wildlife you don't want (rab-bits, moles, deer, etc.) and attract wildlife you do want (bees, birds, butterflies).

Mahnken, Jan
HOSTING THE BIRDS: HOW TO ATTRACT BIRDS TO NEST IN YOUR YARD (Storey, 1989) Covers preferred habitat and food, nestling periods, etc. for 175 species of birds.

Merilees, William
ATTRACTING BACKYARD WILDLIFE (Voyageur Press, 1989) How to make birdhouses, bumblebee nest boxes, toad homes, toad lights, bat houses, rabbit burrows and other things to attract wildlife.

Ortho
HOW TO ATTRACT HUMMINGBIRDS AND BUTTERFLIES (Ortho, 1991) Covers which plants and how to use them to attract hummingbirds and butterflies.

Proctor, Dr. Noble
GARDEN BIRDS: HOW TO ATTRACT BIRDS TO YOUR GARDEN (Rodale Press, 1986) How to recognize and feed all kinds of birds and what to do to your garden to attract more.

SONG BIRDS: HOW TO ATTRACT THEM AND IDENTIFY THEIR SONGS (Rodale Press, 1988) Information on behavior, feeding, song patterns and how to turn your garden into a habitat for song birds; includes an audio cassette of the songs of 100 species.

Schneck, Marcus
BUTTERFLIES: HOW TO IDENTIFY AND ATTRACT THEM TO YOUR GARDEN (Rodale Press, 1990) Identifies 250 of the most common North American butterflies and gives details on attracting them; 300 color photos and illustrations.

Sedenko, Jerry
THE BUTTERFLY GARDEN: CREATING GARDENS TO ATTRACT BEAUTIFUL BUTTERFLIES (Random House, 1991) Covers which annuals, perennials, trees, vines and wildflowers attract butterflies and how to design a butterfly garden; includes details on common American butterflies.

Simonds, Calvin
PRIVATE LIVES OF GARDEN BIRDS: HOW TO UNDERSTAND THE EVERYDAY BEHAVIOR OF THE BIRDS IN YOUR BACKYARD (Globe Pequot, 1991, new edition) Covers the habits, activities, dietary delights and singing of 10 common birds.

Smith, Geoffrey
THE JOY OF WILDLIFE GARDENING (Trafalgar Square, 1990) Using herbaceous perennials, herbs and ground covers to attract butterflies, birds and bees; includes tips on new and unusual plants.

Stokes, Donald and Lillian
THE BIRD FEEDER BOOK: AN EASY GUIDE TO ATTRACTING, IDENTIFYING AND UNDERSTANDING YOUR FEEDER BIRDS (Little, Brown, 1987) How to identify 23 common species and understand their behavior and eating habits.
THE BLUEBIRD BOOK: THE COMPLETE GUIDE TO ATTRACTING BLUEBIRDS (Little, Brown, 1991) How to attract bluebirds with the best nest boxes and landscaping, plus information on bluebird behavior.
THE HUMMINGBIRD BOOK: THE EASY GUIDE TO ATTRACTING, IDENTIFYING AND ENJOYING HUMMINGBIRDS (Little,

Brown, 1989) Includes a section on attracting orioles and photographing hummingbirds.

Stokes, Donald and Lillian, and Williams, Ernest
THE BUTTERFLY BOOK: AN EASY GUIDE TO BUTTERFLY GARDENING, IDENTIFICATION AND BEHAVIOR (Little, Brown, 1991) Details on creating a butterfly garden, butterfly life cycles, raising butterflies, and identifying butterflies and caterpillars.

Sunset
ATTRACTING BIRDS (Sunset Books, 1990) How to attract, identify and feed birds in your garden.

Tekulsky, Mathew
THE BUTTERFLY GARDEN: TURNING YOUR HOME, WINDOW BOX OR BACKYARD INTO A BEAUTIFUL HOME FOR BUTTERFLIES (Harvard Common Press, 1985) Covers the fundamentals of starting a butterfly garden, building a butterfly house and the different species of butterflies.
THE HUMMINGBIRD GARDEN: TURNING YOUR GARDEN, WINDOW BOX OR BACKYARD INTO A BEAUTIFUL HOME FOR HUMMINGBIRDS (Crown, 1990) Advice covers urban, suburban, rural, mountain, desert and seashore gardens.

Terres, John K.
SONGBIRDS IN YOUR GARDEN (Harper, 1953) A best-seller since the 1950s, because he speaks from personal experience on how to attract birds to the garden.

Warren, E. J.
COUNTRY DIARY BOOK OF CREATING A BUTTERFLY GARDEN (Henry Holt, 1988)

Xerces Society/Smithsonian Institute
BUTTERFLY GARDENING: CREATING SUMMER MAGIC IN YOUR GARDEN (Sierra Club Books, 1990) How to create gardens that attract butterflies and help them survive; includes photographing butterflies and 100 close-up color photos of butterflies.

For related books, see:
TREES, SHRUBS AND VINES FOR ATTRACTING BIRDS: A MANUAL FOR THE NORTHEAST by DeGraaf and Witman (page 190)

TROPICAL AND SUBTROPICAL GARDENS

Acrivos, Nick
A GUIDE TO TROPICAL AND SUBTROPICAL VEGETABLES (Brevard Rare Fruit Council, 1988)
Describes a variety of vegetables including some from the Orient, Africa and Central and South America. He also wrote *A Guide to Tropical Fruit Trees and Vines* (1987). Both are available from P.O. Box 2091, Melbourne, FL 32902.

Berry, Fred, and Kress, W. John
HELICONIA (Smithsonian, 1991) Descriptions and color photos of 200 species, varieties, hybrids and cultivars of heliconia, flowers native to Central and South America.

Castner, James L.
RAINFORESTS: A GUIDE TO RESEARCH AND TOURIST FACILITIES AT SELECTED TROPICAL FOREST SITES IN CENTRAL AND SOUTH AMERICA (Feline Press, 1990)

Challis, Myles
THE EXOTIC GARDEN (Trafalgar Square, 1989)
How to create a garden reminiscent of a tropical clime.

Cheers, Gordon
CARNIVOROUS PLANTS (ISBS, 1983) Directions for the care and feeding of carnivorous plants.

Clay, Horace F., and Hubbard, James C.
TROPICAL EXOTICS: THE HAWAII GARDEN (University of Hawaii Press, 1987) Covers cultivation, propagation, landscape uses, pruning, fertilizing and identification of over 100 tropical and subtropical plants.

Courtright, Gordon
TROPICALS (Timber Press, 1988) Descriptions, cultural information, dimensions and 583 color photos of trees, shrubs and vines primarily found in USDA zones 9 and 10.

Grace, Julie (editor)
CLIMBERS AND TRAILERS (Reed, 1983) Descriptions and color photos of over 250 tropical and subtropical vines.

Graf, Alfred Byrd
EXOTICA IV: PICTORIAL CYCLOPEDIA OF EXOTIC PLANTS AND TREES (Scribner's, 1985)

A two-volume set that includes over 2,000 illustrations.

TROPICA IV: COLOR CYCLOPEDIA OF EXOTIC PLANTS AND TREES (Macmillan, 1992, revised 4th edition) Illustrates and describes over 1,600 genera of tropical and subtropical flowering and fruiting trees and shrubs, bulbous plants and vines; includes over 7,000 color photos and an in-depth bibliography.

Jenuwein, H.
AVOCADO, BANANA, COFFEE: HOW TO GROW USEFUL TROPICAL PLANTS FOR FUN (ISBS, 1988) Examines the origin and habitat, soil, water and fertilizing needs, harvest and propagation of 70 species of tropical and subtropical plants.

Kepler, A. K.
EXOTIC TROPICALS OF HAWAII: HELICONIAS, GINGERS, ANTHURIUMS, AND DECORATIVE FOLIAGE (Mutual Publishing, 1990) How to locate and care for these exotics; 200 color photos.

Kingsbury, John M.
TROPICAL PLANTS OF THE CARIBBEAN (Bullbrier Press, 1988) Descriptions plus 600 color photos of 200 trees, shrubs, vines and perennials of the Caribbean.

Kuck, Loraine, and Tongg, Richard
HAWAIIAN FLOWERS AND FLOWERING TREES: A GUIDE TO TROPICAL AND SUBTROPICAL FLORA (C. E. Tuttle, 1958) Colored drawings and brief descriptions of 140 plants from Africa, South and Central America, the Caribbean, the South Pacific and the Far East.

Lecoufle, Marcel
CARNIVOROUS PLANTS: CARE AND CULTIVATION (Sterling, 1991) Describes plants for a variety of sites, plus information on propagation, prey, growing needs, and pests and diseases.

Leigh Jr., Egbert (editor)
ECOLOGY OF A TROPICAL FOREST: SEASONAL RHYTHMS AND LONG-TERM CHANGES (Smithsonian, 1983)

Lloyd, Francis
THE CARNIVOROUS PLANTS (Dover, 1976) Reprint of a 1942 classic.

Mathias, Mildred (editor)
FLOWERING PLANTS IN THE LANDSCAPE (University of California Press, 1982) Covers hundreds of tropical and subtropical plants; 240 color photos.

Menninger, Edwin A.
FLOWERING TREES OF THE WORLD FOR TROPICS AND WARM CLIMATE (Hearthside Press, 1962) Describes approximately 500 flowering trees; 400 color photos.

Miller, Helen
TOP PLANTS FOR TROPICAL GARDENS (AGPS, 1990)

Perry, Frances, and Hay, Roy
A FIELD GUIDE TO TROPICAL AND SUBTROPICAL PLANTS (Van Nostrand Reinhold, 1982) Describes approximately 200 trees, shrubs, vines and water plants.

Pietropaolo, James and Patricia
CARNIVOROUS PLANTS OF THE WORLD (Timber Press, 1986) Describes all the presently recognized genera and includes comprehensive propagation information.

Slack, Adrian
CARNIVOROUS PLANTS (MIT Press, 1980)
INSECT-EATING PLANTS AND HOW TO GROW THEM (University of Washington Press, 1988) Describes over 200 species from 15 genera.

Sohmer, S. H., and Gustafson, R.
PLANTS AND FLOWERS OF HAWAII (University of Hawaii Press, 1987) Describes 130 species whose habitat is either coastal, bogs, lava flow or rain forest.

Swenson, Allan
CULTIVATING CARNIVOROUS PLANTS (Doubleday, 1977) Growing information for a variety of carnivorous plants.

Temple, Paul
CARNIVOROUS PLANTS (Wisley Handbook) (Sterling, 1990) Covers indoor and outdoor plants and how to care for them.

Thornton, Elizabeth and Sharon
THE EXOTIC PLUMERIA (1985, Plumeria Specialties, P.O. Box 431132, Houston, TX 77243) Introduction that includes descriptions, propagation, cultivation, dormancy and overwintering.

Van Atta, Marian
GROWING AND USING EXOTIC FOODS (Pineapple Press, 1991) Covers over 100 tropical and subtropical fruits, herbs, vegetables and wild edibles; includes recipes and seed and plant sources.

Vanderplank, John
PASSION FLOWERS AND PASSION FRUIT (MIT Press, 1991) Descriptions of 100 species, plus information on cultivation, propagation, hybridization, pests and diseases.

Villegas, Marcello (editor)
TROPICAL BAMBOO (Rizzoli, 1990) Over 300 color photos of *Bambusa guadua*, the bamboo used for construction in Central and South America.

Warren, William
THE TROPICAL GARDEN (Thames & Hudson, 1991) Describes exotic gardens in Hawaii, Thailand, Malaysia, Singapore, Indonesia and Bali; 365 color photos.

For related books, see:
FLORIDA GARDENING MONTH BY MONTH by Smiley (page 194)
MARGARET MEE: IN SEARCH OF FLOWERS OF THE AMAZON FORESTS by Morrison (page 220)
THE WORLD GROWS ROUND MY DOOR by Fairchild (page 3)

LOW MAINTENANCE GARDENS

Brooklyn Botanic Garden
LOW MAINTENANCE GARDENING (BBG #100) How to reduce maintenance with native plants, rock gardens, easy annuals and vegetables.

Caplin, James and Adam
INSTANT GARDENING (Trafalgar Square, 1991) How to get what you want from your garden quickly, easily and enjoyably.

Colburn, Nigel
LEISURELY GARDENING: THE ART OF THE LOW-MAINTENANCE GARDEN (Trafalgar Square, 1990) Covers design and plants for mixed borders, wildlife gardens, rock gardens, roses, bulbs, lawns, wall plants and climbers.

Fish, Margery
CAREFREE GARDENING (Faber & Faber, 1989 reprint) Surveys plants that require less attention and whose use results in a natural and informal garden.

Loewer, Peter
TOUGH PLANTS FOR TOUGH PLACES: HOW TO GROW 101 EASY-CARE PLANTS FOR EVERY PART OF YOUR YARD (Rodale Press, 1992) Includes 25 color-illustrated low-mainte-nance garden designs using American wildflowers, pe-rennials, bulbs, ground covers and native shrubs and trees.

Rose, Graham
THE LOW MAINTENANCE GARDEN (Viking Penguin, 1983) Fifteen plans for gardens that don't require a lot of work and are full of color and texture.

Roth, Susan A.
THE WEEKEND GARDEN GUIDE: WORK-SAVING WAYS TO A BEAUTIFUL BACK-YARD (Rodale Press, 1991) Covers which plants, including food plants, are best and which are worst for a low-maintenance garden.

Stout, Ruth
GARDENING WITHOUT WORK FOR THE AGING, THE BUSY AND THE INDOLENT (Devin-Adair, 1960) How to have a successful garden without plowing, hoeing, cultivating, weeding, water-ing or spraying.

HOW TO HAVE A GREEN THUMB WITH-OUT AN ACHING BACK (Cornerstone Library, 1973) Details on her mulch gardening methods, interwoven as always with details of her life and her wonderfully sensible philosophy for living.

Stout, Ruth, and Clemence, Richard
THE RUTH STOUT NO-WORK GARDEN BOOK (Rodale Press, 1971) A collection of their articles published in *Organic Gardening and Farming* from 1953 to 1971.

Sunset
EASY-CARE GARDENING (Sunset Books, 1988) Encyclopedia of trees, shrubs, ground covers and flowers suitable for a low maintenance garden; includes planning and maintenance tips.

Taylor, Patricia
THE WEEKENDER'S GARDENING MANUAL: EASY CARE GARDENS IN TWO HOURS (OR LESS!) A WEEK (Henry Holt, 1985)

Tilgner, Linda
TIPS FOR THE LAZY GARDENER (Garden Way, 1985) Hundreds of tips for saving time in the garden.

For related books, see:
COUNTRY GARDENING, COUNTRY STYLE by Thompson (page 162)
EASY CARE PERENNIALS by Taylor (page 84)
LANDSCAPING WITH NATURE by Cox (page 39)
LAWNS AND GROUND COVERS by Time-Life (page 50)
THE NATURAL GARDEN by Druse (page 39)
TIPS FOR CAREFREE LANDSCAPING by Binetti (page 38)

GARDENING FOR PROFIT

Ball, Vic (editor)
BALL RED BOOK: GREENHOUSE GROWING
(G. J. Ball Publishing, 1991, 14th edition) Covers the newest varieties of 100 major bedding, pot and foliage plants, plus market trends, accounting, labor-saving techniques, scheduling, mechanizations and much more information for operating a garden business.

Bartholomew, Mel
CASH FROM SQUARE FOOT GARDENING
(Storey, 1985) How to grow produce to sell to restaurants and other businesses and make a nice profit.

Fazio, James
THE WOODLAND STEWARD: A PRACTICAL GUIDE TO THE MANAGEMENT OF SMALL PRIVATE FORESTS (The Woodland Press, 1985, 2nd edition) How to earn money with firewood, maple sugar, Christmas trees, timber and holly production.

Genders, Roy
INDOOR GARDENING FOR PROFIT (Robert Hale, 1982)

Hamilton, David L.
BIDDING YOUR SERVICE FOR PROFIT
(Hamilton's Publishing, no date) A business plan for interior landscapers that includes preparing contracts and bids, keeping records, accounting and more.
COMMERCIAL INDOOR PLANTS (Hamilton's Publishing, 1985) Advice on how to select and maintain the right plants for a commercial location.
HOW TO SELL MORE INDOOR PLANTS (Hamilton's Publishing, 1986) How to evaluate the marketplace, write proposals, negotiate contracts; includes samples of forms used in an interior plantscape business.
INTERIOR DESIGNER'S HANDBOOK ON PLANTS (Hamilton's Publishing, 1987) Information on plant care, sources for containers, and foliage plants, price guides and more.

Harrington, Geri
CASH CROPS FOR THE THRIFTY GARDENER (Putnam, 1984)

Hill, Lewis
CHRISTMAS TREES: GROWING AND SELLING TREES, WREATHS AND GREENS (Storey, 1989) A manual that covers choosing and preparing the site, what to plant, sources of supply, fertilizing, harvesting, retail and wholesale sales and more.

Hils, Jr., Ralph J.
MARKET WHAT YOU GROW: A PRACTICAL MANUAL FOR HOME GARDENERS, MARKET GARDENERS AND SMALL FARMERS (Chicot Press, 1989) Discusses five ways to market produce; includes worksheets for tracking labor costs, assets, tools, machinery, etc.

Jozwik, Francis X.
PLANTS FOR PROFITS: A COMPLETE GUIDE TO GROWING AND SELLING GREENHOUSE CROPS (Andmar Press, 1984) How to turn a small home greenhouse into a moneymaker.

Lee, Andrew W.
AMERICAN MARKET GARDENER: PROFITABLE ORGANIC AGRICULTURE (Good Earth Publications, 1989) How to make money as a small scale vegetable grower; covers budgets, crop planning, marketing, mail order, equipment and labor needed and more.

Miller, Richard A.
THE POTENTIAL OF HERBS AS A CASH CROP: HOW TO MAKE A LIVING IN THE COUNTRY (Acres USA, 1985)

Nelson, Paul
GREENHOUSE OPERATION AND MANAGEMENT (Prentice-Hall, 1991, 4th edition) Textbook covering energy conservation, root media, automatic watering systems, fertilization, growth regulators, pest and disease control, marketing and more.

Northwind Farm Publications
THE BUSINESS OF HERBS—A bimonthly journal for herb businesses and serious hobbyists. Write Northwind Farm, RR2, Box 246, Shevlin, MN 56676 or call Paula Oliver at 218-657-2478.

Price, Laurence W.
HOW TO START YOUR OWN HORTICULTURE BUSINESS (Botany Books, 1983) What to consider before starting a full- or part-time landscape business, lawn renovation service or home nursery. STARTING AND OPERATING A LANDSCAPE MAINTENANCE BUSINESS (Botany Books, 1989) How to estimate costs, tools needed, recordkeeping, resources, sample forms and more.

Staines, Ric
MARKET GARDENING: GROWING AND SELLING PRODUCE (Fulcrum Publishing, 1991)

Sturdivant, Lee
PROFITS FROM YOUR BACKYARD HERB GARDEN (San Juan Naturals, Box 642, Friday Harbor, WA 98250, 1988) An introduction to growing and marketing culinary herbs; includes which herbs to grow, how to package, label and sell them to local grocers and restaurants, and other herb businesses.

Taylor, Ted M.
SECRETS TO A SUCCESSFUL GREENHOUSE BUSINESS AND OTHER PROFITABLE HORTICULTURAL PROJECTS (T. M. Taylor, 1991) How to get started (part- or full-time), what to grow, who to sell to; includes plans for a simple solar greenhouse and where to get supplies, plants, seeds and equipment.

Wallin, Craig
BACKYARD CASH CROPS: THE SOURCE BOOK FOR GROWING AND MARKETING SPECIALTY PLANTS (Homestead Design, 1989) From the 200 crop ideas listed, select the best specialty crop for your garden, then learn how to grow and sell it; advice on "pick your own" patches, marketing products made from the crop, plus a list of 200 wholesale sources for seeds and plants.

Welcome, Robert
HOW TO MAKE BIG MONEY MOWING SMALL LAWNS (Brick House Publishing, 1984) How to get customers, what to charge, how to choose the best jobs to earn a higher per hour wage (three to four times the minimum wage), how to start with a small investment and much more.

Whatley, Booker T.
HOW TO MAKE $100,000 FARMING 25 ACRES (Rodale Press, 1987) You can do this by growing high-value specialty crops such as kiwis, pecans and watercress, to name just a few; includes case histories of people who are doing it.

Wold, Betty
SPEAKING OF HERBS: TEN INTRODUCTORY PROGRAMS FOR SPEAKERS (Available

from Northwind Farm—see address above) Earn money by speaking about herbs; the 10 topics are pioneer uses of herbs, magic of herbs, herbal legends, natural fragrances, pet care, Biblical herb gardens, cosmetics, business ideas, culinary herbs and scented geraniums; includes copyright-free handouts.

For related books, see:
GROWING AND USING HERBS SUCCESS-FULLY by Jacobs (page 112)
GROWING HERBS by Titterington (page 115)
HERBAL TREASURES by Shaudys (page 132
A SMALL FARM IN MAINE by Silber (page 6)

Part V:

Regional
Gardening

Dwelley, Marilyn
SPRING WILDFLOWERS OF NEW ENGLAND (Down East, 1973) and SUMMER WILDFLOWERS OF NEW ENGLAND (Down East, 1975) are identification guides arranged by the blossom color; each guide contains hundreds of full-color botanical drawings.

Esmonde-White, Anstace
VEGETABLE GARDENING (McGraw-Hill Ryerson, 1981) Covers planning, preparing the soil, planting and growing a variety of vegetables, herbs and fruit; written for Canadian gardeners, but applicable to the northern U.S. also.

Ferguson, Katharine (editor)
SPRING FLOWERS: A HARROWSMITH GARDENER'S GUIDE (Camden House, 1989) Covers perennials, flowering shrubs and bulbs suitable for a northern spring.

Flint, Harrison L.
LANDSCAPE PLANTS FOR EASTERN NORTH AMERICA (John Wiley, 1983) A guide to trees, shrubs and vines for the entire eastern part of the U.S. excluding Florida and the Gulf Coast; drawings and growing information for 500 species and 1,000 cultivars.

Forsyth, Turid, and Simonds, Merilyn
HARROWSMITH SALAD GARDEN (Camden House, 1992)

Gray, Asa
GRAY'S MANUAL OF BOTANY: A HANDBOOK OF THE FLOWERING PLANTS AND FERNS OF THE CENTRAL AND NORTHEASTERN U.S. AND ADJACENT CANADA (American Book Co., 1950, 8th edition) Family, genera, species and subspecies of 8,340 vascular plants.

Hill, Lewis
COLD-CLIMATE GARDENING: HOW TO EXTEND YOUR GROWING SEASON BY AT LEAST 30 DAYS (Storey, 1987) How to deal with early frost, cool summers and a short gardening season; includes both food and ornamental plants.

Kamm, Minnie W.
OLD TIME HERBS FOR NORTHERN GARDENS (Dover, 1971) Gardening and cooking information on more than 125 species of herbs.

Lanner, Ron M.
AUTUMN LEAVES (Northword, date not set) Describes the major tree species of the northeast U.S. and Canada; includes color photos and telephone numbers for information on peak autumn color times.

Lima, Patrick
THE HARROWSMITH ILLUSTRATED BOOK OF HERBS (Camden House, 1986) How to grow herbs in the northern U.S. and Canada; covers designing the garden, container growing and choosing herbs for color, cooking, teas and fragrance.
THE HARROWSMITH PERENNIAL GARDEN: FLOWERS FOR THREE SEASONS (Camden House, 1987) Covers growing approximately 100 species of perennials in northern gardens; includes five plans for borders and beds.

McDonald, Elvin
NORTHEAST GARDENING: THE DIVERSE ART AND SPECIAL CONDITION OF GARDENING IN THE NORTHEAST (Macmillan, 1990) Covers soil evaluation and plant selection for a variety of garden types (cottage, container, vegetable and naturalized) and locations (seashore, urban and far north).

Minnesota State Horticultural Society
FLOWER GARDEN: NORTHERN GARDENER'S LIBRARY SERIES (Voyageur Press, 1991) How to grow perennials, bulbs, annuals and roses in zones 3 and 4.
THE GOOD GARDENER: NORTHERN GARDENER'S LIBRARY SERIES (Voyageur Press, 1991) Details on planning, growing and propagating when the growing season is limited (zones 3 and 4).

Moyle, John and Evelyn
NORTHLAND WILD FLOWERS (University of Minnesota Press, 1986)

New England Wildflower Society
GARDEN IN THE WOODS CULTIVATION GUIDE (1986)

identification guide for 400 native (zones 7,8,9) and introduced trees, shrubs and vines; includes a line drawing and information on each ornamental plant. **WILDFLOWERS IN THE CAROLINAS** (University of South Carolina Press, 1987)

Brown, Claud, and Kirkman, Katherine
TREES OF GEORGIA AND ADJACENT STATES (Timber Press, 1989) Describes 205 species and varieties.

DeFreitas, Stan
COMPLETE GUIDE TO FLORIDA GARDENING (Taylor Publishing, 1987) Covers trees, shrubs, flowers, landscaping, orchids, vines, lawns, citrus, food plants and houseplants; over 500 color photos.

Deschamps, Elizabeth
TOILING IN SOIL: A GUIDE TO SOUTHERN GARDENING (Wyrick and Co., 1990) Information and anecdotes about her successes and failures with flowers, trees, shrubs, ground covers, roses and herbs.

Foote, L. E., and Jones, Jr., S. B.
NATIVE SHRUBS AND WOODY VINES OF THE SOUTHEAST: LANDSCAPE USES AND IDENTIFICATION (Timber Press, 1989) Describes approximately 550 species and illustrates how to use native shrubs and vines in the landscape; includes lists of suggested plants for specific situations.

Halfacre, Gordon, and Shawcroft, Anne
LANDSCAPE PLANTS OF THE SOUTHEAST (Sparks Press, 1981, enlarged 5th edition) Covers 1,500 varieties of trees, shrubs, vines and ground covers for zones 6 to 9.

Hastings, Don
GARDENING IN THE SOUTH: FLOWERS, VINES AND HOUSEPLANTS (Taylor Publishing, 1991) How to grow annuals, perennials and houseplants.
GARDENING IN THE SOUTH: TREES, SHRUBS AND LAWNS (Taylor Publishing, 1987) Covers choosing the plants, caring for them and improving the soil; 400 color photos.
GARDENING IN THE SOUTH: VEGETABLES AND FRUITS (Taylor Publishing, 1989) Details on growing 185 food plants.

Hill, Madalene, and Barclay, Gwen
SOUTHERN HERB GROWING (Shearer, 1987) Covers over 130 herbs and includes 300 color photos and 100 recipes; written from their experience of owning Hilltop Herb Farm in Texas.

Hunt, William L.
SOUTHERN GARDENS, SOUTHERN GARDENING (Duke University Press, 1992)

Justice, William, and Bell, Ritchie
WILD FLOWERS OF NORTH CAROLINA (University of North Carolina Press, 1987)

Kell, J. Carroll
SOUTHERN LANDSCAPE AND GARDEN DESIGN (Pacesetter Press, 1980) Covers designs for traditional homes and townhomes.

Ladendorf, Sandra
SUCCESSFUL SOUTHERN GARDENING: A PRACTICAL GUIDE FOR YEAR-ROUND BEAUTY (University of North Carolina Press, 1989) How-to information for growing trees, shrubs, vines, food plants, ground covers, lawns, azaleas, camellias, roses and more in zones 7 and 8.

Lawrence, Elizabeth
A SOUTHERN GARDEN (University of North Carolina Press, 50th anniversary edition, 1991) For 50 years, this book has guided zone 8 gardeners; now, it is enhanced with 19 watercolors by Shirley Felts.

Luer, Carlyle A.
THE NATIVE ORCHIDS OF FLORIDA (New York Botanical Garden, 1972) Covers over 100 terrestrial or epiphytic orchids in Florida.

MacCubbin, Tom
FLORIDA HOME GROWN: LANDSCAPING (Sentinel Books, 1987) Covers all aspects of gardening and all types of plants used throughout the state; includes resources and 10 garden plans.
FLORIDA HOME GROWN TWO: THE EDIBLE LANDSCAPE (Sentinel Books, 1989)

Mackey, Betty, and Brandies, Monica
A CUTTING GARDEN FOR FLORIDA (B. B. Mackey Books, 1985) A month-by-month guide to

growing flowers including some that are considered northern flowers.

Magill, Anne
DESIGNING AND GARDENING WITH THE PLANT MATERIALS AND CONDITIONS OF NORTH CENTRAL FLORIDA (Melrose Garden Press, 1990) She covers the topic by charmingly sharing her personal experiences.

Martin, Laura
SOUTHERN WILDFLOWERS (Longstreet Press, 1989) Covers 70 plants, how they got their names, myths, growing information and more.

McEachern, George
GROWING FRUITS, BERRIES AND NUTS IN THE SOUTHWEST AND SOUTHEAST (Gulf Publishing, 1989, 2nd edition) Covers growing and harvesting over 20 species and 130 varieties; includes selecting the right variety, preparing the soil, planting, watering, pruning and maintenance to ensure maximum yield.

Minar, Bill
GREENHOUSE GARDENING IN THE SOUTH (Pacesetter Press, 1976) How to build a greenhouse, maintain ideal growing conditions, start plants from seeds or cuttings and keep potted plants healthy; covers heating, ventilation, lighting, evaporative cooling and suggested plants.

Miranda, Evelyn
FRAGRANT FLOWERS OF THE SOUTH (Pineapple Press, 1991) Growing information, blooming season and illustrations for 80 species.

Odenwald, Neil G., and Turner, James R.
IDENTIFICATION, SELECTION AND USE OF SOUTHERN PLANTS FOR LANDSCAPE DESIGN (Claitor's Publishing, 1987, revised edition) Details and drawings on over 1,000 species of trees, shrubs, vines, perennials, wildflowers, ferns, water plants, ground covers and grasses.

Oser, Helen, and Stewart, Mary
GARDENING IN NEW ORLEANS (Celestial, 1987, 2nd edition) Because of heavy rainfall, pests, its below-sea-level location and long hot summers, New

Orleans has unusual garden requirements; includes a month-by-month calendar and covers roses, azaleas, camellias, shrubs, perennials, annuals, bulbs, herbs and ground covers.

Perry, Mac
LANDSCAPING IN FLORIDA: A PHOTO IDEA BOOK (Pineapple Press, 1990) Covers design, construction and selection of plants for city and suburban gardens.

Robinette, Gary O.
TREES OF THE SOUTH (Van Nostrand Reinhold, 1985) Covers 190 species of deciduous, ericaceous and coniferous trees native to the southeast U.S.; three drawings of each show the tree in silhouette, winter and summer appearances.

Rogers, David and Constance
WOODY ORNAMENTALS FOR DEEP SOUTH GARDENS (University Presses of Florida, 1991) Covers trees, shrubs, woody vines and ground covers for USDA zone 8.

Seidenberg, Charlotte
THE NEW ORLEANS GARDEN (Silkmont-Count, 1990) From personal experience, she discusses growing every imaginable type of plant in the unique climate of New Orleans.

Smiley, Nixon
FLORIDA GARDENING MONTH BY MONTH (University of Miami Press, 1986, revised 3rd editon) Written by a director of the Fairchild Tropical Garden, this guide is intended for south Florida.

Smith, Ken
SOUTHERN HOME LANDSCAPING (HP Books, 1982) Covers design, plant selection, maintenance and irrigation systems; 400+ color photos.

Southern Living
GARDENING TREES AND SHRUBS (Oxmoor House, 1980) How to select, plant and care for trees, shrubs, ground covers and vines.
GROWING VEGETABLES AND HERBS WITH RECIPES FOR THE FRESH HARVEST (Oxmoor House, 1984) How to plan, plant, grow, harvest and

store a variety of vegetables and 12 herbs; includes 130 recipes.

SOUTHERN LIVING GARDEN GUIDE: HOUSEPLANTS, VEGETABLES, TREES, SHRUBS AND MORE (Oxmoor House, 1981) Arranged in a question and answer format; also covers wildflowers, bulbs, annuals and perennials for the South, excluding subtropical Florida.

Taylor, Walter Kingsley
THE GUIDE TO FLORIDA WILDFLOWERS (Taylor Publishing, 1992) Descriptions and color photos of over 500 wildflowers; includes glossary of botanical terms and 25 botanical illustrations.

Taylor's
GUIDE TO GARDENING IN THE SOUTH (Houghton Mifflin, 1992) Color photos and descriptions of over 250 species of trees, shrubs, perennials, ground covers, vines, ferns and grasses suitable for southern gardens; includes information on regional favorites, native plants, lawns, garden design, soil, pests and maintenance.

Watkins, John, and Sheehan, Thomas
FLORIDA LANDSCAPE PLANTS: NATIVE AND EXOTIC (University Presses of Florida, 1975, revised edition) Describes and gives growing information on 400 trees, ferns, palms, conifers, shrubs, bulbs, perennials, succulents and vines.

Watkins, John, and Wolfe, Herbert
YOUR FLORIDA GARDEN (University Presses of Florida, 1987, 5th abridged edition) The basics of Florida gardening, plus information on growing azaleas, hibiscus, camellias, roses, orchids, bromeliads, food plants and more.

Welch, William C.
PERENNIAL GARDEN COLOR (Taylor Publishing, 1989) Covers 125 perennials, over 100 old roses, cottage gardens and companion plants in the South; includes 500 color photos.

Zak, Bill
A FIELD GUIDE TO FLORIDA CRITTERS: COMMON HOUSEHOLD AND GARDEN PESTS OF THE SUNSHINE STATE (Taylor Pub-

lishing, 1986) How to identify and control them; 647 color photos.

For related books, see:
BUTTERFLY GARDENING FOR THE SOUTH by Ajilvsgi (page 178)
THE LOUISIANA IRIS by Caillet and Mertzweiller (page 86)
ODENA'S TEXAS HERB BOOK by Conrad and Murray (page195)
A ROCK GARDEN IN THE SOUTH by Lawrence (page 157)

SOUTHWESTERN U.S.

Brookbank, George
DESERT GARDENING: FRUITS AND VEGETABLES (Fisher Books, 1991) Covers which plants do well, how to save water and a weekly schedule of what to do.

Conrad, James, and Murray, Stephen
ODENA'S TEXAS HERB BOOK: HOW TO GROW, USE AND SELL (Lavendar Hill Herb Farm, 1990) Master herb grower Odena Brannam explains how to grow, harvest and market herbs and herbal products.

Coons, Harriet Edmunds
NATURAL GARDENING IN THE LOWER RIO GRANDE VALLEY (Coons, 805 Acacia Lake Drive, Brownsville, TX 78521) Organic gardening information for *all* of Texas, despite its title.

Cotner, Dr. Sam
THE VEGETABLE BOOK: A TEXAN'S GUIDE TO GARDENING (Texas Gardener Press, 1985) For the newcomer to Texas or the old hand at dealing with the peculiarities of gardening in Texas; includes 200 color photos.

Doolittle, Rosalie, and Tiedebohl, Harriet
SOUTHWEST GARDENING (University of New Mexico Press, 1967, revised edition)

Garrett, Howard
LANDSCAPE DESIGN: TEXAS STYLE (Taylor Publishing, 1986) How to design, select the plants,

install and maintain a landscape in any part of Texas; includes 38 case studies and 450 color photos. **TEXAS ORGANIC GARDENING BOOK** (Gulf Publishing, 1992)

Knoop, William
THE COMPLETE GUIDE TO TEXAS LAWN CARE (Texas Gardener Press, 1986) How to establish a new lawn, renovate an existing one and maintain a healthy one.

Latymer, Hugo
THE MEDITERRANEAN GARDEN (Barron, 1990) Covers over 300 trees, shrubs, flowering plants and cacti for the Southwest and California climates, plus design and growing information.

Meier, Leo, and Reid, Jan
TEXAS WILDFLOWERS (Portland House, 1990) Botanical, ecological and historical information on species native to the state.

Meltzer, Sol
HERB GARDENING IN TEXAS (Gulf Publishing, 1992, 2nd edition revised and expanded) How to propagate, grow and use over 90 herbs; covers zones 6 to 10 and includes recipes.

Miller, George
LANDSCAPING WITH NATIVE PLANTS OF TEXAS AND THE SOUTHWEST (Voyageur Press, 1991) Details on over 350 trees, shrubs, vines, wildflowers and cacti.

Niehaus, Theodore, and Ripper, Charles
A FIELD GUIDE TO SOUTHWESTERN AND TEXAS WILDFLOWERS (Houghton Mifflin, 1984)

Nokes, Jill
HOW TO GROW THE NATIVE PLANTS OF TEXAS AND THE SOUTHWEST (Pacesetter Press, 1986) Propagation, collection, and landscape use of over 350 species of native trees, shrubs and woody vines.

O'Kennon, Lou Ellen and Bob
TEXAS WILDFLOWER PORTRAITS (Gulf Publishing, 1987) Collection of 260 color photos of the large variety of Texas wildflowers.

Phillips, Judith
SOUTHWESTERN LANDSCAPING WITH NATIVE PLANTS (Museum of New Mexico Press, 1987)

Rundell, Mary Gail
TEXAS GARDENER'S GUIDE TO GROWING TOMATOES (Texas Gardener Press, 1984) How to grow tomatoes in Texas.

Shuler, Carol
PLANTS FOR SOUTHWEST GARDENS (Fisher Books, 1992) Details and color photos on 200 plants.

Sitton, Diane M.
TEXAS GARDENER'S GUIDE TO GROWING AND USING HERBS (Texas Gardener Press, 1987) Covers 49 herbs that grow well in Texas; includes history, description, cultivation requirements, plus harvesting and using for crafts and recipes.

Sperry, Neil
NEIL SPERRY'S COMPLETE GUIDE TO TEXAS GARDENING (Taylor Publishing, 1991, revised and updated 2nd edition) Includes landscape planning, trees, shrubs, vines, ground covers, lawns, flowers, food plants, pests and diseases and more; over 800 color photos.

Taylor's
GUIDE TO GARDENING IN THE SOUTHWEST AND SOUTHERN CALIFORNIA (Houghton Mifflin, 1992) For gardeners in New Mexico, Arizona, western Texas and southern California; covers trees, shrubs, perennials, ground covers and vines suitable for the area, and explains regional differences within the Southwest.

Terrell, Lorna (editor)
A GARDEN BOOK FOR HOUSTON AND THE TEXAS GULF COAST (Pacesetter Press, 1989, 4th revised edition) Everything you need to know to garden successfully in this sometimes difficult climate.

Vines, Robert
TREES, SHRUBS AND WOODY VINES OF THE SOUTHWEST (University of Texas Press, 1960) Describes and illustrates 1,231 native and naturalized plant species.

Wasowski, Sally and Andy
NATIVE TEXAS PLANTS: LANDSCAPING REGION BY REGION (Gulf Publishing, 1991) Describes and illustrates 364 native plants and includes 21 landscape plans.

Weniger, Deb
CACTI OF TEXAS AND NEIGHBORING STATES: A FIELD GUIDE (University of Texas Press, 1984) Descriptions and color photos of approximately 200 cacti of Texas, New Mexico, Oklahoma, Arkansas and Louisiana.

Zak, Bill
A FIELD GUIDE TO TEXAS CRITTERS: COMMON HOUSEHOLD AND GARDEN PESTS (Taylor Publishing, 1988) How to identify and control; 500 color photos.

For related books, see:
THE HERB GARDEN COOKBOOK by Hutson (page 107)
PERENNIAL GARDEN COLOR by Welch (page 195)

MIDWEST & WESTERN U.S.

Abrams, Leroy
ILLUSTRATED FLORA OF THE PACIFIC STATES (Stanford University Press, 1960) Covers every species of fern, flower, grass, tree and shrub native to Oregon, Washington and California; a four-volume reprint of the 1940 classic.

Benson, Lyman
THE NATIVE CACTI OF CALIFORNIA (Stanford University Press, 1969)

Colebrook, Binda
WINTER GARDENING IN THE MARITIME NORTHWEST: COOL SEASON CROPS FOR THE YEAR-ROUND GARDENER (Sasquatch Books, 1989, 3rd edition) How to have a continuous vegetable garden.

Craighead, John J., et al.
A FIELD GUIDE TO ROCKY MOUNTAIN WILDFLOWERS (Houghton Mifflin, 1974)

Emery, Dara
SEED PROPAGATION OF NATIVE CALIFORNIA PLANTS (Santa Barbara Botanic Garden, 1988)

Gordon, Don
GROWING FRUIT IN THE UPPER MIDWEST (University of Minnesota Press, 1990) Covers growing pears, peaches, cherries, plums, apricots, grapes, strawberries, currants, blueberries, apples, brambles and gooseberries.

Grant, John and Carol
TREES AND SHRUBS FOR PACIFIC NORTHWEST GARDENS (Timber Press, 1990, 2nd edition) Describes plants that are available in nurseries, hardy and not excessively difficult to grow; originally published in 1943, this revised edition includes new species.

Gundell, Herb
COMPLETE GUIDE TO ROCKY MOUNTAIN GARDENING (Taylor Publishing, 1985) Covers trees, shrubs, vines, landscaping, lawns, ground covers, flowers, food plants, and houseplants; almost 700 color photos.

Houk, Rose
WILDFLOWERS OF THE AMERICAN WEST (Chronicle Books, 1987) Covers coastal, desert, mountain and plains wildflowers; includes 60 color photos and watercolors.

Jacobsen, Arthur Lee
TREES OF SEATTLE: THE COMPLETE TREE-FINDERS GUIDE TO 740 VARIETIES (Sasquatch Books, 1990) Includes how to care for them and where to find the best specimens.

James-Palmer, Robert M.
HAWAIIAN ORGANIC GROWING GUIDE (Oasis Maui, 1988)

Jones, Carolyn
BEDDING PLANTS: THE COMPLETE GUIDE FOR AMATEURS AND EXPERTS (Voyageur Press, 1989) How to grow, propagate and use bedding plants in the Pacific Northwest; source list included.

Keator, Glenn
COMPLETE GARDEN GUIDE TO THE NA-
TIVE PERENNIALS OF CALIFORNIA (Chroni-
cle Books, 1990) Details and growing information on
over 500 species; includes sources and a list of societies.

Keith, Rebecca, and Giles, F. A.
DWARF SHRUBS FOR THE MIDWEST (Univer-
sity of Illinois Press, 1980) Covers over 100 shrubs
under 4' tall.

Kenady, Mary
THE PACIFIC NORTHWEST GARDENER'S
ALMANAC (Alaska Northwest, 1988) How to grow
a vegetable garden in the Pacific Northwest.

Kite, Pat, and Mackey, Betty
A CUTTING GARDEN FOR CALIFORNIA (B.
B. Mackey Books, 1989) Written from personal experience, it covers growing the annuals, biennials, perennials, bulbs, and flowering trees and shrubs that are
suitable for use in bouquets.

Kruckeberg, Arthur
GARDENING WITH NATIVE PLANTS OF
THE PACIFIC NORTHWEST: AN ILLUS-
TRATED GUIDE (University of Washington Press,
1989) Written from his personal experience with
growing native plants.

Lenz, Lee, and Dourley, John
CALIFORNIA NATIVE TREES AND SHRUBS:
FOR GARDEN AND ENVIRONMENT (Rancho
Santa Ana Botanic Garden, 1981) Descriptions, color
photos, drawings and landscape uses of ornamental
native plants; includes a list of plants divided into
seven regions.

Lovejoy, Ann
THE YEAR IN BLOOM: GARDENING FOR
ALL SEASONS IN THE PACIFIC NORTH-
WEST (Sasquatch Books, 1987) Covers a variety of
topics and plants (roses, lilacs, clematis, daylilies etc.)
for northwestern gardeners.
THE BORDER IN BLOOM: A NORTHWEST
GARDEN THROUGH THE SEASONS (Sas-
quatch Books, 1990) A sequel to *The Year in Bloom*,
this time concentrating on borders and what works
well with what.

McKeown, Denny
COMPLETE GUIDE TO MIDWEST GARDEN-
ING (Taylor Publishing, 1985) For zones 5 and 6 in
the middle of the U.S.

McNeilan, Ray, and Ronningen, Micheline
PACIFIC NORTHWEST GUIDE TO HOME
GARDENING (Timber Press, 1989) Covers vegetable, fruit and nut growing with a section on kiwi
cultivation.

Minnich, Jerry
WISCONSIN GARDEN GUIDE (Northword,
1989) Covers flowers, lawns, trees, shrubs and food
plants hardy to all cold climates.

Niehaus, Theodore, and Ripper, Charles
A FIELD GUIDE TO PACIFIC STATES WILD-
FLOWERS (Houghton Mifflin, 1981)

Niering, William, and Olmstead, Nancy
THE AUDUBON SOCIETY FIELD GUIDE TO
NORTH AMERICAN WILDFLOWERS: WEST-
ERN REGION (Knopf, 1979)

Perry, Bob
TREES AND SHRUBS FOR DRY CALIFORNIA
LANDSCAPES (Land Design Publications, 1981)
How to select the best trees and shrubs for erosion and
fire control.

Ross, Robert; Chambers, Henrietta; Stevenson,
Shirley
WILDFLOWERS OF THE WESTERN CAS-
CADES (Timber Press, 1988) A field guide of descrip-
tions and 182 stunning color photos and 102 line
drawings.

Schmidt, Marjorie G.
GROWING CALIFORNIA NATIVE PLANTS
(University of California Press, 1980) Everything
needed for growing California wildflowers.

Smaus, Robert
LOS ANGELES TIMES PLANNING AND
PLANTING THE GARDEN (Abrams, 1990) Cov-
ers which plants do best in sun, which in shade, seasonal plants and plans for paths, borders, beds and
patios; he is gardening editor of the *Los Angeles Times*.

Smith, Ken
WESTERN HOME LANDSCAPING (HP Books, 1985, revised edition) Covers plant selection, cost, low maintenance garden design, drip irrigation and more; 500+ color photos.

Snyder, Leon C.
GARDENING IN THE UPPER MIDWEST (University of Minnesota Press, 1985, 2nd edition)

Snyder, Rachel
GARDENING IN THE HEARTLAND (University Press of Kansas, 1991) Offers solutions to Midwestern gardening problems.

Solomon, Steve
GROWING VEGETABLES WEST OF THE CASCADES (Sasquatch Books, 1989 revised edition) Based on his personal experience of organically growing vegetables in the Pacific Northwest.

Staw, Jane Anne, and Swander, Mary
PARSNIPS IN THE SNOW: TALKS WITH MIDWESTERN GARDENERS (University of Iowa Press, 1990) Portraits of 12 very different amateur vegetable gardeners.

Stebbins, Richard
WESTERN FRUITS, BERRIES AND NUTS: HOW TO SELECT, GROW AND ENJOY (HP Books, 1981) Covers over 400 varieties.

Sunset
THE WESTERN GARDEN BOOK (Sunset Books, 1988, 5th edition) Detailed descriptions of over 6,000 plants, keyed to 24 western zones, plus planting and growing data.

Thomasson, Joseph R.
GROWING VEGETABLES IN THE GREAT PLAINS (University Press of Kansas, 1991) How to combat the variable weather and the insects and produce a vegetable garden in the Midwest.

Waters, George, and Harlow, Nora (editors)
PACIFIC HORTICULTURE BOOK OF WESTERN GARDENING (Godine, 1990) A selection of articles from *Pacific Horticulture* magazine.

Wolfe, Pam, and Irving, Gary
MIDWEST GARDENS (Chicago Review Press, 1991)

For related books, see:
GARDENING UNDER COVER by Head (page 121)
HOME LANDSCAPING IN THE NORTHEAST AND MIDWEST by Smith (page 192)

GARDENS AROUND THE WORLD

GARDENS OF THE U.S. & CANADA

Alcosser, Murray (photographer)
AMERICA IN BLOOM: GREAT AMERICAN GARDENS OPEN TO THE PUBLIC (Rizzoli, 1991) Over 200 color photos of 40 of the best public gardens in the U.S.

Baron, Robert (editor)
THE GARDEN AND FARM BOOKS OF THOMAS JEFFERSON (Fulcrum, 1987) A transcription of the journals recording his horticultural successes and failures over nearly 60 years, his thoughts and observations on gardening and relevant letters to friends; includes information on the restoration work done at Monticello.

Brooklyn Botanic Garden
AMERICAN GARDENS: A TRAVELER'S GUIDE (BBG #111) Surveys 250+ public gardens and arboreta in the U.S.; arranged by state, it gives hours, fees and special collections.

Bry, Charlene, et al.
A WORLD OF PLANTS: THE MISSOURI BO-TANICAL GARDEN (Abrams, 1990) A full-color tour of the 79 acres of the oldest U.S. botanical garden; includes rock garden, rose gardens, Japanese garden, scented garden, English woodland garden and more.

Cameron, Louisa P.
THE PRIVATE GARDENS OF CHARLESTON (Wyrick, 1992) Covers 25 varied gardens including an historic restoration and a tropical garden.

Cheek, Richard (photographer)
OLD WESTBURY GARDENS (Old Westbury Gardens, 1985) Seventy color photos of the Long Island, New York estate and arboretum.

DeForest, Elizabeth
THE GARDENS AND GROUNDS AT MOUNT VERNON: HOW GEORGE WASHINGTON PLANNED AND PLANTED THEM (University Press of Virginia, 1982)

Dunhill, Priscilla, and Freedman, Sue
GLORIOUS GARDENS TO VISIT: 61 GAR-DENS WITHIN 3 HOURS OF NEW YORK CITY (Crown, 1989) Information, including hours and fees, on 61 gardens in New York, New Jersey, Pennsylvania and the Delaware Valley, Connecticut, Massachusetts, and Rhode Island.

Dutton, Joan P.
ENJOYING AMERICA'S GARDENS (Reynal and Co., 1958) An Englishwoman who came to the U.S. for six months specifically to tour the gardens ends up staying three years and traveling around the perimeter of the U.S. She gives her impressions of well-known (Longwood, Magnolia, Middleton, etc.) and unknown gardens.

Eaton, Nicole, and Weston, Hilary
IN A CANADIAN GARDEN (Rizzoli, 1989) A variety of 35 gardens are described by the people who created them; 250 color photos.

Emmerling, Mary
AMERICAN COUNTRY GARDENS (Clarkson Potter, 1991) Contains 100 color photos and verses from favorite poets that capture the spirit of the American country garden.

Favretti, Rudy and Joy
FOR EVERY HOUSE A GARDEN: A GUIDE FOR REPRODUCING PERIOD GARDENS (University Press of New England, 1990) Describes four types of American gardens popular between 1620 and 1940—farmstead gardens, city merchant/country gentleman gardens, gardens of prosperity and gardens of workmen or craftsmen; includes lists of the plants used.

Fell, Derek
DEERFIELD: AN AMERICAN GARDEN THROUGH FOUR SEASONS (Pidcock Press, 1986) One hundred one color photos of this 35-acre private garden near Philadelphia.

Griswold, Mac, and Weller, Eleanor
THE GOLDEN AGE OF AMERICAN GARDENS: PROUD OWNERS, PRIVATE ESTATES 1890-1940 (Abrams, 1991) Designs of Beatrix Farrand, Jens Jensen, Frederick Law Olmsted, Stanford White and Fletcher Steele; includes 300 illustrations, 100 of which are made from hand-colored lantern slides created originally for the Garden Club of America.

Herb Society of America
TRAVELER'S GUIDE TO HERB GARDENS (Herb Society, 9019 Kirtland-Chardon Road, Mentor, OH 44060) Covers over 500 herb gardens in the U.S. and Canada.

Hockaday, Joan
THE GARDENS OF SAN FRANCISCO (Timber Press, 1988) A history of the development of gardens in San Francisco, plus descriptions and plans for 23 city gardens.

Jacob, Irene and Walter
GARDENS OF NORTH AMERICA AND HAWAII: A TRAVELER'S GUIDE (Timber Press, 1986) Describes and rates over 1,400 U.S., Canadian and Hawaiian gardens, arboreta, and conservatories.

Johnson, Eric A., and Millard, Scott
BEAUTIFUL GARDENS (Ironwood Press, 1991) Describes over 50 botanical gardens, arboreta, estates, garden centers and demonstration gardens in southern California, Arizona, Nevada and New Mexico.

Johnson, Jory
MODERN LANDSCAPE ARCHITECTURE (Abbeville, 1991) Plans and information on the designs of Louis Kahn, Isamu Noguchi, Lawrence Halprin, Peter Walker and Russell Page; 175 color photos.

LeBlanc, Joyce
THE PELICAN GUIDE TO GARDENS OF LOUISIANA (Pelican, 1989, 2nd edition)

Leighton, Ann
EARLY AMERICAN GARDENS: FOR MEATE OR MEDICINE (University of Massachusetts Press, 1986) Describes 17th century food and medicine gardens and lists which plants were used.
AMERICAN GARDENS IN THE 18TH CENTURY: FOR USE OR FOR DELIGHT (University of Massachusetts Press, 1986) How gardeners become interested in beauty and start importing and using ornamental plants; includes plant list.
AMERICAN GARDENS IN THE 19TH CENTURY: FOR COMFORT AND AFFLUENCE (University of Massachusetts Press, 1987) Includes list of plants used in this period.

Lewis, Taylor (photographer)
MARTHA'S VINEYARD: GARDENS AND
HOUSES (Simon & Schuster, 1992) This very special
island is captured in over 450 color photos of 40 houses
and gardens.
NANTUCKET: GARDENS AND HOUSES (Lit-
tle, Brown, 1990) Over 300 color photos bring this
beautiful island to life and present great design ideas
for the seaside gardener.

Loewer, Peter
AMERICAN GARDENS: A TOUR OF THE
NATION'S FINEST PRIVATE GARDENS
(Simon & Schuster, 1988) Describes 30 private U.S.
gardens from a Manhattan penthouse to a California
xeriscape; 200 color photos.

Logan, Harry B.
A TRAVELER'S GUIDE TO NORTH AMERI-
CAN GARDENS (Scribner's, 1974) Covers over
1,200 gardens.

Martin, Peter
THE PLEASURE GARDENS OF VIRGINIA:
FROM JAMESTOWN TO JEFFERSON (Princeton
University Press, 1991)

Massachusetts Horticultural Society, and Punch,
Walter (editor)
KEEPING EDEN: A HISTORY OF GARDEN-
ING IN AMERICA (Little, Brown, 1992) Covers
500 years of gardening.

McEwan, Barbara
WHITE HOUSE LANDSCAPES: HORTICUL-
TURAL ACHIEVEMENTS OF AMERICAN
PRESIDENTS (Walker, 1992)

Miller, Everitt, and Cohen, Jay
THE AMERICAN GARDEN GUIDEBOOK:
EAST (Evans, 1987) Covers 339 gardens in eastern
North America; includes hours, fees, collections, etc.
THE AMERICAN GARDEN GUIDEBOOK:
WEST (Evans, 1990) Covers 240 gardens west of the
Mississippi River including Hawaii, western Canada,
and Alaska; includes hours, fees, collections, etc.

Mitchell Jr., William
CLASSIC SAVANNAH: HISTORY, HOMES
AND GARDENS (Golden Coast, 1987) Covers approximately 30 houses and gardens.
GARDENS OF GEORGIA (Peachtree, 1989) Describes a variety of public, private, historic and modern
gardens; 300 color photos by Richard Moore.

Moore, Barbara, and Weener, Gail (editors)
HIDDEN GARDENS OF BEACON HILL (Bea-
con Hill Garden Club, no date) Description and a
color photo for each of the 38 gardens presented.

Morris, Karen, and Craker, Lyle
HERB GARDENS IN AMERICA: A VISITOR'S
GUIDE (HSMP Press, 1991) Covers public and private gardens, how to locate them, and what services
they offer (gift shops, classes, plant sales, etc.).

Mulligan, William
COMPLETE GUIDE TO NORTH AMERICAN
GARDENS: THE NORTHEAST (Little, Brown,
1991) Covers history, design and travel information,
plus 100 color photos.
COMPLETE GUIDE TO NORTH AMERICAN
GARDENS: THE WEST COAST (Little, Brown,
1991) Companion book to the above.

Oakley, Myrna
PUBLIC AND PRIVATE GARDENS OF THE
NORTHWEST (Beautiful America Publishing,
1990) Brief descriptions of public gardens, arboreta,
nurseries as well as wildlife preserves, scenic areas and
historic homes; includes addresses and phone numbers.

Olwell, Carol
GARDENING FROM THE HEART: WHY GAR-
DENERS GARDEN (Antelope Island Press, 1990)
Interviews with 21 gardeners, none of whom are famous, but all passionate gardeners. They explain why
they garden and what benefits they derive from this
very personal endeavor.

Ottesen, Carole
THE NEW AMERICAN GARDEN (Macmillan,
1988)

Panich, Paula, and Trulsson, Nora (editors)
DESERT SOUTHWEST GARDENS (Bantam, 1990) Over 250 color photos of a variety of garden styles in California, Arizona, Texas and New Mexico.

Prentice, Helaine
THE GARDENS OF SOUTHERN CALIFORNIA (Chronicle Books, 1990) Surveys 25 of the best public gardens in the counties of Los Angeles, Orange, San Diego, Riverside and Santa Barbara; includes over 200 color photos.

Ray, Mary Helen and Nicholls, Robert P. (editors)
THE TRAVELER'S GUIDE TO AMERICAN GARDENS (University of North Carolina Press, 1988, revised edition) Describes over 1,000 public and private gardens that have been in existence for over 75 years and which represent their time period; arranged by state.

Sigg, Eric
CALIFORNIA PUBLIC GARDENS: A VISITOR'S GUIDE (John Muir, 1991) Describes approximately 150 gardens plus information on fees, hours and tours; includes maps.

Southern Accents Magazine editors
GARDENS OF THE SOUTH (Simon & Schuster, 1985)

Tanner, Ogden
GARDENING AMERICA: REGIONAL AND HISTORICAL INFLUENCES IN THE CONTEMPORARY GARDEN (Viking Penguin, 1990) A tour of 50 magnificent public and private gardens across the U.S.; includes 300 color photos.

Tanner, Odgen, and Auchincloss, Adele
THE NEW YORK BOTANICAL GARDEN: AN ILLUSTRATED CHRONICLE OF PLANTS AND PEOPLE (Walker, 1991) Covers the history and a tour of this famous garden in celebration of its 100th anniversary.

Thorpe, Patricia, and Sonneman, Eve
AMERICA'S COTTAGE GARDENS (Random House, 1990) How Americans around the country have created their version of the traditional English cottage garden: 145 color photos depict the results.

Valentine, James (photographer)
CALLAWAY GARDENS: THE UNENDING SEASON (Longstreet Press, 1989) A full-color tour of the 2,500-acre Georgia garden, famous for its azaleas.

Van Ravenswaay, Charles
A NINETEENTH CENTURY GARDEN (Universe Books, 1977) Selections from 19th-century U.S. nursery garden catalogues.

Verey, Rosemary
THE AMERICAN MAN'S GARDEN (Little, Brown, 1990) Covers a variety of U.S. and Canadian gardens.

Verey, Rosemary, and Samuels, Ellen
THE AMERICAN WOMAN'S GARDEN (Little, Brown, 1984) Covers over 30 U.S. private gardens including those of Eleanor Perenyi and Ann Leighton.

Warner, Jr., Sam B.
TO DWELL IS TO GARDEN: A HISTORY OF BOSTON'S COMMUNITY GARDENS (Northeastern University Press, 1987)

Williams, Dorothy
HISTORIC VIRGINIA GARDENS: PRESERVATIONS BY THE GARDEN CLUB OF VIRGINIA (University Press of Virginia, 1985)

Wilson, Jim
MASTERS OF THE VICTORY GARDEN: SPECIALTY GARDENERS SHARE THEIR EXPERT TECHNIQUES (Little, Brown, 1990) Eleven gardeners from around the U.S. describe how they grow, propagate and exhibit their specialized plants (lilies, peonies, peppers, antique fruit trees, herbs, hostas, wildflowers, rhododendrons, roses, dwarf conifers, daylilies); includes advice on how to get started in each of the specialties.

Wine, Wauneta
GARDENS FOR ALL SEASONS: THE PUBLIC GARDENS AND ARBORETA OF MARYLAND (Vandamere, 1987) Details on 33 gardens and arboreta including the best season to visit, hours, fees, directions, garden maps, suggestions for day trips, how much time to allow, wheelchair information and more.

Wood, Louisa F.
BEHIND THOSE GARDEN WALLS IN HIS-
TORIC SAVANNAH (Historic Savannah, 1982)
Plans and lists of plants for 28 private gardens.

For related books, see:
TIMELESS TREES: THE U.S. NATIONAL
BONSAI COLLECTION by Bloomer (page 152)

GARDENS OF GREAT BRITAIN & IRELAND

Alexander, Rosemary, and Pasley, Anthony D.
THE ENGLISH GARDENING SCHOOL (Grove
Weidenfeld, 1987) The complete master course on
garden planning and landscape design for the American gardener from the Chelsea Physic Garden.

Bartholomew, James (photographer)
THE MAGIC OF KEW (New Amsterdam Books,
1988) Includes 100 black-and-white photos of Kew
and Wakehurst Place taken before the damaging 1987
storm.

Batey, Mavis, and Lambert, David
ENGLISH GARDEN TOUR: A VIEW INTO
THE PAST (Trafalgar Square, 1991) History of more
than 50 notable English gardens from the Middle Ages
to the beginning of the 20th century.

Bean, W. J.
TREES AND SHRUBS HARDY IN THE BRIT-
ISH ISLES (Timber Press, 1991, 8th revised edition
consists of four volumes plus a supplement issued in
1988) Extensive descriptions of woody plants that
grow in all parts of the British Isles; a classic work for
almost 80 years because of its reliable information and
charming plant descriptions.

Bisgrove, Richard
THE NATIONAL TRUST BOOK OF THE EN-
GLISH GARDEN (Viking Penguin, 1990) Discusses
the changes that have occurred in garden design from
medieval times to the present.

Blomfield, Reginald
THE FORMAL GARDEN IN ENGLAND (Tim-
ber Press, 1985) Originally published in 1892, it covers
history, garden architecture, symmetry and symbolism.

Boney, A. D.
THE LOST GARDENS OF GLASGOW UNI-
VERSITY (Trafalgar Square, 1989)

Bowe, Patrick
THE GARDENS OF IRELAND (Little, Brown,
1986)

Brown, Jane
THE ART AND ARCHITECTURE OF EN-
GLISH GARDENS (Rizzoli, 1989) How ornaments,
bridges, furniture and decorative structures have
played their part in the history of English garden
design; 320 watercolors.
EMINENT GARDENERS (Viking Penguin, 1991)
Covers influential British gardeners and their gardens
in the period 1880 to 1980.
THE ENGLISH GARDEN IN OUR TIME:
FROM GERTRUDE JEKYLL TO GEOFFREY
JELLICOE (ISBS, 1986) Covers 20th century English
garden design with special emphasis on Sissinghurst
and Hidcote; includes garden plans.
SISSINGHURST: PORTRAIT OF A GARDEN
(Abrams, 1990) Over 100 color photos of this magnificent garden in all seasons and at all times of day;
includes history of the manor and details of plantings.

Chivers, Susan, and Woloszynska, Suzanne
GARDENS OF THE HEART (Chatto & Windus,
1988) Describes 24 gardens of such well-known people
as Barbara Cartland, Sir John Gielgud and David
Hicks.

Clarke, Ethne
ENGLISH COTTAGE GARDENS (Viking, 1986)
Over 120 color photos of cottage gardens throughout
England.
HIDCOTE: THE MAKING OF A GARDEN (Mi-
chael Joseph, 1989)

Clarke, Ethne, and Wright, George
ENGLISH TOPIARY GARDENS (Clarkson Pot-
ter, 1988) Examples of the finest and most eccentric
English topiary; includes the history of topiary and of
the English gardens.

Clayton-Payne, Andrew, and Elliott, Brent
FLOWER GARDENS OF VICTORIAN EN-
GLAND (Rizzoli, 1989) Over 130 watercolors of more
than 120 different Victorian gardens.

Coats, Peter
THE HOUSE AND GARDEN BOOK OF EN-
GLISH GARDENS (Little, Brown, 1988) A selection of his favorite gardens from the ones he has
written about for *House and Garden* magazine.

Cooper, Guy, and Taylor, Gordon
ENGLISH HERB GARDENS (Rizzoli, 1986) Detailed descriptions and color photos of some of the best
herb gardens in England.
ENGLISH WATER GARDENS (Little, Brown,
1987) A great source of ideas for all types of water
gardens from the simple to the elaborate; 135 color
photos.

Cotton, Sarah (editor)
GUIDE TO THE SPECIALIST NURSERIES
AND GARDEN SUPPLIERS OF BRITAIN AND
IRELAND (Antique Collector's Club, 1989) Where
to find the best and most unusual plants and ornaments
for the garden.

Cowan, May
INVEREWE: A GARDEN IN THE NORTH-
WEST HIGHLANDS (Geoffrey Bles, 1964) How
this great Scottish garden was created.

Davies, Jennifer
THE VICTORIAN KITCHEN GARDEN (Nor-
ton, 1988) Covers the plants and gardening techniques of 19th century kitchen gardens and the
restoration of a traditional Victorian kitchen garden
in Berkshire.

DuBoulay, Shirley
GARDENERS (Trafalgar Square, 1986) Twelve well-
known British gardeners talk about how their careers
started and their personal gardening preferences.

Elliott, Brent
VICTORIAN GARDENS (Timber Press, 1986)
Covers the origins and development of the Victorian
concepts of gardening and landscaping.

Fearnley-Whittingstall, Jane
HISTORIC GARDENS: A GUIDE TO ONE
HUNDRED SIXTY BRITISH GARDENS OF IN-
TEREST (Viking Penguin, 1991)

Findhorn Community
THE FINDHORN GARDEN (Harper & Row,
1975) Story of how the Scottish garden on a peninsula
in the North Sea was founded by Peter and Eileen
Caddy, and the unbelievable results they achieved
with vegetables, fruits and flowers.

Fisher, John
MR. MARSHALL'S FLOWER ALBUM: FROM
THE ROYAL LIBRARY AT WINDSOR CAS-
TLE (Trafalgar Square, 1987)

Gibson, Michael
THE ROSE GARDENS OF ENGLAND (Globe
Pequot, 1988) Covers 70 public rose gardens arranged
by county with information on hours and directions
for locating.

Girling, Richard (editor)
THE MAKING OF THE ENGLISH GARDEN
(Macmillan, 1988) Describes how the various compo-
nents of the garden are created.

Greenoak, Francesca
FRUIT AND VEGETABLE GARDENS: THE
NATIONAL TRUST GUIDE TO PRODUC-
TIVE GARDENS (Trafalgar Square, 1991) De-
scribes the orchards, kitchen gardens and herb gardens
belonging to the National Trust.

Hemphill, John and Rosemary
THE FRAGRANT GARDEN (Harper Interna-
tional, 1992) A tour of beautiful gardens in England
and France that emphasize herbs and old-fashioned
flowers.

Hinde, Thomas
STATELY GARDENS OF BRITAIN (Norton,
1983)

Hobhouse, Penelope
A BOOK OF GARDENING: A PRACTICAL
GUIDE (Little, Brown, 1986) A tour of some Na-
tional Trust gardens and visits with the head gardeners
(Charlecote Park, Clivedon, Mottisfont Abbey,

Hardwick Hall and others); includes plans and plant lists.

PRIVATE GARDENS OF ENGLAND (Harmony Books, 1987) Covers 33 well-known private gardens such as Hatfield House, Brockenhurst Park, Great Dixter, Levens Hall and Dower House.

Hollis, Sarah
THE SHELL GUIDE TO THE GARDENS OF ENGLAND AND WALES (Trafalgar Square, 1989) Describes over 350 gardens from parks of stately homes to small private gardens; includes directions for reaching them, opening times and more.

Hyams, Edward S.
ENGLISH COTTAGE GARDENS (Viking Penguin, 1988)

Innes, Miranda (editor)
THE PASSIONATE GARDENER (Trafalgar Square, 1990) Interviews with 23 famous English people (Germaine Greer, Sir Terence Conran, Mary Keen, Beth Chatto, Hugh Johnson, Robin Lane Fox among others) who tell what their gardens, both grand and working, mean to them.

Jacques, David
GEORGIAN GARDENS: THE REIGN OF NATURE (Timber Press, 1984) Covers the period 1730 to 1830 which produced some of the greatest gardens and gardeners, Capability Brown among them.

Johnson, Judy, and Berry, Susan
ENGLISH PRIVATE GARDENS: OPEN TO THE PUBLIC IN AID OF THE NATIONAL GARDEN SCHEME (Trafalgar Square, 1991) A detailed presentation of 36 private gardens that are very different in size, design and location; includes interviews with the owners.

Joyce, David (editor)
THE CHELSEA YEAR 1988/89 (Random House, 1989) A variety of essays by well-known British gardeners (Christopher Lloyd, Stephen Lacey, Michael Gibson, etc.) covering the newest varieties of plants and the highlights of the Chelsea Flower Show; includes a list of exhibitors.

Keen, Mary
THE GLORY OF THE ENGLISH GARDEN (Little, Brown, 1989) Covers over 150 gardens of every style, size and design type; 300 color photos.

Lees-Milne, Alvilde, and Verey, Rosemary
THE ENGLISHMAN'S GARDEN (Viking, 1988) Covers 33 gardens, including those of Beverley Nichols, Graham Thomas and Christopher Lloyd.
THE ENGLISHWOMAN'S GARDEN (Chatto & Windus, 1980) The 36 contributors include Beth Chatto, Penelope Hobhouse and Rosemary Verey.
THE NEW ENGLISHWOMAN'S GARDEN (Trafalgar Square, 1990) A sequel to the above with 28 more gardens.

Lennox-Boyd, Arabella
PRIVATE GARDENS OF LONDON (Rizzoli, 1990) Includes 40 planting plans and 225 photos.

Lennox-Boyd, Arabella; Perry, Clay; Thomas, Graham
TRADITIONAL ENGLISH GARDENS (Rizzoli, 1987) Descriptions and 135 color photos of 28 gardens.

Llewellyn, Roddy
ORNAMENTAL ENGLISH GARDENS (Rizzoli, 1990)

Lloyd, Christopher
THE YEAR AT GREAT DIXTER (Viking, 1987) How this famous garden designed by Edwin Lutyens looks throughout the year; 100 color photos.

Lycett-Green, Candida, and Lawson, Andrew
BRILLIANT GARDENS: A CELEBRATION OF ENGLISH GARDENING (Trafalgar Square, date not set) Describes 75 small gardens all around England that, because of their uniqueness and eccentricity, attract a large number of sightseers.

Morgan, Joan, and Richards, Alison
A PARADISE OUT OF A COMMON FIELD: THE PLEASURES AND PLENTY OF THE VICTORIAN GARDEN (HarperCollins, 1990) Describes the elegance of the gardens, food and interiors of the Victorian Age; developed from the British radio series of the same name.

Mott, George, and Aall, Sally S.
FOLLIES AND PLEASURE PAVILIONS
(Abrams, 1989) Describes over 100 18th and 19th
century gazebos, belvederes, temples, pagodas, ruins
and tree houses in England, Ireland, Scotland and
Wales, most of which are open to the public; 141 color
photos.

National Gardens Scheme Charitable Trust
GARDENS OF ENGLAND AND WALES (pub-
lished annually by the Trust, Hatchlands Park, East
Clandon, Guildford, Surrey GU4 7RT, England; also
available from Green Shade, P.O. Box 547, Cape
Neddick, Maine 03902) A county-by-county guide to
over 2,500 private gardens, the majority of which are
not normally open to the public; gives open dates, fees,
whether tea is served, directions, etc. (I love browsing
through this book and coming across entries like "a
garden perpetually changing to accommodate needs of
obsessive gardener with too little time for gardening.")

National Trust
THE NATIONAL TRUST GARDENS HAND-
BOOK (Trafalgar Square, 1991) Guide to 140+ gardens in England, Wales and Northern Ireland giving
opening and closing hours, fees, best visiting times,
nearby gardens and more.

Ottewill, David
THE EDWARDIAN GARDEN (Yale University
Press, 1989) Describes the incredible gardens the En-
glish created prior to World War One.

Owen, Jane
ECCENTRIC GARDENS (Random House, 1990)
Twenty-five unusual gardens are described.

Page, C. N.
THE FERNS OF BRITAIN AND IRELAND
(Cambridge University Press, 1983)

Pearson, Robert, and Mitchell, Susanne (editors)
THE ORDNANCE SURVEY GUIDE TO GAR-
DENS IN BRITAIN (Norton, 1987) Another guide
book for the wonderful gardens in the U.K.

Peplow, Elizabeth and Reginald
HERBS AND HERB GARDENS OF BRITAIN
(Salem House, 1985) Covers approximately 90 of their
favorite herb gardens.

Phillips, R.
WILD FLOWERS OF BRITAIN (Mad River, 1977)

Plumptre, George
COLLINS BOOK OF BRITISH GARDENS: A
GUIDE TO 200 GARDENS IN ENGLAND,
SCOTLAND AND WALES (Collins, 1985) Ar-
ranged by region and then by county.
LATEST COUNTRY GARDENS (Trafalgar
Square, 1990) A survey of the history of British gardens
since 1945.

Read, Miss (introduction)
THE ENGLISH VICARAGE GARDEN:
THIRTY GARDENS OF BEAUTY AND INSPI-
RATION (Viking Penguin, 1989) Includes the gar-
dens of Canon Charles Kingsley, Gilbert White, Dean
Hole and Rev. William Wilks.

Robinson, William
THE ENGLISH FLOWER GARDEN (Timber
Press, 1984) Originally published in 1883, this edition
has been updated by Graham Stuart Thomas with the
current nomenclature for Robinson's encyclopedic
plant lists.
GRAVETYE MANOR OR TWENTY YEARS
WORK ROUND AN OLD MANOR HOUSE
(Sagapress, 1984) A record of the plantings and garden
work done from 1885 to 1908 at his estate.

Rose, Graham, and King, Peter (editors)
THE GOOD GARDENS GUIDE 1992: OVER
1,000 OF THE BEST GARDENS OPEN TO THE
PUBLIC IN GREAT BRITAIN AND IRELAND
(Trafalgar Square, 1991) Includes addresses, phone
numbers, locations by county, opening times, best
season, fees, ratings, maps, listings by type of garden
(rose, herb, water, etc.) and a section on great gardeners.

Russell, Vivian
DREAM GARDENS: A MAGICAL CORNER OF
ENGLAND (Trafalgar Square, 1989) Interviews with
owners of large and small gardens in England's Lake

District; includes Wordsworth's and Beatrix Potter's gardens.

Marchioness of Salisbury
THE GARDENS OF QUEEN ELIZABETH, THE QUEEN MOTHER: A PERSONAL TOUR WITH THE MARCHIONESS OF SALISBURY (Viking Penguin, 1991) Includes the history and design of the gardens and 130 color photos.

Saville, Diana
GARDENS FOR SMALL COUNTRY HOUSES (Viking Penguin, 1989)

Scott-James, Anne, and Lancaster, Osbert
THE PLEASURE GARDEN: AN ILLUSTRATED HISTORY OF BRITISH GARDENING (Trafalgar Square, 1992) An entertaining survey of the development of British gardens from Roman times to the present; covers design, plants and gardeners over the last 2,000 years.

Stevens, John
THE NATIONAL TRUST BOOK OF WILDFLOWER GARDENING: HOW THE BRITISH USE NATIVE PLANTS TO CREATE NATURAL-LOOKING GARDENS (Globe Pequot, 1988) Plenty of ideas for wildflower garden design, and also covers rock, water and seaside gardens.

Stewart, Joyce (editor)
ORCHIDS AT KEW (Unipub, 1992)

Strong, Roy
LONDON'S PRIDE: THE GLORIOUS HISTORY OF THE CAPITAL'S GARDENS (Anaya Publishers, 1990) Covers London's gardens from Elizabethan to modern times.
THE RENAISSANCE GARDEN IN ENGLAND (Thames & Hudson, 1979)

Stuart, David
THE GARDEN TRIUMPHANT (HarperCollins, 1988) Covers the origins, techniques and well-known creators of the Victorian garden.
GEORGIAN GARDENS (Hale, 1979) Covers English landscaping from 1730 to 1830; includes flower gardens, kitchen gardens, the deer park, town and country gardens, wildernesses and pleasure grounds.

Tait, A. A.
THE LANDSCAPE GARDEN IN SCOTLAND (Columbia University Press, 1988)

Triggs, H. Inigo
FORMAL GARDENS IN ENGLAND AND SCOTLAND: THEIR PLANNING AND ARRANGEMENT, ARCHITECTURAL AND ORNAMENTAL FEATURES (ISBS, 1989) A reprint of the 1902 classic work on historic formal gardens; includes 44 modern color photos.

Truscott, James
PRIVATE GARDENS OF SCOTLAND (Harmony Books, 1988) One hundred seventy photos illustrate the diversity of these gardens.

Turner, Tom
ENGLISH GARDEN DESIGN: HISTORY AND STYLES SINCE 1650 (Antique Collectors Club, 1986) Covers how and why the English garden evolved and how later developments changed the original ideas.

Whaley, Jack
GARDENS OF IRELAND (Dufour, 1990)

Wheeler, David
PANORAMAS OF ENGLISH GARDENS (Little, Brown, 1991) From the publisher of *Hortus*, this book covers formal and informal, known and less well-known gardens.

Whitsey, Fred
HIDCOTE: A GARDEN OF GENIUS (Antique Collector's Club, 1989) Covers the design, history, personalities and plants of one of the loveliest of the National Trust gardens.

Young, Fay
THE BOOK OF THE SCOTTISH GARDEN (Timber Press, 1991) A survey of 52 gardens; 236 color photos.

GARDENS OF FRANCE

Cox, Madison
PRIVATE GARDENS OF PARIS (Harmony, 1989) Describes 30 terrace, courtyard and patio gardens near famous sites in Paris.

Girard, Jacques (photographer)
VERSAILLES GARDENS: SCULPTURE AND
MYTHOLOGY (Vendome, 1985) Over 260 color
photos and illustrations.

Jones, Louisa
THE GARDENS OF PROVENCE (Abbeville
Press, 1992) Includes 250 color photos.

LeDantec, Denise and Jean-Pierre
PARIS IN BLOOM (Abbeville Press, 1991) De-
scribes the history, botany and legends of Paris's parks
and gardens; includes maps and 260 color photos.
READING THE FRENCH GARDENS: STORY
AND HISTORY (MIT Press, 1990) A discussion of
French garden design interspersed with snatches of
fiction that re-create the mood of the time.

de Montclos, Jean-Marie Perouse
VERSAILLES (Abbeville Press, 1991) Covers the
transformation of Louis XIII's hunting lodge to the
Palais de Versailles; 392 color photos of the exterior,
interior and gardens.

Murray, Elizabeth
MONET'S PASSION: IDEAS, INSPIRATION
AND INSIGHTS FROM THE PAINTER'S GAR-
DENS (Pomegranate Press, 1989) From a year spent
at Giverny, she discusses Monet's color theories, design ideas and growing advice; includes plans, a list of
the plants Monet used and sources for locating them.

Racine, Michel; Binet, Francoise; Boursier-
Mougenot, Ernest
THE GARDENS OF PROVENCE AND THE
FRENCH RIVIERA (MIT Press, 1987) Describes 50
gardens from the simple to the elaborate; 375 color
photos.

Scully, Vincent
FRENCH ROYAL GARDENS: THE DESIGNS
OF ANDRE LE NOTRE (Rizzoli, 1992) Describes
the gardens that Le Notre designed for Louis XIII and
Louis XIV at Versailles, Les Tuileries and other royal
residences.

Valéry, Marie-Françoise
FRENCH GARDEN STYLE (Barron, 1990) Covers
30 of the best gardens located throughout France; 250
color photos.

Weckler, Charles (photographer)
IMPRESSIONS OF GIVERNY (Abrams, 1990)
Over 60 color photos capturing the magic of Monet's
house and garden at Giverny.

Wiebenson, Dora
THE PICTURESQUE GARDEN IN FRANCE
(Princeton University Press, 1978)

For related books, see:
THE FRAGRANT GARDEN by Hemphill (page
205)

GARDENS OF ITALY

Agnelli, Marella
GARDENS OF THE ITALIAN VILLAS (Rizzoli,
1987) Many of the gardens shown and discussed have
not been in any previous books; 225 photos, 112 in
color.

Chatfield, Judith
THE CLASSIC ITALIAN GARDEN (Rizzoli,
1991) The evolution of the Italian garden from Roman
times to the 20th century revivals.
GARDENS OF THE ITALIAN LAKES (Rizzoli,
1992) Describes 30 terraced gardens of villas situated
around Lake Como, Lake Maggiore and Lake Garda;
180 color photos.
A TOUR OF ITALIAN GARDENS (Rizzoli, 1988)
A guide to over 50 gardens, most open to the public,
that includes a history of Italian gardening plus family
histories and garden plans.

Clarke, Ethne, and Bencini, Raffaello
THE GARDENS OF TUSCANY (Rizzoli, 1990)
History, location and descriptions of gardens of Flor-
ence, Sienna and Lucca.

James, Geoffrey (photographer)
THE ITALIAN GARDEN (Abrams, 1991) Includes
93 panoramic black-and-white photos, plus an essay
by Robert Harbison.

Lazzaro, Claudio
THE ITALIAN RENAISSANCE GARDEN: FROM THE CONVENTIONS OF PLANTING, DESIGN AND ORNAMENT TO THE GRAND GARDENS OF 16TH CENTURY ITALY (Yale University Press, 1990)

Masson, Georgina
ITALIAN GARDENS (Antique Collector's Club, 1986) Covers the classical Italian garden that flourished from 1550 to 1700; reprint of 1962 edition.

de' Medici, Lorenza
RENAISSANCE OF ITALIAN GARDENS (Fawcett, 1990) Descriptions and 200 color photos of gardens in Lombardy, Piedmont, Genoa and Tuscany.

Pool, Mary Jane
THE GARDENS OF FLORENCE (Rizzoli, 1992) Color photos and descriptions of over 30 gardens.
THE GARDENS OF VENICE (Rizzoli, 1989) Contains 125 color photos of the gardens you don't see as you travel the canals of Venice.

Ramsay, Alex, and Attlee, Helena
ITALIAN GARDENS: A VISITOR'S GUIDE (Seven Hills Books, 1990) Description, history, location, hours and other details on approximately 50 of the best gardens in Italy.

Shepherd, J. C., and Jellicoe, G. A.
ITALIAN GARDENS OF THE RENAISSANCE (Princeton Architectural Press, 1986)

Wharton, Edith
ITALIAN VILLAS AND THEIR GARDENS (DaCapo, 1976)

GARDENS OF JAPAN & CHINA

Itoh, Teiji
THE GARDENS OF JAPAN (Kodansha, 1984) Discusses the history of Japanese garden design with added side trips into such areas as exactly what to do before a garden tea ceremony.
THE IMPERIAL GARDENS OF JAPAN: SENTO GOSHO, KATSURA, AND SHUGAKU-IN (Weatherhill, 1970) Explores the famous gardens in Kyoto.

Katsuhiko, Mizuno (photographer)
TSUBONIWA: THE JAPANESE COURTYARD GARDEN (Books Nippan, 1991) Over 100 color photos of 78 courtyard gardens at shrines, temples, private homes and public places.

Ohashi, Haruzo (photographer)
JAPANESE COURTYARD GARDENS (Japan Publications, 1988) Over 80 color photos explore design ideas for peaceful gardens.
THE JAPANESE GARDEN: ISLANDS OF SERENITY (Japan Publications, 1987) Brief descriptions and 98 color photos.
JAPANESE GARDENS OF THE MODERN ERA (Japan Publications, 1987) A continuation of the above book covering gardens from the end of the Edo period to the present; 98 color photos.
THE TEA GARDEN (Books Nippan, 1990) Contains 96 color photos and brief descriptions of 60 tea gardens from around Japan.

Rambach, Pierre and Susanne
GARDENS OF LONGEVITY IN CHINA AND JAPAN (Rizzoli, 1987) A guide to stone, not plant, gardens in China and Japan.

Rimer, Thomas
SHISENDO: PAVILION OF THE GREAT POETS (Weatherhill, 1991) Details on one of Kyoto's loveliest gardens, which was designed and built by the poet, Ishikawa Jozan (1583 to 1672); includes a biography of Jozan.

Yamamoto, Kenzo (photographer)
INVITATION TO KYOTO GARDENS (Books Nippan, no date given, 2nd edition) Describes 47 public gardens of various historical periods and styles; includes map, fees and hours.
KYOTO GARDENS: SEASONAL IMAGES IN MOSS AND STONE (Mitsumura Suiko Shion, 1989) Fifty-six full-page color photos.

Yamashita, Michael S. (photographer)
IN THE JAPANESE GARDEN (Starwood, 1991) Contains 73 panoramic color photos of a variety of Japanese gardens.

Yoshikawa, Isao
STONE BASINS: THE ACCENTS OF THE JAPANESE GARDEN (Books Nippan, 1989) Over 290 stone basins in a variety of styles and Japanese garden settings.

CHINESE GARDENS: GARDENS OF THE YANGTZE RIVER (Books Nippan, 1990) Descriptions and 230 color/120 black-and-white photos of 37 gardens.

THE WORLD OF ZEN GARDENS (Books Nippan, 1991) History and 200 color photos cover Zen gardens from all around Japan.

MISCELLANEOUS GARDENS

Bowe, Patrick
GARDENS OF CENTRAL EUROPE (Antique Collector's Club, 1991) Covers a variety of central European gardens giving design history and information on climate and flora.

Brookes, John
GARDENS OF PARADISE: THE HISTORY AND DESIGN OF THE GREAT ISLAMIC GARDENS (New Amsterdam Books, 1987) Covers the development of the Islamic gardens in Spain, the Middle East, northern Africa and India.

Carita, Helder, and Cardoso, Homem
PORTUGUESE GARDENS (ISBS, 1991) Reference work on gardens with a Moorish influence; includes 362 photos and illustrations, over 150 in color.

Marquesa de Casa Valdes
SPANISH GARDENS (ISBS, 1987) An in-depth study of Spanish garden design and history; includes 118 black-and-white illustrations and 405 color photos.

Dohna, Ursula
PRIVATE GARDENS OF GERMANY (Harmony Books, 1986) Covers 30 of the best private gardens in Germany.

Guest, Sarah
PRIVATE GARDENS OF AUSTRALIA (Crown, 1990)

Henty, Carol
FOR THE PEOPLE'S PLEASURE: AUSTRALIA'S BOTANIC GARDENS (Rizzoli, 1989) Covers 14 botanic gardens in tropical, temperate and desert regions of Australia.

GARDENS WORLDWIDE

Adams, William H.
NATURE PERFECTED: GARDENS THROUGH HISTORY (Abbeville Press, 1991) Covers the history of western gardens from their beginnings in Greece, Egypt and Rome to modern times.

Angel, Heather
A VIEW FROM A WINDOW (Salem House, 1988) Views of public and private gardens around the world seen through windows and openings in walls or hedges.

Bazin, Germain
PARADEISOS: THE ART OF THE GARDEN (Little, Brown, 1990) The development of Eastern and Western gardens from antiquity to the present.

Brown, Richard
MOMENTS IN EDEN: GARDEN PHOTOGRAPHS (Little, Brown, 1989) Over 80 color photos of gardens around the world, including Versailles, Holland's Keukenhof Garden, Winterthur, Sissinghurst, Giverny and Kyoto, plus simpler ones such as a Swiss window box and a Cotswold cottage.

Hobhouse, Penelope, and McDonald, Elvin (editors)
GARDENS OF THE WORLD: THE ART AND PRACTICE OF GARDENING (Macmillan, 1991) Companion to the PBS television series; includes 200 color photos of 60+ gardens and chapters by John Brookes (country gardens), Ann Lovejoy (flower gardens), Katherine Whiteside (tropical gardens), Elvin McDonald (rose gardens), Allen Paterson (tulip and bulb gardens), Madison Cox (public gardens), Teiji Itoh (Japanese gardens) and Penelope Hobhouse (formal gardens).

Hobhouse, Penelope, and Taylor, Patrick (editors)
THE GARDENS OF EUROPE (Random House, 1990) A travel guide to 700 gardens open to the public in Europe and Russia; includes opening hours and days and entrance fees.

Hyams, Edward S.
GREAT BOTANICAL GARDENS OF THE WORLD (Macmillan, 1969) Covers gardens in Europe (Italy, Netherlands, Scotland, Ireland, Belgium, Germany, France, Austria, England, Scandinavia), North America (U.S. and Canada), USSR (as it was called in 1969), Tropics (Java, Ceylon, Singapore, India, Uganda, Brazil), Southern Hemisphere (Australia, New Zealand, South Africa, Argentina) and Japan; includes numerous color and black-and-white photos and a world map pinpointing the location of each of the 525 gardens.

King, Ronald
THE QUEST FOR PARADISE: A HISTORY OF THE WORLD'S GARDENS (W. H. Smith, 1979) Covers major gardens.

Littlefield, Susan, and Schinz, Marina
VISIONS OF PARADISE: THEMES AND VARIATIONS ON THE GARDEN (Stewart, Tabori & Chang, 1985) A survey of Western gardens divided by type (rose gardens, perennial borders, herb gardens, landscapes, formal, etc.).

Loxton, Howard (editor)
THE GARDEN: A CELEBRATION (Barron, 1991) Describes gardens through history in all parts of the world; includes list of famous gardens, garden organizations and 500+ color photos.

Martin, Peter, and Maccubbin, Robert (editors)
BRITISH AND AMERICAN GARDENS IN THE 18TH CENTURY (University Press of Virginia, 1984)

McFadden, Dorothy Loa
TOURING THE GARDENS OF EUROPE (David McKay, 1965) Excellent for planning a personalized garden tour of Europe; contains "wheel maps" allowing the traveler to stay in a centralized city and travel within a 30-mile radius; covers 10 countries.

Messervy, Julie M.
CONTEMPLATIVE GARDENS (Howell Press, 1990) Examines 35 unusual gardens from around the world with approximately 170 breathtaking color photos.

Mosser, Monique, and Teyssot, Georges (editors)
THE ARCHITECTURE OF WESTERN GARDENS (MIT Press, 1991) Over 70 essays and 650 illustrations trace the Western garden from Renaissance times to the present.

Rose, Graham; King, Peter; and Ottesen, Carole
GARDENING WITH STYLE (Trafalgar Square, 1989) Interviews with 30 outstanding garden designers from around the world; includes detailed plans and photographs.

Saudan, Michael, and Saudan-Skira, Sylvia
FROM FOLLY TO FOLLIES (Abbeville Press, 1988) Covers 15th to 18th century grand European gardens; includes 226 photos, 168 in color.

Seebohm, Caroline, and Sykes, Christopher
PRIVATE LANDSCAPES: CREATING FORM, VISTA AND MYSTERY IN THE GARDEN (Clarkson Potter, 1989) The owners of 19 private gardens in England and America describe their successes and failures; contains garden plans and 400 color photos.

Taylor, Patrick
PERIOD GARDENS: NEW LIFE FOR HISTORIC LANDSCAPES (Atlantic Monthly, 1991) Describes 12 historic gardens on both sides of the Atlantic that have recently been restored; includes U.S. sources for plants and ornaments.

Vercelloni, Virgilio
EUROPEAN GARDENS: A HISTORICAL ATLAS (Rizzoli, 1990) Surveys European gardens from early Egypt to the 20th century.

Part VI:

Miscellaneous
Gardening
Topics

GARDENING FOR KIDS

Bonnet, Bob, and Keen, Dan
BOTANY: 49 SCIENCE FAIR PROJECTS (TAB Books, 1989) For ages 8 to 13, a variety of projects covering germination, propagation, photosynthesis, composting, hydroponics and more.

Brown, Marc
YOUR FIRST GARDEN BOOK (Little, Brown, 1981) For first grade and up.

Chesanow, Jeanne R.
HONEYSUCKLE SIPPING: THE PLANT LORE OF CHILDHOOD (Down East, 1987) Covers childhood games involving plants (do you remember making an acorn tea set?).

Eckstein, Joan, and Gleit, Joyce
FUN WITH GROWING THINGS (Avon, 1991)

Fell, Derek
A KID'S FIRST BOOK OF GARDENING: GROWING PLANTS INDOORS AND OUT (Running Press, 1989) Includes growing unusual plants such as a potato-tomato plant, chocolate peppers and a money plant; how to start plants from seeds and cuttings.

A KID'S FIRST BOOK OF GARDENING WITH GREENHOUSE AND SEEDS (Running Press, 1990)

Fryer, Lee, and Bradford, Leigh
A CHILD'S ORGANIC GARDEN (Acropolis, 1990)

Garland, Sarah
PETER RABBIT'S GARDENING BOOK (Warne, 1983) Covers growing flowers, vegetables and herbs outdoors or in; includes the plants' needs, different ways of growing, friends and enemies of plants, and preparation and serving suggestions.

Hunken, Jorie
BOTANY FOR ALL AGES: LEARNING ABOUT NATURE THROUGH ACTIVITIES USING PLANTS (Globe Pequot, 1989) For individuals and groups, the activities include how to estimate the number of leaves on a tree and how to use a pine cone to measure amount of rainfall.

Jekyll, Gertrude
CHILDREN AND GARDENS (Antique Collector's Club, 1982)

Kains, M. G.
GARDENING FOR YOUNG PEOPLE
(Scarbrough House, 1978) Reprint of a 1937 book that
explores germination, the needs of plants, soil content,
compost, green manure, names of plants, how to dig
correctly and caring for tools; for ages 10 and up.

Kinney, R. R.
A GUIDE TO GARDENING WITH YOUNG
PEOPLE (Prentice-Hall, 1955)

Krementz, Jill
A VERY YOUNG GARDENER (Dial Books, 1991)
A story told by a six-year-old gardener.

Lopez, Ruth K.
Ruth and John Lopez own Gardens for Growing People, a business devoted to gardening supplies for children. Contact them at P.O. Box 630, Point Reyes Station, CA 94956 for the following:
A CHILD'S GARDEN DIARY A coloring and activity book to help kids aged five to 12 track their garden's progress.
GARDENS FOR GROWING PEOPLE: A GUIDE TO GARDENING WITH CHILDREN Explains how a child's interest and motor skills determine to what extent he or she can plan, plant and care for a garden; includes selecting vegetable plants that children enjoy growing.

Markmann, Erika
GROW IT! AN INDOOR/OUTDOOR GARDENING GUIDE FOR KIDS (Random House, 1991)

McCann, Sean
GROWING THINGS (Dufour, 1989)

Mintz, Lorelie M.
VEGETABLES IN PATCHES AND POTS: A CHILD'S GUIDE TO ORGANIC VEGETABLE GARDENING (Farrar, Straus & Giroux, 1976)

Ocone, Lynn, and Pranis, Eve
THE NATIONAL GARDENING ASSOCIATION'S GUIDE TO KIDS' GARDENING: A COMPLETE GUIDE FOR TEACHERS, PARENTS AND YOUTH LEADERS (John Wiley, 1990) Over 70 activities for gardening with kids ages six to 16.

Oechsli, Helen and Kelly
IN MY GARDEN: A CHILD'S GARDENING
BOOK (Macmillan Child Group, 1985)

Porter, Wes
THE GARDEN BOOK (Workman, 1989) Packaged
in a little plastic greenhouse.

Raftery, Kevin and Kim
KIDS GARDENING: A KID'S GUIDE TO MESSING AROUND IN THE DIRT (Klutz Press, 1990)

Skelsey, Alice F., and Huckaby, Gloria
GROWING UP GREEN: CHILDREN AND PARENTS GARDENING TOGETHER (Workman, 1973) Simple projects help parents and children discover the world of gardening together.

Tilgner, Linda
LET'S GROW: 72 GARDENING ADVENTURES WITH CHILDREN (Garden Way, 1988) Indoor and outdoor projects for toddlers to 12-year-olds and for disabled children.

Verey, Rosemary
THE HERB GROWING BOOK (Little, Brown, 1980)

Waters, Marjorie
THE VICTORY GARDEN KIDS' BOOK: A BEGINNER'S GUIDE TO GROWING VEGETABLES, FRUITS AND FLOWERS (Houghton Mifflin, 1988) Step-by-step guide to an entire gardening season with 30 easy crops and an explanation of all gardening tasks; includes guidelines for teachers and parents.

Wilkes, Angela
MY FIRST GARDEN BOOK (Knopf, 1992) Step-by-step activities for a variety of mostly indoor projects for ages seven to 10.

Wilner, Isabel
A GARDEN ALPHABET (Dutton, 1991) Shows a garden unfolding from winter planning, spring planting and fall harvesting.

Wright, Sally
GARDENING: A NEW WORLD FOR CHILDREN (Macmillan, 1957)

GARDENING FOR THE DISABLED AND ELDERLY

The National Library Service publishes *Gardening for Handicapped and Elderly Persons*, a free bibliography available from the Library of Congress, Washington, DC 20542.

Gardens for All (180 Flynn Avenue, Burlington, VT 05401) sells a booklet, *Tools and Techniques for Easier Gardening*, for $3.

The American Horticultural Therapy Association (9220 Wightman Road, Suite 300, Gaithersburg, MD 20879, 800-634-1603) publishes a yearly journal and a newsletter 11 times a year.

The Canadian Horticultural Therapy Association (c/o Royal Botanical Garden, Box 399, Hamilton, ON, Canada L8N 3H8, 416-529-7618) publishes a quarterly newsletter.

Chaplin, Mary
GARDENING FOR THE PHYSICALLY HANDICAPPED AND THE ELDERLY (Batsford Press, 1978)

Cloet, Audrey, and Underhill, Chris
GARDENING IS FOR EVERYONE: A WEEK-BY-WEEK GUIDE FOR PEOPLE WITH HAND- ICAPS (Souvenir Press, 1982) Covers the basics, plus projects for the entire growing year.

Kramer, Jack
GARDENING WITHOUT STRESS AND STRAIN: SHORTCUTS FOR LESS ACTIVE GARDENERS (Scribner's, 1973)

Moore, Bibby
GROWING WITH GARDENING: A 12 MONTH GUIDE TO THERAPY, RECREATION AND ED-UCATION (University of North Carolina Press, 1989) Covers over 250 activities suitable for a variety of ages and abilities, plus information on cost and resources needed for developing a program.

Please, Peter (editor)
ABLE TO GARDEN: A PRACTICAL GUIDE FOR DISABLED AND ELDERLY GARDENERS (Trafalgar Square, 1990) Step-by-step guide through the fundamentals of gardening, plus planning a garden for easy access, special tools, gardening without bending, raised beds, gardening from a sitting position and more; includes detailed instructions and illustrations and diagrams.

Schweller, Frank J.
**CONTAINER GARDENING FOR THE HAND-
ICAPPED: VOLUME 1** (Hand-D-Cap Publishing,
1990)

Yeomans, Kathleen
**THE ABLE GARDENER: OVERCOMING
BARRIERS OF AGE AND PHYSICAL LIMI-**
TATIONS (Storey, 1992) How to lessen the work
involved in gardening.

For related books, see:
LET'S GROW by Tilgner (page 215)

GARDEN PHOTOGRAPHY

Angel, Heather
A CAMERA IN THE GARDEN (Quiller, 1984)

Blacklock, Craig and Nadine
PHOTOGRAPHING WILDFLOWERS: TECH-NIQUES FOR THE ADVANCED AMATEUR AND PROFESSIONAL (Voyageur Press, 1987) Advice for photographing wildflowers in open fields and woodlands.

Brooklyn Botanic Garden
GARDEN PHOTOGRAPHY (BBG #120) An introduction to photographing gardens, plus photos for inspiration.

Fell, Derek
HOW TO PHOTOGRAPH FLOWERS, PLANTS AND LANDSCAPES (HP Books, 1980) Covers close-ups, f-stops, using artificial and natural light, depth-of-field, equipment needed, solutions to common problems, where to sell your photos and more.

Fitch, Charles M.
THE RODALE BOOK OF GARDEN PHOTOG-RAPHY (Amphoto, 1981) Covers equipment and techniques.

Lefkowitz, Lester
THE MANUAL OF CLOSE-UP PHOTOGRA-PHY (Amphoto, 1979) Covers lenses, positioning, supporting the camera, lighting, exposures and more.

Rokach, Allen, and Millman, Anne
FOCUS ON FLOWERS: DISCOVERING AND PHOTOGRAPHING BEAUTY IN GARDENS AND WILD PLACES (Abbeville Press, 1990) Instruction plus the inspiration of 255 beautiful color photos; includes the effects achieved with a variety of lenses, filters, positions and sources of light.

Wignall, Jeff
LANDSCAPE PHOTOGRAPHY: A KODAK GUIDE (McGraw-Hill, 1988)

BOTANICAL ILLUSTRATION

Anderson, Frank
THE COMPLETE BOOK OF 169 REDOUTE ROSES (Abbeville Press, 1979) Covers the 169 different species and varieties of roses that Empress Josephine grew and Redoute painted.

Blunt, Wilfrid
THE ART OF BOTANICAL ILLUSTRATION (Scribner's, 1951) A survey of botanical illustration from antiquity to the 20th century.

deBray, Lys
THE ART OF BOTANICAL ILLUSTRATION: THE CLASSIC ILLUSTRATORS AND THEIR ACHIEVEMENTS FROM 1550 TO 1900 (Wellfleet Press, 1989) Covers all the major artists up to 1900, plus a final chapter discusses artists since 1900.

Brickell, Christopher, and Grierson, Mary
AN ENGLISH FLORILEGIUM (Abbeville Press, 1987) Botanical watercolors of 17th century English flowers, trees, shrubs, fruit and herbs.

Johnson, Cathy
PAINTING NATURE'S DETAILS IN WATERCOLOR (North Light Books, 1991) Covers the suc-cessful use of light, texture and color when painting with watercolor.

Mabey, Richard
THE FLOWERS OF KEW (Atheneum, 1989) A selection of 150 of the most beautiful flower paintings from the Royal Botanic Gardens at Kew; includes history of Kew and the artists who created the paintings and illustrations over the last 350 years.
THE FRAMPTON FLORA (Prentice-Hall, 1986) More than 230 color reproductions of the Victorian botanical prints found in the attic at Frampton Court, Gloucestershire, England.
A VICTORIAN FLORA: THE FLOWER PAINT-INGS OF CAROLINE MAY (Viking Penguin, 1991)

Mallary, Peter and Frances
A REDOUTE TREASURY (Wellfleet Press, 1986) Contains 468 botanical plates of lilies, iris, amaryllis, tulips, pineapple and banana from *Les Liliacées*; organized by genus and species.

Monahan, Patricia
YOU CAN PAINT FLOWERS, PLANTS AND NATURE (North Light Books, 1986) Covers various

media (pencil, oil pastel, charcoal, watercolor, oil, acrylic) and techniques.

Morrison, Tony (editor)
MARGARET MEE: IN SEARCH OF FLOWERS OF THE AMAZON FORESTS (Antique Collector's Club, 1989) Photos and illustrations of Mee's paintings of flowers in the Amazon rain forests, plus selections from her diary.

Parsons, Alfred
A GARDEN OF ROSES (Salem House, 1987) Watercolors painted around 1900 for a wealthy rose enthusiast; each of the almost 70 plates is accompanied with notes by Graham Stuart Thomas.

Redouté, P. J.
THE ROSES (Wellfleet Press, 1990) Contains 167 botanical illustrations with pertinent information on each rose.

Reid, Charles
FLOWER PAINTING IN WATERCOLOR (Watson-Guptill, 1986) Covers a variety of techniques and flower and leaf shapes.

Rix, Martyn and Alison
THE REDOUTE ALBUM (Dorset Press, 1990) A selection of 60 of Redouté's flower paintings from all of his classic books; includes cacti, roses, lilies, heathers and pelargoniums.

Rix, Martyn, and Stearn, Dr. William T. (editors)
REDOUTE FAIREST FLOWERS (Prentice-Hall, 1987) Contains 144 color reproductions of roses, lilies, lilacs, honeysuckles, dahlias, peonies and more.

Robertson, Bruce
DRAWING WORKBOOKS: TREES AND PLANTS (North Light Books, 1987) Over 100 projects for learning how to draw trees and plants.

Sitwell, Sacheverell, and Blount, Wilfrid
GREAT FLOWER BOOKS 1700–1900 (Atlantic Monthly, 1990) Lists over 750 of the best illustrated flower books; includes 51 full-page and full-color reproductions of botanical illustrations from well-known artists.

Sprunger, Samuel (editor)
ORCHIDS FROM "CURTIS'S BOTANICAL MAGAZINE" (Cambridge University Press, 1987)

Stearn, Dr. William T.
BOTANICAL MASTERS: PLANT PORTRAITS BY CONTEMPORARY ARTISTS (Prentice-Hall, 1990) Contains 56 full-color works of 19 modern botanical artists who have worked at Kew Gardens.

Stiff, Ruth
FLOWERS FROM THE ROYAL GARDENS OF KEW: TWO CENTURIES OF "CURTIS'S BOTANICAL MAGAZINE" (University Press of New England, 1988) A selection of 48 plates.

Thomas, Graham Stuart
THE COMPLETE FLOWER PAINTINGS AND DRAWINGS OF GRAHAM STUART THOMAS (Timber Press, 1987) Over 170 illustrations, 58 of them in color, plus history and cultivation information.

Vojtech, Anna, and Prance, Ghillean T.
WILDFLOWERS FOR ALL SEASONS (Crown, 1989) Detailed watercolors and descriptions of 129 wildflowers.

Walsh, Wendy, and Nelson, Charles
AN IRISH FLORILEGIUM II: WILD AND GARDEN PLANTS OF IRELAND (Thames & Hudson, 1988) Contains 48 full-page watercolors of plants connected with the botanic gardens at Trinity College.

West, Keith R.
HOW TO DRAW PLANTS: THE TECHNIQUES OF BOTANICAL ILLUSTRATION (Watson-Guptill, 1983) Advice and illustrations on depicting botanically correct flowers and plants whether using pencil, pen, watercolor or acrylics.

Wunderlich, Eleanor B.
BOTANICAL ILLUSTRATION IN WATERCOLOR (Watson-Guptill, 1991) Step-by-step instruction from the teacher of botanical illustration at the New York Botanical Garden.

ORNAMENTS IN THE GARDEN

Balston, Michael
THE WELL-FURNISHED GARDEN (Simon & Schuster, 1987) How to use statues, benches, trellises, etc. to add to a garden's beauty; includes 600 photos (180 in color) and drawings.

Blandford, Percy
BACKYARD BUILDER'S BONANZA (TAB Books, 1989)

Brooklyn Botanic Garden
GARDEN ORNAMENTS (BBG #113) Guidelines for using benches, gazebos, sundials and more.

Buchanan, George
GARDEN FURNITURE (Sterling, 1991) Step-by-step plans for building tables, chairs, benches, trellises, etc. in a variety of styles; includes 300 illustrations.

Burgess, Lorraine
GARDEN ART: THE PERSONAL PURSUIT OF ARTISTIC REFINEMENTS, INVENTIVE CONCEPTS, OLD FOLLIES AND NEW CONCEITS FOR THE HOME GARDENER (Walker, 1981) Ways to use structures and ornaments in the garden.

Chamberlin, Susan, and Pollock, Janet
FENCES, GATES AND WALLS: HOW TO DESIGN AND BUILD (HP Books, 1983) Money-saving ideas for using concrete, rocks, brick, railroad ties, wood and wire in building fences, gates and wall.

Conran, Terence
GARDEN STYLE (Crown, 1991) Describes a variety of build-it-yourself projects, materials and tools needed, and step-by-step instructions; projects include benches, tree seat, garden and tool houses, fencing, containers and more.

Davis, John
ANTIQUE GARDEN ORNAMENT (Antique Collector's Club, 1991) Surveys garden ornaments from the 17th century to today; covers statues, vases, fountains, balustrades and furniture of lead, bronze, marble, iron, stone, terracotta and cast-iron; includes illustrations from trade catalogues and addresses the problem of fakes.

Driemer, John
OPEN AIR DESIGNS: HOW TO CREATE A DECK, PATIO, GARDEN AREA AND PLAY SPACE THAT REALLY WORKS (HP Books,

1988) How to budget, plan and build an attractive and functional outdoor living space; includes information on materials, building codes, safety and more.

Engler, Nick
OUTDOOR FURNITURE (Rodale Press, 1989) Instructions and materials lists for making 20 wood projects (Adirondack chair, canvas sling chair, planter box, benches, tables, etc.).

Fell, Derek
GARDEN ACCENTS: THE COMPLETE GUIDE TO FEATURES FOR CREATIVE LAND-SCAPES (Henry Holt, 1987) How to include sculpture, fountains, paths, pools, gazebos, trellises, arbors, fences, benches, containers and birdbaths into a landscape plan.

Foley, Daniel J.
THE COMPLETE BOOK OF GARDEN ORNA-MENTS, COMPLEMENTS AND ACCESSO-RIES (Crown, 1972) A picture book of a variety of garden ornaments and structures.

Fraser, Stewart
GARDEN MATTERS: BRICKWORK FOR BE-GINNERS (Sterling, 1991) Covers pouring concrete, replacing damaged brick, pointing, cleaning and painting old brick; includes a variety of projects to make.

Garnock, Jamie
TRELLIS: THE CREATIVE WAY TO TRANS-FORM YOUR GARDEN (Rizzoli, 1991) Details all the many ways to use trellises, the various styles and how to construct and maintain them.

Gaze, John
FIGURES IN A LANDSCAPE: A HISTORY OF THE NATIONAL TRUST (Trafalgar Square, 1989)

Green, Michael
BUILDING FOR THE GARDEN (ISBS, 1989) Step-by-step instructions and diagrams for building paving, paths, driveways, retaining walls, raised garden beds, fences, wood decks, pergolas, screens and barbecues.

Harrod, Julie
THE GARDEN WALL (Atlantic Monthly, 1991) Covers planning and planting fences, hedges and walls; includes descriptions of 300 cultivars that do well on or near walls.

Holloway, David
STEP-BY-STEP OUTDOOR BRICKWORK: OVER 20 EASY-TO-BUILD PROJECTS FOR YOUR YARD AND GARDEN (Storey, 1992)

Home Planners
DECK PLANNER: TWENTY-FIVE OUT-STANDING DECKS YOU CAN BUILD (Home Planners, 1990) Plans and material lists for 25 single, double and multilevel decks in a variety of architectural styles.

Hunt, Peter (editor)
THE BOOK OF GARDEN ORNAMENT (Architectural Book Publishing, 1974) Covers an enormous number of decorations (statues, fountains, containers, walls, gates, ironwork, paving, furniture, topiary, etc.) and garden buildings (gatehouses, temples, dovecotes, etc.).

Jackson, Anthony
GARDEN FURNITURE: DESIGN AND CON-STRUCTION (Trafalgar Square, 1988) Instructions for 16 structures such as bench, pergola, trellis, nesting box, footbridge and summerhouse.

Jekyll, Gertrude
GARDEN ORNAMENT (Antique Collector's Club, 1982) Ways to use ornaments, furniture and structural elements such as bridges in a garden; 600 photos.

Jerome, John
STONE WORK: REFLECTIONS ON SERIOUS PLAY AND OTHER ASPECTS OF COUNTRY LIFE (Viking Penguin, 1989) Describes a year spent in building a stone wall in the Berkshire Hills of Massachusetts.

Landis, Michael, and Molholt, Ray
PATIOS AND DECKS: HOW TO PLAN, BUILD AND ENJOY (HP Books, 1983) Hundreds of ideas and 350 color photos.

Lawrence, Mike (editor)
BACKYARD BRICKWORK: HOW TO BUILD
WALLS, PATHS, PATIOS AND BARBECUES
(Storey, 1989) From designing to building patios,
walls, planters, steps, arches, paths and other projects;
includes 200 color photos, detailed plans, how to estimate costs and quantities of materials, and information
on drainage and mixing concrete.

Library of Garden Detail
Each tiny book in the series (Simon & Schuster, 1992)
is written by a famous gardener and contains color
photos and ideas for using a special ornamental garden
feature.
THE GARDEN BENCH by Mirabel Osler
THE GARDEN GATE by Rosemary Verey
THE GARDEN PATH by Patrick Taylor
THE GARDEN TRELLIS by Roy Strong

McHoy, Peter
GARDEN ORNAMENTS AND STATUARY:
GARDENING BY DESIGN (Sterling, 1990) Ad-
vice, instructions and color photos using ornaments in
the garden.

Ortho
HOW TO DESIGN AND INSTALL OUTDOOR
LIGHTING (Ortho, 1984) Covers lighting for paths,
plantings, pools and more; includes techniques, power
needs, annual maintenance and sources.

Penberthy, Ian
BUILDING YOUR GARDEN (Macmillan, 1989)
Over 350 color photos and illustrations, plus step-by-
step instructions for designing and building all types of
garden features (brick walls, pools, patios, fences,
planters, trellises, rock gardens, waterfalls, etc.).

Plumptre, George
GARDEN ORNAMENT: FIVE CENTURIES OF
NATURE, ART AND ARTIFICE (Doubleday,
1990) Covers the history of ornament in Western gardens, how to use ornaments in today's gardens and illustrations of ornaments that can be found for sale today.

Rustic Hickory Furniture Co. Staff
PORCH, LAWN AND COTTAGE FURNITURE
(Dover, 1990) Two complete catalogues from around
1904 and 1926 describe "Adirondack" and other rustic

furniture giving dimensions, weight and original
prices.

Smith and Hawken
Their *Catalog of Garden Furniture* contains absolutely
beautiful wood, steel and metal garden furniture. Write
to 25 Corte Madera, Mill Valley, CA 94941 or call
415-383-2000.

Stevens, David
PERGOLAS, ARBORS, GAZEBOS, FOLLIES
(Sterling, 1991) Building information on many different styles, plus design ideas for using these structural
garden elements to frame a view, emphasize seclusion,
define a path, etc.
SIMPLE GARDEN PROJECTS: A COLLEC-
TION OF ORIGINAL DESIGNS TO BUILD IN
YOUR GARDEN (Globe Pequot, 1992) With a minimum of labor and expense, build arbors, raised beds,
seating, plant supports, paths, patios, fences, walls,
gates, and more; includes a directory of techniques
explaining the basics of construction.

Strombeck, Janet and Richard
GAZEBOS AND OTHER GARDEN STRUC-
TURE DESIGNS (Sterling/Sun Designs, 1983) Covers 55 various styles (rustic, oriental, modern,
traditional, Victorian) of gazebos, plus seven designs
for arbors, 13 designs for strombrellas and 18 bird house
and bird feeder designs.

Sunset
FENCES AND GATES (Sunset Books, 1981) How
to plan, build, and landscape with fences, gates and
screens.
GARDEN AND PATIO BUILDING BOOK (Sun-
set Books, 1983) Ideas for quick and inexpensive projects.
OUTDOOR FURNITURE (Sunset Books, 1979)
Step-by-step directions for 35 easy projects for patio
and lawn furniture.
PATIO ROOFS AND GAZEBOS (Sunset Books,
1988) Plans and instructions for building a weather-
proof garden shelter.

Vivian, John
BUILDING FENCES OF WOOD, STONE,
METAL AND PLANTS (Williamson Publishing,

1987) A step-by-step guide for all types of fences (rail, fieldstone, flagstone, picket, electric and hedges).
BUILDING STONE WALLS (Storey, 1979) How to prepare the foundation, plus height/weight ratios, whether or not to use mortar, pointing, and more.

White, J. P.
GARDEN FURNITURE AND ORNAMENT (Antique Collector's Club, 1987) A reprint of his Pyghtle Works catalogues (1910 and before) which featured seats, sundials, treillage, trellises, pottery, gates, sculpture, summerhouses, bridges and more; contains almost 1,000 illustrations and diagrams. J. P. White was the largest supplier of garden furniture and ornament in his time. His clients included Jekyll, Lutyens and Sackville-West.

Wilkinson, Elizabeth, and Henderson, Marjorie (editors)
DECORATING EDEN: A COMPREHENSIVE SOURCEBOOK OF CLASSIC GARDEN DETAILS (Chronicle Books, 1992) Covers ornamental objects for the garden with suppliers listed.

For related books, see:
FOLLIES AND PLEASURE PAVILIONS by Mott and Aall (page 207)
STONE BASINS by Yoshikawa (page 211)

GARDENING VIDEOS

For additional gardening videos—this list only scratches the surface—consult *The Video Source Book* at your library.

One Up Productions (P.O. Box 410777, San Francisco, CA 94141, 800-331-6304) and The Matrix Group (P.O. Box 1176, Southport, CT 06490) offer catalogs of gardening videos.

Baker, Jerry
HOUSE PLANT TIPS AND TRICKS (Simon & Schuster, 1984, 40 minutes) Basics of houseplant care.
LAWN CARE TIPS AND TRICKS (Simon & Schuster, 1986, 60 minutes) How to grow a healthy lawn.

Ball, Jeff
YARDENING (1986, various lengths) These videos are endorsed by The National Gardening Association and won the 1987 Quill and Trowel Award from the Garden Writers Association of America:
How to Care for Your Lawn (53 minutes): Discusses choosing the right lawn, seeding, mowing, dethatching, controlling weeds and revitalizing an old lawn.
How to Design a Flower Garden (48 minutes): How to choose the right plants and garden site, design a layout and mulch, plus ways to keep the garden productive and low maintenance.
How to Design and Build a Vegetable Garden (53 minutes): Step-by-step instructions for creating a 200-square-foot garden that produces 400 pounds of vegetables.
How to Grow and Cook Fresh Herbs (60 minutes): Covers growing herbs and using them to enhance ordinary dishes.
How to Grow and Nurture Seedlings (49 minutes): Discusses watering, feeding and setting out.
How to Grow Cool-Weather Vegetables (57 minutes): How to extend your growing season by three months with "tunnels" and special methods.
How to Grow Flowers (50 minutes): Covers growing perennials, annuals and bulbs for use as cut flowers.
How to Grow Healthy Houseplants (60 minutes): Covers selecting containers, making potting soil, cleaning, pruning and more.
How to Grow Plants in a Greenhouse (47 minutes): Covers design options, where to put the greenhouse and maintenance needed to grow vegetables, flowers and houseplants in a greenhouse.

How to Grow Plants in Sunspaces (54 minutes): Covers selecting the right plants, where to put them, feeding and pest control.

How to Grow Roses (48 minutes): How to test the soil, transplant container and bare-root roses, mulch and control pests.

How to Grow Warm-Weather Vegetables (55 minutes): Discusses the special techniques needed for warm-weather vegetable gardening.

Better Homes and Gardens
FOOLPROOF FLOWER BEDS (1988, 55 minutes) How to select the right plants for your climate, choose the best site, prepare the soil and plan a succession of color; winner of the 1988 Quill and Trowel Award from the Garden Writers Association of America.

British Broadcasting Corporation (BBC)
75 GOLDEN YEARS: THE CHELSEA FLOWER SHOW (40 minutes) A celebration of the last 75 years of this annual London event.

Brooklyn Botanic Garden
The Brooklyn Botanic Garden has produced a number of videos. The ones listed here are from their latest list, but check your library for additional ones.

BONSAI: THE ART OF TRAINING DWARF POTTED TREES (22 minutes) Describes how to shape and maintain bonsai, plus selecting the container, repotting, pruning, wiring, and general care and culture.

DRIED FLOWERS AND PLANTS (20 minutes) How to dry and preserve flowers and other plant parts, plus ways to use them.

FOR THE LOVE OF ROSES: A YEAR IN THE LIFE OF A ROSARIAN (47 minutes) Covers growing and caring for roses year-round.

GET READY, GET SET, GROW!: A KID'S GUIDE TO GOOD GARDENING (15 minutes) A kit consisting of the video and two books with all the information needed to teach kids how to grow flowers and vegetables.

HERBS: USE AND TRADITION (17 minutes) Covers folklore and using herbs in medicine, cosmetics, perfumes and in cooking.

NATURE'S COLORS: THE CRAFT OF DYEING WITH PLANTS (10 minutes) How to get color from roots, leaves, stems, flowers and fruits, plus how to treat and dye yarn.

PLANTING AND TRANSPLANTING (22 minutes) Covers bulbs, annuals, perennials, trees, and shrubs, and offers tips on preparing the soil, potting, and root and top pruning.

Bryan, John
GARDENING FROM THE GROUND UP Series (PBS, 1980, 28 minutes each):

Alternative Pest Control: Covers the disadvantages of chemicals and gives natural alternatives.

Annuals, Biennials and Perennials: How to grow them for a good show of color in your garden.

Bulbs and Rhododendrons: Covers planning a year-round bulb garden, selecting bulbs, planting and cultivating the bulbs, and requirements of growing rhododendrons.

Cacti and Succulents: Covers selection, propagation and cultivation, plus includes a tour of the Desert Garden at the Huntington Botanical Gardens in California.

Cover-ups: Covers using trellises to hide eyesores and enhancing posts, pillars and fences with climbers.

Ground Covers: Discusses a variety of ground covers, their different uses and how to care for them.

Growing Roses: How to plant, prune and grow roses in various climates, plus how to identify and treat black spot, aphids, rust and mildew.

Herbs: Discusses the history and characteristics of a variety of herbs, plus selection tips, soil requirements and uses.

Landscaping: How to plan and design taking into consideration existing buildings, trees, views, etc.

Lawns: Covers thatching, feeding, reseeding, returfing, watering and fertilizing.

Propagation: Covers cuttings, layering and division.

Pruning: Discusses the correct tools and methods of pruning.

Salad Days: How to grow lettuce, tomatoes, cucumbers and radishes.

Seeds of Spring: How to start seeds, care for and plant the seedlings.

Soils: Discusses the different types of soils, the advantages and disadvantages of clay and sand, and how to improve your soil.

War of the Weeds: How to use cultivators and mulch and ways to create and use compost.

Burkhart, Loren
THE ORGANIC GARDENER (1985, 30-minutes) Covers composting, double digging, bed layout, companion planting and transplanting; includes the French intensive method of raised bed gardening.

Encyclopedia Britannica
THE QUEEN'S GARDEN (1987, 52 minutes) Covers the four seasons in the Queen's Garden at Buckingham Palace.

Flagg, Bob
HOUSEPLANTS (1986, 28 minutes) How to choose and maintain beautiful houseplants.

Gainey, Ryan
CREATING THE ROMANTIC GARDEN (58 minutes) Describes how to create a cottage garden using flowers, shrubs, native plants, topiary, borders, ground covers, ornaments, vegetables, herbs, water, arbors, walks and more; filmed in his famous cottage garden in Atlanta, Georgia.

Garrett, Howard
THE ART OF LANDSCAPING (1985, 52 minutes) How to achieve a professional look without the high cost; covers budget, site analysis, layout, irrigation, grading, lighting, planting plans and more.
THE ART OF LANDSCAPING: SHOPPING AND PLANTING (1985, 60 minutes) A guided tour through a nursery that covers how to tell good plants from bad plants, container sizes and soils; includes tips for getting good results from your planting effort.

Gielgud, Sir John (narrator)
THE ENGLISH GARDEN SERIES (Thames Television, 1986, Seven 30-minute videos)

Hublein, Kelle G.
PERENNIAL GARDENING (1980, 45 minutes) How to design a perennial island, prepare the soil, select the plants, plant and maintain the bed; taped at Oregon Bulb Farms.

Hume, Ed
Columnist Ed Hume has a variety of videos including:

GROUND COVERS (60 minutes) Covers a very large variety of ground covers.
PRUNING (60 minutes) Discusses and demonstrates pruning.
SPECTACULAR ROSES (56 minutes) Covers hybrid teas, grandifloras, pillars, miniatures, climbing and tree roses.
VEGETABLE GARDENING (60 minutes)

Kramer, Fay, and Sakai, Soho
IKEBANA (1987, 45 minutes) Covers the basics of getting started in this ancient form of Japanese flower arranging.

Lancaster, Roy
THE GREAT PLANT COLLECTIONS (Granada Television, 1984, 30-minute videos) One video on each of the following United Kingdom gardens:
Birr Castle in the Republic of Ireland is known for its parterres, hornbeam allee and the tallest box hedge in the world.
Bodnant in the Conwy Valley of North Wales specializes in rhododendrons, azaleas and the Viburnum Bodnantense.
Bressingham Gardens of Alan Bloom in Norfolk contain over 5,000 species and varieties of perennials, alpines, heathers and conifers from all over the world.
Caerhays Castle on the Cornwall coast features rhododendrons, magnolias, camellias and daffodils.
Inverewe in Scotland features all the exotic plants that the creator, Osgood Mackenzie, knew did well in Devon, Cornwall and the west of Ireland.
Mount Stewart in Northern Ireland comprises over a dozen gardens started by the Marchioness of Londonderry in 1919.
The Sevill and Valley Gardens in Windsor Great Park in Berkshire feature magnolias, rhododendrons, dwarf conifers and holly.
Wakehurst Place in West Sussex was created from the plants Gerald Loder, Lord Wakehurst, brought back from his botanical expeditions to Asia, South America and Australia.
Westonbirt Arboretum in Gloucestershire was started in 1829 by Robert Holford who collected trees from all over the world.

Loyd, Toady
THE VIDEO HERBALIST: VOLUME I, GARDENING WITH HERBS (47 minutes) Covers planning the garden, buying plants, propagation and harvesting.
THE VIDEO HERBALIST: VOLUME II, COOKING WITH HERBS (81 minutes) A demonstration of using herbs in seasonings, appetizers, salads, soups, sauces and more.

Macqueen, Sheila, and Ord, Ann
THE JOY OF FLOWER ARRANGING I (1985, 61 minutes) How to select, cut, prepare and design floral arrangements.
THE JOY OF FLOWER ARRANGING II (1986, 60 minutes) How to dry and preserve flowers and foliage and use them in arrangements.

Martin III, Clair G.
A COLLECTION OF ROSES (1984, 22 minutes) Tour through the Shakespeare and Rose Gardens at the Huntington Gardens with the resident Rosarian; covers many varieties and shows the historical evolution of the modern rose.

Mason, James (narrator)
THE GLORY OF THE GARDEN (55 minutes) A tour through the Rothschilds' Exbury Gardens, home of the famous azaleas and rhododendrons; includes information on the creation of the garden and its 1,204 new hybrids.

Meuninck, Jim, and Duke, Dr. Jim
EDIBLE WILD PLANTS (60 minutes) A field guide to 100 useful wild herbs and how to use them in teas, salads and desserts.
TREES, SHRUBS, NUTS AND BERRIES (60 minutes) Identifying trees and shrubs across North America; includes recipes using wild berries and nuts.

Meuninck, Jim, and Philip, Dr. Sinclair
COOKING WITH EDIBLE FLOWERS AND CULINARY HERBS (60 minutes) Nine chefs identify the best flowers and herbs to eat and how to gather, preserve and cook with them; includes visits to herb farms and restaurants.

Moulton, Gary
EASY STEPS TO FRUIT TREE PRUNING (Cedardale Orchards, 55 minutes) How to prune both new and mature trees; covers open center, central leader and espalier systems.

National Trust
THE FOUR SEASONS: THE GARDENS AND THE GARDENERS are video tours of the finest gardens in Britain at their peak:
Spring and Autumn (40 minutes) Covers Trengwainton, Lanhydrock, Sheffield Park, Winkworth Arboretum, Stourhead and others.
Summer and Winter (43 minutes) Covers Powis Castle, Clivedon, Hidcote Manor, Polesdon Lacy, Claremont, Leith Hill and others.

Reynolds, Renny
THE SECRETS OF ENTERTAINING WITH FLOWERS (House Beautiful, 40 minutes) How to use flowers, crystal and candles to set a beautiful table, plus ways to use flowers in other parts of your home.
THE SECRETS OF DECORATING WITH FLOWERS (House Beautiful, 40 minutes) How to use containers in unusual ways and how to ensure the flower arrangement is compatible with the room's decor; includes a visit to New York's Flower Market.

Rodale
GETTING THE MOST FROM YOUR GARDEN (1981, 28 minutes) Covers intensive gardening in raised beds to produce more food with less work.
HOME-GROWN FOOD ALL YEAR 'ROUND (1980, 55 minutes) Covers intensive gardening techniques and how to preserve and store home-grown produce.
REDISCOVERING HERBS (1981, 20 minutes) Cyrus Hyde, herbalist of Well-Sweep Herb Farm in New Jersey, discusses how to grow, dry, store and use herbs.
REDISCOVERING HERBS: OVERVIEW (1981, 28 minutes) Cyrus Hyde identifies various herbs and discusses their uses.

Royal Horticultural Society
CHELSEA FLOWER SHOW 1987 (60 minutes) A tour of the gardens, exhibits and displays of such fa-

mous British gardeners as David Austin (roses), Jim Fisk (clematis) and Beth Chatto (perennials).

Sunset
WATERWISE GARDENING: BEAUTIFUL GARDENS WITH LESS WATER, WESTERN EDITION (32 minutes) Techniques and tips on how often to water, irrigation equipment that saves water and plants that are drought-resistant; specifically created for Western gardens; includes a 24-page pamphlet.

Thompson, Bob, and Wilson, Jim
THE VICTORY GARDEN (1986, 60 minutes) A month-by-month tour through an entire year of vegetable gardening.

Thompson and Wilson also host a series of 13 videos covering a variety of gardening techniques and tours of gardens around the world.

Turner, Mary and Al
THE FRUGAL GARDENER (88 minutes) How to garden year round and save money by making an inexpensive basement greenhouse, germinating seeds, recycling disposable household items, propagation and much more.

York, Suzannah (narrator)
A VISION OF PARADISE (27 minutes) A tour of Knightshayes Court, a 40-acre National Trust garden in Devon, England.

MAGAZINES

American Horticulturist, 7931 E. Boulevard Drive, Alexandria, VA 22308, 800-777-7931. A monthly magazine whose subscription fee is included with membership in the American Horticultural Society; the magazine alternates between a glossy format one month and a newsletter format the next month.

Fine Gardening, 63 S. Main St., P.O. Box 5506, Newton, CT 06470, 203-426-8171; bimonthly glossy magazine.

Flower and Garden, 4251 Pennsylvania Ave., Kansas City, MO 64111, 816-531-5730; bimonthly glossy.

Garden Design, 4401 Connecticut Ave. NW, Suite 500, Washington, DC 20008; five times a year glossy.

Horticulture, the Magazine of American Gardening, 20 Park Plaza, Suite 1220, Boston, MA 02116, 617-482-5600; 10 times a year glossy.

National Gardening, 180 Flynn Ave., Burlington, VT 05401, 802-863-1308; bimonthly glossy from the National Gardening Association.

Organic Gardening, 33 E. Minor St., Emmaus, PA 18098, 215-967-5171; nine times a year glossy.

Two regional magazines of interest are:

Pacific Horticulture, P.O. Box 485, Berkeley, CA 94701, 415-524-1914; quarterly glossy.

Texas Gardener, P.O. Box 9005, Waco, TX 76714, 817-772-1270; bimonthly glossy.

In addition, *Green Prints* (P.O. Box 1355, Fairview, NC 28730) is a marvelous, non-glossy, small (5"x8"), quarterly magazine. It contains essays on the "soul of gardening" written by garden lovers, some well-known, some unknown, all interesting. The issue I'm holding has pieces by Henry Mitchell, Eric Grissell and Rebecca Rupp, plus nine other garden enthusiasts.

For help in locating magazine articles on specific gardening topics, get a copy of *The Gardener's Index* by Joy McCann. The index for 1986 to 1990 covers articles from *Flower and Garden*, *Fine Gardening*, *Horticulture*, *National Gardening* and *Organic Gardening*. The 1991 to 1992 index includes those five magazines plus additional ones which, though not primarily gardening magazines, contain excellent gardening articles (e.g., *Harrowsmith Country Life*). More information on *The Gardener's Index* is available from CompuDex Press, P.O. Box 27041, Kansas City, MO 64110. The *Index* is a must-have if you enjoy gardening magazines and want to find specific articles you may have missed.

For a complete listing of gardening publications, consult the latest edition of *Ulrich's International Periodicals Directory* at your library. It contains names, addresses, phone numbers and subscription information for both United States and international publications.

Subject
&
Author
Indexes

SUBJECT INDEX

AUTHOR INDEX

C

X

Y

Z